ADVANCE PRAISE FOR
*Japanese America on the Eve of the Pacific War*

"Researching the 1930s is a challenge in Japanese American history, as it raises unsettling questions about patriotism, loyalty, and citizenship of those who maintained ties with their ancestral homeland, the Empire of Japan. This anthology guides us through the complicated research terrain of the past and provides a roadmap for the future."

—Yuma Totani, professor of history, University of Hawai'i

"In following the lead of a pioneering scholar, the contributors not only have opened up the critical decade of the 1930s regarding the Japanese diaspora but also have engaged in larger discussions of geopolitics, international trade, and immigrant/ethnic nationalisms. A noteworthy achievement deserving of wide readership."

—David K. Yoo, vice provost and professor of Asian American studies and history, University of California–Los Angeles

"This landmark collection adds new dimensions to Japanese American history in Hawai'i, California, and the East Coast, illuminating the complicated dynamics of generational relations, immigrant nationalism, Japanese-language education, and US military surveillance of Nikkei loyalties during the critical decade of the 1930s."

—Valerie J. Matsumoto, professor of history and Asian American studies, George and Sakaye Aratani Chair on the Japanese American Incarceration, Redress, and Community, University of California–Los Angeles

D1555040

# Japanese America on the
# Eve of the Pacific War

# Japanese America on the Eve of the Pacific War

## An Untold History of the 1930s

Edited by Eiichiro Azuma and Kaoru Ueda

### Contributing Authors
Rashaad Eshack
Brian Masaru Hayashi
Masako Iino
Michael R. Jin
Masato Kimura
Toshihiko Kishi
Mire Koikari
Teruko Kumei
Tosh Minohara
Yasuo Sakata

HOOVER INSTITUTION PRESS
STANFORD UNIVERSITY     STANFORD, CALIFORNIA

*With its eminent scholars and world-renowned library and archives, the Hoover Institution seeks to improve the human condition by advancing ideas that promote economic opportunity and prosperity while securing and safeguarding peace for America and all mankind. The views expressed in its publications are entirely those of the authors and do not necessarily reflect the views of the staff, officers, or Board of Overseers of the Hoover Institution.*

Hoover Institution Press Publication No. 734

Hoover Institution at Leland Stanford Junior University,
Stanford, California 94305-6003

Copyright © 2024 by the Board of Trustees of the
Leland Stanford Junior University

All rights reserved. No part of this publication may be reproduced, stored in a retrieval system, or transmitted in any form or by any means, electronic, mechanical, photocopying, recording, or otherwise, without written permission of the publisher and copyright holders.

For permission to reuse material from *Japanese America on the Eve of the Pacific War,* ISBN 978-0-8179-2605-2, please access copyright.com or contact the Copyright Clearance Center Inc. (CCC), 222 Rosewood Drive, Danvers, MA 01923, 978-750-8400. CCC is a not-for-profit organization that provides licenses and registration for a variety of uses.

Cover image: "*Taisei Maru* Returns to Japan," Hawai'i, ca. 1939, Dennis M. Ogawa Nippu Jiji Photograph Collection, T58.030. Hoji Shinbun Digital Collection, Hoover Institution Library & Archives. Courtesy of the Hawaii Times Photo Archives Foundation.

Efforts have been made to locate the original sources, determine the current rights holders, and, if needed, obtain reproduction permissions. On verification of any such claims to rights to the materials reproduced in this book, any required corrections or clarifications will be made in subsequent printings/editions.

First printing 2023
30 29 28 27 26 25 24    7 6 5 4 3 2 1

Manufactured in the United States of America
Printed on acid-free, archival-quality paper

Library of Congress Cataloging-in-Publication Data
Names: Azuma, Eiichiro, editor. | Ueda, Kaoru (Kay), editor, translator.
Title: Japanese America on the eve of the Pacific War: an untold history of the 1930s / edited by Eiichiro Azuma and Kaoru Ueda.
Other titles: Hoover Institution Press publication; 734.
Description: Stanford, California: Hoover Institution Press, Stanford University, [2023] | Series: Hoover Institution Press publication; no. 734 | Includes bibliographical references and index. | Summary: 'An anthology of essays explores Japanese American communities and US-Japan relations in the 1930s, a vital history largely obscured by events preceding and following the decade'—Provided by publisher.
Identifiers: LCCN 2023039525 (print) | LCCN 2023039526 (ebook) | ISBN 9780817926052 (trade paperback) | ISBN 9780817926069 (epub) | ISBN 9780817926083 (pdf)
Subjects: LCSH: Japanese Americans—History—20th century. | United States—History—1933–1945. | United States—Relations—Japan. | Japan—Relations—United States.
Classification: LCC E184.J3 J328 2023 (print) | LCC E184.J3 (ebook) | DDC 973.917089956/073—dc23/eng/20230905
LC record available at https://lccn.loc.gov/2023039525
LC ebook record available at https://lccn.loc.gov/2023039526

# Contents

# Foreword

The Hoover Institution Library & Archives was founded by Herbert Hoover (1874–1964) at his alma mater, Stanford University, in 1919, fifteen years before the US National Archives was established. Mr. Hoover was a visionary who believed that collecting and documenting war-related materials would allow future generations to study them in the hope such study would lead to less conflict. Because of his strong belief in the imperative for scholars to have access to primary sources, we have continued to build and preserve global collections for current and future generations.

The generously endowed Japanese Diaspora Initiative continues our core mission to collect, preserve, describe, make available, and encourage the scholarly and educational uses of primary source materials. The initiative focuses on the history of overseas Japanese during the Empire of Japan period (1868–1945) and rests on Hoover's existent and continuously growing archival collections on Japan and overseas Japanese.

The drive behind the establishment of our current core Japan collection was the Stanford Alumni Association of Tokyo. Its members recognized the strong need to document the Pacific War and processes leading up to the final rupture of the US-Japan relationship before the war, and they recommended establishing a Tokyo office of what was then called the Hoover Library on War, Revolution, and Peace. Just three months after the Japanese Instrument of Surrender was signed, the Tokyo office was opened in November 1945, with the permission of the supreme commander for the Allied powers. The Tokyo office collected an extraordinary range of materials during the Japanese occupation period, until it was closed in 1952. This visionary approach to collecting materials just after World War II ended is at the root of Hoover's Japan collection, which has expanded to include many other materials of historical importance. Among the significant papers held by the Hoover Institution Library & Archives are those of Araki Sadao, former general of the Imperial Japanese Army and former minister of war and education, and Hiranuma Kiichirō, prime minister in 1939; as well as the draft Japanese constitution contained in the Milo E. Rowell papers. The Library & Archives continues to place an emphasis on providing access to these important collections to students and scholars worldwide.

With Hoover's long history of collecting and preserving materials on the Empire of Japan, it is a great pleasure to present *Japanese America on the Eve of the Pacific War: An Untold History of the 1930s*. The volume features Yasuo Sakata's translated seminal paper, "Fifty Years after World War II and the Study of Japanese American History: The Untold 1930s," which is the catalyst for this edited volume. Sakata is a pioneer scholar in Japanese migration studies, and his paper stresses the importance of using primary source documents written in Japanese and English for research. He also raises awareness of the issue of memory of key events amid and after World War II: for example, the Japanese attack on Pearl Harbor on December 7, 1941; the ensuing arrests of key Japanese American community leaders by the FBI; and the mass incarceration of Japanese and Japanese Americans on the West Coast, which turned these communities upside down. When not confiscated by the FBI, personal diaries and organization records among the Japanese American community were discarded or left behind, for fear of their being construed as evidence of pro-Japanese sentiments. As Sakata points out, the absence of these documents has left a lamentable gap in our current understanding of Japanese American history. The war and US government actions also created long-lasting consequences, silencing many who experienced the history of the 1930s—a decade crucial to understanding the trajectories leading up to the outbreak of the war. Against this backdrop, the Japanese Diaspora Initiative developed the Hoji Shinbun Digital Collection, the world's largest online collection of overseas Japanese newspapers, to fill this gap.

The enthusiastic collaborations we were able to develop for this publication with leading scholars of Japanese American history as well as of US-Japan diplomatic and economic history owe a lot to Sakata's respected position in these fields. Sakata's reputation was earned by his tireless research energy to study primary sources in multiple countries and languages; his inquisitive mind, which searched for historical evidence down to every detail; and most importantly, his critical thinking to challenge the prevailing paradigms. His broad research scope helped him gain recognition beyond immigration studies, as witnessed by the number of scholars contributing to this volume from outside this immediate field. This is a promising development toward expanding the boundary of immigration and Japanese American histories to reach and include historians of Japan.

Sakata's contributions to the field are not limited to his own research. Like Mr. Hoover, Professor Sakata always had future generations of scholars in mind. To ensure their access, he has generously donated materials he has accumulated over many years of research to Hoover, including primary source surveys of first-generation Japanese Americans. He also has allowed us to host his transcriptions of handwritten Japanese newspapers published in San Francisco—*Aikoku, Jiyū,* and *Daijūkyūseiki*—on the Hoji Shinbun Digital Collection, making the full text searchable online.

With this book, we honor both the ideas of Mr. Hoover and the scholarship of Professor Sakata that emphasize preserving and promoting the use of primary source documents to learn lessons from the past, and we ensure passing their legacies to future generations of scholars.

ERIC WAKIN
*Director, Hoover Institution Library & Archives*
*Deputy Director and Research Fellow, Hoover Institution*

# Acknowledgments

For the publication of this edited volume, we owe so much to Yasuo Sakata for his uncompromising research and leadership in the fields of Japanese American history and US-Japan diplomatic history, which inspired and encouraged many researchers for decades. We thank him, his family, and the Japanese Association for Migration Studies for allowing us to translate his seminal paper, "Sengo 50-nen to Nikkei Amerikajinshi kenkyū—Katararenai 1930-nendai." We also extend our sincere gratitude to John J. Stephan of the University of Hawaiʻi at Mānoa; he shared Sakata's vision and research method, which was firmly based on empirical evidence, as well as his unyielding attitude not to allow research to be compromised amid prevailing academic, popular, and political trends.

Many of the authors in this edited volume have worked with Sakata: Masako Iino, Teruko Kumei, Masato Kimura, Brian Masaru Hayashi, and Tosh Minohara. Their respect for Sakata's scholarship continues to inspire them. We thank them for their willingness to contribute new research works or allow us to translate their outstanding essays initially published in Japanese. We are also grateful to the Japan International Cooperation Agency for granting permission to translate Kumei's essay, "1930-nendai no kibei undō—Amerika kokusekihō tono kanren ni oite," into English.

Sakata's centerpiece in this volume also attracted a group of researchers, some of whom are willing to challenge themselves to enter into unfamiliar territory in Japanese American history. We appreciate the wonderful contributions of new research by Mire Koikari, Toshihiko Kishi, Rashaad Eshack, and Michael R. Jin.

To conduct such research, needless to say, historical resources are essential. Without many repository institutions and collaborators, we could not have made available a large amount of data now found on the Hoji Shinbun Digital Collection at the Hoover Institution Library & Archives. We value its shared vision of giving researchers open access to its historical resources.

Many Hoover Institution Press and Hoover Institution Library & Archives staff members contributed to the process of putting together this edited volume; they range from the preservation department to the digitization team, editors, and the Japanese Diaspora Initiative team. Their visible and invisible contributions also are extremely valuable for us.

Last but not least, we sincerely appreciate the endowed Japanese Diaspora Initiative and its donor for their continuing support to develop robust Japanese diaspora studies with the use of primary source materials, as Yasuo Sakata always insisted.

# Yasuo Sakata and Japanese American History

*Eiichiro Azuma*

The Hoover Institution Library & Archives is home to Yasuo Sakata's personal papers, which include Japanese-language primary source materials and transcripts of rare immigrant newspapers. Sakata's professional career has been dedicated to the development of both scholarship on and research archives for Japanese American and migration history. Combined with the Hoji Shinbun Digital Collection—a massive online database of overseas Japanese newspapers—the Sakata Collection forms an important component of Hoover's Japanese Diaspora collection.

The inspiration for this anthology stemmed from Sakata's seminal essay published in Japanese in 1995—translated and featured here as chapter 1. Organized around the theme of the "untold 1930s," this edited volume not only pays tribute to Sakata's role as a foremost historian of early Japanese America and transpacific migration. It provides an opportunity for younger generations of Anglophone scholars to reflect on Sakata's enormous contributions while also elucidating how closely his scholarship is intertwined with well-known works of other pioneer historians, like Yuji Ichioka and John J. Stephan. Indeed, by carving out a new area of research and interpretation in Japanese American history, Sakata's chapter is full of valuable historiographical insights and methodological innovations.

The wide array of contributors to this anthology, and the diverse historical subjects they explore, reveal Sakata's status as a role model and trailblazer. His influence has not been limited to Japanese American history; he also made his mark in many other associated fields and topics, including the history of diplomacy and geopolitics, international trade, and immigrant/ethnic nationalism. Taking up these topics and more, some contributors here are Japan-based associates of Sakata who have either produced their original essays or permitted their Japanese-language works to be translated for this volume. Other contributors are Anglophone scholars who authored brand-new historical studies in response to Sakata's call for serious empirical research on the "untold 1930s." Directly or indirectly, both groups of contributors share, or are inspired by, Sakata's scholarly interventions.

## Yasuo Sakata as a Trailblazer in Japanese American and Migration History

Sakata's career and scholarship have spanned both US and Japanese academia. Amid the emergence of Japanese American history as an academic field during the 1960s, he pursued his doctoral degree in Japanese history at UCLA, played an instrumental role in the development of the Japanese American Research Project (JARP) collection there with Yuji Ichioka, and eventually returned to Japan in 1990 to take a professorship at Osaka Gakuin University and help establish the Japanese Association for Migration Studies (JAMS). In chapter 2 of this volume and an introductory essay for Sakata's *On a Collision Course* (2020), his close colleague Masako Iino provides a detailed account of his service to the field of migration studies there.[1] I do not intend to replicate her discussion, but suffice it to say Sakata's standing as a founder of migration studies in Japan is well recognized in the Japanese-language scholarly world.

Sakata's historiographical interventions revolve around his view of the 1930s as a "historical vacuum" in the academic literature on Japanese Americans (see page 15). He contends that this vacuum constitutes a chronological and conceptual missing link between the accumulated studies of the pre-1924 immigration exclusion and the massive scholarship on the wartime mass incarceration. In chapter 1, Sakata expounds on key reasons for the existence of this vacuum and the skewed understandings and methodological problems such uneven historiographical coverage engendered in the field of Japanese American history. One factor he touches on in his concluding remarks of that chapter suggests the enduring impact of Sakata's seminal essay, originally published in 1995.

That year marked the fiftieth anniversary of the end of the Pacific War and followed by only a few years the successful conclusion of Japanese Americans' movement for redress and reparations for their unconstitutional imprisonment by the United States government during the same war. Thus, when Sakata published his Japanese essay in the inaugural issue of the JAMS's *Annual Review of Migration Studies*, war-related topics still drew intense attention from the public and scholarly world. In this context, critical reappraisals of the Pacific War and its prehistory merged with the closure of a "taboo" in Japanese American studies: complicated relations between prewar Japanese America and imperial Japan, including the immigrant support for Japan's military aggression in China during the 1930s. Sakata explained how that taboo accounted for the prevailing absence of scholarly attention to that decade:

> Almost every Nikkei researcher in Japanese American studies was directly involved in the fight [redress movement]. They feared that those who still had racially discriminatory views against the Japanese and Japanese Americans would take advantage of the Issei's [Japanese immigrants'] loyalty to their Japanese ancestral land, if disseminated as a historical fact, to support their anti-redress view and claim to be legitimate. . . . One of the prolific researchers of Japanese American history and one of those who showed strong interest in 1930s Japanese America, Yuji Ichioka, was also an activist fighting for the redress. He revealed his concern to me, his friend and a Japanese American historian, over the possible use of Issei's patriotic activities, among others, against the redress by bigots. [See page 38.]

With the successful conclusion of the redress movement, however, Sakata urged us to delve seriously into "the period's impact on the historical research of Japanese America" (see page 19).

Indeed, as Sakata himself cites, it was Ichioka who almost simultaneously spoke about the need to study the 1930s, describing the decade as an "unexplored period" in Japanese American history (see page 15). This is not a coincidence. This author, a disciple of Ichioka at UCLA, recalls him explaining how much the spark of his interest in the post-1924 history of the Issei and their US-born Nisei children emerged from conversations with Sakata. Sakata's centerpiece in this volume, thus, must be read as one that also had a profound impact on the development of Anglophone scholarship on Japanese Americans spearheaded by Yuji Ichioka. Put differently, I daresay that despite language barriers, Sakata's insights have already been transmitted via Ichioka's English-language works to Anglophone scholars. Not only this author but also many US-based contributors of this volume, including those who have not met Sakata in person, are hence beneficiaries of his foresight and accomplishments without even knowing about the transnational connection between two pioneer historians of Japanese America.

Therefore, it is important to delve further into the partnership between Sakata and Ichioka, lifetime friends and intellectual allies who bulldozed to erect the foundation of Japanese American studies when the field was barely at its inception. A Berkeley-born Nisei, Ichioka is widely known as one of the founders—if not the founder—of Japanese American history as an academic field in United States academia. In 1968, he was instrumental in organizing the Asian American Political Alliance in the San Francisco Bay Area; he coined the term "Asian American" to bring hitherto-divided Asian ethnicities together as a unified group based on their shared "racial" experience under Orientalist US racism. In this pivotal moment, his thirst for knowledge about Issei history coalesced with his political activism. A year after he was recruited as the instructor of the first-ever Asian American studies course at UCLA, Ichioka became the associate director of its Asian American Studies Center, where he laid the foundations for historical research and publications in English on the Japanese American experience, including the award-winning monograph titled *The Issei: The World of the First-Generation Japanese Immigrants, 1885–1924* (1988).[2]

Sakata was not only a collaborator with but also an informal teacher to Ichioka on how to read Japanese immigrant sources and how to understand their experience from the perspective of modern Japanese history. Much of Ichioka's work was influenced by Black radical thought and the antiwar movement of 1960s America, but without his association with Sakata, his scholarly perspective and research methodology could not have become nearly as transnational as they did.

They met originally in the 1960s, when both were promising undergraduate students at UCLA. They parted ways after graduation in 1962: Sakata pursuing a doctoral degree in Japanese history at UCLA, and Ichioka graduate study in Chinese history at Columbia University. They were reunited at their alma mater when Ichioka taught the first Asian American studies course in 1969—the year Sakata completed his PhD. It was the beginning of an intellectual partnership that would last through the next two decades. Sakata's professional career is thus inseparable from both the early history of Japanese American studies in the United States and Ichioka's professional career as the foremost historian of the Japanese American experience in Anglophone academia.

Inspired by Sakata's vision as articulated in chapter 1, between the publication of his first monograph and his untimely passing in 2002, Ichioka composed a number of research-based essays on Issei and Nisei experiences in the 1930s. His nearly complete book manuscript was later published posthumously under the title *Before Internment: Essays in Prewar Japanese American History* (2006)—a major milestone that sheds light on many "untold" aspects of Japanese American history of the 1930s.[3] As a co-editor of that volume, this author can also attest to the imprint of Sakata's influence on Ichioka's works on the decade "before [the wartime] internment." At the time of his death, Ichioka argued in a draft of his book's introduction:

> What happened in the interwar period (especially 1931–1941) had a definite influence on events during the internment period, so much so, indeed, that the latter cannot, in my judgment, be properly understood without taking into account the former.[4]

Ichioka's observation neatly corresponds to Sakata's counterpart, as noted in chapter 1. The latter wrote in 1995:

> [T]he 1930s should be considered a close link with and a period preceding the Japanese American incarcerations, and be studied for

their cause-and-effect relationship. . . . Am I the only historian who wonders whether historians have neglected to conduct empirical research based on historical continuity and serious investigations of historical materials? (See page 18.)

Perhaps Sakata was not "the only historian," but he was certainly a primary trailblazer in opening doors for serious historical research on the 1930s, a standard carried by Ichioka and his students.

## Yasuo Sakata's Role in Archival Development and Vernacular Primary Source Research

Chapter 1 underscores another element of Sakata's pioneering role—his tackling of the "challenges in resource collection, organization, and evaluation that researchers face in studying the 1930s" (see page 19). This methodological contribution, too, emerged from his work with Ichioka at UCLA. As Sakata explains, rescuing the 1930s from historical obscurity requires both discovery of immigrant primary source materials and close and critical reading of them. Indeed, Sakata, with Ichioka, was not only responsible for organizing the world's best collection of vernacular Japanese immigrant sources at UCLA, he also catalyzed methodological innovations in analyzing and interpreting them. Organized mainly by Sakata and Ichioka, the JARP collection consists of over 760 archival boxes that include printed matter, personal papers, organizational records, and rare immigrant publications.[5]

Sakata was uniquely qualified for this work because of his training in classical Japanese paleography. Schooled in Japanese in a cursive style (*kuzushiji*), Sakata painstakingly deciphered and cataloged these materials. Over the course of years, he undertook the arduous task of transcribing documents written by hand in a premodern grammar illegible to most people, including native Japanese speakers. Sakata knew every nook and cranny of the landscape of immigrant source materials in the JARP collection and beyond, and his discussion in chapter 1 of the biases embedded in the *History of Japanese in America* (*Zaibei Nihonjinshi*) is a poignant example of how he developed a new approach to primary source analysis—a method that has had enormous influence over other historians of Japanese America, including Ichioka.

Sakata was also instrumental in discovering and assembling a variety of Japanese immigrant vernacular newspapers in the JARP—some were original copies of rare papers, and others microfilmed issues of major Issei dailies.[6] Hoover's Japanese Diaspora Initiative digital collection has expanded on many of these materials Sakata helped preserve for a future generation of researchers. Taking advantage of prewar Japanese immigrant newspapers, many contributors to this volume also benefited from Sakata's work in archival development.

Sakata also identified Japan's diplomatic papers as an important but neglected source of information about Japanese immigrants in the United States, helping to build a massive collection of selected microfilmed materials from the Diplomatic Archives of the Ministry of Foreign Affairs of Japan.[7] These materials remain important in historians' efforts to broaden the scope of migration studies and examine migration as integral to the history of relations between the United States and Japan—and vice versa. Driven by Sakata's emphasis on immigrant-related research in bilateral relations, some diplomatic historians came to take the migration question seriously while migration historians became more keenly aware of the importance of geopolitics upon the everyday experience of Japanese immigrants and their US-born children.

This volume extends Sakata's vision and methodological intervention to the historical study of Japanese Americans in 1930s' Hawai'i. Because his—and Ichioka's—endeavors for research and archival development focused primarily on the continental United States, particularly California, the archive-based scholarship on Hawai'i's Japanese lagged behind; a notable exception is John J. Stephan's work, which illuminates the 1930s as a significant, if not controversial, part of the Issei and Nisei experience in the mid-Pacific Islands.[8] Part III of this anthology reflects our hope to shed light on that regional blind spot in historiography by showcasing original works that draw upon the history Sakata advocated for—and what Stephan has pioneered in the context of Hawai'i's Japanese American experience.

## Book Organization

This anthology is organized into four parts. In Part I, the first chapter—Sakata's centerpiece—presents the rationale for why and how the "untold 1930s" should be studied, thereby setting up a basic conceptual framework that the other contributors adapted for their respective chapters. In chapter 2, his long-term associate Masako Iino explores Sakata's place in the institutional and historiographical development of migration studies in Japan, providing a glimpse of Sakata's vision and leadership in Japanese academia. Compared to its Anglophone counterpart, in which the question of relations between Japan and overseas migrant societies is more contentious, Japanese scholarship on migration has generated more diasporic, albeit generally Japan-centered, perspectives and orientations.

Featuring contributions by eight historians of varied backgrounds and generations, this anthology is then divided into three parts: two regional units and one thematic. In Part II, chapters 3 and 4, Teruko Kumei and Michael R. Jin each explore issues surrounding Kibei (Nisei residents of Japan returning to America). A translation of Kumei's 1993 Japanese essay, chapter 3 exemplifies the outstanding quality of empirical research and the kind of close reading of primary sources advocated and spearheaded by Sakata.[9] Kumei examines the "Kibei encouragement movement," which Issei leaders organized to defend the ethnic farm industry and cope with labor shortages. Intended for Japanese audiences, the chapter reflects sensitivities to their interests—that is, relations between immigrant leadership and their homeland supporters and government officials. It also explores the question of dual nationality and the threat of denaturalization under the United States Nationality Act of 1940, which placed Kibei in a highly precarious position amid volatile and deteriorating US-Japan relations.

A historian of a younger generation who was trained in the United States, Michael R. Jin built on Ichioka's pioneering works, producing scholarship in dialogue with US-based historiography of Japanese American history. To offset the pervasive omissions of Kibei in ethnic historical narratives, chapter 4 offers a detailed account of specific Kibei individuals—their tumultuous transnational experience and their subsequent expulsion from historical memory in postwar Japanese America.

Echoing Kumei's problematization of dual national belonging/non-belonging as a major challenge to Kibei, Jin calls into question the "dominant historical narrative centered on the unquestioned loyalty of the Nisei" that has perpetuated their absent presence in community identity and historiography (see page 113).[10]

Part III offers three original studies—chapter 5 authored by Japan-based historian Toshihiko Kishi, and the sixth and seventh chapters authored by US/UK-based scholars Mire Koikari and Rashaad Eshack. Translated from Japanese, Kishi's study reveals the kind of meticulous research and close reading of vernacular immigrant sources, particularly newspapers, that Sakata promoted, with attention to the "untold 1930s" in Maui, Hawai'i. It is also important to note that Kishi's essay is among the few serious historical studies that look at the Issei experience outside O'ahu (if not Honolulu). So little is known about the history of Japanese in islands other than O'ahu, barring an example of Kona in the Big Island of Hawai'i. Chapter 5 begins to fill that historiographical gap.

Koikari and Eshack revisit some of the central historiographical questions identified by the few existing studies of the 1930s. In chapter 6, Koikari grapples with what Sakata describes as a "taboo" topic: the Issei's nationalistic support of imperial Japan's military aggression in China. Yuji Ichioka and others (including this author) have taken up this topic in part by responding to Sakata's call, but they all look at California and other Pacific Coast states.[11] Koikari's chapter presents a much-needed corrective to this California-centered historiography by documenting the Issei's expressions and practices of external homeland nationalism in prewar Hawai'i. Koikari brings her expertise in gender studies to bear in elucidating Issei and Nisei women's role in community-wide efforts to support their home/ancestral land. Well researched and astutely analyzed, her study defies simple comparison with its better-known West Coast counterpart and signals a new opportunity for empirical research on Hawai'i's Japanese community.

In chapter 6, Eshack applies a transpacific perspective to the Nisei education problem by contextualizing the subject within US-Japan cultural relations. Trained as a historian of Japan at Cambridge University, the author represents a growing cohort of young historians who cross the rigid boundaries between Asian history and Asian American history. Proficient in Japanese and knowledgeable about modern Japanese history, Eshack directs a critical look at connections Issei leaders forged with Japanese educators in their attempt to keep alive ethnic heritage culture—especially Japanese language and morality—among Hawai'i-born Nisei. Their efforts intersected an equally pivotal and inseparable matter of immigrant concern: the meaning of the Nisei's US citizenship and their responsibility as ethnic/diasporic Japanese. Eshack's attention to the local, national, and global dimensions of Nikkei citizenry complicates a mono-national mode of analysis common in the existing historiography.

Part IV features three essays by Sakata's long-term associates in Japan and the United States. Chapter 8 is a translation of Masato Kimura's 1994 essay that originally appeared in a Japanese anthology co-edited by Yasuo Sakata.[12] It examines how Morimura Bros., a major trading firm in New York City, adapted to volatile political and economic conditions under rapidly deteriorating relations between the United States and Japan on the eve of the Pacific War. Morimura's managers were not only movers and shakers of bilateral trade but also leaders of New York's Japanese immigrant society. Kimura's chapter narrates how East Coast Issei merchants negotiated difficulties stemming from geopolitics they had no control over. Beyond its focus on the late 1930s and early 1940s, chapter 8 helps broaden our understanding of Japanese American history, which historically has largely attended to the experience of the laboring and farming class on the West Coast.

The last two chapters reveal how Japanese American ethnic experience was inseparable from poignant aspects of diplomatic and military histories, although they do not concern Japanese Americans centrally. Tosh Minohara offers a rare glimpse into the internal workings of high-level Japanese diplomatic circles when the two governments were on a collision course. Alternatively, Brian M. Hayashi traces the development of US military intelligence systems surrounding the question of national security risks posed by the Nikkei population on the eve of the Pacific War. Both authors have published major research monographs that examine Japanese diplomacy and US military intelligence, respectively, through the lens of the Japanese American experience; their chapters should be considered as culminations of their earlier research interests.[13] They also shared intellectual and personal connections with Sakata, whose expansive vision of history accommodated many themes that do not necessarily fit into the conventional definitions of migration history, diplomatic history, or military history. Thus, chapters 9 and 10 may be read as emblematic of the important nexuses migration studies have forged with other fields of historical research.

Assembling the outstanding historical studies around Sakata's foundational essay, this anthology is an attempt to catalyze further scholarly research and writing based on the kind of thorough and careful analysis of primary source materials that one pioneer historian spearheaded in both the United States and Japan. It is our hope that the publication of this volume will not only deepen public understanding of the still largely "untold 1930s" era of Japanese American history but also promote Japanese American studies in general. Thanks to Sakata's tireless effort and the generous donation of his personal and research papers, scholars of Japanese America and transpacific migration now have access to rich repositories of vernacular Issei-related materials at UCLA, Hoover Institution Library & Archives, and beyond. It is then only fitting to conclude this introduction with the closing sentence of Sakata's chapter:

Shouldn't we, historians of Japanese America, finally prepare to do earnest research on the untold 1930s?

## Notes

1. Masako Iino, "Introduction," in Yasuo Sakata, *On a Collision Course: The Dawn of Japanese Migration in the Nineteenth Century*, ed. Kaoru Ueda (Stanford, CA: Hoover Institution Press, 2020), xxi–xxviii.

2. Yuji Ichioka, *The Issei: The World of the First-Generation Japanese Immigrants, 1885–1924* (New York: Free Press, 1988).

3. Yuji Ichioka, *Before Internment: Essays in Prewar Japanese American History*, eds. Gordon H. Chang and Eiichiro Azuma (Stanford, CA: Stanford University Press, 2006).

4. Ichioka, *Before Internment*, 3.

5. See Yasuo Sakata, *Fading Footsteps of the Issei: An Annotated Check List of the Manuscript Holdings of the Japanese American Research Project Collection* (Los Angeles: Asian American Studies Center, UCLA Center for Japanese Studies, and Japanese American National Museum, 1992); and Yuji Ichioka, Yasuo Sakata,

Nobuya Tsuchida, and Eri Yasuhara, *A Buried Past: An Annotated Bibliography of the Japanese American Research Project Collection* (Berkeley: University of California Press, 1974).

6. See Ichioka et al., *A Buried Past*, 132–40.

7. Ichioka et al., 19–34. There are over one hundred microfilm reels. Until the digital database of the Japanese diplomatic papers became available several years ago, the UCLA microfilmed collection was a valuable resource for those researchers who could not travel to Tokyo.

8. John J. Stephan, *Hawaii under the Rising Sun: Japan's Plans for Conquest after Pearl Harbor* (Honolulu: University of Hawai'i Press, 1986). In Hawai'i, virtually no systematic effort to collect prewar primary sources has existed despite the absence of the wartime mass incarceration that resulted in the loss of many Issei-related materials. This marks a stark contrast to the continental United States, where the JARP managed to identify and preserve what was left in the 1960s. For this reason, there is no equivalent to the JARP collection in Hawai'i, though the University of Hawai'i library has sizable, albeit scattered, rare publications and archival papers relating to the Issei experience. Some community organizations also hold local primary source materials. Through the work of Kaoru Ueda, Hoover's Japanese curator, its Japanese Diaspora Initiative now endeavors to help identify and preserve what has gone uncollected in Hawai'i and elsewhere.

9. Kumei Teruko, "1930-nendai no kibei undō," *Ijū kenkyū* 30 (1993): 149–62. On her monograph dealing partially with the 1930s, see Kumei Teruko, *Gaikokujin o meguru shakaishi: Kindai Amerika to Nihonjin imin* (Tokyo: Yūzankaku, 1995).

10. See also Michael R. Jin, *Citizens, Immigrants, and the Stateless: A Japanese American Diaspora in the Pacific* (Stanford, CA: Stanford University Press, 2021), 14–55.

11. See Ichioka, *Before Internment*, 180–226; and Eiichiro Azuma, *Between Two Empires: Race, History, and Transnationalism in Japanese America* (New York: Oxford University Press, 2005), 163–86.

12. Kimura Masato, "Nichibei kaisen to Zaibei kigyō," in *Tairitsu to dakyō: 1930-nendai no Nichibei tsūshō kankei*, eds. Yamagami Kazuo and Sakata Yasuo (Tokyo: Daiichi Hōki Shuppan, 1994), 347–72.

13. Minohara Toshihiro, *Hainichi Iminhō to Nichibei kankei* (Tokyo: Iwanami Shoten, 2002); and Brian M. Hayashi, *Asian American Spies: How Asian Americans Helped Win the Allied Victory* (New York: Oxford University Press, 2021).

# Part I

# Yasuo Sakata's Place in Migration and Nikkei Studies

# CHAPTER I

# Fifty Years after World War II and the Study of Japanese American History

## The Untold 1930s

*Yasuo Sakata*

*Translated by Kaoru Ueda*

The fifty years after World War II, particularly from 1970 onward, have been an extremely significant, vibrant, and exciting period for researchers of Japanese American history—a time when we could shed light on understudied subjects.[1] Scholars in the United States and Japan published research results based on meticulous and empirical investigations of new material or theoretical analyses based on innovative analytical concepts.[2] However, should we researchers celebrate these accomplishments? Or should we instead be aware of the stagnant water that may exist under the visible current on the surface? We still have what Yuji Ichioka called an "unexplored period" in the historical study of Japanese Americans, even half a century after World War II.[3]

This historical vacuum is sandwiched between two major events of twentieth-century history: the Immigration Act of 1924 and the outbreak of the Pacific War after the Japanese attack on Pearl Harbor. After being enacted in July 1924, the former reportedly angered many Japanese, who regarded it as a national humiliation.[4] This law, legally ruling Japanese as "aliens incligible for citizenship," completely banned the entry of Japanese into the United States as immigrants.[5] The latter, proclaimed as "the Day of Infamy" by President Franklin D. Roosevelt, became a catalyst for propelling the American will to fight. No post–World War II

This paper was originally published in Japanese as "Sengo 50-nen to Nikkei Amerikajinshi kenkyū—Katararenai 1930-nendai" in *Imin Kenkyū Nenpō* 1 (1995): 3–42.

historian of Japanese America would dismiss this so-called interwar period of seventeen years as not worthy of study.

Other fields of historical inquiry, such as US-Japan diplomatic history, deal with the interwar period, and the 1930s in particular, as a concentrated and comprehensive study target to investigate the causes of the Pacific War. But why has the historical study of Japanese Americans left the 1930s as an "unexplored period," although the study of Japanese American history arguably requires an international perspective? Would this gap suggest the historians of Japanese America are dealing with unique conditions or reasons? Of course, we could surmise the presence of some superficial reasons. We can intuitively understand parallel situations between Japanese and Japanese American historians in the 1950s, only ten years after the war; they regarded the 1930s as a past they would not want to touch upon. Many Japanese historians with World War II experience were undeniably hesitant to study the interwar period, particularly the 1930s, because they regarded this period as too close to the immediate and personal past, which would preclude them from conducting objective academic research. Similarly, Japanese American researchers and writers, who were forcibly removed to incarceration camps and experienced hardship behind barbed wire, arguably avoided revisiting the 1930s, a decade considered to hold the potential causes for their disaster, sufferings, and humiliation.[6]

In fact, the 1930s were vividly memorialized with accounts of historical events, personal and family life experiences, and activities of the Japanese in America, which led to the outbreak of the loathsome US-Japanese war.[7] This event turned the lives of Issei and Nisei upside down. Among themselves, they were unwilling to discuss some facts; for example, the "patriotic" fundraising activities that were socially organized and boomed in Japanese America after the Second Sino-Japanese War in July 1937.[8] Even against this backdrop, researchers' personal proximity to the past and mental blocks do not convincingly explain why the 1930s have remained unexplored territory. We need to consider more fundamental reasons. It appears that complex reasons alone can explain why postwar generations of Sansei and Yonsei researchers who collaborate with non-Nikkei scholars rarely study the 1930s even more than half a century after the war.

I argue that this situation in Japanese American history—Nikkei scholars' muted interest in the unexplored late 1920s and 1930s— reflects unignorable disproportionality in the research. Postwar Japanese American historical research is characterized by the concentration on certain topics in which its scholars are interested. To explain concretely, historians in Japan and the United States have frequently selected topics related to two major events that created a fissure in twentieth-century history: the racially biased discriminatory ban of Japanese immigrants' entry into the United States via the Immigration Act of 1924, and the forced removal and incarceration of the Issei and Nisei who lived in the US West, in violation of constitutional human rights, following the president's executive order after the Japanese attack on Pearl Harbor.[9] The other frequently selected topics did not go far beyond these two events but included anti-Japanese movements and incidents at the beginning of the twentieth century that precipitated the enactment of the Immigration Act and its related events and conditions.[10]

What do these research selections tell us about Japanese American historians? The fact that many scholars did not choose to research the seventeen years that link these two major events suggests that historians did not judge this period as significant or had a reason to avoid it. If the latter is the case, [I would argue that] this research decision constitutes a flaw or an issue in the Japanese American historical study. Historians have not yet seriously ascertained the correlation between the two significant historical events based on empirical evidence of historical records. However, the two are inferred to have been racially motivated. Many questions remain unanswered. Can we find any common threads among political decision makers of these two events? If so, what were the linkages? Can we regard the nature of American racial prejudice in 1924 as fundamentally similar to that in 1941?

Historians often discuss whether they can apply the principle of periodization to historical inquiries. However, shouldn't we instead deal with the outstanding issue of why this historical vacuum has remained unanswered? To put it radically, early twentieth-century Japanese American history consists of two chapters with a hiatus in between. The chapter of endurance and suffering starts with the enactment of the Immigration Act of 1924, which led to diplomatic negotiations like the Gentlemen's Agreement, the establishment of the Asiatic Exclusion League, anti-Japanese movements like the San Francisco school segregation, and the rise of Yellow Peril discourse driven by White racism. Once this chapter closes in the 1920s, a new chapter begins with the forced removal and incarceration of Japanese Americans after the outbreak of the Pacific War in December 1941. It continues with Japanese Americans' postwar quest for racial justice and their success stories.

The Immigration Act of 1924 infuriated the Japanese, to the point that it has been represented as a "national outcry." The prevailing story is that the Japanese then tucked it away for the next seventeen years, without rekindling it to impact the US-Japan relationship.[11] However, the reasons are not yet ascertained. What had happened to the serious voices of Tokutomi Sohō and Uchimura Kanzō, who called for the entire nation to stand up to take revenge against American humiliation?[12] White Americans and Japanese emotionally confronted one another at the beginning of the twentieth century; the former brandished White racism, and the latter, having believed themselves de-Asianized, insisted on equal treatment as the subjects of the Empire of Japan, a rising Asian power. This sensitive conflict triggered war scares in the 1900s and 1910s.[13] Yet its presence disappears from many history books as if it had suddenly gone underground in 1924.[14] Can empirical studies support George F. Kennan's argument that American anti-Japanese sentiment irritated sensitive Japanese via immigration issues and led to deteriorating US-Japan relations leading up to the Pacific War?[15] Almost no scholarly research has been conducted on this issue so far.[16] Furthermore, the 1930s should be considered a close link with and a period preceding the Japanese American incarcerations, and be studied for their cause-and-effect relationship. However, the 1930s have been left out of the subject of study, unlike the wartime incarcerations. The latter have been a target of intense and persistent research on a stand-alone basis, triggered by the Japanese attack on Pearl Harbor. Many analyses have been conducted from this perspective.[17] Am I the only historian who wonders whether historians have neglected to conduct empirical research based on historical continuity and serious investigations of historical materials?

One thing I should mention here is that this article never intends to criticize historians for their negligence or disinterest. It instead attempts to emphasize that these unexplored seventeen years have been left out of the Japanese American historical inquiries and to demonstrate this omission's impact on the discipline. I don't intend to present this paper as a lament to the absolute absence of studies covering 1924 to 1941. On the contrary, excellent and interesting, albeit limited in number, research papers dealing with this period have been published in the United States.[18] Moreover, new Nisei leaders, who replaced the Issei leaders after their wartime arrest and became active in postwar Japanese America, published their autobiographies and Japanese American histories starting in 1970. In these publications, they clearly voiced their core beliefs, political views, and historical judgment related to the 1930s, based on their experiences.[19] I would boldly emphasize that these books, written by a small minority of Nisei who shared similar opinions, were published as historical documents, leaving for future generations only one-sided stories by the Nisei leaders who were critical of the Issei's views and judgment as well as their hindsight interpretations—a situation of skewed historical material that researchers should be wary of. Instead, this paper attempts to suggest the danger of this by discussing the unexplored period in Japanese American history.

This paper aims to investigate clues as to why the seventeen years in question, particularly the 1930s, have remained a vacuum in Japanese American history, and to discuss the period's impact on the historical research of Japanese America. I do not attempt to cover all the conditions or examine every individual issue in detail in this limited space. Therefore, I will discuss the overview as a starting point: the challenges in resource collection, organization, and evaluation that researchers face in studying the 1930s; where they should pay attention; and what we researchers should do going forward.[20]

## Bias in *History of Japanese in America* as a Core Study Material

White racism ran deep in the first half of the twentieth century in America; Alexander Saxton suggests it was an "ideology," one that characterized the nature of the political, social, and cultural activities of US citizens.[21] Thus, it's challenging to write a history of Japanese in America in this period truly objectively. Japanese American researchers often strongly oppose or, in some cases, rage at the views and judgment exhibited in historical documents. Considering this type of reaction, I question if Japanese American researchers can write such a history.

When Roger Daniels, a postwar pioneer historian of Japanese America, began serious historical inquiries in the second half of the 1950s, not only were extant and accessible historical resources limited, but the materials that were available primarily reflected White Japanese-exclusion advocates' intentions, prejudice, political views, and judgment.[22] One of these examples sees White supremacists' views expressed in the editorials of the first issue of *The White Man*, put out by the Asiatic Exclusion League. The San Francisco–based organization published it in June 1910 after changing its name from the Japanese and Korean Exclusion League, which was originally founded in 1905.[23]

The popular conception of the Exclusionist is a loud-mouthed agitator, who, wallowing in prejudice, proclaims infinite superiority for his particular branch of the human race, and denounces as "inferior" all those of a different complexion. In comparing the races of the earth the words "superior" and "inferior" have no place. Nature has seen fit to make certain variations in the characteristics, color and environments of the diverse racial groups of mankind. Within these groups centuries of evolution have developed boundaries and barriers, indefinable but insurmountable, and doubtless erected for the well-being of humanity. We have heard Japanese of high understanding speak of the Chinese and negro as "inferior races." The use of such terms is to be deplored and evidences a misinterpretation of biological truths. The jungle negro is still in the childhood of his racial existence. Scientists compute that the negro race is some 20,000 years behind the Caucasian racial development. Two hundred centuries hence a black skin may be the badge of the ascendant race. But leaving these controversies to the biologists and ethnologist[s], the fact remains that it is simply impossible for peoples of radical racial variations to dwell together in harmony. . . . Every acre of ground occupied by Asiatics in the United States is just that much lost to the white man. Should California and the Pacific Coast ultimately become occupied by Japanese, the boundary lines of Japan would be, regardless of flags or geographies, where the

Japanese dwelt. . . . The intermingling of races has hitherto been absolutely destructive of social order, and has acted as a check on human progress. Whatever the cause of the present influx of Japanese, the continuation of Japanese immigration can have but one result of war.[24]

White Americans in 1910 might have regarded this editorial as science-based. However, here at the end of the twentieth century, most Americans would agree that this editorial was a convenient and unfair pretense by racist bigots.

Prescott F. Hall was the chairman of the Boston-based Immigration Restriction League, which advocated for restricting the influx of New Immigrants—White immigrants from Eastern Europe and the Mediterranean region, a target of contempt as undesirable. He regarded Japanese laborers on the West Coast as being even more undesirable than already legally excluded Chinese coolie workers and proposed the absolute need to restrict their immigration.[25]

Of the 14,382 [Japanese] immigrants arriving in 1904, practically all were destined to Hawaii, California, Washington, and Oregon, and were laborers, farm laborers, servants, or persons without occupation. They showed about forty-five dollars in money per capita; and the average illiteracy of those over fourteen years of age was 21.6 percent, or nearly three times that of the select classes of Chinese admitted under the Exclusion Acts. . . . In the opinion of some observers, they are more undesirable than the Chinese coolies who were imported [similarly by the immigration companies] before the passage of the Chinese Exclusion Acts. Wages in Japan are about one-half those in the United States, and this stimulus to emigration is aided by the pressure of population in Japan, constantly seeking for new outlets.[26]

Yamato Ichihashi, a Harvard PhD and professor at Stanford University, published *Japanese in the United States* in 1932 to refute exclusionists' unflattering and erroneous interpretations.[27] Concerned about Whites' reactions, even Ichihashi repeats various unassertive explanations that we today could not help but consider lame excuses.

For example, he explains that Japanese *dekasegi* (migrant) laborers in the 1890s and the early 1900s were judged to be similar to excluded Chinese coolies because "the Japanese inherited the prejudice against the Chinese."[28] He refers to a sympathetic American scholar representing Christian organizations, whose view demonstrated a "paternalistic" understanding of Japanese in America.[29]

> Although we may not agree with this statement in its every detail, there is no denying that the Japanese have inherited the prejudice against the Chinese. The first cry "Japs must go," was heard as early as 1887, or five years after the enactment of the Chinese exclusion law. Its author was Dr. O'Donnell of San Francisco, whose political and professional reputation was of doubtful character. He was unable to make it even a municipal political issue, for the following reasons: There were no more than 400 Japanese in the entire state, most of them engaged in domestic service and a very few as farm hands. They were not competing in any field with whites. The Japanese wore American dress and wore no queue. The general public was still unconscious of their presence and the working classes were indifferent.[30]

He attempts to emphasize that early Japanese *dekasegi* laborers were different from excluded Chinese workers.[31] He writes in *History of Japanese in America*, which was published by the Japanese Association in 1940 as part of the 2,600th Anniversary Celebrations of the Japanese Empire:

> Unlike *dekasegi* rural laborers, [who became the target of the anti-Japanese movement,] Japanese [first-generation] pioneers [who settled] in the United States had sizable land, some education, and experience in social activities in Japan. They came to the States with more ambition than to make money. Although some had arrived with some resources, many came resourceless but studied hard to open up their destinies at new dream frontiers. Therefore, today's *dōhō* [Japanese compatriot] society is entirely dissimilar to the immigrants' settlements centering around pure *dekasegi* workers.[32]

Ichihashi's statement demonstrates his attempt to distance the Japanese *dōhō* from the early *dekasegi* laborers, who settled in the United States and became Issei. Doesn't his counterargument simply underscore the passive attitude and self-defense of the Issei, who were extremely sensitive about anti-Japanese attacks and criticism?[33] Postwar Nisei historians of Japanese Americans depict the prewar Japanese society in America as being susceptible to the intentions and reactions of White American society.

> Japanese immigrants struggled against the anti-Japanese exclusion movement. Always sensitive to criticism, immigrant leaders strove to eradicate what they considered the unsavory features of Japanese immigrant life. . . . [The Japanese Association] tried to control the behavior of all immigrants in various ways and even cooperated with police authorities to have so-called undesirable elements deported.[34]

Positioning himself as a non-Nikkei researcher, Daniels characterizes the prewar history of Japanese in America:

> Unfortunately, much of the Asian American experience is what I call "negative history"; that is, for a significant part of their history in this country, Asians have been more celebrated for what has happened to them than for what they have accomplished. At certain times and places in the past, Asians and their children have been a pariah group at the very bottom of the ethnic escalator of American society, holding legal and social status even below that of oppressed American blacks.[35]

Daniels stresses that most Japanese history in America written in English portrays the Issei as supporting characters on the stage where the excluders brilliantly play the main characters, reflecting the historical American prejudice.[36] Against the backdrop of new postwar awareness and understanding, researchers, particularly Japanese American historians, have widely recognized the need to excavate historical diaries and correspondence that honestly recorded the Issei's experience and emotional responses, conduct detailed empirical research on them, and disseminate the exclusion history from a victim's perspective along with their true feelings and reactions. No doubt, many scholars have made tremendous efforts toward this goal since the 1970s.

Yuji Ichioka, in introducing his book *The Issei*, published in 1988, emphasizes he was one of those who made efforts.

> The early history of Japanese immigrants in the United States, far from being a success story, is, above all, a history of a racial minority struggling to survive in a hostile land. Past studies of Japanese immigration have concentrated heavily on the anti-Japanese exclusion movement from 1900 to 1924, focusing on the excluders rather than the Japanese immigrants.[37]

However, how truthfully can Japanese immigrants tell their history, and what are the challenges in the way of achieving this goal?

## Postwar Collection of Nikkei Research Material—Ideals and Realities

After the 1960s, Japanese Americans called for collecting valuable historical resources and documents for the study of Japanese Americans before they disperse or disappear. In response to this call, university libraries and research institutions, primarily in Hawai'i and on the US West Coast, established collection projects.[38] Japanese Americans played central roles in the collection efforts, which took place in their communities.[39]

In concluding these projects, Japanese Americans assessed them as being on par with or near expectations, saying, "In spite of . . . the manner in which they were acquired, and the obvious gaps in the collection, the Japanese American Research Project Collection is without doubt the most significant body of materials on the history of Japanese immigrants and their descendants."[40]

However, over time, some researchers realized the collections acquired on the West Coast, from which Japanese Americans were forcibly removed, may have been too optimistically praised.

They recognized that bias existed in the resources related to the victims' experiences that emphasized minority experiences, opinions, and judgments in Japanese America—a bias dissimilar to what was in the prewar materials, which had strongly reflected exclusionists' intentions, determination, and ideas. It came to light the main cause was the formerly incarcerated Issei's self-defensive concern toward White Americans and their society.

First of all, the researchers noticed the forced removals and incarcerations caused the dispersals and loss of indispensable resources more than they had initially foreseen.[41] As the collections acquired on the West Coast were getting organized and cataloged, researchers were able to grasp a more defined outline of which records had been lost and how it impacted future research. I must say it was ironic that the forced removals and incarcerations, anti-Japanese symbolic events that spurred the researchers of Japanese America, made many indispensable study materials disappear.

The extent and scope of the damage this human disaster caused on the Japanese American study was considerable. The forcibly removed and incarcerated 120,000 Issei and their families account for about 90 percent of all Japanese Americans in the continental United States.[42] Many of them had been living on the West Coast as a permanent settlement place for more than twenty years and raised their families there. Pursuant to the Executive Order, in principle, they were allowed to take what they could carry to the "relocation centers." They did not have the time to contemplate what to take and leave behind for a long time. Instead, they had to make hasty decisions. How did they decide? I quote my previously published explanation below.

> After the Japanese attack on Pearl Harbor, which was criticized as a disgraceful surprise attack, the Japanese Issei, overnight, became enemy aliens in the United States, for they could not obtain US citizenship on the basis of their being ineligible for naturalization. If the Issei lived in neighborhoods where anti-Japanese sentiment was intense, they worried about their safety. After the US-Japan War began, many Issei, their families, and Japanese groups and organizations, including Nihonjinkai (Japanese associations), Japanese Chambers of Commerce, and *kenjinkai* (prefectural associations), likely attempted to burn, bury, or throw into the sea documents that might be taken as evidence of their loyalty to Japan, their motherland and new enemy nation. It became clear through postwar

research interviews that their foremost criterion for selecting potentially dangerous documents was anything written in the Japanese
language. In some cases, they destroyed materials randomly. The
same research interviews suggest that, to the dismay of historians,
some documents that might have been considered unfavorable or
inconvenient to Japanese individuals and organizations were also
destroyed.[43]

The targeted materials for destruction were the records, correspondences, and documents that may have provided evidence against
Issei, particularly leaders in prewar Japanese America, and proved or
deepened the suspicions that they were dangerous enemies. Therefore,
most of these destroyed or discarded materials were about the 1930s, a
decade of worsening US-Japanese relations leading up to the US-Japanese
war. These documents represent the behavior and activities of the Issei
that showed their attachment to Japan. After all, the ineligible aliens
had no choice but to remain the subjects of the Empire of Japan in the
United States. It is not difficult to guess that these documents could
have trapped them if misinterpreted. To understand the Issei's document destructions, you don't have to look any further than the cat-
alog records of postwar Japanese American collections, such as the
Japanese American Research Project (JARP) collection at the University
of California–Los Angeles (UCLA).[44] In other words, the Issei discarded
the valuable pages and the direct voices of Japanese America in the
1930s without edits or additions. Despite the inevitable circumstances,
historians could not regret this act more—one of the significant reasons
for the challenges in studying the 1930s in the postwar era.

Unfortunately, the Issei's caution about White America kept them
silent, negatively influencing the postwar collections and creating a hin-
drance for scholarly research. To further explain, I need to examine the
Issei's psychology. Since this topic touches the core of this paper, I will
take the risk of repeating myself and explain my experience in the JARP
collection.[45] My experience will reveal that the Japanese American
collections acquired in the 1960s concentrate on the materials of particular individuals who fit into specific criteria, despite the expectations of
the project members.

## Silent Issei in the Postwar Era

The JARP began its work in September 1963 at UCLA after preparations dating from the beginning of 1962. One of its primary objectives was to conduct holistic historical and social studies of Issei. Both the senior members of the Japanese American Citizens League (JACL) and the JARP's first project director, Nisei sociologist T. Scott Miyakawa, were concerned about the aging Issei and wanted to record the Issei's memories as much as possible while they were still alive. Many of them were reaching sixty-five or older by 1960. To achieve this, the JARP embarked on interviewing about one thousand Issei randomly selected in urban and rural America.[46] The questionnaire was as long as seventy-three pages. The project staff conducted interviews based on the questionnaires and recorded oral histories of Issei leaders.[47]

However, this project, which was heralded as epoch-making, was hampered unexpectedly despite the planner's expectations. Being a PhD student in history at UCLA at the time, I was directly involved in the study from the inception of the JARP. I was the coordinator of Issei interviews and selected the interviewees and trained Japanese and English bilingual interviewers. The interviews first started in Los Angeles in 1964. However, we frequently encountered a lack of responses from the Issei that were randomly selected. These nonresponses destroyed the illusion that most Issei shared the wish of the project planner and researchers: to pass down the prewar history of Japanese in America to their descendants.

The project staff had wrongly anticipated that Issei in the 1960s would proactively support and cooperate with the project because their prewar Japanese American organizations had a tradition of compiling histories of Japanese in America, and the Japanese American newspapers published commemorative publications [on every possible occasion]. [And more importantly], the situation was significantly changing by the 1960s.[48] The rejection did not stop there. Many Issei leaders who were chairpersons or senior officers of the Japanese Association, the Japanese chamber of commerce, or prefectural associations did not want to be interviewed, or would bite their tongues when it came to certain events and topics.

The majority of Issei who refused to be interviewed were concerned and critical, saying that they would not cooperate to reveal elements of the past that might rekindle anti-Japanese sentiment, already subsiding by then. They gave the cold shoulder to the project planner's and researchers' know-it-all approach. More unexpectedly to me, the majority of the interviewees in Los Angeles responded "none" to the question of personal anti-Japanese experience.[49] Their responses undoubtedly reflected their caution about White American society. These unexpected Issei responses revealed their hardened attitude against truthfully speaking about past events and experiences that were considered to be linked to the outbreak of the US-Japan war and the incarceration camps, and that were thought likely to ignite a new anti-Japanese movement. In the 1960s, contrary to the project planner's expectations, many Issei continued to keep their mouths shut, and very few were willing to speak about their feelings and ideas as is.

The JARP had another objective, complementary to the interviews, of collecting base material for Japanese American studies.[50] It was the first pan–West Coast project of collecting resources. Thus, the results exceeded the original expectations, particularly in terms of volume. However, the acquired resources too demonstrated unexpected bias, reflecting the minds of Japanese Americans, especially Issei, shortly after World War II.

On one hand, the silent Issei refused to gift their private records and documents to the JARP. On the other hand, most of those willing to donate sizable personal records and documents had no worries about their activities in the 1930s. In other words, the donors were primarily limited to those who were not actively engaged in Japanese patriotic organizations or activities—it was considered taboo even to discuss them in the 1960s—or those who could boast of their critical attitude against Japan's militaristic policies and overseas aggression. For example, Mr. H, a devout Christian, was deeply involved both with the Japanese Christian church and American Christian social activities and continued to maintain a friendship with and the respect of White Americans even in the 1930s, despite his ineligibility for US citizenship and his status as a longtime principal of a Japanese-language school. Another example is Mr. Y, a Kibei Nisei, who donated documents. He was a labor union organizer with a left-leaning ideology, and he publicly and continuously criticized the Japanese government's direction and policies through his political organization.[51] There was an exception such as Mr. A, who donated his entire records and documents to the JARP, despite having been active in prewar Japanese society [in the United States].[52] However, Mr. A's case is regarded as an extremely rare one. More frequently, the donors who wanted to boast of their experience selected records and documents for specific purposes or intentions, and brought their auto-biographies and memories—which were obviously edited.[53] Therefore, from a strict perspective, I consider the JARP collection to contain ma-terial that strongly reflects the background of specific individuals. The history woven from these types of historical resources undoubtedly does not reflect the historical realities.

Japan's defeat was a tragic event for the Japanese in America, anni-hilating their prewar dreams and expectations. The 1960s were not that distant from the horrific defeat of Japan at the end of World War II. It is not hard to imagine that some Issei considered their pa-triotic acts a mistake and regretted behaving the way they did in the 1930s when their motherland's diplomatic policy and military action caused US-Japanese relations to deteriorate. We can understand that their patriotic fundraising activities for the Japanese military during the Second Sino-Japanese War were unpleasant memories they wanted to forget. However, historical events and processes cannot be replaced by hindsight.

For historians, the purpose of our research is not to reflect upon memories. The 1930s extend from and are linked with the thirty years of anti-Japanese incidents and sentiment that Japanese in America suffered in the 1900s through the 1920s. The Immigration Act of 1924, criticized as humiliating, was an unforgettable blow to Issei. It is also not a far-fetched assumption that the Japanese in America had ani-mosity against White Americans who had targeted Japanese for racial discrimination, nor that they continued to resent the Immigration Act of 1924 in the 1930s. Meanwhile, research results show that the Issei, now ineligible for citizenship after the Immigration Act of 1924, real-ized their future was shuttered, and raised their expectation for Nisei to carry the future torch.[54] Doesn't that ring true with the reality of Issei, who continued to have a mixed feeling of hatred and resignation, who worked hard every day as ineligible foreigners, and who felt attached to and protected by Japan without expecting the outbreak of US-Japan war—an emergency that turned their and their families' lives upside down overnight?

However, unfortunately, most of the material that would inform historians of the reality of the 1930s has disappeared through forced removals to incarceration camps. Not only that, but out of fear of remembering the prewar and wartime past, the Issei had already passed away without informing us about the whereabouts of many of their private records and documents. They are no longer traceable. As a result, the Issei's loyalty to the Empire of Japan amid its military invasion of China is placed under the postwar spotlight as a "historical fact" based on what is available to study, such as newspapers, which widely reported the Issei's patriotic activities like fundraising efforts for the military campaign.[55]

The historical background against which the Issei were placed—for example, their ideas, judgment, and mindset, since aliens ineligible for citizenship had no choice of protector but Japan—were no longer considered important in postwar Japanese American historical studies. Aren't what we historians seek true reflections, raw ideas, and real conditions of life, and the honest experiences of Japanese in America in the 1930s, free of adaptations influenced by dynamic postwar trends, ideas, and judgments? Aside from simply concluding that the Issei's actions and ideas in the 1930s were wrong, shouldn't researchers place themselves in the 1930s and try to examine them?

Not only that, but what I am concerned about is an additional recent development that offers an edit of the Issei's prewar history. The Asian American Movement of the 1970s spurred drastic changes in White American ideas and views toward historically prejudiced ethnic minorities, and Asian American pride and ethnic identity. During the 1970s and thereafter, the JACL Nisei leaders that took over for Issei leaders who had been arrested and incarcerated amid the chaos of the Japanese attack on Pearl Harbor, published Japanese American histories that Daniels characterizes as "victims' records."

In their publications, postwar Japanese American leaders retrospectively projected the views, beliefs, and judgment of the 1930s as right, based on the idea that Japanese American citizens are Americans—a notion strongly emphasized since the 1970s. However, I regard their postwar conclusions and interpretations as Americans directly colliding with and challenging the situation and mindset of the Issei. The latter were aliens ineligible for citizenship and subjects of the Empire of Japan. However, many of the Issei, who could have refuted assertive Nisei's critical views and conclusions against them, are no longer with us, although they were the ones who had to navigate through the turbulent sea of the 1930s. As I mentioned earlier, the prewar Issei leaders kept silent and didn't publish their private documents and records before their death.

Future studies will provide a basis for concluding whether the Issei's actions in the 1930s were, as suggested by some postwar Nisei leaders, based on false judgments, or otherwise not beneficial to Japanese American society. However, whether such a study will be possible remains questionable. Nobody is alive anymore to answer our questions, and the possibility of finding their records and documents in the near future is extremely limited.

I take the risk of being interpreted as making an excuse here; I am not denying that the biographies of JACL Nisei leaders and other publications are valuable primary materials for Japanese American historical research. I only attempt to point out that what Nisei leaders present to the world are judgments and interpretations of historical transitions and events—so-called hindsight—reflecting the times that have passed since the events, as well as political and economic standpoints and Japanese American consciousness and pride. No primary sources, such as correspondence, diaries, or records, to support these judgments and interpretations have been made available to the public as comprehensive study material.[56] Researchers should prudently avoid outweighing the viewpoints, judgments, and arguments of a small part of the Japanese American community even if they are prominent individuals who played important roles.

*Nisei: The Quiet Americans* by Bill Hosokawa is one example. One of the Issei gave a stirring speech at a farewell party for two Nisei who volunteered to serve in the US Army in the fall of 1939, saying, "We the Issei gladly offer you, our sons, to the cause of the United States. Be brave and prove yourselves loyal citizens of this country, for by so doing you will prove worthy inheritors of the best of the Japanese heritage as well."

Hosokawa quotes Father Joseph Kitagawa:

At that moment the Issei was in a frame of mind that would easily have led him to fight the Japanese forces, should they invade the Pacific Coast. Emotionally it would have been an extremely painful thing for him to do, but he would have done it just the same, for he saw quite clearly that it was the only thing for him to do as one who had been "wedded" to the United States. The traditional Japanese ethic, when faithfully adhered to, would not only justify, but positively demand, his taking the side of the United States. No Issei, however, articulated his feelings on this extraordinarily touchy subject. Yet, amazingly, this sentiment, in almost everybody's heart, quickly dominated the climate of opinion without anyone's expressing it. There could have been no split within the Japanese American family insofar as the issue of war between the United States and Japan was concerned, for in that eventuality the Issei would stand solidly behind the Nisei.[57]

However, nobody has answered the question of how many Issei agreed with this Nisei pastor in 1939.[58] Keen observers may interpret this speech as a prewar expression conscious of White American society. Rumors were circulating that the executive members of the JACL cooperated with the FBI and military intelligence and provided information in 1939–40.[59] Some in the postwar Japanese American society criticized this act. Togo Tanaka, a JACL leader [and a Nisei poet], defended the organization's executives [in his 1941 diary], saying:

Out of the habit defining loyalty, talking about loyalty, interpreting it for both the Japanese and Caucasian communities, a segment of JACL leadership in 1939 and 1940 began to arrogate to itself authority to judge and evaluate the loyalty of members of the Japanese communities. [Having been asked to cooperate in] guarding against sabotage and espionage by federal agents, the JACL representatives for the most part . . . responded with a patriotic zeal exceeded only by their public expression of American loyalty. . . . From the standpoint within the Japanese community, such JACL leaders were perceived as spies and stooges for the FBI.[60]

It was probably an indisputable fact that JACL leaders determined this was the best course of action for Japanese American society in 1940 and acted accordingly on this belief. Therefore, they openly and confidently stated their views and judgment after World War II. The problem is the silenced voices of Issei—their true feelings and criticism that we could no longer hear because JACL leaders "spied" on Issei whose names were included in the FBI and intelligence list of dangerous individuals and who were arrested and confined immediately after the Pearl Harbor attack. As I mentioned earlier, these Issei had kept silent after the war and passed away without leaving their biographies behind, among others. It's not impossible to understand Nisei patriotism as American citizens in the second half of the 1930s, a decade of worsening US-Japan relations. However, what was the patriotism of Issei who lived in the US as aliens ineligible for citizenship? This question is yet to be answered.

Wouldn't these historical circumstances suggest a new bias of the research material emerging, similar to that bias of the 1950s when exclusionists' views and judgment were strongly reflected in the primary source material, as Daniels pointed out? What researchers should be afraid of is that the 1930s would become not only an untold but also a distorted decade.

## Records at the Time of Incident and Memories—Subtle Discrepancies

When studying autobiographies, one should be aware of discrepancies naturally occurring with records kept at the time of the incident. Many biographies and publications written by JACL Nisei leaders show their retrospective judgment based on their memories and experiences. It's up to the researchers to determine the credibility of these documents. However, if researchers relied solely on these memoirs, needless to say, the history reconstructed this way cannot be valued as objectively reliable. As I have explained thus far, the study of Nikkei history in the 1930s or in the prewar era in general encounters challenges to empirical support, given the extremely limited documentary resources. However, this situation is gradually improving with efforts made by Yuji Ichioka, among others. Private documents, albeit a small number, have been donated to the JARP collection at UCLA since the 1960s.

I will discuss one or two areas for future study in reference to these new materials.

These documents indicate that the Pearl Harbor attack and the outbreak of the war between the US and Japan were extremely shocking.

It's a lie, a lie!! It could not be true. I certainly believed it was a false rumor, but a war finally broke out between the US and Japan. The most scary and unwanted event fell on us. Still, I cannot believe it. Let's wait until tomorrow. Then, I will know better.

It felt like a dream that I compiled three pieces of poem and Shinshū Dansō, sent them to Mr. Matsumoto Shūsui at the Nanka Jihō, and beat my brain to answer three questions in the New Year edition of Rafu Shinpō, just this morning. Anything and everything, Japanese-language newspapers will be finished now. A special issue of the Rafu Shinpō arrived in the dead of the night. I felt hushed.[61]

One Issei wrote in his dairy on December 7, 1941, when the Pacific War broke out, and continued the following day, on December 8:

I was irritated although I went to the store and was conducting business as usual. This and that. That and this. I dealt with nonchalant customers and prepared many items for them. Fortunately, both my relative Miura and our family have US citizenship. We can get by for half a year or a year with the money. However, non-US citizens Japanese had their money all frozen. We had about $4,500 to $5,000 in the store. It's our fate. Finally, the feared worst time has arrived.[62]

His entry from December 8 shows his growing anxiety, desperation, deepening worry, and his concern for his household as the head of the family.

I could not sleep much at night. I think everything and anything are our fate, but I cannot help thinking and worrying because everyone else in my family is women and children. We could not keep our store open. We are not permitted to buy or sell anyway. Finally, the end of the store may have come. Although I have little hope for tomorrow, let's live with hope and allow myself to be present for the day until my last day. If I cannot live, that's God's calling. I was worried about many things today. I sent people to procure food and others.[63]

Compared to the Issei, who had little suspicion about optimistic articles in the Japanese-language newspapers, the Nisei, on the other hand, should have expected the worst situation to some extent, given their exposure to articles in English-language newspapers. However, eventually adult Nisei apparently could not hide their surprise at the outbreak of the war. It's been said that JACL chairman Saburo Kido shouted at the Japanese Navy's attack on Pearl Harbor:

That's too fantastic to believe. The report must be wrong, probably just another rumor. Let's hear what H. V. Kaltenborn has to say when he comes on at 12:15.[64]

An Issei recalls his reaction to a phone call from his neighbor.

As soon as I returned home and sat at the dinner table with my family, I heard an ear-piercing phone ringing. I said "Hello, hello," a voice on the other end sounded impatient and repeatedly shouted, "A serious problem." "A serious problem," but she did not get to the point. It was my immediate neighbor Mrs. Aiiso, who called me on the phone. She seemed to be extremely pressed. "What's the matter?" I asked her. She surprisingly responded, "You still don't know yet?" "The radio is non-stop announcing the Japanese Navy is attacking Pearl Harbor right now." While I appreciated her emergency phone call, to be honest, I still could not believe it immediately.[65]

He clearly records how surprised he was, saying that "Although I was aware that unsettling conditions were in the air between the US and Japan, and the degree was growing day by day, I had not expected that our Navy would make a significant blitz attack on the US Navy's only base in the Pacific, Pearl Harbor."[66]

However, memoirs risk turning records written at the time of the event, which reveal the author's emotional reactions in the moment, into

something different. Mike Masaoka, who served as Executive Secretary
of the JACL under the leadership of Chairman Kido, attempts to distinguish himself from the Issei who became enemy aliens, and to illustrate his calm attitude loyal to the US in his autobiography published in
1988, forty-seven years after the Japanese attack on Pearl Harbor.

> When I reached San Francisco, I found Kido being driven almost
> frantic by the demands of his clients and his JACL responsibil-
> ities. Families of Issei seized by the FBI pleaded with Kido to
> help get them released. Of course, he could do nothing for them.
> Japan's act of war had made them "enemy aliens," even though
> it was discriminatory American laws that had kept them in non-
> citizen status. . . . Businesses found their credit curtailed or bank
> accounts tied up and came to Kido for help. . . . I pitched in to try
> to bring order out of the near-chaos of Kido's office. . . . But that
> changed abruptly.
>
> One morning soon after my return, Kido received a call from
> the FBI office asking him to come in with me. I didn't concern my-
> self greatly about the summons, because we had become acquainted
> with some of the special agents before war's outbreak. Several of
> them were acquaintances from University of Utah days who had
> gone into the Bureau after getting their law degrees. Perhaps be-
> cause of these contacts, Kido and I, as well as other JACL leaders,
> were to be accused by some Japanese Americans of being informers
> for the FBI—inu, "dogs," in the Japanese vernacular—who betrayed
> our people. I do not hesitate to say that I cooperated with the FBI
> to the best of my ability; the FBI was the federal agency entrusted
> with internal security, and it was the patriotic duty of all citizens to
> cooperate with any law enforcement agency.[67]

Mike Masaoka was one of the JACL leaders who were criticized as
one of the FBI's *inu*—as he pointed out. At the time of writing this article, this criticism is only whispered about amid the Japanese American
community. No criticism has been expressed as an opinion to the public
or no discussion has been held based on evidence, though one paper
of interest has been published.[68] Shouldn't researchers deal with such
questions as: how should an ethnic community respond to a sudden

change in international affairs or emergency situations; what issues emerge in the community; and how unexpected impacts may be felt among the community members?

Another problem is the fact that, and the reasons why, Nisei leaders insist that they had to grasp the leadership after the outbreak of the war. Mike Masaoka explains the situation where Nisei had to take over the leadership roles played by Issei during this chaotic period.

> The reality was that the FBI had seized more than a thousand prominent Issei within hours after the outbreak of war, stripping Japanese-American communities of their leaders. Most of the remaining Issei were understandably reluctant to step forward. The result was a gaping leadership vacuum into which JACL, as the only organized civic organization left, was inevitably drawn.[69]

As far as I know, no Issei opinions were made available to the public to support Nisei leaders' self-assertion to emphasize that they were US citizens at the outbreak of the war. As Masaoka points out, the reality was that the Issei, who were Japanese nationals, could not be or were unwilling to be the external face of the community. However, couldn't some Issei have assumed even temporary leadership roles while the Issei leaders were detained? It seems wrong to give the impression that all Issei were deflated over the fact that they became enemy aliens.

> The damage to the Japanese in America is indeed severe. Everything and anything cannot be helped, but I'm sorry for many, Komai and Umetsubo of Yamanashi Prefecture, our store's regular customer, Mr. Kawabata, and the bosses of Star Agriculture, Kita, Hirashiki, Ota among others, Mr. Namekawa and Mr. Nakamura. None of them are bad people. The Japanese power is thwarted in the agricultural wholesale market. S. K. and W. F. have no prospect of reopening, and Star Agriculture may go bankrupt in a bad-case scenario. All heartbreaking developments. Mr. Seki of Nyland sent me green chili peppers before he received my letter. Money, albeit scarce, still comes, and he is doing a good amount of business. Apparently, Joe and Sarabia (a Mexican American shopkeeper who works at the store) are drafted. They must take an examination at

six o'clock tomorrow morning. This is an emergency. Even if we don't make much money, as long as we can continue to run the business, I think it's a blessing. How long will the war last? How deeply will we get involved? Just as writer Vicente Peros observes, I hope the day that US and Japan shake hands will come without wasting a day. I'm about to catch a cold. I had a hot lemon and went to sleep.[70]

The above excerpts are taken from the aforementioned Issei diary recorded on December 17, ten days after the Pearl Harbor attack. From this record, one can sense that Issei tried to deal with the emergency calmly, at least until the forced removal started. I suggest researchers further need to study documents like this to prove the "great chaos" caused by the roundup of Issei leaders that Masaoka suggested.

## Conclusions—Redress and the History of the 1930s

Another reason exists why the researchers of Japanese America could not seriously study the 1930s—and it may be considered the most important reason: the redress that the Japanese American community had hoped to achieve and made incessant efforts toward for forty years. Almost every Nikkei researcher in Japanese American studies was directly involved in this fight. They feared that those who still had racially discriminatory views against the Japanese and Japanese Americans would take advantage of the Issei's loyalty to their Japanese ancestral land, if disseminated as a historical fact, to support their anti-redress view and claim to be legitimate. The history of Japanese in America written by prewar exclusionists indeed teaches us a lesson on how effective and risky intentionally distorted facts are. One of the prolific researchers of Japanese American history and one of those who showed strong interest in 1930s Japanese America, Yuji Ichioka, was also an activist fighting for the redress. He revealed his concern to me, his friend and a Japanese American historian, over the possible use of Issei's patriotic activities, among others, against the redress by bigots.[71]

It would require writing out the entire postwar Japanese American history to investigate the relations between postwar Japanese American society's fight for the Japanese American Evacuation Claims Act and the untold 1930s of Japanese America. This is the most apparent reason I refrained from discussing the influence of the redress on the historical study of the 1930s in this short article. Many scholars are currently studying the redress; therefore, it may not be too late for their work to be published before examining this issue.

In conclusion, I want to stress that the forty-year-long fight for redress and reparations for Japanese Americans' forced removal and incarceration would come to an end when President Reagan signed the redress legislation in August 1988, and the US celebrated the fiftieth anniversary of World War II. Shouldn't we, historians of Japanese America, finally prepare to do earnest research on the untold 1930s?

## Notes

1. As the field of study grew and subjects of research diversified, a more interdisciplinary approach was required, which sparked a rigorous reexamination and definition of the basic terminology used in the field. The term *Japanese Americans*, which came to be used by both Japanese and American researchers after the war, is one such example. Reflecting the late 1960s' Asian American Movement and its purpose and slogans as well as the social and political opinions it stresses, however, the term *Japanese Americans* came to be used to mean Japanese immigrants and persons of Japanese ancestry, including Issei in studies in the United States. However, the postwar term *Japanese Americans* became widespread as America came to be known as a "multiethnic country" from the 1970s onward. *Japanese Americans* became an identity and an ethnicity, one of the ethnicities the United States comprises; the phrase was often used as a contrast to the White Anglo-Saxon Protestant, or WASP, which was thought to be the mainstream of American society. In this case, *Japanese Americans* naturally refers to "citizens" who make up a part of the American population, or those who are assumed to be eligible for citizenship. Should this newly coined term, which reflects the state of the generation following the war, be used to mean Japanese immigrants and persons of Japanese ancestry, including the Issei living in the United States with Japanese nationalities, who prior to the 1953 immigration law were considered aliens ineligible for citizenship? Rather, to express the unique experiences and historical background of the prewar Issei, would it not make sense to use the term *Japanese in America* that they themselves used to refer to themselves? I am one of the researchers who holds this suspicion; however, the purpose of this paper is to study the postwar research trends of this field, so I will set aside my personal pursuit of such questions and use *Japanese Americans* to include Issei in cases directly pertaining to postwar situations and circumstances.

2. For information on postwar Japanese history research trends and results in America, see Roger Daniels, "Westerners from the East: Oriental Immigrants Reappraised," *Pacific Historical Review* 35, no. 4 (1966): 373–83; Roger Daniels, "American Historians and East Asian Immigrants," *Pacific Historical Review* 43, no. 4 (1974): 448–72; Roger Daniels, "Introduction," in *Asian America: Chinese and Japanese in the United States since 1850* (Seattle: University of Washington

Press, 1988), 3–8. For studies in Japan, Imin Kenkyūkai, ed., *Nihon no imin kenkyū: Dōkō to mokuroku* (Tokyo: Nichigai Asoshiētsu, 1994) is a good resource, though it does not encompass the entire extent of research. For new materials that became the cornerstone for research in the postwar United States, see Yuji Ichioka, Yasuo Sakata, Nobuya Tsuchida, and Eri Yasuhara, comps., *A Buried Past: An Annotated Bibliography of the Japanese American Research Project Collection* (Berkeley: University of California Press, 1974); Yasuo Sakata, comp., *Fading Footsteps of the Issei: An Annotated Check List of the Manuscript Holdings of the Japanese American Research Project Collection* (Los Angeles: Asian American Studies Center and Center for Japanese Studies, UCLA, and Japanese American National Museum, 1992); and Sakata Yasuo, "Imin kenkyū no rekishiteki kōsatsu to sono kadai," in *Nihon imin shiryōshū dai 1- ki: Hokubei hen dai 18-kan*, ed. Yasuo Sakata (Tokyo: Nihon Tosho Sentā, 1991), 1–81.

3. "As an interlude between the Japanese exclusion movement period and the dramatic wartime internment of Japanese Americans, the years between 1924 and 1941 comprise an unexplored period in Japanese American history." Yuji Ichioka, "Japanese Immigrant Nationalism: The Issei and the Sino-Japanese War, 1937–1941," *California History* 69, no. 3 (Fall 1990): 260. Ichioka is one of the few scholars who shows a strong interest in the experiences of the Issei and Nisei in the interwar period.

4. The persistently continuing movement beginning in the 1890s to drastically restrict the entry of "undesirable aliens" to the United States as "immigrants" resulted in the federal Congress taking legislative measures on July 1, 1924, to enact and enforce an immigration law that is known today by many names. Some examples include the National Origins Act, which hints at restricted entry based on "quotas by national origins," which was the basic concept on which implementation of such restrictions was based; another is the Johnson-Reed Act, named after the persons in charge of the legislation; and the 1924 Immigration Act, named after the year in which the law was implemented. When such naming is used, one can sense that the writer is trying to imply that such legislation was not based on racial prejudice, nor was it a discriminatory law aimed at a particular people—the Japanese people. (For example, see Maldwyn Allen Jones, *American Immigration*, 2nd ed. [Chicago: University of Chicago Press, 1992], 212–38.) However, for the Japanese people, particularly Japanese living in America, it was an undeniable truth that the enactment of the 1924 act was a discriminatory legal measure based on the legal decision that the Japanese were "aliens ineligible to citizenship," and that it attempted to restrict the entry of Japanese into the United States. Thus, in the field of Japanese American history, it is customary to refer to this law as the Anti-Japanese Immigration Law. On the historical background that led to the enactment of this law, in particular the trends of anti-Japanese sentiment and anti-Japanese movements, Roger Daniels, *The Politics of Prejudice: The Anti-Japanese Movement in California and the Struggle for Japanese Exclusion* (Berkeley: University of California Press, 1962) is the most specific and a good reference. Yuji Ichioka analyzes and discusses the psychological effect that the Anti-Japanese Immigration Law had on Japanese living in America in Yuji Ichioka, *The Issei: The World of the First Generation Japanese Immigrants, 1885–1924* (New York: Free Press, 1988), 176–254 (Tomita Torao, Kumei Teruko, and Shinoda Satae, trans., *Issei: Reimeiki Amerika imin no monogatari* [Tokyo: Tōsui Shobō, 1992], 197–281). On the effect that the law had on the Japanese government and its people,

see Asada Sadao, *Ryōtaisenkan no Nichi Bei kankei: Kaigun to seisaku kettei katei* (Tokyo: Tōkyō Daigaku Shuppankai, 1993), 273–328, and Yoshida Tadao, *Hainichi iminhō no kiseki: 21-seiki no Nichi Bei kankei no genten* (Tokyo: Keizai Ōraisha, 1990). However, the structure of Yoshida's argument is a bit forced.

5. Regarding the ruling that the Japanese were aliens ineligible to citizenship, which became grounds for the enactment of the Japanese immigration law, see Ichioka, *The Issei*, 176–254, or its Japanese translation, *Issei*, 197–281.

6. Though not a research paper, in the postwar *Nihonjinshi* compiled by the Issei, the period between 1924 and 1941 is also an "unspoken time." In Ochi Dōjun, ed., *Minami Kashū Nihonjin shi kōhen* (Los Angeles: Japanese Chamber of Commerce of Southern California, 1956–57), of the 120 pages that make up "Daini taisenmae hen," only twenty pages are allocated to "Chapter 7: Major events in Southern California from 1919 to the start of the war." Regarding the Issei's patriotic activities at the start of the Second Sino-Japanese War in 1937, there is only one line, which states, "July: our compatriots in Southern California support the home front with devotion and send 12,000 comfort bags to the Imperial Japanese Army. It is reported that the donations sent to relieve the soldiers in September amount to 255,600 yen" (114). Furthermore, in 1960, the following year, the Japanese Chamber of Commerce of Southern California organized the Minami Kashū Nihonjin 70-nenshi Kankō, which edited and published the *Minami Kashū Nihonjin nanajūnenshi* as a revised edition. Inserted in it are less than ten lines of an inoffensive description that states, "Especially with the outbreak of the Manchurian Incident and the Second Sino-Japanese War, the community of Japanese living in America were stirred to patriotism. Heimusha Kai (Society of Men Eligible for Military Service) were formed (in Southern California, Zaigō Gunjindan, a reservists' group), and there was widespread development of activities including patriotic donations, plane donations, and comfort bag offerings by the military associations, Japanese associations, *kenjinkai*, and women's associations. On the other hand, the delicate state of international relations resounded with the community of Japanese living in America. Japanese associations, Japanese cultural associations, Japanese churches, and other organizations operated proactively, especially in Southern California with their Jikyoku Iinkai (current affairs committee), and there was a powerful expansion of movements to foster Japanese American friendship" (27–28).

7. The Issei resided in the United States as Japanese citizens, as they were ruled "aliens ineligible for citizenship." Thus, when referring to them, I will be using the term *Japanese in America* that the Issei themselves used to refer to themselves, in contrast with the postwar term *Nikkeijin*. See endnote 1 for more on this topic.

8. Ichioka, "Japanese Immigrant Nationalism," 260–75, 310–11.

9. For example, see Roger Daniels, *Concentration Camps USA: Japanese Americans and World War II* (Hinsdale, IL: Dryden Press, 1971), and Richard Drinnon, *Keeper of Concentration Camps: Dillon S. Myer and American Racism* (Berkeley: University of California Press, 1987).

10. The focus here is from a historical research perspective. It does not touch on research results in the fields of sociology and anthropology; for example, the extensive research developments on acculturation, cultural assimilation, and ethnicity.

11. "In Japan, the widespread emotional opposition against the 1924 Immigration Act was intense. In various locations throughout the country, public rallies were held to protest against the enactment of the law. The Japanese protestors called July 1st the 'day of national humiliation.' From their point of view, the Japanese had

been slighted in being chosen as a target for expulsion. Intellectuals who had been educated in the United States fiercely opposed the law. Nitobe Inazō, who graduated from Johns Hopkins University, vowed to never step foot again in the United States until the 1924 Immigration Act was revised and the exclusion clause was removed. Christian Uchimura Kanzō, graduate of Amherst University and a leading intellectual, was even more intense. Not only did he oppose visiting the United States, he also urged the Japanese not to accept assistance from the United States, not to read anything written by an American, and not to attend American churches. . . . Japanese immigrants took to quieter ways of protesting against the 1924 Immigration Act." Ichioka, trans. Tomita et al., *Issei*, 274. See also Asada, *Ryōtaisenkan no Nichi-Bei kankei*, 308–12; Yoshida, *Hainichi iminhō no kiseki*, 220–33; and Sakata Yasuo, "Iminshi kara mita Nichi Bei kankei: Motsureau 'jihushin' to 'tsuyogari,'" in *Tairitsu to dakyō: 1930-nendai no Nichi-Bei tsūshō kankei*, eds. Ueyama Kazuo and Sakata Yasuo (Tokyo: Daiichi Hōki, 1994), 373–404.

12. Yoshida, *Hainichi iminhō no kiseki*; Asada, *Ryōtaisenkan no Nichi Bei kankei*.

13. For example, see Shoichi Saeki, "Images of the United States as a Hypothetical Enemy," in *Mutual Images: Essays in American-Japanese Relations*, ed. Akira Iriye (Cambridge, MA: Harvard University Press, 1975), 100–114.

14. Sakata, "Iminshi kara mita Nichi Bei kankei," 388–97.

15. George F. Kennan, *American Diplomacy*, exp. ed. (Chicago: University of Chicago Press, 1984), 38–54. "Throughout this long and unhappy story we would repeatedly irritate and offend the sensitive Japanese by our immigration policies and our treatment of people of Japanese lineage, and of oriental lineage in general, in specific localities in this country. The federal government was prepared to plead with local authorities in California and elsewhere for a recognition of the element of national interest in these unhappy problems of residence, of land-ownership, of neighborhood treatment, but it was not prepared to force any issues; and the country as a whole remained unwilling to recognize that the actions and attitudes of state and local authorities might constitute an important element in the creation of foreign policy" (49). See also Sakata, "Iminshi kara mita Nichi Bei kankei"; Ueyama and Sakata, *Tairitsu to dakyō*.

16. Asada, *Ryōtaisenkan no Nichi Bei kankei* is one of the few studies on this topic.

17. As I will explain later in the main text, one cannot deny that the fight to secure redress for incarceration made it difficult to pursue studies of the relationship between the 1930s and incarceration. Consequently, now that the redress bill has been enacted and executed, I expect that research can be done from a different angle.

18. For example, more than one thousand Issei were arrested and detained at Department of Justice Camps before the mass forced removal and incarceration of people of Japanese ancestry. Other than fishers who were suspected of being familiar with coastal security facilities, they were Issei leaders of Japanese America. However, other than Bob Kumamoto, "The Search for Spies: The American Counterintelligence and the Japanese Community, 1931–1942," *Amerasia Journal* 6 (1979): 45–75, no other studies have been published on how these people were considered to be "dangerous individuals" and how the FBI had prepared the list at the outbreak of war.

19. For example, the publications directly related to this time period include Ichioka, "Japanese Immigrant Nationalism," and Kumamoto, "The Search for Spies." Although not comprehensive, other than these works, see also R. W. O'Brien,

"Reaction of the College Nisei to Japan and Japanese Foreign Policy from the Invasion of Manchuria to Pearl Harbor," *Pacific Northwest Quarterly* 36 (1945): 19–28; Roger Daniels, "Japanese America, 1930–1941: An Ethnic Community in the Great Depression," *Journal of the West* 24 (1985): 35–49; Roger Daniels, "The Japanese," in *Ethnic Leadership in America*, ed. John Higham (Baltimore: Johns Hopkins University Press, 1978), 36–63; Yuji Ichioka, "A Study in Dualism: James Yoshinori Sakamoto and the *Japanese American Courier*, 1928–1942," *Amerasia Journal* 13 (1986–87): 49–81; Ichioka, "Japanese Immigrant Nationalism," 260–75, 310–11; Valerie Matsumoto, "Redefining Expectations: Nisei Women in the 1930s," *California History* 73, no. 1 (Spring 1994): 44–53; Jere Takahashi, "Japanese American Responses to Race Relations: The Formation of Nisei Perspectives," *Amerasia Journal* 9 (1982): 29–57; Yasuo Sakata, "Conflicting Identities: Issei and Nisei in the 1930s," *Osaka Gakuin University International Colloquium* (1991), 133–60. Furthermore, interesting studies published in Japanese include Ichioka Yuji, "Dai Nisei Mondai: 1902–1941 Nisei no shōrai to kyōiku ni kanshite hensen suru issei no tenbō to kenkai no rekishiteki kōsatsu" ["*Dai Nisei Mondai*: Changing Japanese Immigrant Conceptions of the Second-Generation Problem, 1902–1941"], in *Hokubei Nihonjin Kirisutokyō undōshi*, ed. Dōshisha Daigaku Jinbun Kagaku Kenkyūsho (Tokyo: PCM Shuppan, 1991), 731–84, and Ichioka Yuji, "Kengakudan-Nikkei nisei ni yoru Nihon kenkyū ryokō no kigen" ["The Origin of Japan Study Trips of Nisei"] in Ueyama and Sakata, *Tairitsu to dakyō*, 281–308. The former criticizes the theory of *kakehashi* ("bridge" Nisei) and the latter discusses Nisei tours to Japan.

20. I only list representative publications in this limited space: Frank Chuman, *The Bamboo People: The Law and the Japanese-Americans* (Del Mar, CA: Publisher's, 1976); Bill Hosokawa, *Nisei: The Quiet Americans* (New York: William Morrow, 1969); Bill Hosokawa, *JACL in Quest of Justice* (New York: William Morrow, 1982); Mike Masaoka and Bill Hosokawa, *They Call Me Moses Masaoka: An American Saga* (New York: William Morrow, 1987). These authors are all JACL leaders who were active from prewar to postwar. These publications are translated into Japanese. The other publications include Edna Bonacich and John Modell, *The Economic Basis of Ethnic Solidarity: Small Business in the Japanese American Community* (Berkeley: University of California Press, 1980); Daniels, *Asian America*; Gene Levine and Colbert Rhodes, *The Japanese American Community: A Three Generation Study* (New York: Praeger, 1981); Ivan H. Light, *Ethnic Enterprise in America: Business and Welfare among Chinese, Japanese and Blacks* (Berkeley: University of California Press, 1972); John Modell, *The Economic and Politics of Racial Accommodation: The Japanese of Los Angeles 1900–1941* (Urbana: University of Illinois Press, 1977); Robert A. Wilson and Bill Hosokawa, *East to America: A History of the Japanese in the United States* (New York: William Morrow, 1980).

21. Ichioka et al., *A Buried Past*; Sakata, *Fading Footsteps of the Issei*; Sakata, "Imin kenkyū no rekishiteki kōsatsu to sono kadai" ["A Historical Study of Migration Research and Its Challenges"]. (The English translation is included in Yasuo Sakata, *On a Collision Course: The Dawn of Japanese Migration in the Nineteenth Century* [Stanford, CA: Hoover Institution Press, 2020].)

22. Alexander Saxton, *The Rise and Fall of the White Republic: Class Politics and Mass Culture in Nineteenth-Century America* (London: Verso, 1990).

23. Daniels, *Asian America*, xiii. "My background and training have focused on United States history in general and immigration history in particular. As the son of immigrants from Britain and Hungary, I began to study the Asian component of our population when the accidents of academic logistics took me to UCLA. There was a twenty-nine-year-old veteran with eastern and southern roots. I was trained by Theodore Saloutos, one of the pioneers of immigration history and a specialist in Greek American history. In an era that stressed consensus—and the notion of the melting pot is perhaps the arch consensual notion—I was more concerned with conflict and with ethnic and racial relations. In 1957 Theodore Saloutos suggested that I survey the literature dealing with Asian immigration and the reactions it aroused. My subsequent dissertation resulted in my first book, *The Politics of Prejudice.*"

24. Acting Japanese consul general of San Francisco Matsui Shōzō reported to minister of foreign affairs Komura Jutarō about the detailed process of how this magazine *The White Man* was published, and sent part of the magazine as an attached document. "The Asiatic Exclusion League in this city has been publishing leaflets to promote its argument and educate the general public about it; however, it had not published regular periodicals thus far. However, it now decided to publish its monthly organ paper *The White Man*. It has already published the first issue. Its reporter A. E. Fowler is not only a well-known demagogue propelling anti-Japanese flame but the ringleader of a campaign calling workers in Vancouver to attack Japanese stores and persecute Japanese on the street when former director of the International Trade Bureau Ishii left this country for Vancouver as part of his North American and European tours. He traveled south to attend the Asiatic Exclusion League convention in Monterey, returned to San Francisco, and stayed here. Since then, he was rumored to be planning something and recently expressed himself in the form of the aforementioned monthly periodical." Letter from San Francisco acting consul general Matsui Shōzō to Minister of Foreign Affairs Komura Jutarō, May 31, 1910, *Hokubei Gasshūkoku ni oite honpōjin tokō seigen oyobi haiseki ikken* (A matter concerning entry restrictions and exclusions of Japanese in the United States), *Kō* no. 115, May 31, 1910, cited in Gaimushō, *Nihon gaikō bunsho,* vol. 17 (Tokyo: Nihon Kokusai Rengō Kyōkai, 1952). Issue no. 2 was published in August 1910 (Meiji 43), no. 3 in December of that year, and no. 4 in March 1911 (Meiji 44). Even though they claimed it to be a monthly magazine, apparently it was impossible to publish regularly.

25. *The White Man* 1, 21–22, *Gaimushō Gaikō Shiryōkan* (Diplomatic Archives of the Ministry of Foreign Affairs), "Hokubei Gasshūkoku ni oite honpōjin tokō seigen oyobi haiseki ikken," cited in Gaimushō, *Nihon gaikō bunsho,* vol. 17.

26. Prescott Hall was a blue-blooded member of the intelligentsia and an advocate for restricting new immigrants into the US. Together with Charles Warren and Robert DeCourcy Ward, he established the Immigration Restriction League in 1894. He was a lawyer by profession and was active as a leader of a new immigrant exclusion movement, including "Orientals" for twenty-five years. Allen Jones, *American Immigration*, 222.

27. Prescott F. Hall, *Immigration: And Its Effects upon the United States*, rev. 2nd ed. (New York: Henry Holt, 1913), 58–59.

28. H. A. Millis, *The Japanese Problem in the United States: An Investigation for the Commission on Relations with Japan Appointed by the Federal Council of the Churches of Christ in America* (New York: Macmillan, 1915), 240.

29. Yamato Ichihashi, *Japanese in the United States: A Critical Study of the Problems of the Japanese Immigrants and Their Children* (Stanford, CA: Stanford University Press, 1932). For Yamato Ichihashi and the background of the publication of *Japanese in the United States*, see "Attorney for Defense: Yamato Ichihashi and Immigration," *Pacific Historical Review* 55, no. 2 (May 1989): 192–225.

30. Millis, *The Japanese Problem in the United States*, 240–41. "The immigration of the Japanese followed that of the Chinese. The whole history of the Japanese has been colored by that fact. The Chinese came to the West under such circumstances that they stood in striking contrast to all other elements in the population. With a different language, with queue and different dress, with no family life, with different customs, and steeled against change as they were, the reaction against them was strong and immediate when they ceased to be objects of curiosity. That they underbid others when seeking employment merely added strength to the reaction and fury to the opposition with which they would have met under any circumstances. As a result of the struggle that ensued they were assigned the inferior place they unprotestingly accepted. The Chinaman was a good loser. Then came the Japanese. They came from the same quarter of the earth, were of related color, had a similar language, accepted the same economic rank as the Chinese, frequently occupied their bunkhouses, and underbid for work as did the Chinaman. What wonder, though they were vastly different peoples, that the Japanese should be set down as being in the same category as the Chinese? In men's minds they were assigned the same place to begin with. Moreover, it was assumed that they should continue to occupy it. Not to do so was to be regarded as undesirable."

31. Ichihashi, *Japanese in the United States*, 228–29.

32. The Japanese government's bureaucrats, Japanese business and intellectual leaders, and community leaders in Japanese America who dealt with the anti-Japanese and immigration issues in the US consistently stressed that the Japanese, both *dekasegi* migrant workers and the Issei who settled in the US, were totally different nationals from their fellow "Orientals"—the excluded Chinese—and tried to demonstrate it in one way or another. These efforts were made from the beginning of the 1890s, when racially discriminatory attacks and harassment started against Japanese laborers in the US, through 1924, when the Immigration Act was enacted, resulting in the banning of Japanese immigrants' entry into the US. "San Francisco is like a confluence of European and Asian races. Therefore, to maintain our country's reputation, it is the most important place. It is extremely important for the Japanese who come to this place to represent our national character and maintain our reputation. Like those who arrive recently, those of shameful occupations, poor, and eccentrically clothed would not help us maintain our national benefits and avoid the Japanese being excluded by chance. The threatening situation is imminent to have a regrettable precursor to having good people to be excluded worldwide." Report from San Francisco consul Chinda Sutemi to Minister of Foreign Affairs Enomoto Takeaki, May 10, 1892, cited in Gaimushō, ed., *Nihon gaikō bunsho* vol. 25 (Tokyo: Nihon Kokusai Rengō Kyōkai, 1952), 702–3. "Japanese reputation in the US is as bad as what people say. Although the Japanese were unlike the Chinese in San Francisco, there are some who exaggerate the bad reputation of the Japanese to win the wishes of the lower class, as part of the usual political faction competition and general elections. It says the Japanese reputation in Vancouver is rather favorable. Among the positive opinions, the Japanese are innocent and honest

while eight to nine out of ten Chinese save money and leave [the US] for home, the Japanese are settlers in this country after making efforts, and they do not save money that can be spent today. Therefore, it says very few Japanese commit crimes like robbers because of their high quality." "Beishū ni okeru Nihonjin no hyōban," *Ajia*, dai 30-gō, July 13, 1891. To reflect the reputation of the Japanese, Sidney L. Gulick, who persistently argued for the protection of Japanese rights in the US, said, "Both the Japanese and Chinese are assimilable like the Italians and the Russians." He also suggested Japanese characteristics: "The Japanese will be loyal to the US because they weigh duty in spite of natural feelings." Sidney L. Gulick, *Evolution of the Japanese* (New York: Fleming H. Revell, 1903). For the view on the Japanese and Chinese as the target of exclusion in the US, see also "Datsua no shishi: Tozasareta Hakusekijin no rakuen—minkenha shosei to Beikoku ni okeru ōshoku jinshu haiseki," in Tamura Norio and Shiramizu Shigehiko, eds., *Beikoku shoki no Nihongo Shinbun* (Tokyo: Keisō Shobō, 1986), 47–194; Sakata Yasuo, "Shōtotsu ten e mukau kidō-Meijiki ni okeru Nihonjin no Amerika dekasegi," in *Osaka Gakuin University International Colloquium* 3:2 (1992-nen 12-gatsu): 35–91; Sakata, "Iminshi kara mita Nichi Bei kankei"; Ichioka, *The Issei*, 249–51. The American exclusionists developed their argument claiming the Japanese are more dangerous than the Chinese, by taking advantage of the Japanese attempt to distinguish the Japanese from the Chinese and stress their superior quality and moral character. "The Japanese are less assimilable and more dangerous as residents in this country than any other of the people ineligible under our laws [the authors note, the yellow race ineligible for citizenship thus includes the Chinese]. . . . With great pride of race, they have no idea of assimilating in the sense of amalgamation. They do not come here with any desire or any intent to lose their racial or national identity. They came here specifically and professedly for the purpose of colonizing and establishing here permanently the proud Yamato race. They never cease being Japanese. . . . They have greater energy, greater determination, and greater ambition than the other yellow and brown races ineligible to citizenship, and with the same low standards of living, hours of labor, use of women and child labor, they naturally make more dangerous competitors in an economic way." Testimony of Japanese exclusion movement leader in California Valentine S. McClatchy at the United States Congress hearing in March 1924, in *Senate Japanese Immigration Hearings, 68th Congress, 1st Session* (Washington, DC: Government Printing Office, 1924), 5–6. To fight against the attack by the Japanese exclusionists, the Japanese in America vindicated themselves, stressing their differences from excluded Chinese, but at the same time distancing themselves from the early Japanese *dekasegi* workers who were criticized as being coolies just like the Chinese laborers. See also Ichioka, *The Issei*.

33. Zaibei Nihonjinkai Jiseki Hozonbu, ed., *Zaibei Nihonjinshi* [History of Japanese in America] (San Francisco: Zaibei Nihonjinkai, 1940), 32.

34. Ichioka, *The Issei*, 5. For the Japanese publication, see Ichioka, trans. Tomita et al., *Issei*, 5.

35. Daniels, *Asian America*, 4.

36. Daniels, "American Historians," 448–72.

37. Ichioka, *The Issei*, 1. For the Japanese publication, see Ichioka, trans. Tomita et al., *Issei*, 1.

38. Ichioka et al., *A Buried Past*, 3–15.

39. The author was one of those who played a role. Ichioka et al., *A Buried Past*, 12–13.

40. Ichioka et al., 12–13.

41. Sakata, *Fading Footsteps of the Issei*, 5–10; Sakata, "Imin kenkyū no rekishiteki kōsatsu to sono kadai," 13–17.

42. Dorothy S. Thomas, *Salvage* (Berkeley: University of California Press, 1952), 571–626.

43. Sakata, "Imin kenkyū no rekishiteki kōsatsu to sono kadai," 15.

44. The records and correspondences of the JARP are held in Special Collections, UCLA University Research Library, boxes 503–518. See also Sakata, *Fading Footsteps of the Issei*, 229–33.

45. Sakata, "Imin kenkyū no rekishiteki kōsatsu to sono kadai," 13–17.

46. The JARP recognized fundamental differences between Japanese Americans in Hawai'i and mainland US; it did not include Japanese Hawai'i in its collection target. Hawai'i-born Sansei historian Ronald Takai, in *Strangers from a Different Shore: A History of Asian Americans* (New York: Penguin Books, 1989), 179–80, says, "[The] Nisei had come from a vastly different place. In Hawaii, Japanese were needed as laborers, and they had been incorporated by the planters in a paternalistic racial hierarchy. A large white working class did not exist in the islands; in fact, most of the people in the islands were Asians and the Japanese alone represented 43 percent of the population. Their problems and difficulties were related mainly to their conditions as laborers. . . . On the mainland . . . Japanese faced a fundamentally different "necessity." . . . [I]n California . . . [the Nisei were] a member of a racial minority. Altogether, Asians were extremely few compared to whites, and the Japanese—the larger Asian group—totaled only 2 percent of the California population. While agricultural and railroad employers of Japanese laborers were willing to include Japanese in subordinate economic and social roles, whites generally scorned their very presence and white workers waged hostile and sometimes even violent campaigns to keep the Japanese out of the labor market. Ethnicity more than class tended to determine social relations on the mainland. The Japanese found certain possibilities that existed to a greater extent on the American continent than in Hawaii."

47. I used my research notes and UCLA JARP Collection, boxes 503–518, for the author's experience at JARP and its related activities.

48. For example, the Issei became the first group to become eligible for citizenship, and their naturalization applications were approved after the establishment of the McCarran-Walter Act in 1952. Furthermore, Japanese—albeit an extremely small number—were permitted to enter the US as immigrants. Allen Jones, *American Immigration*, 246–47.

49. Issei Interview Schedules, Los Angeles–Long Beach Metropolitan Area; UCLA JARP Collection, boxes 400–407.

50. The JARP did not have clear objectives or conduct systematic collecting activities of the basic research and documentary materials outside its headquarters, Los Angeles. Interviewers of the Issei collected materials "on the side." We cannot deny the issue. See Sakata, *Fading Footsteps of the Issei*, 11–14.

51. Hoshimiya Papers, UCLA JARP Collection, boxes 69–77; Yoneda Papers, UCLA JARP Collection, box 152; Sakata, *Fading Footsteps of the Issei*, 65–74, 106–11.

52. The exception was Masaru Akahori, and thus his paper is considered the most valuable private paper in the JARP collection. Akahori Papers, UCLA JARP Collection, boxes 1–40; Sakata, *Fading Footsteps of the Issei*, 1–51.

53. The contents of personal papers in the JARP collection attest to this. See also Sakata, *Fading Footsteps of the Issei*, 1–127.

54. See Ichioka, "Dai Nisei Mondai," among others.

55. For example, see Ichioka, "Japanese Immigrant Nationalism."

56. So far, only materials that spotlight the Nisei's views and ideas, such as the documents in the JARP collection, are selected and cited as historical evidence in Japanese American history and autobiographies. For example, many documents and statements in the JARP collection cited in Hosokawa, *Nisei: The Quiet Americans*.

57. Hosokawa, *Nisei: The Quiet Americans*, 208–10.

58. By 1939, prewar UCLA graduate and English editor in chief of Los Angeles–based Japanese newspaper the *Rafu Shinpō*, Togo Tanaka, mentions he had opposing ideas about the future US-Japan relations with his father to the point he could not even have a conversation with him at the dinner table. His father (pen name Tanaka Hollywood) was from Yamaguchi Prefecture and on friendly terms with Matsuoka Yōsuke. See Sakata, "Conflicting Identities," 143–47.

59. "JACL did cooperate with the Federal Bureau of Investigation, Naval Intelligence, and other agencies by furnishing them with all the information which we might have had at our disposal regarding the suspects the agencies questioned us about. This is the duty of every American. . . . In summary, JACL did not institute a witch-hunt; neither did evade our duty as patriotic Americans interested, as are other Americans; in protecting our nation from espionage and sabotage." Mike Masaoka, "Final Report," 22 April 1944, 43–44, JERS 51; quoted in Ichioka, "A Study in Dualism," 72–73; see also Kumamoto, "The Search for Spies."

60. Ichioka, "Japanese Immigrant Nationalism," 273–74.

61. Togawa Akira Papers, UCLA JARP Collection, box 3. Togawa Akira (1903–80) was a well-known Issei poet who was active in prewar and postwar literary circles. He was involved in editing and publishing *Poston Bungei* during World War II and *Nanka Bungei* after the war. Born in Aza Asakawa, Funatsu village, Minami Tsuru county, Yamanashi Prefecture, he traveled alone to San Francisco in 1907, and in 1922, he came to the US with his father, who later returned to Japan. He worked at M. S. Miura Company in the Los Angeles agricultural produce market before the war. The store mentioned in his diary is Miura Company. He managed the Brooklyn & Ford Market after the war. His family posthumously donated the Togawa Akira Papers to UCLA in 1993. Therefore, his papers should be considered different in nature from the Issei material mentioned in this article, which were donated to UCLA in the 1960s.

62. UCLA JARP Collection, Togawa Akira Papers, box 3.

63. UCLA JARP Collection, Togawa Akira Papers, box 3.

64. Hosokawa, *Nisei: The Quiet Americans*, 224.

65. Fujioka Shirō, *Ayumi no ato* (Los Angeles: Ayumi No Ato Kankō Kōenkai, 1957), 184–85.

66. Fujioka, *Ayumi no ato*, 185.

67. Masaoka and Hosokawa, *They Call Me Moses Masaoka*, 72–73, was not available to me; I used the Japanese translation volume: Mike Masaoka and Bill Hosokawa, *Mōze to yobareta otoko Maiku Masaoka*, trans. Kō Shioya (Tokyo: TBS Buritanika, 1988), 82–83. However, the English translator used the original quote in English. Masaoka admits that he willingly cooperated with the FBI before the outbreak of the war. However, he stops short of making an excuse for being called *inu* in this autobiography. See Masaoka, "Final Report."

68. Kumamoto, "The Search for Spies."

69. Masaoka and Hosokawa, *They Call Me Moses Masaoka*, 75; Masaoka and Hosokawa, *Mōze to yobareta otoko Maiku Masaoka*, 85–86.

70. UCLA JARP Collection, Togawa Akira Papers, box 3.

71. The theme of the international symposium of Japanese American researchers of Nikkei studies organized by Yuji Ichioka, among others, held September 14 and 15, 1985, was initially planned to be the untold decade of the 1930s. I selected a paper topic on *Kashū Mainichi* and the Second Sino-Japanese War. However, some spoke up against a symposium on the Issei, since the wartime redress had not yet been resolved. After discussion, the author remembers that the symposium's theme was changed to "Coming of Age in the 1930s," focusing on the Nisei.

# CHAPTER 2

# Migration Studies in Japan—Development and Future

*Masako Iino*

This chapter focuses on how migration studies in Japan have evolved and developed, including some issues relating to sources and research methods, referring to Dr. Yasuo Sakata, who contributed to migration studies both in Japan and in the United States. There has been, of course, a fair amount of literature that discusses the trend of migration studies, including Sakata's discussion.[1] It is hoped that this chapter adds to it a new perspective dealing with recent research results and adds in what direction migration studies in Japan will develop.

## Beginning

In 1975, a small number of Japanese scholars who were interested in and doing research on Japanese immigration to the United States gathered to discuss which direction they should look to in order to develop their research results. The majority of them were in American studies programs and they were exploring the experiences of Japanese immigrants and their children in the United States. "Immigration studies" was an important part of studies of the United States, a "nation of immigrants," as American people preferred to call their country. Immigrants from all over the world have been drawn to the United States, where their dream would be realized. At the same time, there was a definite idea that all those who came to this promised land would be welcomed and incorporated into American society, with the assimilation theory, represented in the work of sociologists like Milton M. Godon, working effectively.[2] Many researchers in Japan were finding that this theory was not true for Japanese Americans, as they were discriminated against and excluded from the mainstream of American society.

In Japan, migration studies was, for a long time, considered part of Japanese history. The focus of research was mainly an analysis of the so-called push factors of emigration, with reference to the conditions of the areas in Japan that sent out large numbers of emigrants, those we called *Imin-ken* (literally translated as "emigration prefectures"). Naturally the sources researchers mainly used were a part of the local history of Japan, written in Japanese. Research on the emigration policies of the Japanese government was also an important theme of migration studies then.[3]

Thus, with the realization that research on migration should not be limited to the field of American studies, nor to discussions of push factors, researchers started collaborative efforts in migration studies. The idea was that migration should be viewed from both sides—from the perspective of the country people left and that of the country people entered. Naturally the sources researchers used were both in Japanese and English. In order to grasp how Japanese Americans saw themselves being treated by the larger society in the United States, researchers found Japanese-language newspapers published in Japanese American communities—such as the valuable collections that the Hoover Institution Library & Archives now have—quite useful.

At the same time, many researchers studying Japanese immigrants to the United States and their children, i.e., Japanese Americans, realized that their research focus should not be limited to how Japanese immigrants were discriminated against and excluded. Their realization that they should pay attention to how Japanese Americans contributed to American society or to the friendly relations between the two countries led them to apply a comparative approach in their research. They started to see the experiences of Japanese Americans in a larger context, comparing them with those of other ethnic groups in the United States in their research: for example, they compared the history of Japanese Americans with that of Chinese Americans, or that of African Americans and Hispanic Americans.

The comparative approach was also observed in collaborations of Japanese scholars with scholars doing research on migration in other countries, including the United States, Canada, and Australia. For example, Japanese migration to Canada was compared with that to the United States, showing the differences in the ways Japanese immigrants were received by the two countries.[4]

## Developing Migration Studies (the 1980s and 1990s)

In the 1980s, research on migration was growing in various fields; not only in history, sociology, geography, demography, anthropology, and area studies, but also in the fields of literature, legal studies, medicine, psychology, ethnology, philology, gender studies, art, and sports, among others. Also, as researchers considered the areas where Japanese emigrants moved to, as well as those where people crossed the borders as immigrants or refugees, they started to pay attention not only to the Americas but also to Asia and to European countries. The sources they used became more varied across multiple languages. Their research also became interdisciplinary. Results of the changes were clearly seen in international symposiums and journals containing internationally collected papers on the theme of "people on the move over the borders."

Another important change observed then was that a large number of Latin Americans of Japanese descent entered Japan in order to seek employment as temporary workers. They were often called *return migrants* and many of them settled in such areas as Aichi, Tochigi, and Kanagawa; their children went to schools in those areas, creating the phenomenon of multicultural coexistence. This entailed increased research on them in the field of migration studies. In the field of Japanese history, researchers who focused on those return migrants naturally had to deal with questions of why their parents and grandparents had left Japan to go to Latin America in the first place.

This was also the time when discussion among researchers in Japanese history touched on the awareness that migration studies should pay attention to those Japanese who were sent to Southeast Asia, the South Pacific, Russia, Sakhalin, and other areas, by the Japanese government. Researchers paid more attention than before to the government documents to find out the motives and effects of its migration policies. This trend invited more researchers to collaborate with each other in migration studies.

## Establishment of the Japanese Association for Migration Studies (the 1990s)

With such trends as a backdrop, in 1991 the Japanese Association for Migration Studies was established, combining some small groups of researchers on migration, with Sakata as its first president. This meant that migration studies in Japan was very much broadened and became interdisciplinary. It did not focus exclusively on Japanese people who moved beyond Japan's borders, but included research on those who moved from one country to another—for instance, from European countries to the United States, from France to England, or from Mexico to Canada, as well as those who came to work and eventually settled in Japan. Again, the sources researchers needed to analyze the phenomena became multilingual. The association, with a current membership of about four hundred, publishes an academic journal, *The Annual Review of Migration Studies*.

At around the same time, in the United States, the concept of "transnational history" with a transnational perspective became quite popular. It was part of efforts to reconstruct the interpretation of American history without reference to the histories of other countries, or the interpretation based on so-called American exceptionalism. It was considered a natural consequence of the academic criticism of the traditional way of interpreting the history of the United States. Research on "the people on the move over the borders" was placed in that trend. Many young researchers started to apply the paradigm of transnational history to migration studies in Japan.

Interdisciplinary research also started to show definite accomplishments among the results of many international projects in the late 1990s and early 2000s. One such project that became a flagship was the International Nikkei Research Project (INRP), organized by the Japanese American National Museum between 1999 and 2001. It included twenty-one researchers from seven countries, doing research on Japanese immigrants and their children (Nikkei) in North and South America as well as in Japan. Naturally the sources they depended on were multilingual—not only those written in English and Japanese, but also in Spanish and Portuguese, collected in the archives in various countries.[5] Another example of a successful large-scale interdisciplinary project is the one organized by the Institute for Research in Humanities of Kyoto University. It tried to reexamine race theory from a global perspective with international scholars in the fields of the natural sciences as well as the humanities. Researchers in the natural sciences began to present their research results, such as "Racial Science in Japan: Mixed-Blood, Adaptability, and Scientific Racism" and "Race and Ethnic Genome Research."[6]

One of the signs that migration studies in Japan had become interdisciplinary as well as transnational was that academic associations other than the Japanese Association for Migration Studies started to hold sessions on themes related to migration studies in their annual conferences. For instance, the Japanese Association of International Relations in Japan set up a session titled "Reconsideration of Migration Studies in Japan," which tried to present a new perspective on migration studies as early as 2008. The program committee of the association stated the purpose of the session as follows: " 'Migration studies' in Japan has shown conspicuous development. Now we should reconsider the relations between the national authority and 'migrants' not only from the perspective of individual identities or cultural transformation, which have attracted people's attention in the past." The titles of the presentations in the session were: "Immigration Laws and Japanese Americans," "Japanese Policy on the South Sea Islands and Japanese Migration to the South Sea," and "Issues of Japanese Who Returned Home from North Eastern Asia, Where the Japanese Empire Collapsed after World War II." What the session accomplished, according to the journal, was that "the crossroads of individual human perspectives and national policy were made clear and the session gave attendees full satisfaction in considering the importance of history."[7]

In another session, titled "International Relations Built by Human Ties," at the annual conference of the Association for American Studies (2009), three papers were presented: "Nisei in the Occupation Force in Japan," "Japanese American MIS (Military Intelligence Service): The Pacific War and Japanese Language Which Changed Their Lives," and "Senryu Connections across the Pacific Rim." The session was evaluated highly, as it showed the accomplishment of research with transnational perspectives.

Having gone through a period of expansion of the field that includes migration studies as well as an increase in number of researchers and amount of research, in the 1980s some people started to raise such comments as "Are Japanese researchers qualified to do research on people of Japanese descent in the Americas?" and "Would the Japanese be able to truly understand (or appreciate) the hardship Japanese Americans experienced?" Not only in the United States but also in Japan did we hear such comments in the 1990s. After some heated discussion, many Japanese researchers in migration studies now seem to share the idea that the differences in perspective do not mean that Japanese are not qualified to do research on people of Japanese descent in the Americas or in any other countries. Researchers on Japanese Americans in the United States, for example, can be non-Japanese Americans; the first book on Japanese Americans that I found useful was *Politics of Prejudice* (1962 and 1977) by Roger Daniels. And differences in perspective are not only based on where you live or where you come from; even among Asian American scholars and researchers, opinions vary. Japanese researchers believe we can contribute valuable insights and findings to the scholarship in the field.

## Establishment of the Japanese Overseas Migration Museum (the 2000s)

The Japanese Overseas Migration Museum (JOMM), in Yokohama, Kanagawa Prefecture, was established in 2002, with the basic theme of "Dedicated to Those Japanese Who Have Taken Part in Molding New Civilizations in the Americas." The Japanese government felt the need to create a center for preserving the records on Japanese migration, mainly to the Americas, and for helping people in the world, as well as in Japan, to understand its importance. Here again, Sakata's contribution was significant. As the leader of the project team, he was instrumental in presenting important ideas to make the dream of the museum come true. The museum explains its mission as follows: it aims to accurately position in history the paths traced by overseas migrants through exhibits of materials, literature, photographs, etc., while thinking of these migrants as pioneers of international cooperation who took part in the planning and formation of new cultures in new lands.

The museum offers exhibitions on Japanese migration as well as a variety of resources and learning materials. The most recent exhibition, *The History of Immigration from Okinawa and the Ties between Okinawans in the World*, opened in December 2022. The museum also supports research projects dealing with migration and migrants, by funding them and organizing workshops and lectures to invite the general public to participate in learning opportunities. A recent lecture series the museum offered, a collaboration with the Japanese Association for Migration Studies, was on "Japanese and Overseas Migration," with twelve lectures; the series was published in 2018.[8] The museum has been making efforts to establish networks with museums and archives in Japan as well as overseas that deal with migration. The communities that sent out large numbers of immigrants to the world, such as Okinawa, Kagoshima, and Wakayama, have responded to the efforts of the museum and produced collaboratively made exhibits and research results in their own local museums, which have invited local governments to be involved in the activities related to migration studies. The museum publishes the *Journal of the Japanese Overseas Migration Museum, JICA Yokohama* in order to share the museum's accomplishments with a larger audience. The latest issue of the journal includes various results of the research projects the museum supports, such as "Canada-Japan Relations Seen through the Experiences of Japanese Canadians," "Multifaceted Examination of Personal Documents and Account of Immigration History," and "The Global History Seen from Migration, Transfer, and 'Ties.'"

Now migration studies in Japan have reached the stage where many scholars and researchers in the field have transnational perspectives, or place their research in the framework of global migration history. And there is already a proposal arguing that migration studies should be dealt with using the new paradigm or framework of "Pacific history," which is considered a counter to "Atlantic history."[9] In this framework, Japanese immigration to North America, for example, should be discussed as a part of the long history of "people on the move" and the power struggle between the nations in the area. This argument has just started and nobody is certain about what we are moving toward. But at least this is a sign that migration studies in Japan have kept moving and developing.

Also, researchers are focusing their work on "the people on the move" in the world. Some researchers also deal with "the people on the move" not only before and during World War II but also in the postwar period. Using more than two or three languages, such as English, Japanese, and Portuguese, these researchers—with new perspectives and new paradigms or frameworks—have brought new findings that can be an important addition to migration studies in Japan. One example of a research project that illustrates this new change, as well as the transnational perspective, is "Japanese Canadians Who Were 'Repatriated' to Japan Immediately after World War II," which tries to discover what paths those Japanese Canadians who were shipped to Japan by the Canadian government in 1946 followed after the war. Collaborators on the project have interviewed those who were shipped to Japan then and remained in Japan as well as those who eventually returned to Canada.[10] It corresponds to a large-scale seven-year research project based at the University of Victoria, funded by the Social Science and Humanities Research Council of Canada as well as by matching contributions from participating institutions, and includes many Japanese Canadian communities in Canada.[11] Another illustration is the international project planned and led by the Hoover Institution Library & Archives at Stanford University, the Japanese Diaspora Initiative Workshops, held in 2017 and 2022, where participants with international backgrounds gave presentations discussing the Japanese diaspora from a global perspective. These research projects point toward the future of migration studies in Japan.

Some individual researchers also show new perspectives: for example, dealing with immigrants from Japan and Mexico within the context of racism on the side of Whites, including Irish Americans, or analyzing the racist attitude toward the Ainu in Hokkaido, Japan, using the idea of settler colonialism toward Indigenous peoples in the United States.

These changes are signs that migration studies in Japan have kept moving and growing, with an enlarged scope, and are developing further to contribute to the future of international migration studies, reflecting changes in society itself. Research on "people on the move" is on the move!

## Notes

1. The emerging trends and development of migration studies are discussed in the literature such as: Sakata Yasuo, 阪田安雄. 1994. 『移民研究の歴史的考察とその課題』 ([日系移民資料集] 北米編) 解題・解説; *Bulletin of the Center for Pacific and American Studies of the University of Tokyo* 17 (1995); Japanese Association for Migration Studies, ed., *Migration Studies and Multicultural Coexistence* (Tokyo: Ochanomizu Shobo, 2011); Imin Kenkyukai, ed., *Emigration and Immigration Studies in Japan: Survey and Bibliography I, Meiji Era to Sept. 1992* (Tokyo: Akashi Shoten, 2008); Imin Kenkyukai, ed., *Emigration and Immigration Studies in Japan: Survey and Bibliography II, Oct. 1992 to Sept. 2005* (Tokyo: Akashi Shoten, 2008); Fuminori Minamikawa, *Historical Sociology of "Japanese Americans"—Ethnicity, Race, and Nationalism* (Tokyo: Sairyu-sha, 2007); Miya Suga, "Transnational History of People's Migration—Research Trend in Japan," *Journal of the Japanese Association for American History* 30 (2007); Toshio Iyotani, ed., *Experiences in Motion: New Agendas for "Migration Studies" in Japan* (Tokyo: Yushindo, 2013); Japanese Association for Migration Studies, ed., *Japanese and Overseas Migration* (Tokyo: Akashi Shoten, 2018); Japanese Association for Migration Studies, *Annual Review of Migration Studies* 28 (2022).

2. See Milton M. Gordon, "Assimilation in America: Theory and Reality," *Daedalus* 90, no. 2 (Spring 1961): 263–85.

3. Leading scholars in the field were Tomonori Ishikawa, Masaaki Kodama, and Kenji Kimura.

4. For example, see Masako Iino, *A History of Japanese Canadians: Swayed by Canada-Japan Relations* (Tokyo: University of Tokyo Press, 1997).

5. Akemi Kikumura-Yano, ed., *Encyclopedia of Japanese Descendants in the Americas: An Illustrated History of the Nikkei* (Lanham, MD: AltaMira Press, 2002); (邦訳、小原雅代他訳『アメリカ大陸日系人百科事典――写真と絵で見る日系人の歴史』 (明石書店); Lane Ryo Hirabayashi, Akemi Kikumura-Yano, and James A. Hirabayashi, eds., *New Worlds, New Lives: Globalization and People of Japanese Descent in the Americas and from Latin America in Japan* (Stanford, CA: Stanford University Press, 2002); (邦訳、移民研究会訳、レイン・リョウ・ヒラバヤシ、アケミ・キクムラ＝ヤノ、ジェイムズ・A・ヒラバヤシ編, 移民研究会訳『日系人とグローバリゼーション――北米、南米、日本』, 2006).

6. Yasuko Takezawa, ed., *Questioning the Universality of the Concept of Race* (Kyoto: Jinbun Shoin, 2005); Yasuko Takezawa, ed., *The Representation of Race and the Social Reality* (Tokyo: Iwanami Shoten, 2009); Ayako Saito and Yasuko Takezawa, eds., *Dismantling the Race Myth* (Vols. 1, 2, and 3) (Tokyo: University of Tokyo Press, 2016).

7. Symposium, the Japanese Association of International Relations, Kobe International Conference Place, November 6–8, 2009.

8. Japanese Association for Migration Studies, ed., *Japanese and Overseas Migration: History, Present Situation, and Future Prospect of Migration* (Tokyo: Sairyu-sha, 2018).

9. Hiroshi Yoneyama and Norifumi Kawahara, eds., *The International Movements of the Japanese and Their Pacific World* (Kyoto: Bunrikaku, 2015), 5–6.

10. For example, see Masako Iino, Hiroko Takamura, and Kunihiro Haraguchi, "The Japanese Canadians Who Were 'Repatriated' to Japan Immediately after World War II," *Journal of the Japanese Overseas Migration Museum* 11 (2016): 39–59; Kunihiro Haraguchi, "Japanese Canadians Who Were 'Repatriated' to Japan Immediately after WWII: Issues Surrounding Re-Entry to Canada and Documentation in Japan," *Journal of the Japanese Overseas Migration Museum* 13 (2018): 49–70.

11. Landscapes of Injustice: Displacement of Japanese Canadians Project.

# Part II

# Japanese Americans in 1930s' California

# CHAPTER 3

# The Kibei Movement of the 1930s in Relation to US Nationality Law

*Teruko Kumei*

*Translated by Kaoru Ueda*

## 1. Raising the Issue

In reviewing the history of Japanese Americans to date, it can be said that the Issei (first generation) left the spotlight with the passage of the Immigration Act of 1924, while the Nisei (second generation) took the stage during World War II and started playing an active role. The 1930s seem to have been a transition period between these two theatrical acts. However, the absence of "big events" during that transition period does not mean that people disappeared from the historical stage. The Immigration Act of 1924 influenced the Japanese community residing in the United States in the years that followed. The success of Nisei soldiers during World War II was a natural outcome of the Nisei Americanism movement of the late 1930s. In fact, the issue of the identities of Issei and Nisei during the intermission between the acts is increasingly being discussed. In the 1930s, various political, economic, and social orientations—such as views on US-Japan relations, employment, marriage, and other aspects of life—diverged between the Nisei, who grew up as US citizens and wished to be accepted into American society, and the Issei, who could not be naturalized in the United States and lived as subjects of the Japanese empire. It was a matter of self-identities of Issei and Nisei—who they considered they

---

This paper was originally published in Japanese as "1930-nendai no Kibei undō— Amerika kokusekihō tono kanren ni oite," *Ijū Kenkyū* 30 (1993): 149–62.

were and in which country they would make their home base for their future life.[1]

One issue that cannot be overlooked in connection with the inter-generational problems between the Issei and the Nisei in the 1930s is the issue of the Kibei (literally meaning "go home to America," and a term often used in the 1940s to describe Japanese Americans born in the United States who returned to America after receiving their education in Japan). In the 1930s, during the escalation of the Second Sino-Japanese War in particular, many American citizens who were Nikkei (people of Japanese descent) returned to the United States after being educated in Japan. Their Japanese ideology and behavior made them incompatible with Nisei in general. Furthermore, the American loyalty of Japanese immigrants and Nikkei Americans, especially Kibei, was questioned during the Second World War.

This author first became aware of "the issue of Kibei" in the 1930s after studying the citizenship renunciation movement during World War II at the Tule Lake Segregation Center in a joint study of US-Japan wartime exchange ships and postwar repatriation ships.[2] According to statistics collected by the War Relocation Authority (WRA), 5,589 Nikkei citizens renounced their citizenship during World War II.[3] Figure 3.1a displays the percentage of those who renounced citizenship, indicated by the number of years they lived in Japan. The group of pure Nisei who had never lived in Japan accounted for 33.42 percent (1,868 people) of all those who renounced their citizenship. Figure 3.1b (organized by years of education in Japan) shows that 45.37 percent (2,536 people) of this group of Nisei had not received any education in Japan. This means that one-third of the citizenship renouncers were pure Nisei, and about half of them did not receive any education in Japan. If they had stayed in Japan, they did not go to school there and probably had been in Japan for only a short time. These figures suggest that there is little correlation between renunciation of citizenship and the number of years of residence or education in Japan. However, this is a rash conclusion. Figures 3.2a and 3.2b show each group in comparison with Nisei who did not renounce their citizenship. These figures delineate the relationship between the number of years of residence in Japan, the number of years of education, and the renunciation of citizenship. The most common duration of residence was ten to fifteen years; those who lived in Japan for more than fifteen years were slightly less common.

Even among those in the group with the longest duration of residence, only about 40 percent renounced their US citizenship. In the group of those who spent most of their personality-formation periods in Japan and were educated there, less than half of the respondents renounced their citizenship.

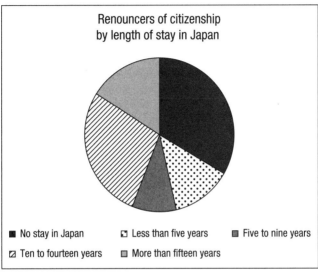

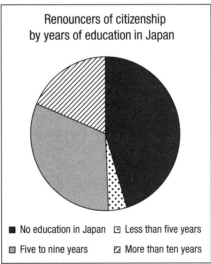

FIGURE 3.1. Renouncers of Citizenship by Length of Stay in Japan (a) and by Years of Education in Japan (b).

Source: War Relocation Authority, *The Evacuated People: A Quantitative Description* (New York: AMS Press, 1975), table 82.

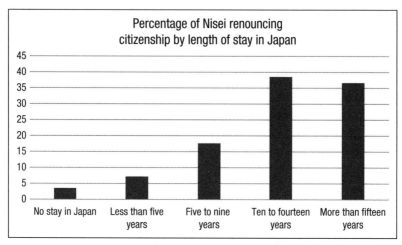

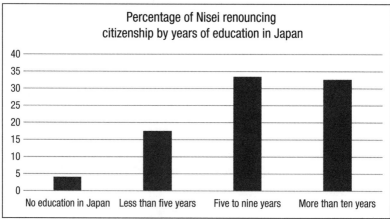

FIGURE 3.2. Percentage of Nisei Renouncing Citizenship by Length of Stay in Japan (a) and by Years of Education in Japan (b).

Source: War Relocation Authority, *The Evacuated People: A Quantitative Description* (New York: AMS Press, 1975), tables 30, 32, and 82.

It is more reasonable to consider that education and length of stay was only one factor, albeit a large one, that contributed to the renunciation of citizenship.[4] While the loyalty of Kibei to the United States was called into question, some believe that the reason they returned to the US was to evade the Japanese draft.[5] John L. Burling, an adversarial member of the Immigration and Naturalization Service (part of the Department of Justice), questioned the loyalty of leaders of the

Sokuji kikoku Hōshidan (Immediate Return to Japan Service) and the Hōkoku Seinendan (Patriotic Young Men's Association), organizations that campaigned for re-segregation at the Tule Lake Segregation Center during World War II, over the "loyalty" to Japan that both groups claimed to have. Burling said that "a great many of the leaders are Kibei, having left Japan after 1937. In that year, Japan started the Second Sino-Japanese War. Although not an officially declared war, it was nevertheless bloody and costly. Since then, Japanese soldiers had fought in China, and compulsory military service was enforced in Japan. Of course, few of those who were drafted actually left Japan, but many young men at ages of seventeen, eighteen, and nineteen left immediately before the draft."[6] But did these Kibei really leave Japan, where they had spent their boyhood, because they did not want to go to war, as Burling suggests? In a joint study of postwar repatriation ships that carried those who renounced their US citizenships and wanted to return to Japan, one interviewee said that he returned home in 1937 in a panic, thinking he would not be able to return to the United States later. What were the circumstances that may have prevented him from returning to the United States? What was the connection between the patriotic movement among the Issei and the movement to encourage young men approaching military service age to return to the United States? This question is the starting point of this research.

## 2. The Kibei Encouragement Movement

### 2.1 The Beginning of the Movement

In the 1930s, a movement to encourage the return of Kibei developed mainly through Nihonjinkai (Japanese associations) in the United States and Japanese overseas associations. This movement was fundamentally spurred by the Immigration Act of 1924. According to *Zaibei Nihonjinshi* (History of Japanese in America), a nationwide movement encouraging Japan-based Nisei to return to the United States developed around 1935, led by Japanese associations in the US, local *kenjinkai* (prefectural associations), and overseas associations, who cooperated to provide travel expenses, employment, and other support. As a result, it was estimated that about ten thousand Kibei had gone back to the

United States by around 1940.[7] Yamashita Sōen, in his book *Nichibei o tsunagu mono*, wrote that between 1936 and 1937 "a heartrending hue and cry to encourage Nisei to return to the US" was raised. Nihonjinkai in San Francisco, Seattle, and Los Angeles, along with prefectural associations in Wakayama and Hiroshima, and other overseas associations from Japan's prefectures, responded to the call and "propelled a fiery movement around the state of California."[8] According to Yamashita, several thousand people returned to the United States in the three or four years following 1938.[9]

However, Japanese-language newspapers in the United States indicate that the movement had started earlier than that, and by the end of 1929 there was already some organizing in place to encourage the return of Kibei. The December 16, 1929, issue of the *Nichibei Shinbun* (*Japanese-American News*), Southern California edition, reported that "the overseas associations in Hiroshima, Wakayama, and Fukuoka prefectures primarily led a plan to invite Nisei of the appropriate age to the US," and a concrete plan was discussed early the following year. At the *kenjinkai* level in San Francisco, too, the Sōkō Hiroshima Kenjinkai, in cooperation with more than thirty Hiroshima *kenjinkai* and overseas associations in California, requested that the prefectural authorities conduct an investigation on the number and addresses of Nisei residing in Hiroshima, and send a representative at an appropriate time to invite them to return to the United States, as well as take steps to do so.[10] The Sōkō Wakayama Kenjinkai adopted a resolution on January 26, 1930, to encourage its Nikkei citizens to return to the United States.[11] The Fukuoka Prefecture Overseas Association Branch conducted "Kibei encouragement campaigns" through newspapers in Fukuoka Prefecture alongside the overseas association's official magazine; in addition, it ruled that its volunteers should provide financial assistance to these Kibei. Its members also decided that the branch director would discuss the matter with the San Francisco branch of Nippon Yūsen Kaisha (NYK Line), a flagship Japanese shipping company that carried passengers across the Pacific.[12]

Furthermore, in January 1930, the Sōkō Nihonjinkai passed a resolution at its general meeting to "encourage the travel of Nisei children residing in Japan and Hawai'i to the continental United States. We will make efforts to achieve this goal."[13] On February 17, representatives from more than thirty organizations in San Francisco were summoned to discuss concrete plans for implementation.[14] The invitation letter to the meeting reads in part: "The matter of the campaign inviting Nikkei citizens to return to the US, which is now becoming a problem in various areas, is very timely, and it is urgent that the general public cooperates in its implementation." The Sōkō Nihonjinkai submitted the following eleven items as part of its Citizens' Travel Encouragement Proposal.

First, request each Governor-General's Office throughout Japan to report on Nikkei citizens residing or staying in their jurisdictions.

Second, request that each overseas association and other Japanese organization affiliated with overseas Japanese investigate and report the names and addresses of Nikkei citizens in Japan.

Third, send a letter of invitation to each of the aforementioned organizations, explaining the important status of Nikkei citizens residing in Japan and Hawaii, their honorable future, their mission, rights, and duties, and forward a letter of invitation of return to the United States to each of the aforementioned organizations, and request they deliver the letters to each Nikkei citizen.

Fourth, introduce in detail the rich resources, conditions of agriculture, industry, culture, education, and economy, and so on, in California and other US states, and to inform them of the development of Japanese fellow countrymen residing in the US with photographs and other articles.

Fifth, petition the Japanese and US authorities to facilitate the return of the Nisei to the U.S.

Sixth, take measures to assist Kibei who wish to return to the US and, if necessary, advance their travel expenses, act as their mediator for boarding ships, and act as guarantors for identification after landing in the US.

Seventh, propose practical ways to assist them in their career, marriage, and other issues, to the best of our ability after their arrival in the US and communicate this to the recipient.

Eighth, ask each organization to make every effort to establish contact with Nikkei citizens residing in Japan and in Hawaii.

Ninth, ask politicians, businessmen, educators, and other influential persons with a connection or interest in the United States to
encourage Nikkei citizens to return to the United States.

Tenth, assist Nikkei citizens residing in Japan and Hawaii
whose births were not recorded in the United States, especially in
establishing the fact of their birth and travel to the United States.

Eleventh, regarding the expenses required for the execution of
the items above.[15]

Nanka Chūō Nihonjinkai (Japanese Association of Southern California) also unanimously approved the proposal to encourage Nisei
Kibei residing in Japan to return to the United States at its regular representative meeting held on February 14 and 15.[16] However, it does
not appear that the entire Nihonjinkai was making a concerted effort
to promote the Kibei encouragement movement at that time. Rather,
it seems that the branches of overseas associations in prefectures with
large numbers of emigrants were more active in this area. The *Nichibei
Shinbun* reported: "the overseas association of each prefecture is currently enthusiastically engaged in activities through its local chapters."
It also reported that forty-five Yobiyose Nikkei Shimin (Call to Return
Japanese American Citizens) from Hiroshima, Fukuoka, and Wakayama
arrived at a port in the United States on the *Tatsuta Maru*. According
to the same article, the majority of Kibei were between the ages of seventeen and twenty-three and had either dropped out of or graduated
from junior high school. There were more boys than girls. Usually, as
soon as they landed, they dispersed toward their destinations to engage
in labor. However, "the Fukuoka Overseas Association, in cooperation with the California branch association, is making a great effort
to recruit citizens residing in the prefecture and instruct them on how
to travel to the US."[17] In Wakayama Prefecture at the time, there
were 5,586 Nikkei citizens, while Fukuoka had 1,200; this brought
the total number of Nikkei citizens residing in Japan to approximately 23,000. There were almost as many Nikkei citizens residing
in Japan as there were residing in the United States (that is, about
30,000). Anticipating that such a large number of Nisei residing in
Japan would "continuously travel to the US" at the current pace of
the Kibei encouragement movement, the *Nichibei Shinbun* urged that

"some measures be taken to unify and politically validate the rights of Nikkei citizens."[18] Although the prefectural movement to encourage the return of Kibei did not produce the results predicted by the *Nichibei Shinbun*, it is reasonable to assume that this movement began in the early 1930s.

## 2.2  Reasons for Encouraging Kibei

One reason for the Kibei encouragement movement was the decline in the number of Japanese people residing in the United States. Figure 3.3 shows the changes in the number of returnees and travelers to the US in Hiroshima Prefecture.[19] It makes clear that after 1920, the number of returnees to Japan generally outnumbered that of travelers to the United States, except in the years 1933 and 1934, and from 1939 to 1941. This does not indicate that the number of Nikkei decreased. But for the Japanese residing in the US, the interruption of the influx of

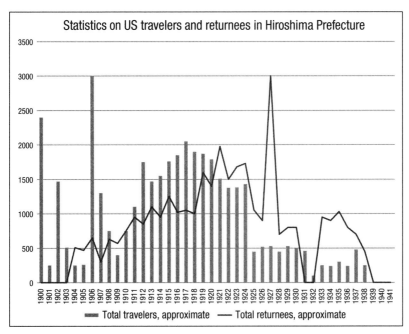

FIGURE 3.3. Travelers to the United States from Hiroshima Prefecture and Returnees, by Year.

Source: Compiled from statistical data prepared by the Hiroshima Kenritsu Monjokan.

migrant laborers due to the Immigration Act of 1924 diminished the margin of future population growth. Furthermore, Issei leaders feared for the future of agriculture, the core industry of the Japanese people— and by extension, the future of the Japanese community living in the United States—because they noted a trend of disdain toward working in agriculture among the Nisei raised in the US, as well as their subsequent move to the cities.

According to the *Zai Nihon dai nisei kibei no shiori* (Guide for Nisei Kibei residing in Japan), a report compiled in 1936 primarily by Zaibei Nihonjinkai and Nanka Chūō Nihonjinkai, the reason for encouraging Kibei was based on the difficulty of finding successors in the agriculture business due to the aging of the Issei population.[20] It calculated that the working population of the Issei in California (adult males under sixty years of age) was 21,500 (12,000 in rural areas and 9,500 in urban areas), and this was projected to decrease to 12,000 (7,000 in rural areas and 5,000 in urban areas) in five years. On the other hand, the number of Nisei males aged twenty or older, even including those who relocated from Hawai'i, was estimated to be less than 8,000, and since they would tend to migrate toward urban areas, the number in rural areas was estimated to be about 3,500. The report, concerned about the prospect, then predicted that "in five years' time, as mentioned previously, the farms of our Japanese fellows in California will have no choice but to be maintained and managed by 7,000 Issei, with an average age of 58 years, and working-aged Nisei population of a little more than 3,000." At the time of writing, the Japanese farms already had no choice but to rely on Filipino and Mexican migrant laborers. Drawing conclusions from the consequences of the 1882 Exclusion Act on the Chinese community residing in the United States and the Japanese Americans' own fate, the report argued,

> The Issei, the pioneers of a new land, are facing anti-Japanese sentiment, and the farming villages that they have developed over the past 40 years with their patient and unaided efforts are facing the same fate as the Chinese people of 40 years ago, because they are having difficulty finding successors. The decline of the agricultural industry, which supports sixty-five percent of the population, is truly unbearable to the expectations of our entire society. However,

it is a challenge that our compatriots residing in California cannot do anything about.

The report admitted that the situation was critical and deeply worrisome.

Therefore, they turned their attention to the Nisei who had grown up in Japan. In order to make a breakthrough in this "challenge," the report hoped that young American citizens who had grown up in rural Japan would return to the United States.

> The only solution falls on the shoulders of the 50,000 people resid-
> ing in Japan who were born in the continental United States and in
> Hawaii. Only if about 5,000 Nisei men who live in rural Japan re-
> turn to the US it will be solved. I want them to return to the US with
> a determination to complete the new history of our Japanese race,
> considering the plight of our fellow Japanese residing in California,
> who are making unprecedented new history in the land of the
> Anglo-Saxons.

Thus, *Zai Nihon dai nisei kibei no shiori* strongly hoped that the Nisei residing in Japan would return to the United States.

A few years before the publication of the above report, in an edito-rial titled "The Mission of the Nisei Raised in Their Home Country," on January 21, 1931, the *Nichibei Shinbun* expressed the hope that the Nisei raised in Japan would be the successors to the Issei farmers. The editorial asserted:

> Particularly promising candidates to take over the Issei's farming
> business these days are Kibei boys who were born in the US and
> spent their elementary or junior high school years in Japan.

Moreover, the editorial also praised them, saying,

> Those who grew up in Japan have developed a patient spirit of per-
> severance that enables them to endure the hardships of life better
> than the Nisei who grew up free and easygoing, with comfortable
> lives, in the US. They have excellent qualities to carry on the work
> of the Issei in the agricultural industry.

In other words, the Kibei who grew up in Japan were closer in spirit to the Issei who faced hardships and built the original foundations for Japanese in America.

In addition to wanting successors for the farming industry or workers in agriculture, some had another hope: that the increasing number of travelers from Japan would lead to practical benefits for shipping companies and Japantowns based in port cities such as San Francisco. A February 17, 1930, editorial in *Nichibei Shinbun* titled "Nikkei Citizens' Call to Return Movement" noted that the return of tens of thousands of Nisei from Japan to the United States would increase the number of ship passengers, "which would be the best thing that could happen to Japantown in San Francisco, as it would bring prosperity to our community."[21]

The Kibei encouragement movement also served to educate people on how to return to the United States without problems, so that they would not be detained or deported due to inadequate procedures. Between the summers of 1930 and 1931, sixty-three Kibei Nisei were sent to immigration authorities in San Francisco every month.[22] In Los Angeles, the number of Kibei Nisei detained by the immigration authorities increased to more than thirty in June 1931. There were cases of Kibei who went to Japan at the age of two or three and later returned to the United States with no birth certificates, witnesses, or photographs of their time in America, and were subsequently detained due to their ignorance.[23]

### 2.3 Development of the Kibei Encouragement Movement

The Kibei encouragement movement began to gain momentum at the end of the 1920s. It is interesting to note that just prior to the movement, the Ministry of Foreign Affairs' Trade Bureau requested a survey be conducted in twelve prefectures, mainly those with large numbers of emigrants, regarding "the number of people born in North America and Hawai'i who wish to travel to North America, and the reasons why they are unable to do so."[24] Of this survey's respondents who had been born in the continental United States, 39 out of 121 (32 percent) from Fukushima Prefecture, 40 out of 170 (23.5 percent) from Fukuoka Prefecture, 755 out of 2,759 (27.4 percent) from Hiroshima Prefecture, and 1,072 out of 2,785 (38.5 percent) from Yamaguchi

Prefecture all indicated they would like to return to the United States. The most common reason for not returning despite their desire to do so was that they were still in school. This implied that many would return to the United States in the next few years were they to achieve their academic goals. Other reasons given, for example, in Yamaguchi Prefecture, included the death of parents, family circumstances, the lack of an accompanying guardian, and the lack of citizenship. In Fukuoka Prefecture, some reported not having money for travel, or finding themselves in the process of applying for birth certificates. The survey was sent on February 21, 1929, and responses were received between March and July. The survey revealed that some Nisei residing in Japan were unemployed, some did not have birth certificates, and some wished to return to the US, which may have served as a catalyst for the movement.[25] Nevertheless, the movement itself did not gain momentum quickly. The Sōkō Nihonjinkai could not make good on its resolutions, due to its own internal circumstances.[26] The Nanka Chūō Nihonjinkai also did not otherwise specify its activities in its history.[27] In addition, the overall number of Pacific Ocean ship passengers declined in 1933 and 1934.[28]

And yet, the movement did not disappear. The *Kashū Mainichi Shinbun* reported on October 5, 1935, that the Kibei movement was developing in various regions. According to the same article, the Sōkō Nihonjinkai estimated that out of the fifty thousand US-born Nisei residing in Japan, about 10 percent of them, or five thousand, were willing to return to the United States, and that the association intended to invite them to return to work on farms. Furthermore, the Nihonjinkai in Los Angeles also asked its secretary, Idehara Kōzō, who was returning to Japan, to give lectures on how to recruit Kibei. However, the president of the Seattle Nihonjinkai was reluctant to engage in the recruiting campaign itself, and considered it more important to properly inform people about procedures for returning to the United States.[29]

A few years later, Aoki Fukuitsu, of the Rikkōkai (an organization that promoted and arranged emigration from Japan), who traveled to the United States in connection with the Kibei encouragement movement, wrote in his *Beikoku Hōmonki* that even within California, different attitudes toward the movement held sway depending on the region.[30]

The fifty thousand Nisei residents in Japan, as reported in the *Kashū Mainichi Shinbun*, is believed to be the figure generally accepted at the time. The aforementioned *Zai Nihon dai nisei kibei no shiori* also estimated the number of Nisei in Japan at fifty thousand. Yamashita Sōen put the figure at about forty thousand.[31] By contrast, a survey compiled by each prefecture and the Tokyo Metropolitan Police Department at the end of October 1933 at the request of the Ministry of Foreign Affairs put the total at fifteen thousand.[32] However, it is not easy to conclude that this figure is accurate. According to this survey, there were 945 Nisei with US citizenship residing in Kumamoto Prefecture, but the figure compiled by the Kumamoto Prefecture Overseas Association itself, in April 1935, was 3,250. Of these, 320 were junior high school students and 1,263 were elementary school students—a very large number.[33] In Hiroshima Prefecture, the earlier survey from March 1929 had shown 4,160 US- and Hawai'i-born, and the July 1932 survey had shown over 10,000.[34] But according to a response to the Ministry of Foreign Affairs survey at the end of October 1933, the number was apparently only 4,446. It is unclear whether the number did or did not rapidly increase to more than double in a couple of years, whether one of the figures was incorrect, or whether there was a difference in the survey methods. Fukuoka Prefecture also conducted a survey in January 1931 but added a note that the list of names in the survey results could contain errors due to the lack of official notification rules of travel to and from the prefecture.[35] According to a survey published by Fukuoka Prefecture, 1,769 Nikkei American citizens resided there; of these, 485 out of 846 (57.32 percent) male respondents and 458 out of 923 (49.62 percent) female respondents expressed the intention to return to the United States.[36] Even if the Fukuoka respondents were only slightly inclined to return to the United States if they had the chance, the fact that about half of them expressed the intention to return to the US was very significant to the leaders of the Kibei encouragement movement.

The Kibei encouragement movement gained the cooperation of overseas associations in prefectures with large numbers of emigrants, such as those of Hiroshima, Wakayama, Fukuoka, and Kumamoto (see fig. 3.4). In February 1931, the Fukuoka Prefecture Overseas Association issued *Nikkei Beikoku (Hawai) Eiryō Kanada shimin kenka taizai jūshoroku*, or the Residence Record of Nikkei residing in the

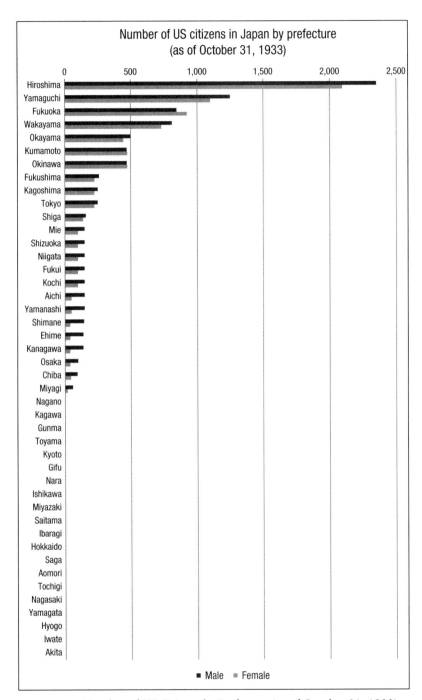

FIGURE 3.4. Number of US Citizens by Prefecture (as of October 31, 1933).

Note: The chart was reproduced from the original article with approximated numbers.

Source: Prepared from the Diplomatic Archives, K1109.

United States (Hawai'i) and British Canada. The reason for its publication was, "in an era of population, food, and employment problems, it was extremely regrettable that such a large number of Nikkei American and Canadian citizens resided in Japan. It would help to recruit them to return to the US and Canada to join the Kibei movement to contribute to the national transplantation policy and the development of the nation."

In September 1932, Hiroshima Prefecture also published the *Hiroshima-ken taizai Beifu shusseisha meibo* (Directory of American and Hawaiian citizens residing in Hiroshima Prefecture) as an extraordinary edition of the *Dai Hiroshima-ken* (Great Hiroshima Prefecture). In "On the Occasion of Publication," it claimed that the purpose for compiling the directory was as follows.

> Those born in the US and Hawaii can freely return to the US and Hawaii at any time during their stay in Japan, regardless of gender, and without limitation with regards to the age at the time of their return to Japan. The return of as many US citizens as possible to the US and Hawaii will help break the deadlock in our immigration policy and will also alleviate the marriage difficulties of the Nisei fellows.

Hiroshima Prefecture, "the largest emigration prefecture in Japan," expressed its responsibility as an emigrant mother prefecture, saying, "It is keenly felt that some measures must be taken." Naturally, it was implied that the Nisei had the freedom to travel to the United States and could exercise this right without any reservations. However, the Hiroshima Overseas Association must have thought this would be a new form of migration that would lead to the overseas development of the Japanese people and solve a food shortage problem Japan faced at that time. Along with a list of Nisei resident in Hiroshima, this issue also contained a question-and-answer page about travel. The Kōbe Gaikō Ryokan Kumiai (Kobe Oceangoing Ryokan Association) featured an advertisement, saying, "Are there any Nisei who want to go to the US but can't? You can go from Kobe." Furthermore, it also included the addresses of the Hiroshima-ken Overseas Association branch and the Hiroshima Kenjinkai in America and Hawai'i, along with the tariffs of various shipping companies on the Pacific Ocean route, including Honolulu, Los Angeles, and Seattle.[37]

This cooperation on the part of home prefectures was probably in response to the requests of the overseas association branches and *kenjinkai* in the United States in the early 1930s. However, the Kibei movement probably did not gain momentum in the United States until around 1936. The consul general of San Francisco, Tomii Shū, claimed that the previously mentioned report, *Zai Nihon dai nisei kibei no shiori* was compiled "as the first step" in the Nisei Yobiyose (Call to Return) Movement.[38] The procedures required for returning to the US were described in the report, which also claimed that Nihonjinkai could offer advice and assistance in the following areas:

1. No relative or acquaintance when returning to the US
2. Obtain a birth certificate
3. Employment

In addition, "plenty of work on farms from late February to late November" would pay about $500 a year. Even for those who were not as physically strong as farm laborers, "there is plenty of work available, such as household labor, helping at the merchants' houses, cleaning buildings, and so on," the report states. The report also claimed that if returnees were willing to work diligently, they would not have to worry about their livelihoods after coming back to the United States.[39]

The Chūō Nihonjinkai sent the leaflets to Japanese overseas associations and Rikkōkai and requested a distribution campaign.[40] However, it was not possible to obtain Consul General Tomii's approval and support, and thus whether it was widely distributed or not is unknown. Nevertheless, Fujioka Shirō of the Nihonjinkai of Los Angeles and the Japanese Chamber of Commerce was dispatched in March 1936, and prior to that, the director of the Japanese Association in America, Tsukamoto Matsunosuke, visited Japan and traveled to Kumamoto and other places.[41]

The Rikkōkai became involved in this movement around the end of 1937. In the November 1937 issue of *Rikkō Sekai*, chairman Nagata Shigeshi regarded this as "a nationalistic request of the Japanese residing in the US," and expressed his full support for the project. According to

Nagata, Kibei youth possessed all the virtues of the Japanese, including honesty, gentleness, docility, enthusiasm, and agility. They understood the Japanese language. In short, they were the "spiritual comforters and heirs of spirit" to the Issei residing in America. He believed not only that bringing these young men back to the United States would support the development of the Japanese race but that it was crucial to do this.[42] In the following month's issue, there was a one-page advertisement for the "Newly Established Youth Club for Kibei." In the following year's New Year's issue, an article titled "Newly Established Youth Club for Kibei" specifically explained that the Rikkōkai, in cooperation with Zaibei Nihonjinkai and the prefectural overseas associations, had begun preparing for the assistance of Nisei Kibei.[43]

There were many ways to assist the Kibei, including applying for a US birth certificate for American-born Kibei who did not have one, acting as guarantor for the immigration authorities upon arrival to the United States, and helping to secure employment. Such assistance would be provided by Zaibei Nihonjinkai and the employers of the farms where the Kibei youth would be working, rather than by the Rikkōkai. Instead, the Rikkōkai would provide them with learning opportunities about the "good aspects of Japan" and education to prepare them to be "unashamed citizens of the United States." Namely, the purpose of Rikkōkai was to provide preparatory education for Kibei within six months at the Rikkō Kōtō Kaigai Gakkō (Rikkō Overseas High School). If necessary, this school's tuition (¥200) would be loaned to the student (but would need to be paid back after the student's return to the United States). In addition, it lent Kibei two hundred yen for the boat fare (also to be repaid upon return to the US). The Rikkōkai emphasized the advantages of coming back to the States, claiming that "once you arrive in the U.S., an obligation to work awaits you." They would be paid "two dollars and fifty cents a day," and "in one year, one can save five to six hundred dollars," around fifteen hundred to two thousand Japanese yen.

Eligible persons were those born in the continental United States and Hawai'i. Even those who did not possess a birth certificate were eligible if the birth certificate was already on file with US government offices and the name of that office and the date of birth were known. Candidates had to be under twenty-one years of age. Those who had some cash were desirable, but this was not an absolute requirement. The obligation on the part of the Kibei was to receive a preparatory education of six months or less at a Rikkō Overseas High School; work as much as possible for the benefactors who took care of them after their return to the United States; and repay the loans for the school tuition and ship fare.

This explanation implied that very specific arrangements were made between the Rikkōkai, the prefectural overseas associations, and the Nihonjinkai in the United States. It was believed that the Rikkōkai planned to accept young men recommended by the overseas associations, provide them with preparatory education for their trips to the United States, and send them to the US-based Nihonjinkai. In fact, Nagata Shigeshi discussed and agreed with Kumamoto Prefecture in December 1937 that the overseas association would bring Nisei who wished to come back to the United States to the Rikkōkai, which would educate them at the Rikkō Overseas High School before their journeys to the US.[44] Furthermore, the report of Aoki Fukuitsu, who traveled to the United States on behalf of the Rikkōkai, claims, "Mr. Tsukamoto Matsunosuke recommended that the Rikkōkai is best suited to carry out a Kibei citizens' movement, so I accepted the request." He then discussed the matter with Takimoto Tamezō, general secretary of the San Francisco Japanese Association.[45]

The Ministry of Foreign Affairs was rather indifferent to this movement to encourage Kibei. The view of the America Bureau of the Ministry of Foreign Affairs can be found in Chapter VIII, "Honpō seiiku Nikkei shimin no kibei shōrei mondai" (The Issue of Kibei Encouragement for Citizens Who Grew Up in Japan) in *Hokubei Nikkei Shimin Gaikyō* (Overview of Japanese Americans in North America) issued by Amerikakyoku Dai-ikka (America Bureau No. 1) in November 1936. According to the book, with the passage of the Immigration Act of 1924, the Japanese community in the United States saw the influx of young workers cease, while the number of Japanese returning to Japan increased. Furthermore, "Nikkei citizens have a marked dislike of agriculture and a tendency to concentrate in urban areas," making the future of agriculture, the economic foundation of the Japanese community in the US, uncertain. The impact of this situation was "a sudden decline in the vitality of the Japanese community in the cities." To break the deadlock, the Kibei encouragement movement got underway. Every ship associated with this movement carried about twenty people returning from Japan to America—but there was no call from farmers to encourage Kibei. The America Bureau noted, "Some have even coldly commented that the [Kibei] movement was ultimately a desperate attempt by Issei farmers who wanted to find a successor to live lazily," which may have also been the view of the Bureau itself.

The above view comports in many ways with the added and revised version of the report "Kimitsu 38-gō," dated February 6, 1936, from Tomii Shū, consul general in San Francisco, to Hirota Kōki, the minister of foreign affairs.[46] In Consul General Tomii's view, the leaders of the movement were "Nihonjinkai and Japanese residents who have earned their livelihood mainly from the arrival and departure of Issei immigrants, including newspaper businessmen and city innkeepers," and he argued that the movement was motivated by the private interests of these leaders. Nevertheless, the consul general said that while it would be "acceptable" for the Nisei and Issei to "carry on quietly," the Japan side "should not openly promote such assistance." Moreover, he expressed caution, stating that the first step in the movement was to carefully assess the job situation in the United States and the number of people who wished to return. The consul general assumed that Nisei who were willing to come back to the US would be able to pay their travel expenses by relying on family connections rather than on the encouragement movement, and he estimated that the number of Nisei who would not be able to return to the US without borrowing money for travel expenses would be small. The consul general also worried that the movement would affect not only US-Japan relations but also the legal status of the Nisei in the United States, saying, "if we, in large numbers, try to attract what amounts to labor immigrants . . . we will be baiting and enticing the anti-Japanese crowd, which will impede the future of Nisei citizens." Ultimately, the Ministry of Foreign Affairs' America Bureau concluded that the Kibei encouragement movement was "propaganda and futile rabble rousing." It warned the overseas associations that such a movement "would not be good measure" because it could provide an adverse stimulus to the enactment of a law that would deprive Nisei of their citizenship.[47]

The Kumamoto Overseas Association regarded the Ministry of Foreign Affairs' opinion as a "groundless fear" and judged that there would be no problem in "giving travel expenses in moderation to a small number of people in order to return to the U.S. in a moderate manner." Its members also expressed their support: "We cannot stand idly by and do nothing to help the Nisei youth residing in Japan, who wish to return to the US with travel expenses paid, to become commanders of their farms, pioneering over the countryside where their ancestors have toiled for a half century." The Kumamoto Overseas Association decided to send back twenty physically and mentally healthy young men who were willing to engage in agriculture, with travel expenses lent by the US branch. The association estimated that there were approximately four thousand Nisei residing in Kumamoto Prefecture.[48]

The Rikkōkai showed consideration for the prudent stance of the Ministry of Foreign Affairs, saying, "Regarding the Kibei youth movement . . . it is wise to stay clear of those who foment anti-Japanese business, since they will interpret anything between Japan and the U.S. in a bad light." To avoid the "failure to achieve great deeds," the Rikkōkai stated clearly, "the movement needs to be as stealthy as possible"; so in the United States and in Japan, Zaibei Nihonjinkai and the Rikkōkai, respectively, were to take care of the Kibei youth. They decided that it was better to avoid fighting over Kibei youths, which would result in delivering them back to the United States in a disorganized mass.[49]

In the summer of 1938, the Rikkōkai encouraged Kibei to return to the United States in Kyushu, Yamaguchi, Hiroshima, Okayama, and Wakayama prefectures. As a result, "energetic young men gathered."[50] In early 1939, Keizaburo Koda returned to Japan aboard the *Asama Maru*, which arrived in Yokohama on January 23. He asked if he could bring a few young men to the United States when he returned in early March. The Rikkōkai was going to send Nisei who were in training there, but the number of Nisei who accompanied him was fewer than he had hoped. Thus, "they decided to increase their efforts to recruit a large number of Nisei."[51] It seemed as if the movement had somehow gotten off the ground.

In Wakayama Prefecture, the "Encouragement of Nisei Kibei" program was implemented as an overseas association project in the fiscal years 1937, 1939, and 1941. In 1937, a reception was held in Wakayama

Prefecture and pamphlets were distributed. In 1939, these stated, "we encourage all current residents of the prefecture who were born in the US to return to the US," and decided to provide one person with a loan for his travel expenses. In 1939, in conjunction with the Wakayama Kenjin Dai Nisei Kibei Shōreikai in Los Angeles, they decided to select a guarantor for Kibei and organize a loan for travel expenses.[52] From the perspective of this project, it cannot be said that the Kibei encouragement movement had yet taken off. However, the establishment of the Wakayama Kenjin Dai Nisei Kibei Shōreikai in Los Angeles in 1941 implied that it was gradually beginning to take root.[53]

## 3. Revision of the US Nationality Laws

Even without the cooperation of the Ministry of Foreign Affairs, and despite San Francisco Consul Tomii's fear of anti-Japanese attacks and the general uncertainty surrounding the movement's effectiveness, it appeared that the initiative to encourage the Kibei to return finally began to show signs of life after the mid 1930s.[54] This may have been due in part to the support the movement received from prefectural overseas associations and Rikkōkai. However, it was mainly because of the effort to revise the nationality laws, which concerned the citizenship of Nisei residing in Japan.

One of the goals of the Kibei encouragement movement was to educate people about the proper procedures for returning to the United States—that is, to inform them of the loss of citizenship provisions in the Civil Rights Act. The Civil Rights Act of 1866, dated April 9, 1866, provided that "all persons born in the United States and not subjects of a foreign state, except Indians who are not subject to taxation, are hereby declared to be citizens of the United States."[55] Furthermore, the Fourteenth Amendment of the United States Constitution of 1868 declared that anyone born in the United States was a citizen of the United States. However, the Expatriation Act, approved on March 2, 1907, stipulated that naturalization to a foreign country would result in the loss of US citizenship "upon taking an oath of allegiance to any foreign country."[56] Under this provision, if a person served in the military in Japan, he was considered to have renounced his citizenship, and entry into the United States was denied in some cases. This provision was sometimes spotlighted in the newspapers.[57]

The Nationality Act of 1940 further detailed the existing provisions for loss of citizenship. On April 5, 1933, by presidential decree, a commission consisting of the secretary of state, the attorney general, and the secretary of labor was established to overhaul the existing immigration and naturalization provisions. On June 13, 1938, the president sent a letter to Congress indicating the need to review the law. After a draft was submitted to Congress, a subcommittee headed by Representative Edward Rees (R-KS) was formed within the Immigration and Naturalization Service; it would hold more than thirty hearings in two years.[58] A draft passed the House during the 1938 session, but did not go further.[59] Finally, the H.R. 9980 bill passed the House without a dissenting vote on September 11, 1940, after President Roosevelt requested its passage "without any possible delay." The following day, on September 12, the *New York Times* reported that the House of Representatives had passed a new nationality bill: "FIFTH COLUMN BAR IS VOTED IN HOUSE; Citizenship Bill, Urged by Roosevelt, Is Passed without Dissenting Voice; DRASTIC RULES INCLUDED; Measure Is Expected to Cost Rights Here to Those Called 'Nominal' Citizens."[60]

The Nationality Act, as passed by the House of Representatives, was not so much about targeting Nisei as it was about preventing the naturalization of fifth column activists, Nazis, fascists, and communists, by revoking the citizenship of "nominal citizens" who had not resided in the United States for years or who had served in a foreign military or voted in a foreign country. The bill's sponsor, Rep. Samuel Dickstein (D-NY), said in a speech that "the committee feels that people who are so interested in other countries that they go abroad, support, or vote for other governments are not fit to be citizens of the United States." He opposed "American citizens possessing [American] citizenship while voting in Italy or Germany or any other dictatorship." Believing that "Americans should be for Americans," he actively supported the bill.[61] Representative Rees also expressed support for the proposal, citing as a reason that it would fix the situation where people who became naturalized US citizens would, upon their return to Italy, still retain US citizenship for themselves and their children. The fact that a person claiming citizenship needed to prove that he or she had not violated the provisions for loss of citizenship was "particularly important in the current world situation," he said.[62] Simply put, the disenfranchisement provision of the bill was intended to keep out citizens who were deemed to be unaligned with full Americanism.

Even though it was not aimed solely at Japanese Americans, the nationality bill was a matter of concern for the Nisei residing in Japan. By June 1936, rumors had already begun spreading that "Japanese nationals with US citizenship (dual citizenship) would have to return to the US within two years from the date of their return to Japan due to the recent amendment to the US Constitution" or else they would not be able to return to the United States.[63] In Hiroshima in May 1937 and in Wakayama in June 1937, local newspapers reported that US citizens would lose their citizenship if they stayed abroad for an extended period of time, as a measure intended to prevent Nisei from returning by the US government.[64] In Wakayama Prefecture, the situation was "more than a little upsetting," and its governor inquired about the authenticity of the story to the America Bureau of the Ministry of Foreign Affairs of Japan.[65] A person from Hiroshima Prefecture who was interviewed in connection with the joint research on wartime exchange ships and postwar repatriation ships testified that he hurriedly went back to the States in 1937 after reading an article in the *Chūgoku Shinbun* that implied he would not be able to return to the United States.[66]

Another native of Hiroshima Prefecture was repeatedly urged by his father to return to the United States as soon as possible. In 1939, he was given an ultimatum that if he did not return, he would not return at all.[67] His father was a reporter for the *Shin Sekai Asahi Shinbun (New World Sun)* and may have been concerned about his son's age and the impending nationality bill when he learned of the bill's provision for loss of citizenship.

Back in Washington, DC, a proposed Nationality Act—revisions to provisions of law concerning US citizenship and naturalization—passed the House of Representatives and went to the Senate for amendment. The provision for loss of citizenship raised the issue of triggering the automatic loss of citizenship upon joining the armed forces of a foreign country, whether the individual in question was US-born or naturalized. At the time, many Americans had joined or wanted to join the Canadian or United Kingdom armies as volunteer soldiers; therefore, the Senate Committee on Immigration decided to make an amendment specifically for dual citizens who join the armed forces of another country. The *New York Times* editorialized on this amendment and welcomed it, saying, "An amendment to the bill along these lines would be in keeping with the wishes of a great many people."[68] In addition, the Senate included a new provision that would allow a person to forfeit US citizenship if he or she were to hold an official position that only a citizen of another nation would be entitled to hold. The Senate bill sponsor, Rep. Lewis B. Schwellenbach (D-WA), explained to the press that the new ban would have no effect in the case of the United Kingdom and Canada, since they did not claim the nationality of the descendants of their citizens.[69]

The Senate amendment to the proposed Nationality Act was clearly developing into a pro-British-and-Canadian policy. It clarified the question of existing nationality laws so that American citizens could support the British against the Germans. Although the way the debate unfolded in the House of Representatives would seem to indicate that the bill also targeted those of Italian and German descent, some commentators suggested that the amendments in the Senate were actually aimed at dual Nikkei citizens. The October 19, 1940, issue of the *Rafu Shinpō*, and the following day's English-language edition of the same newspaper, featured commentary by Washington columnists Pearson and Allen, who wrote, "The bill recently signed by the president to prevent the entry and naturalization of the Fifth Foreign Legion is aimed at Japanese nationals." The column reported that "Japanese American citizens are now going to Japan, receiving military training, returning to the US, and reverting to US citizenship. We are trying to prevent this," citing the argument that "their parents are obligated to dedicate their sons to His Majesty the Emperor." In fact, the issue of dual citizenship for the Nisei had been attacked by anti-Japanese groups at every turn since around the 1920s. When the Treaty of Commerce and Navigation between the United States and Japan expired on January 26, 1940, James K. Fisk, who succeeded V. S. McClatchy as chairman of the California Joint Immigration Committee, wrote an op-ed in the *Los*

*Angeles Times* attacking the 60 percent of Nisei citizenship holders who could have renounced their Japanese citizenship but did not do so.[70] In order to clear doubts about their loyalty, many Nisei, led by the Japanese American Citizens League, campaigned for the renunciation of Japanese nationality, claiming that "hyphenated Americanism is hyphenated loyalty."

While the issue of dual citizenship and enlistment of Nikkei citizens was being debated in Congress, the Japanese government conducted a census of the overseas Japanese population. The survey was nothing out of the ordinary, yet the *New York Times* reported with interest that the Japanese government was collecting detailed data on "men of military age in 1941," as well as the wealth and occupations of the general Japanese population residing in both North and South America.[71] In addition, on the same day, the same newspaper reported that the Japanese vice minister of foreign affairs, Ōhashi Chūichi, said that although American pressure was increasing, Japan "has become 100 times stronger than it was in Perry's era, so there is no need for us to fear them" and that "the European and American imperialists who supported Chiang Kai-shek are the true enemies of Japan." Furthermore, the *New York Times* described the speech as a call to prepare for the imminent storm.[72] This was the kind of article that would deepen concerns about the Nisei for American readers.

After the bill was signed by the president, the *Rafu Shinpō*, in a commentary dated November 22, 1940, stated: "a. If a person takes an oath of allegiance to a foreign country; b. If a dual national serves in the armed forces of that country; c. If a person holds an official position that only a citizen of that country can hold; or d. If a person has the right to vote and cast a vote in a foreign country, then he loses his nationality." The report also warned, in bold, that "e. If a person's parents are foreigners and he stays in the country of the parents for more than six months, he is presumed to fall into categories b and c, and thus loses citizenship unless proof to the contrary can be shown." However, the *Rafu Shinpō* provided an optimistic summary, stating, "In short, the new nationality law clarifies the previous general provision that 'a person shall forfeit his US citizenship if he takes an oath of allegiance to a foreign government,' by further detailing the provision. Therefore, the revision of US nationality laws at this time should not be interpreted as a significant disadvantage to the Nisei." This was probably added to avoid upsetting readers unnecessarily. On the other hand, on November 17, 1940, the English-language edition of the same newspaper had featured a large, alarming two-page headline: "CITIZENSHIP FORFEITURE FACE NISEI NOW IN JAPAN," "Congress Passes New Act Effective from January 12 to Citizens," and "Nisei Remaining in Japan Longer Than Six Months Must Forfeit American Citizenship Unless They Abide by Law." This demonstrated the great interest in the Nisei.

The provision of the new nationality law that pertained to the Nisei is Article 402, which clarified that they would be "presumed" to have renounced their nationality under Article 401, paragraphs c and d, if they were to "stay for more than six months in any foreign country in which they or their parents are nationals under the law of such foreign country." This meant that the consequence of deprivation of citizenship is only "presumed"—not confirmed. In practice, this meant that returning to Japan within six months of January 13, 1941, or submitting satisfactory rebuttal evidence to the US consulate in Japan, was sufficient. Nevertheless, if a Nisei with dual citizenship was residing in or going to Japan, the fear of losing citizenship increased. If one went to Japan to seek employment and obtained a government position available only to Japanese citizens, or if one was drafted, one would not be able to provide evidence to retain American citizenship. It became increasingly necessary for those who expected to stay in Japan for an extended period of time to renounce their Japanese citizenship before going there. This was because, under Japan's nationality laws at the time, it was not possible to renounce one's nationality inside Japan. In other words, for a Nisei with dual nationality who was already in Japan, it was actually necessary to leave Japan in order to renounce Japanese nationality.[73]

## 4. Conclusion

The Kibei encouragement movement of the 1930s was spurred by the need of the Japanese community residing in the United States to find successors to their agriculture industry. Since Japanese leaders viewed this movement as one that would contribute to the overseas development of the Japanese people, it does not appear to have been inconsistent with the patriotism of that time. Fujioka Shirō spoke for the leaders of the movement of Kibei encouragement, saying that "we want them to return to the US as long as circumstances permit," and to "take advantage of their natural-born US citizenship and be active in this resource-rich land of North America to their heart's content."[74] In these statements we can detect a deep sense of pride in America as a wonderful country where young people could play an active role, as well as a fervent desire for US citizenship that they could not obtain even if they had wished and fought for it. It does not seem that the pursuit of one's own interests was the primary concern, despite what a Ministry of Foreign Affairs official apparently perceived. However, I also suggest that the movement did not produce significant outcomes. If some actually did return to the United States as a result, it would have been very few. One may argue that the war broke out before the movement gained momentum.

From the mid 1930s, the effort to revise US nationality laws sparked the Kibei encouragement movement, which became an additional factor in promoting the Kibei's return to the United States. As the clouds of war expanded in Europe, the loss of citizenship provisions in the new nationality law was one result of a growing exclusionary trend that demanded loyalty only to the United States. At the same time, however, it was also intended to clarify what happens to citizenship for those who intended to actively support the United Kingdom at the national level, and to solve the problem of dual citizenship for undesirable nationals from countries such as Japan, Italy, and Germany. With the enactment of the Nationality Act of 1940, Nisei with dual citizenship residing in Japan were now required to return to the United States in order to maintain their US citizenship. If the Kibei did not want to be drafted in Japan, it was only because of the law's stipulation that they would lose their US citizenship if they were drafted.

Future studies should investigate the following topics. This paper did not cover what specific measures were actually implemented in the emigrant-dominated prefectures. Neither were the relevant discussions in the US Congress, especially at the committee level, sufficiently analyzed. The relationship between Japanese ministries beyond the Ministry of Foreign Affairs, especially the Army and Navy, has also not yet been examined.

## Notes

1. For example, Ichioka Yuji, "Dai Nisei Mondai, 1902–1941," in *Hokubei Nihonjin Kirisutokyō undōshi*, ed. Dōshisha Daigaku Jinbun Kagaku Kenkyūjo (Tokyo: PMC Shuppan, 1991), 731–84, and Yasuo Sakata, "Conflicting Identities: Issei and Nisei in the 1930s," *Osaka Gakuin University International Colloquium* (1992), 133–60.

2. Murakawa Yōko and Kumei Teruko, *Nichi-Bei senji kōkansen sengo sōkansen "kikoku" sha ni kansuru kisoteki kenkyū: Nikkei Amerikajin no rekishi no shiten kara* (Tokyo: Toyota Foundation, 1992).

3. A renounced citizen here refers to a person who was approved by the attorney general between December 1944 and April 1946. War Relocation Authority, *The Evacuated People: A Quantitative Description* (New York: AMS Press, 1975), 177–79.

4. For the correlation between renunciation of citizenship and years of residence and education in Japan, refer to my article, Teruko Kumei, "Senji tenjūsho karano 'saiteijyū' — Nikkei Amerikajin no chūsei o meguru ichi oboegaki," Nagano-ken Tanki Daigaku kiyō 47-gō, December 1992.

5. Ichioka, "Dai Nisei Mondai," 774–75.

6. Letter from John L. Burling to Sakamoto Masao and Higashi Tsutomu, dated January 9, 1945, National Archives and Records Administration (NARA), Department of State, Decimal File 740.0015PW, 2-1445 Appendix.

7. Zaibei Nihonjinkai, *Zaibei Nihonjinshi* (Tokyo: PMC Shuppan, 1984), 1117–18.

8. Yamashita Sōen, *Nichibei o tsunagu mono* (Bunseisha, 1938), 186–87. Yamashita also noted that it was not until the latter half of 1932 that the movement emerged as a social movement (188).

9. Yamashita, *Nichibei o tsunagu mono*, 175.

10. "Zai Nihon no dai nisei kibei shōrei o ketsugisu," *Nichibei Shinbun*, December 25, 1929.

11. "Wakayama Kenjinkai sōkai giketsu futatsu," *Nichibei Shinbun*, January 28, 1930.

12. "Shimin kibei undō e Fukuoka Kaikyō Shibu chakushu," *Nichibei Shinbun*, February 21, 1930.

13. "Mazu mazu heion ni Sōkō Nikkai sōkai owaru," *Nichibei Shinbun*, January 27, 1930.

14. "Zai-Nichi shimin yobiyosede shinai sanjūyo dantai no daihyōsha kyōgikai," *Nichibei Shinbun*, February 14, 1930.

15. "Dai nisei yobiyose undō jikkō fukuan naru," *Nichibei Shinbun*, February 15, 1930.

16. Fujioka Shirō, *Beikoku Chūō Nihonjinkaishi* (Los Angeles: Beikoku Chūō Nihonjinkai, 1940), 205.

17. "Dai nisei yobiyose undō jikkō fukuan naru," *Nichibei Shinbun*, February 15, 1930.

18. "Rikuzoku tobei suru yobiyose Nikkei shimin," *Nichibei Shinbun*, September 17, 1930.

19. Compiled from statistical data prepared by the Hiroshima Kenritsu Monjokan. Data compiled by the Monjokan was obtained from Hiroshima-ken Tōkeisho, Hiroshima-ken Jinkōsho, and so on.

20. The quotations from *Zai Nihon dai nisei kibei no Shiori* are found in Gaimushō (Ministry of Foreign Affairs), Amerikakyoku Dai-ikka, *Hokubei Nikkei Shimin Gaikyō* (Tokyo: Gaimushō Amerikakyoku Dai-ikka, 1936), chapter 8; Murayama Tamotsu, *Amerika Nisei* (Tokyo: Jiji Press, 1964), 178–83; and Iwasaki Tsugio, *Kumamoto-ken Kaigai Kyōkaishi* (Tōkyō: Tōyō Gogaku Senmon Gakkō, 1943), 204–6.

21. "Nikkei shimin no yobimodoshi undō," *Nichibei Shinbun*, February 17, 1930.

22. Murayama, *Amerika Nisei*, 183–84. To show the trend concerning Kibei, Murayama listed the number of Nisei detained by the San Francisco immigration authorities for each ship that entered the US. However, it is not known if this figure covers all ships that entered the port.

23. "Chihō Shinbun no kyohō kara iminkyoku ni yokuryū no ukime," *Nichibei Shinbun*, June 11, 1931, Southern California edition.

24. "Tomitake Tsūshōkyokuchō yori Wakayama, Hiroshima, Fukuoka, Okayama, Fukushima, Kumamoto, Okinawa, Mie, Shizuoka, Shiga, Nara, Kagoshima kakuken chiji ate" (from Tomitake, chief of the trade section to Governors of Wakayama, Hiroshima, Fukuoka, Okayama, Fukushima, Kumamoto, Okinawa, Mie, Shizuoka, Shiga, Nara, and Kagoshima Prefectures), February 21, 1929, Futsū no. 138, Diplomatic Archives K1109-1. The appendix includes a letter from the US Consul General to Ōhashi Chūichi (dated March 23, 1929), responding to the procedure for Kibei applicants who did not have US birth certificates to return to the US.

25. In Hiroshima Prefecture, there were 301 and 167 elementary and junior high school students who were born in the continental United States or Hawai'i, respectively, who did not have a US birth certificate, in the 1929 survey. *Dai Hiroshima-ken* (March 1930): 53, 15th anniversary special issue.

26. "Rikuzoku tobei suru yobiyose Nikkei shimin," *Nichibei Shinbun*, September 17, 1930.

27. Fujioka, *Beikoku Chūō Nihonjinkaishi*, 207–55.

28. The number of Kibei Nisei who were detained by the San Francisco immigration authorities from March to May 1931 was 142, and for the same period in 1932, the number decreased to 95. Murayama, *Amerika Nisei*, 183–84.

29. In fact, in Los Angeles too, there were cases of people being detained by immigration authorities and eventually deported for lack of witnesses or guarantors at the time of their birth. On November 9, 1935, the *Kashū Mainichi Shinbun* carried an article seeking witnesses for a young man born in Ogden, Utah, who went to Japan at the age of five and returned to the US via the *Chichibu Maru* two weeks earlier but was denied landing.

30. From the *Beikoku hōmonki* series, it seems that the San Francisco area was the most enthusiastic about the Kibei encouragement movement. *Rikkō Sekai* (August 1938–February 1939).

31. Yamashita, *Nichibei o tsunagu mono*, 175.

32. *Honpō ni kyojyū suru Beika shussei Nikkeijinsū shirabe no ken*, Ministry of Foreign Affairs of Japan Archives, K1109-1. The statistical reports were compiled from each prefecture. Ōita and Tokushima prefectures are not included in the report. The data for Okayama Prefecture is based on the 1931 survey by the Okayama Prefecture Overseas Association. Fukuoka Prefecture conducted a survey in January 1931, which was published in the Fukuoka Prefecture Overseas

Association's *Hakkō*, Appendix, *Nikkei Beikoku (Hawai) Eiryō Kanada shimin kenka taizai jyūkyoroku* (February 15, 1931).

33. Iwasaki, *Kumamoto-ken Kaigai Kyōkaishi*, 195.

34. A chart in "Nihon taizai Beifu shussei Hiroshimakenjin sirabe," *Dai Hiroshima-ken, rinji-gō* (September 1932).

35. Diplomatic Archives K1109-1. Even though Okayama Prefecture conducted a survey in June 1931, it suggests the possibility that some people had been omitted from the survey.

36. Hirohata Tsunegorō, *Zaibei Fukuoka Kenjinshi* (Los Angeles: Zaibei Fukuoka-kenjin hensan jimusho, 1931), 48–49.

37. The *Chūgoku Shinbun* reported on June 18, 1932, that the list was being compiled to help Hiroshima Prefecture play a role of "a god to connect the Japanese residing in the US."

38. "Kimitsu 38-gō," from Tomii Shū, Consul General of San Francisco, to Hirota Kōki, Minister for Foreign Affairs, dated February 6, 1936, Diplomatic Archives K1109-2. The report states, "One of the main advocates of the movement is Takimoto Tamezō, Secretary General of the Japanese Association in the US."

39. Murayama, *Amerika Nisei*, 182–83.

40. Fujioka, *Beikoku Chūō Nihonjinkaishi*, 302.

41. Iwasaki, *Kumamoto-ken Kaigai Kyōkaishi*, 206.

42. "Kibei seinen ni tsuite," *Rikkō Sekai* (November 1936): 2–5.

43. "Kibei seinenbu shinsetsu," *Rikkō Sekai* (January 1937): 26–28.

44. Iwasaki, *Kumamoto-ken Kaigai Kyōkaishi*, 208.

45. "Beikoku Hōmonki (Sanfuranshisuko no maki)," *Rikkō Sekai* (August 1938): 16.

46. Diplomatic Archives K1109-2.

47. The North American citizen overview is cited by Iwasaki, *Kumamoto-ken Kaigai Kyōkaishi*, 206–7. The director of the America Bureau wrote to the Hiroshima Prefectural Overseas Association, dated May 31, 1937: "There is some doubt as to whether (the Kibei) movement is in the best interest of Nikkei citizens residing in the US" and that "it is not something that should be actively supported or promoted in government circles." Diplomatic Archives K1109-3.

48. Iwasaki, *Kumamoto-ken Kaigai Kyōkaishi*, 207–9.

49. "Chū," *Rikkō Sekai* (January 1938): 28.

50. "Beikoku hōmonki," *Rikkō Sekai* (November 1938): 22.

51. "Kaigai hatten mondō," *Rikkō Sekai* (February 1939): 13.

52. Wakayama Prefecture, *Wakayama-ken Iminshi* (Wakayama Prefecture, 1957), 231–38.

53. The Wakayama Kenjin Dai Nisei Kibei Shōreikai was organized by residents of Southern California and volunteers from Wakayama Prefecture to encourage Nisei from Wakayama Prefecture to return to the US. Its headquarters were located in Los Angeles. In cooperation with the Overseas Association of Wakayama Prefecture, the members decided to assist Nisei—specifically those who were over eighteen years of age, had "good conduct, physical fitness, and firm resolve," and had the personal guarantee of the mayor of their municipality—in their return to the US. Furthermore, "for the purpose of facilitating the procedures related to Kibei, we will loan a fixed amount of money, as agreed upon by the board of directors, to those who are able to find a job for Kibei after their return to the US." The framework of

the activity was set forth. Yamashita, *Nichibei o tsunagu mono*, 196–97. However, loaned expenses had to be repaid later.

54. V. S. McClatchy, one of the spearheads of the anti-Japanese movement, posted a commentary in a newspaper on the Pacific Coast that attacked the Kibei encouragement movement as "purely Japanese immigration." The *Nichibei Shinbun* quoted the article on June 10, 1936. McClatchy also referred to dual nationality and criticized the fact that although they could renounce their Japanese nationality at twenty years of age, two thirds of them still had not done so. The original text of McClatchy's article and the articles in the *Nichibei Shinbun* can be found in Diplomatic Archives K1009-2.

55. Immigration and Naturalization Service, United States Department of Justice, *Laws Applicable to Immigration and Nationality* (Washington, DC: Government Printing Office, 1953), 753. Enacted April 9, 1866, Sec. 1992 (8 U.S.C. §1).

56. Immigration and Naturalization Service, 814 (34 Stat. 1228, 8 U.S.C. §17).

57. "Nijū kokusekisha to Beikokusekisha tono kankei," *Nichibei Shinbun*, December 6, 1929. The article warns that Nisei residing in Japan with dual nationality were required to appear at a consulate or other appropriate facility upon turning twenty-one to declare their intention to choose American citizenship, and that they would lose their American citizenship if drafted into the military in Japan.

58. "New Citizenship Code Is Pushed; May Permit British Enlistments," *New York Times*, September 22, 1940; US Congressional Record, 76th Congress, 3rd session, 1940–41.

59. 84 Cong. Rec. 4,944 (1939).

60. "Fifth Column Bar Is Voted in House," *New York Times*, September 12, 1940.

61. 84 Cong. Rec. 4,944 (1939).

62. 84 Cong. Rec. 11948–50 (1939).

63. Letter from Kuniyasu Denkichi, Mayor of Agenoshōchō in Ōshima-gun, Yamaguchi-ken, to Gaimushō Amerika kyokuchō, dated June 26, 1936, Diplomatic Archives K1104-3.

64. On May 6, 1937, the *Chūgoku Shinbun* reported that McClatchy, "executive secretary of the California Immigration Commission," supported the proposal by Congressman Cannon to set the extended period of time as more than one year. In a letter dated May 21, 1937, from Tomita Aijirō of the Hiroshima Prefecture Overseas Association to the director of the America Bureau, Aijirō inquired about the authenticity of the rumor, stating that "many Nisei in the prefecture seem to be quite shaken up." The *Osaka Mainichi Shinbun*, dated June 11, 1937, Wakayama edition, reported that the revocation of US citizenship for those who have been in Japan for more than two years would take effect on July 1. Furthermore, in a communication to Foreign Minister Hirota Kōki dated June 29, 1937, Consul Hori Kōichi of Los Angeles stated that the mayor of Kusumi-mura in Kaisō-gun, Wakayama Prefecture, had inquired about the introduction of a bill in the California legislature to ban Kibei. "I think that the above rumor is spreading to Wakayama, Hiroshima, and other areas where many North American emigrants are originating from." Diplomatic Archives K1109-3.

65. Diplomatic Archives K1109-3.

66. Murakawa and Kumei, *Nichi-Bei senji kōkansen sengo sōkansen "kikoku,"* 138. The purpose of the ships was both repatriation for those who renounced their US citizenship and expatriation for the US-born minors who accompanied their parents.

67. Unnamed subject, interviewed in Hiroshima-shi on August 11, 1992.

68. Editorial, "To Permit British Enlistment," *New York Times*, September 23, 1940.

69. "New Citizenship Code Is Pushed; May Permit British Enlistments," *New York Times*, September 22, 1940.

70. "Anti-Alien Drives Hit by N.Y. Times," *Rafu Shinpō*, January 10, 1940, English-language page.

71. L. C. Speers, "Japan Enrolling Nationals Abroad," *New York Times*, October 23, 1940.

72. "New Citizenship Code."

73. In Diplomatic Archives K1101, the shortening of the procedure period and the renunciation of nationality inside Japan are considered.

74. Fujioka, *Beikoku Chūō Nihonjinkaishi*, 417–18 ("Nichibei kankei to nisei").

# CHAPTER 4

# Kibei Transnationalism and Japanese American History in the 1930s

*Michael R. Jin*

Twenty-year-old college dropout Itami Akira barely spoke English when he left Tokyo in July 1931 to seek a new life in California. The next summer he found a job as a cannery worker in Alaska to support himself. A learned man, well versed in Classical Chinese, modern Japanese literature, and Indian philosophy, he was nevertheless a quick study when it came to language acquisition. He taught himself to speak English well enough to represent Japanese cannery workers during their wage negotiations that summer.[1] By 1934, he had moved to Southern California to study at Los Angeles City College and work as a reporter for the Japanese American newspaper *Kashū Mainichi Shinbun* (Japan-California Daily News). Within three years, he joined the newspaper's editorial board and had begun penning articles analyzing volatile international developments affecting US-Japan relations.[2]

There was much more to Itami's role as an emerging voice in the Japanese immigrant community in the United States in the 1930s, as this chapter will show. However, he was not a Japanese immigrant. Born David Akira Itami, he was an Oakland, California, native who had gone to Japan as a toddler in 1914 to grow up in his parents' hometown of Kajiki in Kagoshima Prefecture. He was among the thousands of Kibei, the Nisei who returned to the United States after spending their formative years in Japan throughout the 1920s and 1930s.

By the eve of the Pacific War, tens of thousands of young Nisei like Itami had lived, traveled, studied, and worked in Japan and Japanese colonial frontiers in Asia, putting an ocean between themselves and pervasive anti-Japanese xenophobia in the United States.[3] Like Itami, many young Nisei children were sent to Japan by their immigrant parents to be raised by their relatives and to receive a Japanese education. Others came along on their Japanese immigrant parents' return migration to Japan when exclusionary measures like alien land laws threatened their families' future in the American West. Many Nisei teenagers and young adults were there to acquire practical skills in agriculture, trade, or management, with a goal of one day returning to the United States and helping sustain an immigrant family business. A significant number of Nisei also moved to the rising Japanese empire to pursue opportunities denied to them in the United States due to systemic racial discrimination. In addition, throughout the 1920s and 1930s it was not uncommon for many Nisei to embark on transpacific journeys to the Japanese archipelago to participate in short-term study tours, to visit relatives, and for a variety of other personal circumstances. All in all, at least one in four Nisei had spent various amounts of time in their parents' homeland before World War II in the Pacific.[4]

Despite this ubiquity of Nisei transpacific encounters with Japan throughout the interwar period, the stories of these Japanese American sojourners and returnees remain at the margins of Japanese American history. The life experiences of David Itami and other Nisei migrants can help us rethink Japanese Americans' subjectivities as an ethnic group, as citizens, and as a community in diaspora. They were a unique group of American migrants who traversed multiple national and colonial borders in the US-Japan borderlands. And their experiences and their struggles for survival were intimately shaped by their social relations with diverse groups of people in both empires. This chapter explores the 1930s in Japanese American history from the perspectives of young Kibei returnees and the critical role they played in shaping the cultural and political dynamics of the prewar Japanese American community in the United States. These Kibei's visions for the future of the Japanese American community were actively informed by their exposure to the volatile sociopolitical changes afoot in the Japanese colonial world in Asia and the anti-Japanese xenophobia in the United States that intimately intersected with them.

## Nisei Biculturalism and Japanese American History

Pioneering historian Yuji Ichioka has recognized that the Kibei remain a critical missing link whose experiences shed light on "significant continuities and discontinuities between the 1930s and 1940s."[5] Ichioka's work demonstrates that the Kibei's role in shaping the intergenerational dynamics of prewar Japanese America defies the assimilationist framework that engendered popular biases against these Nisei educated in Japan as "unacculturated, pro-Japan, and disloyal" during World War II. Even after the war, such a sweeping characterization of the Kibei would continue to shape the common public perceptions that the Kibei's cultural and political orientations were incompatible with the loyal Americanized Nisei.[6]

However, as Ichioka has shown, the circumstances that influenced the Kibei's transnational identities and experiences reflected the internationalist ethos of both Japanese immigrant intellectuals and emerging Nisei community leaders in their articulations of Japanese American respectability at the turn of the 1930s.[7] In the post-1924 era of exclusion that completely shut America's gates on Japanese immigration, Issei intellectuals like Abiko Kyūtarō actively promoted the role of Nisei not only as the future of the Japanese American community but as *kakehashi* (a bridge of understanding) between the United States and Japan. Because increasingly souring US-Japan relations compounded the pervasive Japanese exclusionist movement, these Issei leaders called for US-born Nisei's exposure to Japanese culture and society to gain insights that would dispel White America's negative perceptions of Japan.[8]

A growing number of Nisei intellectuals shared such a vision for the second-generation Japanese Americans' role as cultural brokers. James Yoshinori Sakamoto, the publisher of the *Japanese-American Courier* and one of the founding fathers of the Japanese American Citizens League (JACL), emphasized the Nisei's position as the future of what he conceived of as a new "Pacific Era." Born and raised in Seattle at the turn of the twentieth century, Sakamoto recognized that the Nisei would surpass their parents' generation, both in number and influence, in the coming decades. While emphasizing the importance of the

Nisei's "Americanism," and even going so far as to refuse to use the
Japanese word *Nisei*, Sakamoto nevertheless saw that cultivating certain elements of Japanese culture would foster the second generation's
Americanization. Sakamoto believed that the Japanese virtue of loyalty
instilled in Nisei children would enable them to become model citizens
of the United States. Furthermore, Sakamoto's view was in line with
the Issei intellectuals' belief that the Nisei's biculturalism would make
them ideal *kakehashi* between the United States and Japan. Sakamoto
encouraged Nisei to learn the linguistic and cultural nuances of Japan
so that they would develop a greater understanding of the volatile international conditions in the transpacific world and promote better relations between the two nations.[9]

The proliferation of Nisei study tours (*kengakudan*) in Japan
throughout the second half of the 1920s and the 1930s catered to such
a vision for cultivating Nisei biculturalism. After the San Francisco–
based *Nichibei Shinbun* sponsored the first *kengakudan* in 1925, other
Japanese American community and religious organizations funded their
own study tours and excursion programs.[10] These tours lasted several
weeks and offered young Nisei students opportunities to visit major
Japanese industrial centers, cultural heritage sites, and even Japanese
colonies in Korea and Manchuria.[11] Southern California native Kay
Tateishi visited Japan in 1934 on a high school study tour sponsored
by the Young Buddhist Association. A son of struggling strawberry
farmers, Tateishi found himself in awe of Tokyo's modernity, which
served as a stark contrast to the humbleness of Japanese immigrant
families in rural California towns. Five years later, Tateishi moved to
Tokyo to study journalism.[12] In less than three years after his relocation
to Japan, he secured a job as an English-language correspondent for
the state-run Domei News Agency.[13] To young Nisei like Tateishi who
felt frustrated by the limited opportunities for socioeconomic mobility
outside Japanese American enclaves, international education in Japan
served as a way out of their ethnic community in the American West.

As demonstrated in Tateishi's case, the 1930s saw an increasing
number of United States–born Nisei in Japan with long-term plans
for education and vocational trainings. According to Issei community
leader and intellectual Yamashita Sōen, more than seventeen hundred
Nisei were in Tokyo, the cities of Kansai, and other metropolitan areas

in 1935 exclusively to seek education.[14] For many other Nisei, study tours and personal visits turned into extended stays in Japan as they sought more permanent professional opportunities there. According to Japanese immigrant historian Takeda Junichi in 1929, the internationalist ideal had opened doors to young Nisei in California who had felt frustrated by the racial prejudice that had led to job discrimination in America; they increasingly looked to Japan as a place to pursue a second life.[15] In 1931, another Issei leader and Los Angeles–based businessman, Hirohata Tsunegorō, estimated that nearly a third of the Nisei children in Los Angeles with family ties to Fukuoka had relocated to the prefecture to study or find work.[16]

Throughout the 1930s and until the eve of the Pacific War in 1941, the Nisei's transpacific movements in both directions remained remarkably common, as many Nisei in Japan began to return to their homes in the United States. In the mid 1930s, Japanese American community organizations such as the Japanese Association of North America led Kibei Undō—the movement to bring Nisei back to the United States—to accommodate the needs of Japanese immigrant parents nearing the retirement age.[17] The deteriorating diplomatic tension between the United States and Japan also compelled an increasing number of Nisei facing an uncertain future as American citizens living in Japan to make their way home. Up to twenty thousand of the fifty thousand Nisei who had gone to Japan had resettled in the United States throughout the 1930s and on the eve of the Pacific War.[18] Confronting intense anti-Japanese racial hostility again, these Kibei represented a unique group of return migrants with diverse perspectives on Japanese society.

By the time he joined *Kashū Mainichi Shinbun*'s editorial board in 1937, David Akira Itami seemed primed to fulfill the bridge-building role that Abiko, Sakamoto, and other Japanese American intellectuals had envisioned for the Nisei transnational generation. Itami used his multilingual reading skills to analyze reports from Asia on the volatile international developments that shaped the increasingly hostile US-Japan relations. He was especially mindful of the impact that Japan's aggression in China was having on the ever-intense anti-Japanese sentiment in the United States. Several major newspapers in the Anglophone world throughout late 1937 and 1938 actively reported on the Japanese invasion of Nanjing and the atrocities against Chinese civilians that ensued.[19] Itami also paid close attention to related events that compounded the widespread anti-Japanism among the American public, such as the infamous December 1937 *Panay* Incident, in which Japanese forces sank the United States' gunboat *Panay* and three American oil tankers on the Yangtze River. In an effort to mend diplomatic relations with the United States and curtail negative international publicity, the Japanese government claimed that the attack on Americans had been unintentional and promptly paid an indemnity to the US government. In addition, nearly eight thousand individuals and more than two hundred organizations in Japan sent money and personal letters of apologies to US consulates and the US Department of the Navy.[20] Itami's *Kashū Mainichi Shinbun* editorial in June 1938 highlighted this development as an earnest desire by the Japanese to restore amicable US-Japan relations. As the State Department affirmed that none of the private donations from Japan would be paid to the families of the deceased, Itami suggested that the US government could instead spend the money to sponsor talented Japanese international students to pursue education in the United States. Here, Itami deployed his own internationalist vision in service of a potential role for young Japanese students as the bridge of understanding between the United States and Japan through their transnational education in America.[21]

Although Itami's biculturalism indeed served as a model for the bridge-building role envisioned by Issei and Nisei leaders in the prewar Japanese American community, what remains distressingly understudied are the perspectives of the Kibei themselves. Itami and other Kibei's education in Japan, their exposure to Japanese society, and their perspectives on US-Japan relations require an alternative approach to Nisei biculturalism, loyalty, and intergenerational relations beyond the framework centered on immigrant leaders' visions. As migrants who spent various amounts of time in Japan, their experiences were shaped by their physical presence on both sides of the Pacific. Their identities were both socially constructed and self-defined through their interactions with Issei and Nisei within the Japanese American community as well as with people of multiple generations in Japan. Therefore, tracing their movements and experiences offers a unique analytical lens that can help

explore how embedded Nisei lives were in multiple transnational sociopolitical fields, as they engaged complex legal, political, and social
transformations in the United States and Japan throughout the 1930s.

## Japanese American Returnees and the Making of Japanese America before World War II

David Akira Itami and other young Nisei migrants in Japan became
exposed to the dynamic social changes of the Taishō and early Shōwa
periods that deeply influenced their formal and informal education.
These Japanese American migrants contributed to the circulation of
ideas across the Pacific between Japan and the United States. Itami spent
his formative years in the small southern Kagoshima town of Kajiki in
the 1910s and 1920s amid the social transformations of the volatile
Taishō period. When he turned five, he started his education at a local
fraternity modeled after the old samurai education system, and learned
to read Confucian classics. Nevertheless, Itami was as much a product
of the Taishō era's modernity as he was a student of the old Japan.
Growing up in a remote coastal town did not stop Itami from immersing
himself in the works of political commentators, women's suffragists,
and socialist intellectuals that were widely circulated throughout the archipelago. An ardent reader of literary magazines since his days at Dajo
Primary School, he developed a keen interest in writing as a form of
social commentary, modeling himself after leading Japanese modernist
authors like Akutagawa Ryūnosuke and Natsume Sōseki.[22]

After finishing middle school in Kagoshima, Itami moved to the center
of the empire to study at Daito Bunka Gakuin (Academy of Greater
East Asian Culture), a postsecondary institution in Tokyo that offered
degrees in Asian culture and civilizations. The school offered courses in
languages and cultures from all the major regions of Asia, effectively
serving as a training ground for future propagandists, industrialists, and
cultural experts for the Japanese empire in Asia. The institution's pan-
Asian curriculum nevertheless bolstered Itami's knowledge of classical
Chinese as well as his new intellectual pursuit of Indian philosophy.
More importantly, Itami chose Daito Bunka Gakuin as a practical way
out of Kagoshima Bay because the school provided monthly stipends in
addition to tuition-free education.[23]

Like Itami, other young Nisei migrants had varied experiences in Japan that illuminate how their engagement with Japanese society was actively shaped by the circulation of new ideas—both homegrown and from abroad. For example, Karl Goso Yoneda was a seven-year-old child of poor Japanese immigrant farmers just outside Los Angeles when he moved to Japan with his family in 1913; he then grew up in a poverty-stricken rural village in Hiroshima Prefecture. Yoneda's family hardly benefited from Japan's unprecedented industrial boom after World War I. The family's struggle for survival in California and Hiroshima deeply affected this young Nisei's intellectual development. He became a student of socialist and anarchist literature in Japan, which in the 1920s was home to a burgeoning Marxist intellectual movement as well as militant social unrest. Yoneda spent his youth studying the works of Nagatsuka Takashi and other leading Japanese Marxist writers, alongside those of noted anarchist intellectuals such as Vasili Yakovlevich Eroshenko, a Russian writer who had lived in Japan and worked with the Japanese Socialist Party before he was kicked out and moved to Beijing. Yoneda traveled through the Japanese colonial frontiers in Korea and Manchuria to Beijing to work for Eroshenko.[24]

In 1926, Yoneda became one of the first Kibei to return to the United States when he left Japan to escape being conscripted into the Japanese armed forces. A seasoned labor organizer who had participated in protests throughout Japan, often led by workers from Korea and other corners of the Empire of Japan, Yoneda joined the Communist Party in Los Angeles under the pseudonym Karl Hama, borrowing the given name from the author of *The Communist Manifesto*. Karl G. Yoneda would eventually become a household name in the history of the Asian American labor movement, but he and other Kibei socialists did not necessarily fit the ideal of *kakehashi* that Issei and Nisei leaders had envisioned for them. Instead, joined by James Oda, George Ban, and other young Kibei who had been radicalized in Japan throughout the 1920s and 1930s, Yoneda was primed to lead the Japanese American contingent of the labor movement in the United States. These Kibei leftists were critical of the conservatism of their parents' generation. Instead of pursuing careers in professional fields and entrepreneurship, or inheriting their parents' agricultural businesses, these radical Kibei devoted much of their time to political activism and participating in militant labor struggles. They also would emerge as ardent critics of Japanese imperialism in Asia throughout the rest of the 1930s and during World War II.[25]

Thus, although both Yoneda and Itami reached adulthood in Japan in the 1920s, they had drastically different intellectual and life trajectories that demonstrate the complexity and multiplicity inherent in the Kibei's transpacific engagement with both Japan and the United States. Even Itami's self-identity proved far more complex than the idealized bridge-building role of the Kibei. His role as a writer and emerging community leader upon his return to California illuminates the critical ways in which Kibei perceived the world around them and shaped Japanese American cultural dynamics. Itami was among the young Kibei intellectuals who played a critical role in organizing creative and political spaces of their own within the larger Nisei community as a way to sustain their voice outside the dichotomous Issei-Nisei intergenerational dynamics.[26]

In a time of deepening chasms between Issei elders and emerging Nisei leaders that would only be exacerbated by the Pacific War, the Kibei intellectuals' voices offered alternative perspectives to the generational polarization within the Japanese American community. Despite efforts of Sakamoto and other community leaders to promote Nisei biculturalism, the second half of the 1930s also saw the emergence of young leaders within the Japanese American Citizens League who actively promoted Americanization of Nisei in the face of mounting anti-Japanese sentiment. Frustrated by what they saw as the failure of the bridge-building model of Nisei biculturalism to improve relations between the United States and Japan, JACL leaders aggressively sought to rebrand the Nisei as loyal Americans.[27] Although the Kibei were expected to be the cultural link between Japan and the United States, they found themselves increasingly marginalized by this generational polarization within the Japanese American leadership.

Itami joined a circle of young bilingual writers like himself who used literature as a creative venue to grapple with their transnational experiences. Although the majority of these writers were Kibei, the group included a number of young Japanese immigrants who were called Yobiyose (呼び寄せ; "called over"). Yobiyose were born in Japan but raised or educated in the United States. Typically, after their birth one or both of their parents left for America to find work. After establishing residence and employment the parents would then send for their children to join them in the United States. Thus, many Yobiyose and Kibei shared similar experiences, such as being raised in Japan by relatives while their parents were in the United States. Many Kibei and Yobiyose experienced varying stages of schooling in both Japan and the United States. These Yobiyose and Kibei emerged as some of the most active and influential literary figures in the Japanese American community before World War II. The leader of this cultural movement was in fact Yobiyose poet and essayist Kagawa Bunichi, whom Japanese literary scholars have considered the father of prewar Kibei literature for his influence on young bilingual Kibei writers like Itami.[28] Born in Yamaguchi Prefecture in 1904, Kagawa joined his parents in Los Altos in Northern California at the age of fourteen. Kagawa's intellectual struggle to define his transnational identity made him turn to poetry early on, and he started publishing poems in both English and Japanese in the 1920s. In the 1930s, with the help of noted poet and literary critic Yvor Winters, who had admired the Yobiyose's works, Kagawa saw the publication of a collection of his poems, *Hidden Flames*.[29]

In Kagawa, Itami found another literary figure to model himself on. In 1936, Itami joined Kagawa in Los Angeles to found Hokubei Shijin Kyokai (Association of Poets in North America), a group of primarily Kibei and Yobiyose writers in California.[30] In the first issue of the club's organ *Shukaku* ("Harvest"), Kagawa and the members of Hokubei Shijin Kyokai declared their magazine the collective work of artists who also happened to be ordinary immigrants and sojourners. They used the publication as a means to wrestle with the meanings of their "inevitable" daily struggles as transnational individuals who did not fit the binary intergenerational conceptualizations of Issei and Nisei.[31]

Itami further developed his keen interest in writing social commentary through his work as an editor for *Shukaku*. The literary magazine in fact offered Itami and other Kibei writers more substantial creative space than *Kashū Mainichi Shinbun* ever could in their attempt to grapple with political issues affecting the lives of Japanese Americans. For example, a number of the magazine's short stories published after the outbreak of the Second Sino-Japanese War in 1937 dramatized the day-to-day impact that international events had on anti-Japanese xenophobia in the United States. In these stories Japan's war of aggression in China compelled even those White Americans on the US West Coast who had been friendly toward the Japanese to exhibit contempt against Japanese Americans. However, *Shukaku* went much further in illustrating how the war had complicated race relations beyond one-dimensional snapshots of anti-Japanese sentiment. In other stories the Second Sino-Japanese War shattered the once amicable relationship between Japanese and Chinese immigrants in the American West as they turned against one another. These stories defied monolithic representations of Japanese and Japanese Americans by featuring varied reactions within the Japanese American community: enthusiastic support for Japanese imperialism, cautious criticism of the increasing signs of Japanese militarism, and the fear of renewed racial hostility and the loss of Japanese American respectability.[32]

In this way, creative writing functioned as a cultural and political outlet for young Japanese-speaking Kibei to address issues that they believed were the immediate part of everyday Japanese American lives. The writers' responses to the transpacific implications of Japan-China relations were not far removed from the concerns of others within the Japanese American community. When the mainstream press described China as the victim of Japan's military aggression, many Japanese Americans felt they in turn would fall victim to intensified anti-Japanese agitation.[33] However, the work of the Kibei and Yobiyose writers was deeply influenced by their self-identifications as transnational individuals who had traversed the boundaries of both nations. They found themselves in a position to articulate the place of the Japanese American amid a complex set of sociopolitical fields actively shaped by volatile developments in international relations.

Itami's interactions with intellectuals of various backgrounds continued to inform his commentary on Japan's aggression in China in *Kashū Mainichi Shinbun*. The newspaper's outspoken publisher, Fujii Sei, served as another influential figure who recognized Itami's insights as a Kibei writer. A native of Yamaguchi Prefecture, Fujii moved to California in 1901 at age twenty-one. As an alien ineligible for citizenship, Fujii was denied a license to practice law despite his degree from the University of Southern California School of Law. Fujii nevertheless established himself as a civil rights advocate for the Japanese American community, working closely with fellow USC law graduate J. Marion Wright to challenge anti-Japanese policies. In 1927 and 1928, with Fujii's support, Wright successfully represented Japanese doctors in the United States Supreme Court case *Jordan v. Tashiro*. The case restored the doctors' right to build a community hospital in Boyle Heights despite the California state government's refusal to certify the incorporation of the hospital based on the Alien Land Law. In addition to serving as a civil rights activist on behalf of the Japanese American community, Fujii founded *Kashū Mainichi Shinbun* in 1931 as a platform for his advocacy.[34]

Fujii served as an influential mentor to Itami after hiring the young Kibei in 1934. Itami studied Fujii's style of editorializing on volatile transpacific geopolitical relations and proposing what they meant for Japanese America. Fujii used his columns in *Kashū Mainichi*'s Japanese and English sections following the launch of the Second Sino-Japanese War to carefully deflect the mainstream press's negative publicity on Japan's campaigns in Asia. In late 1937, he began to run daily "Uncle Fujii Speaks" columns in the English section, which, according to Ichioka, were written in a type of broken English that Fujii believed would be more appealing to young Nisei readers. Many of the "Uncle Fujii Speaks" pieces dealt with mundane topics, including stories from the publisher's own history as a young student in the United States, to humanize the immigrant generation's experiences. However, Fujii devoted his columns to implicitly mobilizing the Nisei's sympathy for their immigrant parents' perspectives on the Second Sino-Japanese War. It was far from a secret that many among the Issei were rooting for Japan despite the conflict's contribution to anti-Japanese hostility—some were even raising funds to support Japan's war efforts on the China front. Fujii admonished the Nisei to consider their immigrant parents' position of dependency on the Japanese state as aliens ineligible for US citizenship; that their allegiance to Japan should not be interpreted as anti-American.[35]

Itami's writings dovetailed with Fujii's call for unity across generations in the Japanese American community as the generational divide continued. Like Fujii, Itami was concerned that criticism of the Issei's patriotism toward Japan would compound the political tension within the community. Itami wrote sympathetically about many Issei's support

for Japan's actions in China in their precarious position as Japanese citizens living in a country that rejected them. He was reluctant to accept
the concept of loyalty as complete severance of one's allegiance to either
of the two nations. He suggested that many Issei's expression of loyalty
to Japan during the Second Sino-Japanese War was not equivalent to
their rejection of American society. In his view, such a one-dimensional
notion of patriotism would do more harm to the Japanese American
community and US-Japan relations by dividing Issei and Nisei along
generational lines.[36]

Itami continued to articulate his optimistic outlook on relations between the United States and Japan at the turn of the 1940s, amid the
heightened diplomatic tension between the two. In the wake of the
January 1940 resignation of Japanese prime minister Abe Nobuyuki,
who had called for an end to the Second Sino-Japanese War and for
Japan's neutrality, the imminent cabinet change prompted the Western
media's warning that Japan was well on its way to joining Nazi Germany
and Fascist Italy. Itami worked diligently to dispel any prospect of a
more hard-line Japanese diplomatic stance against the United States.
He also assured his readers that "whoever becomes the next prime minister," the diplomatic ties between the two nations would remain intact, quoting "an American journalist" in Tokyo in insisting that the
inauguration of the new cabinet would not mean a swift change of any
Japanese foreign policies.[37]

Both Itami and Fujii used the pages of *Kashū Mainichi Shinbun* to
assure their readers that the political developments abroad would not
jeopardize the future of Japanese Americans. Fujii's "Why America
Won't Fight," which he ran as a seven-day special serial column in
June 1940, insisted that the United States' entrance into the World War
was highly unrealistic even if Japan were to join the Axis powers. Fujii
argued that American society had not yet fully recovered from the Great
Depression, and any attempt by the Roosevelt administration to enter
the war would not withstand opposition from both corporate leaders
and the general public.[38]

Itami buttressed Fujii's position in his "Air Mail" column and urged
the Japanese American community to heed the veteran publisher's
opinion about the unlikelihood of the United States declaring war
against the Axis powers.[39] He insisted that the people in Japan had

no desire to go to war with the United States, and the newspapers in Japan quoted Fujii's argument rejecting the prospect of US involvement in the war.[40] Itami was also frustrated by negative public opinion about Japan, which he believed had much to do with the reporting practices of the US press. Itami phrased his criticism very carefully in order to direct readers' attention toward what he viewed as American newspapers' fearmongering tactics that seemed to violate democratic principles and journalistic integrity. Itami refrained from criticizing US government policies or the American public itself, but instead highlighted what he felt was the mainstream media's encouragement of the United States' entrance into the war against Japan and its allies. His method often involved calling out the mainstream press for its distortion of what he saw as more realistic and positive developments in US-Japan relations. For example, in early 1940 Itami claimed in "Air Mail" that the mainstream US newspapers had refused to report on a statement by the US Department of State that had assured the continuation of normalized trade relations between the two countries even in the case of suspended diplomacy.[41] Itami also emphasized that Secretary of State Cordell Hull had told the Japanese ambassador, Horinouchi Kensuke, that diplomatic tensions would not affect the rights and interests of Japanese living in America. He used his criticism of the US papers to convince his readers that the threat of imminent war between the United States and Japan was part of the anti-Japanese agitation fueled by the mainstream papers, and that it contradicted the goodwill of both the US government and the American public.[42] Unlike Yoneda and the Kibei leftists who were vocal in their public denouncement of Japanese imperialism, Itami was concerned that demonizing Japan would compound the still-intense anti-Japanese sentiment in the United States.

### The War, Memory, History, and Kibei Transnationalism

The wartime language of loyalty and Americanism suppressed the dynamic celebration, debates, and critiques of Nisei's cultural dualism and the "bridge of understanding" ideal in the Japanese American community. Itami's work as a leading political columnist for *Kashū Mainichi Shinbun* and his close relationship with Fujii helped him emerge as a leader of the Kibei community in Southern California; in late 1940, Itami was elected vice president of the JACL Los Angeles Chapter's Kibei Division.[43] But in the wake of Pearl Harbor, Itami was targeted as a potential pro-Japan element and his name was turned over to the FBI in early 1942 because of his status as a Kibei leader and his work as a Japanese-language newspaper columnist before the war. Like the rest of the Japanese Americans in the United States, Itami and other Kibei were compelled to demonstrate their allegiance to Uncle Sam. He did what he could to prove his loyalty. He joined the US Army's Military Intelligence Service out of the Manzanar incarceration camp in late 1942, and won the Legion of Merit award for translating over four thousand Japanese-language documents during the Pacific War.[44] He went on to become a language monitor at the Tokyo war crimes trials after the war, interpreting for Tōjō Hideki and other wartime Japanese leaders indicted at the tribunal. In 1950, though, he committed suicide for reasons unknown while stationed in Tokyo as a member of the US Occupation Force.[45] Despite his critical role as a language monitor and his stellar military record, Itami became an obscure figure in Japanese American history. The wartime experiences of Kibei in general have remained at the margins, as the dominant nation-centered narrative focusing on the Nisei's loyalty and Americanism had little room for their multifaceted transnational experiences and their varied reactions to the war.

In 1983, more than thirty years after Itami's death, the Kibei's life story attracted some attention in Japan. As the postwar Japanese American movement for redress and reparation for wartime mass incarceration was gaining momentum in the United States, the Japanese national broadcasting company, NHK, planned its fifty-one-episode period drama series *Sanga Moyu* (Mountains and Rivers Are Burning). Based on acclaimed novelist Yamasaki Toyoko's 1983 bestseller *Futatsu no Sokoku* (Two Homelands) and starring contemporary and future international stars like Mifune Toshiro and Watanabe Ken, the drama followed a plot set in the United States and Japan during and after World War II. Yamasaki used David Akira Itami's life as a model for her tragic hero, Amo Kenji, a Kibei man who spent his childhood in Kagoshima during the 1920s. Like Itami, Amo joins the US Army out of Manzanar, works as a chief language monitor at the Tokyo tribunal, and takes his own life after the conclusion of the trials.

For the Japanese audience unfamiliar with the history of Japanese Americans in the United States, Amo's tragic life offered a unique perspective on the war and what it meant to be Japanese. However, without substantive discussions about the social realities that had shaped US-born Nisei migrants' transnational experiences, Yamasaki's one-dimensional representation of her main character depicted Kenji Amo as a quintessential victim of the war and racism, a man torn between the country of his birth and the country of his parents. Unable to overcome his conflicting loyalties, Amo commits suicide as the only way to resolve his "failure to find his own country" in the story's dramatic ending. While the dominant historical memory of the Japanese American wartime experience rejected Kibei's cultural dualism, Yamasaki's characterization of Itami also operated within a nationalistic framework—this time centering on his Japanese identity—and was similarly reductive about Kibei's alleged inability to choose between two homelands.

Yamasaki's novel and the NHK's premiere of *Sanga Moyu* had a far-reaching transnational impact as they created a heated controversy in the United States in the mid 1980s, when the movement for redress and reparations was in full swing. Encouraged by the popularity of *Futatsu no Sokoku* in Japan, NHK scheduled the US premiere of *Sanga Moyu* on West Coast Japanese-language cable stations for the spring of 1984. The announcement of the series' stateside debut, however, was met with a fierce backlash from the Japanese American community on the West Coast. In particular, the story of a Nisei with split loyalties did not sit well with the leaders of the JACL, who, during the three decades after the war, had vigorously promoted the history of Japanese Americans' 100 percent Americanism in their campaign for redress for the wartime incarceration. Influential lobbyist and former JACL national secretary Mike M. Masaoka demanded that NHK withdraw its plan to premiere *Sanga Moyu* in the United States. In early 1983, the bipartisan Commission on Wartime Relocation and Internment of Civilians unanimously recommended a formal government apology and monetary compensation for the detention of Japanese American civilians.[46] Masaoka believed that Japanese Americans' continued demonstration of unquestioned loyalty to the United States would be crucial for American society's broad support for the commission's recommendation. He and other JACL leaders were determined to prevent

*Sanga Moyu* from airing on American television, even if the viewership would be limited to Japanese-speaking cable subscribers.[47] The controversy prompted NHK to cancel the series' premiere in the United States market. Yamasaki and the NHK executives failed to grasp the centrality of loyalty and Americanism in the dominant collective historical memory in the Japanese American community.

Despite the controversy, David Itami has remained an obscure figure in Japanese American history. The dominant historical narrative centered on the unquestioned loyalty of the Nisei has had little room for the multifaceted transnational experiences of Itami and other Kibei. They lived through complex and unpredictable circumstances brought about by multiple historical developments on both sides of the Pacific. Moreover, their perspectives illuminate the diverse and contentious articulations of Nisei cultural dualism throughout the 1930s that complicate intergenerational relations within the Japanese American community. The historically grounded lived experiences of Itami and other Japanese American migrants illuminate how these diasporic individuals, displaced in the transpacific borderlands, navigated the geopolitical, social, and ideological exigencies of their two homelands.

## Notes

1. David Akira Itami, "Itami Akira no jihitsu no hennenshiki kubun ichidaiki" ("The Chronicle of Akira Itami's Life as Written by Himself"), *Ryūmon* (September 1987): 42. Itami wrote about his factory life in Alaska for the San Francisco–based *Nichibei Shinbun*: Akira Itami, "Arasuka yori," *Nichibei Shinbun*, June 21, 1932; Akira Itami, "Dock," *Nichibei Shinbun*, July 26, 1932.

2. *Kashū Mainichi Shinbun*, January 1, 1937.

3. See Kumei Teruko, "1930-nendai no kibei undō—Amerika kokusekihō tono kanren ni oite," *Ijū kenkyu* 30 (1993) (also see chapter 3 of this book, which is a translation of this essay); and Paul R. Spickard, *Japanese Americans: The Formation and Transformations of an Ethnic Group* (New York: Twayne Publishers, 1996), 89, 167.

4. Although a number of vernacular Japanese American newspapers in Hawai'i, Los Angeles, and San Francisco throughout the 1930s and 1940s suggested an even larger number of United States–born Nisei in the Japanese empire, I use the Japanese government's figures and the total number of US-born Japanese Americans based on United States census records to estimate that about one-fourth (fifty thousand) of all Nisei (200,194) had gone to the Japanese empire by the eve of Pearl Harbor to work, study, join their parents' return migration to Japan, or for other reasons—such as short-term study tours and personal visits that turned into long-term stays. The Japanese Consulates General in the United States counted forty thousand US-born

Nisei from the contiguous United States and Hawai'i who had gone to Japan by the mid 1930s. This number represented one-fourth of the total Japanese American population based on the 1930 US Census, and one-fifth based on the number of Nisei counted by the Japanese Foreign Ministry in 1935. See Kumei, "1930-nendai no kibei undō"; Spickard, *Japanese Americans*, 89, 167; Robert Lee, "Introduction," in Mary Kimoto Tomita, *Dear Miye: Letters Home from Japan, 1939–1946* (Stanford, CA: Stanford University Press, 1995), 18–19; and Yuji Ichioka, "Introduction," in Karl G. Yoneda, *Ganbatte: Sixty-Year Struggle of a Kibei Worker* (Los Angeles: Asian American Studies Center, University of California–Los Angeles, 1983), xii.

5. Yuji Ichioka, "Introduction," in *Before Internment: Essays in Prewar Japanese American History*, eds. Gordon H. Chang and Eiichiro Azuma (Stanford, CA: Stanford University Press, 2006), 3.

6. Eiichiro Azuma, "Editor's Introduction: Yuji Ichioka and New Paradigms in Japanese American History," in Ichioka, *Before Internment*, xxi.

7. See Yuji Ichioka, "*Dai Nisei Mondai*: Changing Japanese Immigrant Conceptions of the Second-Generation Problem, 1902–1941," in Ichioka, *Before Internment*; Yuji Ichioka, "A Study in Dualism: James Yoshinori Sakamoto and the Japanese American Courier, 1928–1942," *Amerasia Journal* 13, no. 2 (1986): 49–81.

8. Ichioka, "*Dai Nisei Mondai*," 24–5; Eiichiro Azuma, "Nisei no Nihon ryūgaku no hikari to kage: Nikkei Amerikajin no ekkyō kyōiku no rimen to mujun," in *Amerika Nihonjin imin no ekkyō kyōikushi*, ed. Yoshida Ryō (Tokyo: Nihon Tosho Center, 2005), 223–27.

9. Ichioka, "A Study in Dualism," 49–81.

10. Yuji Ichioka, "Kengakudan: The Origin of Nisei Study Tours of Japan," in Ichioka, *Before Internment*, 53–54, 72–73.

11. John J. Stephan, "Hijacked by Utopia: American Nikkei in Manchuria," *Amerasia Journal* 23, no. 3 (Winter 1997–1998): 7; Kay Tateishi, "An Atypical Nisei," *Amerasia Journal* 23, no. 3 (Winter 1997–1998): 201.

12. Tateishi, "An Atypical Nisei," 203.

13. "Heishikan kiroku," *Heishikan News*, June 5, 1942, Heishikan Collection, Japanese Overseas Migration Museum, Yokohama, Japan.

14. Yamashita Sōen, *Nichibei o tsunagu mono* (Tokyo: Bunseisha, 1938), 266; Yamashita Sōen, *Nikkei shimin no Nihon ryūgaku jijō* (Tokyo: Bunseisha, 1935), 2–6.

15. Takeda Junichi, *Zaibei Hiroshima kenjinshi* (Los Angeles: Zaibei Hiroshima Kenjinshi Hakkojo, 1929), 43.

16. Hirohata Tsunegorō, *Zeibei Fukuoka kenjinshi* (Los Angeles: Zeibei Fukuoka Kenjinshi Hensan Jimusho, 1931).

17. Zaibei Nihonjinkai Jiseki Hozonbu, ed., *Zaibei Nihonjinshi* (San Francisco: Zaibei Nihonjinkai, 1940), 1117–8; Matsumoto Nagai, ed., *Nichibei bunka kōshōshi* (Tokyo: Yōyōsha, 1952).

18. See Kumei, "1930-nendai no kibei undō"; Spickard, *Japanese Americans*, 89, 167. *Zaibei Nihonjinshi* (History of Japanese in America) in 1940 reported that ten thousand Nisei returned to the United States from Japan, which left the number of Nisei remaining in Japan to be twenty thousand; Zaibei Nihonjinkai Jiseki Hozonbu, *Zaibei Nihonjinshi*, 1117–8. Brian Hayashi notes that figures suggested by contemporary estimates were likely too low; see Brian Masaru Hayashi, *Democratizing the Enemy: The Japanese American Internment* (Princeton, NJ: Princeton University Press, 2004), 44–45, 238 n11.

19. See, for example, "Terror in Nanking," *The Times* (London), December 18, 1937; "Butchery Marked Capture of Nanking," *New York Times*, December 18, 1937; "Japanese Troops Kill Thousands: 'Four Days of Hell' in Captured City Told by Eyewitness," *Chicago Daily News*, December 15, 1937; "Survivor Tells of Nanking Fall," *Seattle Daily Times*, December 16, 1937; "Witness Tells Nanking Horror as Chinese Flee," *Chicago Daily Tribune*, December 17, 1937; "Japanese Atrocities Marked Fall of Nanking after Chinese Command Fled," *New York Times*, January 9, 1938; "Nanking's Fall to Be Told," *Los Angeles Times*, March 18, 1938.

20. Trevor K. Plante, "'Two Japans': Japanese Expressions of Sympathy and Regret in the Wake of the *Panay* Incident," *Prologue* 33, no. 2 (Summer 2001).

21. "Ea-me-ru," *Kashū Mainichi Shinbun*, June 8, 1938.

22. Kōzō Kinashi, *Itami Akira no shōgai* (Tokyo: Paru Shuppan, 1985); Steve Sameshima, *Tennō o sukutta otoko: Amerika rikugun jōhōbu, nikkei kibei nisei Akira Itami* (Kagoshima: Nanpō Shinsha, 2013), 12.

23. Sameshima, *Tennō o sukutta otoko*, 17–19.

24. Yoneda, *Ganbatte*, 6–9; Pedro Iacobelli, Danton Leary, and Shinnosuke Takahashi, eds., *Transnational Japan as History: Empire, Migration, and Social Movements* (New York: Palgrave Macmillan, 2016), 173–75.

25. Ichioka, "*Dai Nisei Mondai*," 35; Yoneda, *Ganbatte*, 3–5, 13–17.

26. Sakaguchi Mitsuhiro, "Kibei nisei o meguru danshō: Shiatoru kibei nikkei shimin kyōkai no soshiki to katsudō o chūshin ni," *Imin Kenkyū Nenpō* 7 (March 2001): 30.

27. Lon Kurashige, *Japanese American Celebration and Conflict: A History of Ethnic Identity and Festival, 1934–1990* (Berkeley: University of California Press, 2002), 58–59, 68–69.

28. Mizuno Mariko, "Kagawa Bun'ichi no bungeikan to kyōsei shūyōjo taiken: Iminchi bungei kara kibei nisei bungaku no hatten ni oite," *Shakai Shisutemu Kenkyū* 11 (February 2008): 169–82.

29. Shinoda Sataye, "Tessaku: Hatten tojō no kibei nisei bungaku," in *Tessaku: Nikkei Amerika bungaku zasshi shūsei*, 5–6 (Tokyo: Fuji Shuppan, 1997), 7–10.

30. Zaibei Nihonjinkai Jiseki Hozonbu, *Zaibei Nihonjinshi*, 701.

31. Kagawa Bun'ichi, "Sōkan no kotoba," *Shūkaku* 1 (November 1936): 1.

32. *Shūkaku* 5 (October 1938).

33. David Yoo explains that many English-language newspaper articles written by Nisei also attempted to convince the public that Japanese Americans were the targets of racial hostility during this time in their response to the anti-Japanese press. David Yoo, *Growing Up Nisei: Race, Generation, and Culture among Japanese Americans of California, 1924–49* (Urbana: University of Illinois Press, 2000), 87–90.

34. Jeffrey Gee Chin and Fumiko Carole Fujita, *A Rebel's Outcry: Biography of Issei Civil Rights Leader Sei Fujii* (Los Angeles: Little Tokyo Historical Society, 2021); Jordan, Secretary of State of California v. K. Tashiro, 278 U.S. 123 (1928); Kurashige, *Celebration and Conflict*, 26.

35. See "Uncle Fujii Speaks" in *Kashū Mainichi Shinbun*, 1938–1942, English sections; Yuji Ichioka, "Japanese Immigrant Nationalism: The Issei and the Sino-Japanese War, 1937–1941," *California History* 69, no. 3 (Fall 1990): 263–67.

36. Itami's columns from 1940 to 1941, when there was a growing concern among Japanese Americans about a potential war between the United States and Japan, especially sought to make this appeal to his readers. See "Ea-me-ru," *Kashū Mainichi Shinbun*, 1940–1941.

37. "Ea-me-ru," *Kashū Mainichi Shinbun,* January 10, 1940.

38. See Sei Fujii, "Naze Beikoku wa tatakanuka," *Kashū Mainichi Shinbun,* June 1–7, 1940, Japanese section.

39. "Ea-me-ru," *Kashū Mainichi Shinbun,* June 3, 1940.

40. "Ea-me-ru," *Kashū Mainichi Shinbun,* June 7, 1940.

41. "Ea-me-ru," *Kashū Mainichi Shinbun,* January 13, 1940.

42. "Ea-me-ru," *Kashū Mainichi Shinbun,* January 20, 1940.

43. "Kibei bu yakuin senkyo iinkai," *Kashū Mainichi Shinbun,* October 8, 1940; "Hori Named Chief of JACL Kibei," *Kashū Mainichi Shinbun,* December 11, 1940.

44. War Department General Orders No. 82, Washington, DC, August 1, 1946; "Nisei Gets Medal," *Pittsburgh Press,* August 15, 1946; "Nisei Wins Fight to 'Prove Self': Downs FBI Distrust, Gets Merit Award," *Minneapolis Morning Tribune,* September 16, 1946.

45. Itami, "Itami Akira no jihitsu"; Certificate of Death, Akira Itami, 26 December 1950, published in *Ryūmon* (September 1987): 41.

46. Commission on Wartime Relocation and Internment of Civilians, *Personal Justice Denied: Report of the Commission on Wartime Relocation and Internment of Civilians* (Seattle: University of Washington Press and Washington, DC: Civil Liberties Public Education Fund, 1997), 459.

47. "Hard Soap: A TV Series Reopens Old Wounds," *Time,* April 23, 1984; Clifford Uyeda, "Futatsu no sokoku: Synopsis and Comments," *Pacific Citizen,* December 23–30, 1983.

# Part III

# Japanese Americans in 1930s' Hawai'i

CHAPTER 5

# Perceptions of the 1930s in Local Japanese American Newspapers in Hawai'i

## The Nikkei Community and Japan as Portrayed in the *Maui Shinbun*

*Toshihiko Kishi*
*Translated by Kaoru Ueda*

This chapter focuses on the Japanese-language newspaper *Maui Shinbun*, which was first published in Wailuku on the island of Maui, in the territory of Hawai'i, in 1906, and continued publication until two days before the Japanese attack on Pearl Harbor (see fig. 5.1).[1] The articles featured in this small newspaper with a staff of only ten people reveal the connection between the local history from the islanders' perspective and the global history of the 1930s.[2] In this chapter, I want to examine how the *Maui Shinbun* communicated to its Nikkei readers its perception of the times during the ten years leading up to the outbreak of war between the United States and Japan, and its regional perception based on the framework that the United States was the sovereign nation and Japan was the so-called motherland. I also want to explore the essential issues contained within the paper's articles.

The island of Maui is rich in natural beauty, and its main industries are primary products such as sugar, pineapples, and vegetables. On the island of O'ahu, located 120 kilometers northwest of Maui, the US Navy's Pacific Fleet, reestablished in February 1941, built the Pearl Harbor Naval Base and Hickam Air Force Base, established in 1935. However, Maui, located on the periphery of the Territory of Hawai'i (hereinafter referred to as "Hawai'i"), had a completely different environment. The first section of this chapter discusses Maui in light of its geopolitical characteristics of double peripherality: it is located on the periphery of Hawai'i, which itself is on the periphery of the United States. It will also focus on the first half of the life of Yasui Satosuke

FIGURE 5.1. The *Maui Shinbun* (January 1, 1930).
Hoji Shinbun Digital Collection, Hoover Institution Library & Archives.

(1881–1950), a pro-Japanese chief editor and president of the *Maui Shinbun* (see fig. 5.2).[3] The following section investigates the nature of interest in mainland Japan, Manchuria, and mainland China in the 1930s as gleaned from the local Japanese-language newspapers. This study not only inherits the results of a joint research project with Doshisha University—an impetus for writing this article—but furthers it by applying a media-theoretical analysis that was lacking in previous studies.[4] The third section will provide a fuller picture of the motherland tour groups (*bokoku kankōdan*) that traveled across the Pacific to visit these regions, incorporating perspectives from farther afield than Oʻahu, and especially Honolulu.[5] In the final section, I will discuss the changes that have taken place since 1941, which have completely overturned the perceptions of the 1930s.

Inspired by Eiichiro Azuma's concept of "crossing the boundaries between Japanese American and Japanese studies by delving into areas that have been overlooked by both fields," this article aims to examine the regional linkages between the Pacific and Asia from a transnational ethnic community's perspective.[6]

## Background: Maui in the 1930s

### The Shaken Nikkei Community and Media as a Linking Apparatus

The Great Depression had an undeniable impact in Maui, on the periphery of Hawaiʻi, although not to the same extent as it did in the other islands. The market prices of major primary products such as sugar, in four of its plantations (Puʻunene, Pāʻia, Wailuku, and Lahaina), and pineapples (in Lahaina and Haiku) started declining from around the fall of 1931. Bankruptcies amid the construction industry and the food-processing industry, as well as among small stores, ensued, and unemployment skyrocketed.[7] As a result of this regional economic depression, the *tanomoshi-kō*, a collective savings and credit association that had functioned as a bond within the Nikkei community, was shaken up, leading to more bankruptcies and even to the threat of the collapse of the Nikkei community (*MS*, July 8, 1932). Against this backdrop, the island of Maui began the decade of the 1930s.

Although many social problems occurred during this period, Maui was relatively stable compared to the more urbanized areas on Oʻahu

FIGURE 5.2. Yasui Satosuke (date unknown).

Dennis M. Ogawa Nippu Jiji Photograph Collection, JA4722.004, Hoji
Shinbun Digital Collection, Hoover Archives, courtesy of the Hawaii Times
Photo Archive Foundation.

and other islands. This was because the effects of the Depression were not as severe as expected for sugar plantations, and above all, the oligarchic ownership system of plantations by the so-called haole oligarchs, descendants of the Baldwin family from Scotland and other Christian missionaries who had monopolized the development of the island for many years, did not collapse. Unlike in Oʻahu and the island of Hawaiʻi, the political orientation of these haole families was consistently pro-Republican and anti-Democrat with regard to the politics of the United States, and pro–Constitutional Democratic Party (Rikken Minseitō), anti–Association of Friends of Constitutional Government (Rikken Seiyūkai), and anti–Japanese Communist Party (Nihon Kyōsantō) with regard to Japanese politics in Maui (*MS*, September 9, 1932; February 28, 1933).

Still, these families were antagonistic to plantation workers' strikes, Japanese-language schools, and dual citizenship, which would have encouraged ethnic groups to become independent. At any rate, the patron-client relationships that continued on Maui, while concealing the Baldwin family's substantive intention to secure plantation labor, helped establish the so-called Spirit of Maui, or "Maui nō kaʻoi" (Maui is the best)—protectionism and ethnic harmony as a pillar of the social ethic that rested on American Protestant ideals.[8] Even in the 1930s Maui, unlike the other islands, boasted organizations that embodied this ethos, such as the Futaba-kai, which connected Issei and Nisei women, and the Maui Japanese and Chinese Civil Association (Maui Nikka Shimin Kyōkai), which sought to promote cooperation between Japanese and Chinese Americans.

Nonetheless, it's noteworthy that Japanese-language newspapers and radio functioned to maintain the human network in the flustered Nikkei community. The 1930s were the heyday of Japanese-language newspapers and magazines in Hawaiʻi against this backdrop.[9] Maui readers enjoyed local Japanese-language newspapers such as the *Maui Shinbun*, the *Maui Rekōdo* (*Maui Record*, first published in 1917), and the *Shin Jidai* (first published in 1931), as well as Japanese media such as the *Nippu Jiji* and the *Hawai Hōchi*, which were carried in twice weekly from Honolulu, the largest city in Hawaiʻi, 95 miles away.

By the end of 1939, the community was also listening to not only Japanese-language radio broadcasts from Honolulu, Hilo, and other off-island locations (beginning in May or June 1936), but to the Japan Broadcasting Corporation's broadcasts (beginning in June 1935) to comfort their compatriots overseas (Kaigai dōhō imon hōsō, or literally "overseas compatriot care broadcasting").[10] This phenomenon reflects the fact that readers on a remote island like Maui, where information tends to get skewed, sought information from Honolulu, the core area within the region.

### From Educator to Media Person—The First Half of Yasui Satosuke's Life

In this chapter, I will focus on one of Maui's media figures, Yasui Satosuke, an Issei who was the president and editor in chief of the *Maui Shinbun*. First, let me trace Yasui's footsteps up to the 1920s, when he came to be known as Maui's leading figure in the world of journalism.[11]

Yasui Satosuke was born on January 12, 1881, the third son of Yasui Kyūtarō, in Asahara Village (now Hatsukaichi City), Saeki County, Hiroshima Prefecture; and after graduating from Hiroshima Prefectural Normal School in 1900, he became a teacher at an elementary school in Furuta Village (now Furuenishi-machi, Nishi-ku, Hiroshima City), a place so "crowded with successful returnees from the United States and Hawai'i that no one was in poverty." However, in July 1907, when he was twenty-six years old and after his teaching obligations had expired, he and his wife went to Hawai'i on a merchant visa. However, they had only $175 in their possession at the time. Unable to start a business and physically unfit for plantation labor, he ended up teaching at the Honolulu Hongwanji Elementary and Middle School for Girls on O'ahu in August of the same year, even though he said, "I had made up my mind that I would not teach for I bid farewell to the profession" (*MS*, September 17, 1937).

After the death of his first wife, he moved to the island of Hawai'i in May 1911 to take up a position as principal of Papaikou Hongwanji School; two years later, in September 1913, he became principal of Wailuku Hongwanji School in Maui, a position he held for six years (*HT*, January 23, 1950; April 4, 1966).[12] This movement from one place to another within the Hawaiian community was an effective way of networking and was common among members of the Nikkei community.

In April 1919, Yasui's life as a media person finally began at the age of thirty-eight. Because of his enthusiasm for contributing to the *Maui*

*Shinbun*—and because he shared a home prefecture, Hiroshima, with the president, Kaneko Tetsugo —Yasui began his career as a supervisor of the paper. This nimbleness in his choice of profession was due, in part, to the local shortage of human resources. In January of the following year, Yasui took over all authority over the paper from President Kaneko, and began his new position as president; in May of the same year, he was given the new title of chief editor, and in order to expand the paper's readership, the paper moved to a new building on Central Avenue in Wailuku and began mechanizing its facilities. In his personal life, however, his second wife died of illness in March 1922, and he was busy with his three young children (*MS*, April 8, 1919; January 23, 1920; March 10, 1922).

### The Editorial Tone of the Maui Shinbun *in the 1930s*

When discussing the 1930s from the perspective of East Asia, one cannot help but be aware of the constant presence of local conflicts in the region at the time. In fact, there was a series of armed conflicts, such as the Musha Incident, involving Taiwanese Indigenous people, in 1930; the Manchurian Incident in 1931; the Battle of Rehe in 1933; two North Chahar Incidents, in 1934 and 1935; the Marco Polo Bridge Incident in 1937; the Nomonhan Incident in 1939; and World War II.[13] In comparison, Hawai'i, because of its geopolitical position, was far away from the United States, Japan, China, and the Philippines, and enjoyed an environment where it was possible "first of all, to be in the middle of the Pacific Ocean and to criticize the general situation of the world without any grudge" and to comment freely (*MS*, November 14, 1933).

The 1930s began for Yasui personally with his third marriage, to Kuranaga Matsuno, a former teacher at the Japanese Language School in Spreckelsville.[14] He became a prominent Japanese figure in Wailuku in the 1930s, serving as the president of the Japanese Association of Maui, the consulate general agent (*toritsuginin*) in Maui, the president of the Maui Education Association, the president of the Japanese Baseball League of Maui, the executive director of the Wailuku Gakuen, the president of the Wailuku Hongwanji, and the advisor to the Wailuku Agricultural Association (*MS*, January 14, 1931; *HH*, October 10, 1918). He was involved in multiple public activities, and he was so busy that in mid 1933, he began suffering from stomach ulcers and duodenal ulcers, and his health began to deteriorate (*MS*, January 1, 1934).

### Nisei Issues Rather Than Current Affairs

In 1931, the year that marked the twenty-fifth anniversary of the first issue of the *Maui Shinbun*, the Manchurian Incident broke out. Rather than report on the conflict in detail, Yasui focused on criticizing Chiang Kai-shek and Chang Hsüeh-liang (Zhang Zueliang), who had joined him (*MS*, September 30, 1931; January 15, 1932). Furthermore, he developed a hard-line argument, saying, "Since the low-down of the League of Nations, with no authority, has been exposed, Japan should definitely withdraw from it" (*MS*, November 23, 1931). On Maui, however, the Nikkei and Chinese did not engage in a full-scale confrontation. Yasui himself wrote in the paper as follows:

> In Honolulu, we hear that the Chinese are anti-Japanese, but the Japanese and Chinese on this island, young and old alike, get along well and coexist in harmony (no need to fight in Hawai'i ).

Even though the newspapers were stirring up trouble, the Spirit of Maui remained intact (*MS*, November 11, 1931).

However, Hawai'i, being so far away from Manchuria, undeniably lacked information and context about the situation in that region. As if to fill the void of information, video footage of the Manchurian Incident, filmed by the Army Ministry and the South Manchurian Railway (Mantetsu), entered Maui. Using this film, Naramaru Entertainment (Naramaru Kōgyōbu) toured the island, showing it in Wailuku, Waihe'e, Pu'unene, Pā'ia, Kahului, Lahaina, Pu'ukoli'i, and other locations, quickly spreading the "legitimacy" of Japan (*MS*, February 29, 1932). These media events certainly increased interest in Manchuria. The Manchurian Incident was also an impetus for adding a tour of Manchuria to the booming motherland tours, which I will discuss later.

One example of this growing interest in Manchuria can be seen in the case of Matsumura Tadashi, who used to work for the *Maui Shinbun*. Matsumura was granted permission to volunteer for the army during a visit to Japan in 1932, and in November of the following year, he was drafted and enlisted into the Japanese Manchurian Garrison Army. Matsumura was engaged in teaching English to Japanese army officers, and after finishing his military duty, he asked to be reassigned a new role to teach in the Manchurian Garrison. The *Maui Shinbun* also mentioned his ulterior motive: that six years of military service in Manchuria was considered equivalent to twelve years in Japan, and that he would receive higher military benefits. His brother Atsushi Matsumura also volunteered, to serve in the Engineers and Signal Corps (*MS*, March 2, 1934).

However, the lack of mutual understanding between the Issei and Nisei was a more serious problem for Maui at the time than the Manchurian issue. In his editorial, Yasui explained the reason for establishing an English-language section on the occasion of the *Maui Shinbun*'s thirtieth anniversary:

We must communicate with the first generation and the next generation through current affairs. The times are now rapidly shifting to the second generation. Not only that, a lack of communication between the two generations sometimes results in a lack of unity of opinion, and in many cases, both parties are groping in the dark. This is the case with current affairs, which should always be addressed through newspapers in order to promote mutual understanding and reconciliation between the two generations [*MS*, November 10, 1936].

Therefore, Yasui proceeded with a stock issue with a capital of $20,000 and added an English-language section to the paper to appeal to the Nisei, starting on November 10 (*MS*, July 1, 1941).

Indeed, the 1930s were a period marked by a generational shift. Ōzu Yoshihiko, the principal of the Kahului Japanese Language School, wrote in his article "The Mission of the Next Generation Compatriots and Japanese Language Schools" in the same newspaper:

The decrease of so-called Issei has been accelerating in recent years, and we are now in the era of Nisei and Sansei. Some have entered politics, some have entered business, some have entered education, and some have entered medicine. Their expansion and development are particularly remarkable. Today, more than 120,000 Nikkei citizens attend public schools and Japanese language schools because of their dual citizenship. Currently, the number of Japanese language schools on the islands of Hawai'i nears two hundred, with about forty thousand students. . . . The total number of teachers is over six hundred, and more than half of them are Japanese American citizens.

In addition to teaching the Japanese language, these schools began instructing pupils in Japanese-style moral teaching (*shūshin*) in the late 1930s, as a means of planting Japanese identity (*MS*, August 25, 1939). From the perspective of Western society, this educational policy was viewed with alarm as adhering to Japanese nationalistic ideology.

### Newspaper Media Divided by Wartime Positions

After the Marco Polo Bridge Incident in July 1937, the *Maui Shinbun* began to focus more on breaking news of the war, unlike at the time of the Manchurian Incident.

> We are more than satisfied with receiving praise from all quarters for its diligent reporting of conflict news in our every issue. Our readers are so pleased because the newspapers from Honolulu do not arrive on the day of our publication, and even if it does, we deliver news one day ahead (*MS*, November 12, 1937).

They understood that breaking news significantly impacted the circulation of a newspaper.

On the other hand, the editorials in the *Maui Shinbun* were still decorated with sensationalism. They carried statements such as "As for the Chinese and Japanese military movements in North China since the Marco Polo Bridge Incident, while the Japanese forces have been determined not to expand the incident and have been patient, the attitude of the Chinese forces has become more and more provocative, and today we are facing a new crisis of imminent confrontation" (*MS*, July 13, 1937), and "If there is such a thing as a divine soldier, the Japanese army would be it" (*MS*, November 16, 1937). But did the residents of Maui feel more threatened by the Marco Polo Bridge Incident by reading these editorials? The following observation from Tashima Masaru, once a resident of Maui, clarifies this point.

> I did not consider much of the gravity of the situation because the radio telegrams put up on the bulletin board during the conflict reported that the case seemed to be nearing resolution two or three days before the landing. However, when I landed, I found that a special session of the Diet had been held in the imperial capital (Tokyo), and the streets were thumping with cheers for the soldiers going to war. My home country was amid a state of emergency, and I was back in the midst of it [*MS*, October 8, 1937].

Although significant tension was felt in Japan during the Second Sino-Japanese War, there was considerably less of it in the United States, which had not yet actively interfered in the war between the two countries. Perhaps for this reason, the residents of Hawai'i still felt it was somebody else's problem. Although the articles in the *Maui Shinbun* were similar in content to those distributed by Japan's National News Agency, Dōmei Tsūshinsha, in reality they only served to arouse readers' interest in China.

The Japanese-language newspapers published in Hawai'i were more concerned about the perceptions of the Nisei regarding the war than about the actual course of the Second Sino-Japanese War. The Nisei, with insufficient Japanese reading skills, read English-language newspapers published on the United States mainland and in Hawai'i as an important source of information, and the Issei thought that they might believe criticisms of Japan unconditionally (*MS*, August 6, 1937). An editorial in the *Maui Shinbun* also stated,

> The reports on the Second Sino-Japanese War were completely opposite on the Japanese and the Chinese sides, and in Hawai'i, even the English-language newspapers were reporting the same as the China side, so I couldn't help but wonder which side to believe. It is an unquestionable fact that not only third-country nationals, but even our second-generation compatriots believed the Chinese side reported in English- and Chinese-language newspapers.

Therefore, the Japanese-language newspapers in Hawai'i took pains to promptly improve their coverage of the war for Nisei readers.

At the end of 1937, the magazine *Jitsugyō no Hawai*, published in Honolulu, commented on the stances of the Japanese-language newspapers regarding their coverage of the Second Sino-Japanese War as follows (*JH*, December 1, 1937). First, the *Jitsugyō no Hawai* considered it "regrettable" that the *Hawai Hōchi*, one of the two major Japanese-language newspapers in Hawai'i, carried news of the war in its English-language section that was similar to what was in the English-language newspaper. Similarly, the *Jitsugyō no Hawai* also harshly criticized the way the *Yōen Jihō* wrote about the Second Sino-Japanese War, as the paper, published by Reverend Higa Seikan, a native of Koloa, Kaua'i, and an Okinawan, was full of unflattering words about the Japanese military. On the other hand, it gave rave reviews to the *Nippu Jiji*, another major newspaper, with the longest history in Japanese Hawai'i, praising it as "more meritorious than any other newspaper" and "demonstrating one hundred percent patriotism," because it excluded reports from the Associated Press and United Press International in the US and published articles in English that were similar to those distributed by the Dōmei News Agency two months into the Second Sino-Japanese War. The local island publications *Maui Shinbun*, *Maui Rekōdo*, and *Hawai Mainichi* were also praised as being "patriotic" in the same way as the *Nippu Jiji* (*JH*, December 1, 1937). Through the coverage of the battle reporting after the Marco Polo Bridge Incident, Nikkei readers developed interest in wartime China as well as Manchuria.

## Wartime East Asia and Motherland Tours

### Motherland Tour Boom

The Nikkei community in Hawai'i became aware of the changes in Japan after the withdrawal from the League of Nations, and they showed interest in the unknown region of Manchuria after the Manchurian Incident and in mainland China after the Second Sino-Japanese War. As a result, motherland tours boomed in the 1930s, reaching their peak in 1940. This phenomenon was similar to the popularity of Japanese tours to battle sites and school excursions to Manchuria during the First Sino-Japanese and Russo-Japanese wars.[15]

The first motherland tour was organized in Hawai'i in May 1912. It was a Honolulu-based media project; its main organizer was Tasaka Yōkichi, an editorial member of the *Nippu Jiji*, with the *Hawai Shinpō*, *Hawai Nichi Nichi Shinbun*, and *Nippu Jiji* as supporting organizations. The tour group consisted of thirty-six men, seventeen women, and four children, for a total of fifty-seven people. They were originally from Hiroshima Prefecture (sixteen of them), Yamaguchi Prefecture (eleven), and Okinawa Prefecture (six), as well as Wakayama, Fukuoka, Kumamoto, and Niigata prefectures. The group toured the famous and historic sites from Tokyo to Kyushu in fifty-three days, an itinerary that would later become a standard route for motherland tours (*NJ*, April 4, 1912; April 10, 1912). The Japanese media also paid attention to this first large tourist group from Hawai'i (*TA*, June 21, 1912). Maui's first motherland tour was also organized by a coalition of Maui and O'ahu media, sponsored by various Honolulu newspapers, the Honolulu Japanese Ryokan Association, the *Maui Shinbun*, and the *Maui Rekōdo*. The tour was led by Maeda Yoshimi, chief of the *Nippu Jiji* Wailuku bureau, and departed from Honolulu in March 1921, following the standard tour route from Yokohama to Hiroshima (*NJ*, December 3, 1920).

Anticipation of an immigration quota being applied to the Japanese after the Quota Immigration Act of May 1921 was enacted, and the ensuing Immigration Act of 1924, made a dent in the demand for motherland tours. However, an idea dreamed up by Tanabe Sannojō, the principal of a Japanese-language school in Kahului—to organize a tour group to give the Nisei a firsthand look at the culture and conditions in their ancestral home—brought them back into the limelight. The June 1927 tour group consisted of twenty-seven Japanese American citizens who had passed the eligibility test: United States nationals who had completed the seventh grade of public school or higher, or were currently enrolled in school (*MS*, April 28, 1927; May 2, 1927).

The real boom in Hawai'i's motherland tours came in the 1930s. An article appeared as early as 1930 that claimed, "The large number of tourist groups to Japan this year must be considered a rare fact in recent years. During the spring and summer vacation, four groups were organized on the small island of Maui alone, about 10 in the city of Honolulu, and several more on the islands of Hawai'i and Kaua'i, for a total of about 20" (*MS*, January 1, 1930).

The Japanese Colonial Industry Tours (Nihon Shokumin Sangyō Shisatsudan, later renamed the Japanese Pineapple Industry Tour, or Nihon Hōrigyō Shisatsudan), organized by Nakamura Tetsuo, an employee of the Libby, McNeill and Libby pineapple plantation in Haiku, Maui, was unique among the tourist-oriented groups. In addition to the major industries in the Japanese archipelago, the group went to Taiwan to investigate the pineapple industry with the cooperation of the Home Ministry, the Ministry of Colonial Affairs, and the governor-general of Taiwan. In the early 1930s, Maui was experiencing a fever of emigration to Taiwan because landowners did not want to extend the leasing agreements with pineapple growers, and the Japanese could not compete with Filipinos, who were the main plantation workers. The Society for Encouraging the Disposal of Taiwan Public Land (Taiwan Kan'yūchi Haraisage Undō Kiseikai, established in February 1930) decided to dispatch Nakamura and his group to Taiwan. Twenty-five members of the group boarded the *Tenyō Maru* on February 28, half of whom were Nisei. After visiting the Okazaki and Tatara farms in Tainan, the group also visited pineapple plantations in Taichung and Taitung, returning home in June (*MS*, October 7, 1929; January 8, 1930; June 6, 1930; February 27, 1931).

The tours up until the first half of the 1930s were characterized by the presence of many religious groups, including those to attend the Buddhist memorial service for the eight hundredth anniversary of the birth of Hōnen Shōnin in 1932; the great Buddhist memorial service for the thousandth anniversary of the passing of Kōbō Daishi in 1933; the second Pan-Pacific Young Buddhist Association conference in 1934; and the fiftieth anniversary of Tenrikyō Oyasama in 1936, among others. Buddhist groups such as followers of Jōdo-shū, Shingon, and Tenrikyō in Honolulu also formed a delegation (*NJ*, January 12, 1932; October 4, 1933; January 13, 1934; August 3, 1935).

Another characteristic is that many of the delegations were organized by educators, who inherited the spirit of the above-mentioned Tanabe Sannojō. These tours targeted Nisei: the tour group organized by Itō Tatsuo, a teacher at the Pu'unene Japanese Language School; the Hawai'i motherland tour group interacting with university students in Tokyo; the Maui Judo motherland tour; the Hawai'i youth men and women homeland tours; and the educational tour group of public school teachers were all designed for the Nisei (*MS*, April 21, 1930; May 16, 1930; July 4, 1930; *TA*, June 19, 1930). The popularity of the motherland tours grew partly because of the Nisei issue, but also because the yen continued to depreciate; one could fully enjoy sightseeing in Japan with only $500 or $600, making expenses less of a problem (*MS*, July 29, 1932).

The number of sightseeing groups temporarily declined immediately after the Marco Polo Bridge Incident in July 1937, but two years later, six groups set sail in the spring, and two more groups in the summer and fall. "One of the notable features of this year's [1939] tour groups was that they all included sightseeing tours of China, Manchuria, and Korea in their programs, as interest in China had increased since the Incident." Another feature: "several new tours were planned on Kauai and Maui, apart from Hawai'i [island], in addition to the existing group of Kauai resident Nōnin Kuwaichi" (*NJ*, February 8, 1939).

Of these, I would like to examine the motherland tours for the Imperial Japanese Army organized by Kurisu Sadato, an employee of the *Maui Rekōdo* in Wailuku. With the outbreak of the Second Sino-Japanese War, tours named "consolatory delegations" (*imondan*) rather than sightseeing groups (*kankōdan*) increased. Although the consolation groups did some literal activities, such as bringing comfort money and comfort bags to both the Army and Navy ministries, army hospitals, and Red Cross hospitals, the majority of the group ended up on sightseeing trips (*MS*, January 10, 1939). Sixty-five members of Kurisu's group boarded the NYK *Tatsuta Maru* in Honolulu on April 4, arriving in Yokohama in about ten days. From there, they headed west and disbanded in Beppu, Oita Prefecture, in September. The fifteen participants (seven of them residents of Maui) on the optional tour visited Beijing, Tianjin, Dalian, Fushun, Mukden (today's Shenyang), and Harbin before moving on to the Korean Peninsula to visit P'yŭngyang, Keijō or Gyeongseong (today's Seoul), and Mount Kumgang. Many members of the delegation returned to Honolulu on July 21 with tour leader Kurisu (see, for example, *MR*, June 9, 1939; June 13, 1939; June 23, 1939; June 30, 1939).

As if to compete with its rival newspaper, the *Maui Rekōdo*, the *Maui Shinbun* also launched a plan for an Imperial Japanese Army Comfort

Tour and East Asia Tour in January 1939. The trip was to last approximately four months, from August to November of the same year. Yasui was to be the leader of the group. As with the *Maui Rekōdo* tour, it was advertised that there would also be optional tours to Manchuria, Korea, and China (*MS*, January 10, 1939). However, around the time this plan was announced, Yasui developed wet pleurisy and was hospitalized in a sanatorium in Kula for six months, so the tour was canceled (*MS*, April 4, 1939; August 29, 1939). Having lost the opportunity to lead the tour group, Yasui never experienced either mainland China or the United States mainland, due in part to his subsequent health failure. This was one of the reasons Yasui was unable to overcome his pro-Japanese views.

The motherland tours had become a social phenomenon, almost a boom. However, because Japan was then at war, various restrictions were placed on tours to mainland China. For example, one had to show identification issued by the police station or village office in one's hometown to purchase a boarding ticket. In addition, those wishing to visit the front lines had to obtain special permission from the Ministries of War and Navy (*NJ*, February 8, 1939). Furthermore, in 1940, exchange controls were further tightened: those entering Japan from Hawai'i were allowed to carry only two hundred yen or less of Japanese currency (up to five hundred yen when combined with foreign currency). When entering mainland China, one was also allowed to carry no more than five hundred yen, and after November 1939, the entire amount of money carried had to be exchanged for Japanese military currencies (*NJ*, March 19, 1940). Thus, the boom in motherland tours was not the result of just one aspect, the depreciation of the yen—but it should not be overlooked that regulations on entry into and exit from Japan were becoming stricter.

### Motherland Tour Boom Reaches Its Peak

In January 1940, the Treaty of Commerce and Navigation between the United States and Japan expired, leaving Japan and the US without a treaty. Despite this, the motherland tour frenzies did not wane; in fact, this year was said to be "the best year for tours at all" and was "truly unprecedented and was even described as a flood of tour groups" (*NJ*, October 26, 1939; *MS*, March 22, 1940). This was no coincidence. Although the Second Sino-Japanese War was in progress, festive performances were still being staged throughout Japan that year.[16] Although the Tokyo Olympic Games and the Japan World Exposition (commemorating the 2,600th anniversary of the founding of the Empire of Japan) were canceled due to the military's reluctance to spend money on them, the tours, which had been building up their reserves for several years earlier, did not cancel their trips. In fact, in mid March 1940, quite a few tourists from Hawai'i wanted to see other various events held in Japan, including some different 2,600th-anniversary events happening in November 1940 (*NJ*, November 20, 1939).

In fact, from mid March to June 1940 alone, approximately two thousand people from about twenty different groups from Hawai'i visited Japan on a truly unprecedented scale. It's not hard to imagine how crowded it must have been, since more than ten ships operated by NYK and Dollar Steamship Company were fully booked for almost every voyage. Moreover, some of the sightseeing groups planned to continue to Manchuria, Korea, and China, or to participate in the Tokyo Conference of Overseas Japanese (Kaigai Dōhō Tōkyō Taikai), held on November 4–8 (*NJ*, January 18, 1940; October 1, 1940).

The Honolulu Japanese Ryokan Association's Tourism Department took advantage of this series of celebrations and organized four tours for the first time in 1940 (*NJ*, November 1, 1939, and elsewhere). The first group, the fifty-four-member East Asia Tourist Group, departed on March 20, 1940, aboard the *Asama Maru*. The tour leader was Shōji Jinshichi, a native of Fukushima, who was the leader of the Second Imperial Army Wounded and Sick Officers' Tour, organized by the association. The itinerary included a visit to the Matsushima area in Japan's Tohoku region, in addition to standard tourist attractions. Joining this group was a sightseeing group of Fukushima Prefecture compatriots, many of whom were residents of Hawai'i island's Keauhou area (*NJ*, November 24, 1939).

The second group, the Japan-Manchuria-China Tour, departed on April 1 aboard the *Tatsuta Maru*. The tour leader was Koide Yūichi, who had led sightseeing groups to Japan four times and to Manchuria twice. In addition to stopping at the regular sightseeing spots, the tour was scheduled to focus primarily on the Seto Inland Sea. Most of the twenty members of the group were second-generation Japanese Americans. Optional excursions to Manchuria and China were also offered.

The third tour, the Commemorative Tour of the 2,600th Anniversary of the Empire of Japan, departed on April 14 aboard the *Kamakura Maru*, headed by Baba Tokuji, chief of the tourism department and a native of Niigata; it planned to extend its course to the Sea of Japan in the Tohoku region, but for various reasons, this tour was canceled (*NJ*, April 10, 1940).

The fourth group, the Second-Generation Japan-Manchuria-China Inspection Tour, consisted mainly of students who were selected (based on their fluency in both Japanese and English) to join a group from the Ryokan Association, led by Yamashiro Masayoshi, owner of the Yamashiro Hotel in Honolulu, and Miho Katsuichi, owner of the Miho Ryokan in Kahului, departing on the *Rakuyō Maru* on June 16 and returning to Honolulu on the *Asama Maru* on August 14 (*MS*, April 12, 1940).

As mentioned above, the *Maui Shinbun*'s tour was canceled, but the "Hawai'i Consoling Mission for Wounded and Sick Soldiers of the Imperial Japanese Army," organized by Hirose Kōsuke, who worked with Yasui as an executive of the Wailuku Japanese Association, did set sail from Maui. Hirose believed that "the year 1940 was a once-in-a-lifetime event that coincided with the victory in the war and the historical celebration of the 2,600th anniversary of the Japanese Empire." According to the recruitment program in the newspaper advertisement, the itinerary covered about three months from April 1940. The sponsors were the Fukuoka Kenjinkai of Wailuku and volunteers from various parts of Maui. The caretakers included Hirose, the organizer; Hirotsu Masujirō (from Yamaguchi Prefecture), owner of Hirotsu, at one time the oldest clothing store on Maui, as an advisor; Mori Akizō, owner of the Nanmeikan Ryokan in Yokohama; and Kai Shizuya (from Kumamoto Prefecture), a self-proclaimed South Manchurian Railway lecturer, as guide and facilitator to mainland Japan, Korea, and mainland China (*MS*, December 5, 1939).

Kai Shizuya's extraordinarily good offices were noteworthy. Kai had previously served as a missionary at Nishi Hongwanji Temple in Wailuku, and through that connection, he accepted the role of sponsor for this tour—but that was not his only motive. This group was notified that "Hawai'i encourages emigration to Manchuria and offers special assistance to those who wish to emigrate to Manchuria," and also sent material titled *Guidelines for Emigration to Manchuria*.

In other words, it is believed that Kai planned to solicit tour participants to join the Manchurian Agricultural Emigration Plan for One Million Households (May 1936), prepared by the Kwantung Army Headquarters. Kai served as its de facto collaborator. The guidelines stated the following:

(1) It is possible to enter Manchuria as free people and build a Hawaiian village.

(2) Land is leased from the Manchurian Development Company (Manshū Takushoku Kaisha) and repaid in 20-year installments or purchased in cash.

(3) The Manchurian Development Company provides a subsidy of 500 yen per family.

(4) Land leased from the Manchurian Development Company is ten chōho (about 1 hectare) or 20 chōho (about 2 hectares) per family.

(5) Crops are mainly beans, corn, wheat, etc., and can be sustained for ten years without fertilizer.

(6) Winter cold-proofing facilities are provided for a better living environment (*MS*, September 19, 1939).

The newspaper article shows that this group received various arrangements in Japan (*MS*, July 2, 1940). But no articles turned up about the outcome of recruitments to settle in the target destinations of the program, such as Korea, Manchuria, North China, and central China, etc. Therefore, it is not clear whether any of the twenty-two members of this group were ultimately recruited to settle in Manchuria. However, what we know is that the intent of some of the groups involved more than just sightseeing and comforting the soldiers.

Meanwhile, Kurisu Sadato, of the *Maui Rekōdo*, wrote in detail about his tour to Manchuria. The eighty members of Kurisu's consolation tour and the sixth Fujimoto Kenkichi tour group were on the same ship with the Hirose-led group. The joint group experienced life under wartime control in various parts of Japan (*MS*, May 14, 1940). In addition, fifteen people (including eight Maui residents) who participated in an optional excursion from Beppu traveled from Shimonoseki to Busan, met with Minami Governor-General in what today is Seoul, and visited a kisaeng school in P'yŭngyang (*MS*, May 14, 1940). They then toured Shenyang, Harbin, Shinkyō or Xinjing (today's Changchun), and Dalian; south of the Great Wall, they visited Tianjin, Beijing, and Tsū Shū (or Tongzhou), where a massacre of Japanese nationals took place. They then returned to Beijing, transferred to the Peking-Paotow line, and visited the Great Wall after deboarding at Ching-lung-Chiao railway station. However, they were not able to get to Mongolia due to the intensifying battle, and instead visited Qingdao and Shanghai. The group left Shanghai for Japan on the *Nagasaki Maru* on June 26 and returned to Honolulu on July 11, but one can imagine that it was by no means a leisurely tour (*MS*, May 28, 1940; June 14, 1940; June 21, 1940; June 25, 1940; July 12, 1940).

## The Nikkei Community at a Standstill

*Differences in the Perception of Current Affairs between Hawai'i and Japan*
In an article in the *Maui Rekōdo* dated April 1, 1941, the dark clouds of war loomed over Hawai'i as well; it stated,

> As a base for operations in the Pacific, all Hawaiian islands are being fortified into impregnable walls as the first line of defense on the continent. The Honolulu area is the spearhead for the military expansion of the entire nation.

However, the following sentence suggests a relaxed atmosphere in the area.

> Even though the world is in a state of emergency and Honolulu is painted in military colors, the people who pass by are smiling; their appearance, words, and actions are all at ease.

The *Maui Shinbun* and other Hawai'i Japanese-language newspapers continued to publish articles about the motherland tours that were organized in the first half of 1941. As for tour plans related to Maui, the Second Japan Tour, organized by Hirose Kōsuke, and the Seventh Japan Tour, organized by Kurisu Sadahito, were arranged. The fact that a motherland tour was put together in the first half of 1941 suggests a gap in perceptions of current affairs between Hawai'i and mainland Japan. The sense of crisis on the Japanese mainland was considerable, as many Nisei students and businessmen had returned to Hawai'i (*NJ*, May 23, 1941).

Hawai'i broke off from Japan abruptly. On July 28, 1941, the United States government announced a freeze on Japanese assets in the US (the same day the Japanese government implemented similar measures). On August 1, 1941, it announced a halt to oil exports to the Axis powers, making clear the US government's hard-line stance against Japan. In this situation, Nikkei living in Hawai'i would lose all means to return to Japan, both as members of motherland group tours and as individuals. The last chances to return to Japan would be the final two voyages of the *Taiyō Maru* from Honolulu to Yokohama on November 1, or the final journey of the *Tatsuta Maru* from Honolulu to Yokohama (via San Francisco) on November 24 (*MR*, October 14, 1941).

### Hawai'i under Martial Law

For many Nikkei living in Hawai'i, the Japanese attack on Pearl Harbor was a surprise.[17] Even after the US government's policy toward Japan became clear, Japanese-language newspapers in Hawai'i were full of optimistic articles that expressed hopes for negotiations between the United States and Japan (see, for example, *NS*, August 29, 1941).

However, the situation changed drastically when martial law was declared throughout Hawai'i on the day of the attack. Yasui wrote a tanka poem about the situation at that time.[18]

Breaking news of the war and the order to prohibit the use of the Japanese language stunned us.
 The Japanese garments suddenly faded away at the sound of the war.

Not only were the Japanese language and all other representations of Japan banned, but logistics in the city also halted. From 4 p.m. that day to the following day, the FBI, police, and military police arrested about fifty leaders of the Nikkei community, including Japanese organization leaders, religious leaders, Japanese-language school principals, and *toritsuginin* (consulate agents), based on a blacklist of Nikkei leaders that had been prepared before the war began. They were first detained at the Immigration Bureau, and then at the Maui County Jail. The president of the *Maui Shinbun*, Yasui, and that of the *Maui Rekōdo*, Ōtsuka Nagao, were no exception. Yasui, who was suddenly confined, wrote a tanka poem about his feelings at the time.[19]

> The US-Japan war broke out, and I, a sick man, was taken prisoner and chained in a prison cell.
>
> Every time the door opens with a heavy sound, I wonder if a soldier called me to be shot.
>
> Yesterday has passed, and today is coming to an end, and the year will pass away while I wait to be shot to death.

As such, Yasui must have spent many anxious days in prison under the fear of being shot to death. Of course, the Japanese-language newspapers, such as the *Maui Shinbun* and *Maui Rekōdo*, were also suspended under General Order No. 14, dated December 10.[20] The *Maui News*, an English-language newspaper, was the only paper that was allowed to publish on Maui.

Fortunately for Yasui, he was in a sickbed, released from confinement at the Maui County Jail, and placed on home confinement. But unlike Yasui, by February 1946, more than two hundred Nikkei from Maui were confined at the Sand Island Incarceration Camp on O'ahu under the jurisdiction of the 35th US Army Regiment.[21] Furthermore, from among the detainees collected from all the Hawaiian islands, 694 men and eight women (less than eighty from Maui) were sent to the Tule Lake Segregation Center and other locations in North America. Among the individuals mentioned in this chapter, we can confirm that Hirose Kōsuke, the organizer of the motherland tours, was incarcerated at the Santa Fe Department of Justice Camp.[22] In addition, more than three hundred people were incarcerated at Honouliuli Incarceration Camp on O'ahu. Tasaka Yōmin and Koide Yūichi, who led the aforementioned motherland tours, were also incarcerated there.[23]

On December 22, 1941, the second secretary of war, Lieutenant General Delos C. Emmons, issued General Order No. 40, amending section 1 of General Order No. 14, which lifted the suspension of publication of the *Nippu Jiji* and the *Hawai Hōchi*, as well as General Order No. 49, dated January 6 of the following year, allowing both papers to be published again (*NJ*, January 8, 1942). This was done so the United States Army Intelligence Agency could use the two newspapers to pacify the Issei, who could only read Japanese.[24]

The Pacific War became a thorny path for the Yasui family as well as for the Japanese-language newspapers in Hawai'i. Yasui's two sons— Yoji, the eldest, and Rikuji, the second—went off to war as Japanese American volunteers, perhaps in part to wipe away their father's stigma. Yoji was deployed to the European front as a member of the 100th Infantry Battalion and was killed on the Italian front on December 1, 1943 (*HT*, November 16, 1945). He was twenty-six years old. The total number of Maui residents like him who died in the war was 117, of which 91 were Japanese Americans (*HT*, March 30, 1948).

## Conclusion: The Discontinuation and Rebirth of the *Maui Shinbun*

The 1930s was the decade leading up to the outbreak of war between Japan and the United States. However, despite the tensions of the time, the Nikkei community on Maui was aware that the cultural gap between the rising Nisei and Issei was a more serious social problem.

The *Maui Shinbun* periodically captured the motherland of Japan in its military expansion, but the United States, as the sovereign nation, was kept far away. The vernacular press was unable to distinguish between the genuine and falsified news coming from the Japanese mainland, and continued to publish articles that projected the dreams and hopes of the pro-Japanese community on Maui. Despite the rise of dual-nationality and Nisei American citizens in the 1930s, the *Maui Shinbun* continued to distrust the English-language information that the Nisei obtained and disseminated. Although the *Maui Shinbun* opened an English-language section in its Japanese-language newspaper, it did not cover the sovereign nation of the United States and its progress.

However, from a social standpoint, it can be concluded that in the first half of 1933, with the rise of the second generation, the shift to Americanization was already underway at a rapid pace. A total of 1,880 people were born in Hawai'i, of which only 412 (21.9 percent) submitted notifications of their Japanese nationality reservation. The remaining 1,468 (78.1 percent), including those who submitted notifications of renunciation of nationality, selected United States citizenship.[25] It was for this reason that the Nisei problem always emerged as an essential agenda. Against this backdrop, the gap between the newspaper's reporting and the facts led to Yasui's arrest and detention and the discontinuation of the *Maui Shinbun*.

Nevertheless, after the war, on August 2, 1946, the *Maui Shinbun* was reborn with twenty-eight pages in Japanese and forty pages in English (although the author did not have access to the English section to research). The editorial staff consisted of his second son, Rikuji Yasui, as president and chief editor; Hirose Kōsuke as manager; and Yasui's daughter Iao, who had returned from New York as a secretary and who also temporarily collaborated (*HT*, August 30, 1946). Six months earlier, at the first postwar general meeting held at the *Maui Shinbun*, Yasui Satosuke had resigned as president, and Rikuji was to succeed him as the new president (*HT*, February 21, 1946).

The new president, Rikuji Yasui, decided to purchase the management rights to the English-language newspaper *Valley Isle Chronicle* and to publish the newspaper himself under the same name from September 23, 1947 (*HT*, September 25, 1947). With this decision, the *Maui Shinbun* was officially discontinued. Although this new newspaper also portrayed the island of Maui, there was no longer any image of Japan as the mother country, but rather the United States as the sovereign nation. However, this new newspaper did not see Hawai'i as the fiftieth state of the US in August 1959—because it ceased publication four years earlier.

Yasui Satosuke contributed a column to the *Hawaii Times* immediately after the war. Still, not only was he unable to share the *Maui Shinbun* with the public again, his health did not improve, and on November 6, 1949, he was confined to absolute bed rest. The following year, on January 23, 1950, at 3 a.m., he passed away at his home in Wailuku. He was sixty-nine years old.[26]

Just three months after Yasui's death, the SS *General Gordon* visited Japan with 814 passengers, the largest number of tourists in the postwar period (*TA*, April 24, 1950). This event undoubtedly marked the beginning of a new era between Hawai'i and Japan.

## Notes

1. This chapter was translated from "Hawai no nikkei rōkaru shinbun ni miru 1930-nendai ninshiki–'Maui Shinbun' ga egaku nikkei komyunitī to Nihon," written in Japanese by the author for this volume. The abbreviations of newspapers in this chapter include *TA*, for *Tōkyō Asahi Shinbun*, as well as the following newspapers published in Hawai'i that are found in the Hoji Shinbun Digital Collection (www.hoji shinbun.hoover.org), created by the Japanese Diaspora Initiative, Hoover Institution Library & Archives, Stanford University: *HH, Hawai Hōchi*; *HT, Hawaii Times*; *JH, Jitsugyō no Hawai*; *MR, Maui Rekōdo*; *MS, Maui Shinbun*; *NJ, Nippu Jiji*; and *NS, Nichibei Shinbun*. The romanization of the Japanese titles uses the library convention based on the Japanese phonetics.

2. The author published his research results based on this methodology, such as in Kishi Toshihiko, *Ajia Taiheiyō sensō to shūyōsho: Jūkei seikenka no hishūyōsha no shōgen to kokusai kyūsaikikan no kiroku kara* (Tokyo: Kokusai Shoin, 2021).

3. I was enlightened about the needs for various methodologies to aid the study of Nikkei in America by publications such as Ichioka Yuji, G. H. Chang, and Azuma Eiichiro, eds., *Yokuryū made: Senkanki no zaibei Nikkeijin* (Tokyo: Sairyūsha, 2013).

4. Okita Yukizi, ed., *Hawai nikkei shakai no bunka to sono hen'yō: 1920-nendai no Mauitō no jirei* (Kyoto: Nakanishiya Shuppan, 1998); Yoshida Ryō, *Ekkyō suru nisei: 1930-nendai Amerika no nikkeijin to kyōiku* (Tokyo: Gendai Shiryō Shuppan, 2016).

5. Moribe Hiromi, "Hawai nikkei nisei to sokoku kengaku-dan—sedai to jinshu o koeru Nihon bunka no kyōju," in Yoshida, *Ekkyō suru nisei*. While this is a valuable previous study, it is too limited in the quantity and quality of the tours it covers, and does not succeed in painting a complete picture.

6. Azuma Eiichirō, Iijima Mariko, Konno Yūko, Sahara Ayako, and Tsukuda Yōko, *Teikoku no frontia o motomete—Nihon no Kantaiheiyō idō to nyūshokusha shokuminchi shugi* (Nagoya: Nagoya Daigaku Shuppankai, 2022). The original publication is Eiichiro Azuma, *In Search of Our Frontier: Japanese America and Settler Colonialism in the Construction of Japan's Borderless Empire* (Oakland: University of California Press, 2019).

7. The population of Maui in 1933 was approximately fifty-eight thousand, of which twenty-eight thousand (48.3 percent) were Nikkei. The ratio of Japanese nationals to dual nationals and Nisei with US citizenship is estimated at 4:6. *MS*, November 14, 1933.

8. Yoshida Ryō, "Amerika shimin kyōiku to Maui seishin," in Yoshida, *Ekkyō suru nisei*, 225–27.

9. Kankō Iinkai, ed., *Hawai Nihonjin iminshi* (Honolulu: Hawai Nikkei Rengō Kyōkai, 1964), 302.

10. Nippu Jijisha, ed., *Nippu Jiji Hawai nenkan narabi jinmei jūshoroku (1941-nendo)* (Honolulu: Nippu Jijisha, 1941), 119–21.

11. Watanabe Shichirō, *Hawai rekishi* (Tokyo: Kōgaku Kyōikubu, 1936), 209.

12. See also Yasui Matsuno, "Yasui Satosuke ryakureki," in Yasui Shōsō (Satosuke), *Kashū: Ginkensō* (Nagoya: Tanka Zasshi Henshūbu, 1950), 189–90.

13. For these battles, see Kishi Toshihiko, *Teikoku Nihon no puropaganda sensōnetsu o aotta senden to hōdō* (Tokyo: Chūō Kōronsha, 2022).

14. Matsuno was a member of the Maui poets' group Shinju, who worked to promote and educate the public about tanka poetry. See also Yasui Matsuno, *Kashū yashino kage* (Hiroshima: Shinjusha, 1951).

15. Kishi Toshihiko, *Manshūkoku no bijuaru media posutā · ehagaki · kitte* (Tokyo: Yoshikawa Kōbunkan, 2010), chapter 2.

16. Kenneth J. Ruoff, *Imperial Japan at Its Zenith: The Wartime Celebration of the Empire's 2,600th Anniversary* (Ithaca, NY: Cornell University Press, 2010).

17. The last issue of the *Maui Shinbun* was on December 5, 1941. Although the top news on the front page refers to the eighth meeting between the United States and Japan, no article implied a possible US-Japan war.

18. Yasui, *Kashū*, 149.

19. Yasui, *Kashū*, 34–35.

20. Tamaru Tadao, *Hawai ni hōdō no jiyū wa nakatta–senjika no hōji shinbun o henshūshite* (Tokyo: Mainichi Shinbunsha, 1978), 14.

21. Ōtsuka Nagao, the president of the *Maui Rekōdo*, died in Pāʻia Hospital on May 11, 1942, the year after he was detained. *NT*, May 15, 1942.

22. For the Hawaiʻi wartime Japanese American incarceration, see Akiyama Kaori, *Hawai nikkeijin no kyōsei shūyōshi—Taiheiyō sensō to yokuryū no hensen* (Tokyo: Sairyūsha, 2020).

23. Kankō Iinkai, ed., *Hawai Nihonjin iminshi*, 188–90.

24. Tamaru, *Hawai ni hōdō no jiyū wa nakatta*, 15, 214.

25. "Hawai shussei hōjin oyobi Nihon kokuseki ridatsu todoke tōkei 1933-nen 8-gatsu 3-kka fu," *Imin Jōhō* 5, no. 9 (1933): 37.

26. Yasui, "Yasui Satosuke ryakureki," 189–90.

# CHAPTER 6

# Crafting Japanese Immigrant Nationalism

## *Imon Bukuro, Imon Bun,* and *Senninbari* in 1930s' Hawai'i

### *Mire Koikari*

In his 1995 essay titled "Fifty Years after World War II and the Study of Japanese American History: The Untold 1930s," Yasuo Sakata discerned a staunch silence surrounding the 1930s in the historiography regarding Japanese Americans. Situated between the two landmark events that each have generated voluminous scholarship—the passage of the Immigration Act of 1924 and the onset of incarceration in 1942—the 1930s, in contrast, have resisted researchers' scrutiny and remained a "*katararenai* (untold) decade."[1] Among the issues left underexamined is Japanese immigrant nationalism. Issei and Nisei have long insisted on their loyalty to the United States, an assertion necessitated by relentless charges of anti-Americanism before, during, and even after World War II.[2] However, pro-Japanese sentiments, pronouncements, and practices were in wide circulation among overseas *dōhō* (compatriots; literally, "those born from the same womb") in the years before Pearl Harbor, an "untellable" (*katarenai*) fact few scholars have addressed.[3]

Hawai'i was a place where Japanese immigrant nationalism flourished prior to World War II. At the center of this phenomenon were the *imon bukuro* (comfort bag), the *imon bun* (comfort letter), and the *senninbari* (one-thousand-stitch amulet)—gendered items originating in Japan. The custom of *imon bukuro* reached Hawai'i in the early twentieth century and took root in subsequent decades. Issei and Nisei women sewed large quantities of cotton bags and filled them with candies, cigarettes, and other domestic objects to "comfort" (*nagusameru*) Japanese soldiers.

Often included in these care packages were *imon bun*, personal letters written by immigrant women or school-age children, an important morale booster for those in combat. The making of *senninbari*,
another Japanese practice, also became a common sight in the islands.
A piece of rectangular fabric, embellished with a thousand stitches by
a thousand women, was turned into an amulet believed to protect its
wearer from danger in battle. The vernacular press fed the patriotic passion of island *dōhō* by reporting on the relief campaigns proliferating
across the homeland in which women from all walks of life—royals,
housewives, schoolgirls, movie stars, café waitresses, and geisha—
enthusiastically took part. Embodying the "sincere hearts" (*sekisei*) of
the Japanese immigrants in Hawai'i, the comfort bags, comfort letters,
and protective amulets were bundled with other offerings—monetary
donations variously called *imon kin*, *juppei kin*, or *kokubō kenkin* and
material contributions such as clothing, bedding, and even scrap metal
and rubber—and shipped across the ocean to fuel Japan's expansionist
ambitions.

This essay examines the rise of Japanese immigrant nationalism in
Hawai'i. Prior to World War II, Japanese patriotism gained traction in
overseas Nikkei communities wherein the crafting of comfort bags, comfort letters, and protective amulets symbolized *dōhō* loyalty to Japan.
Though a widespread phenomenon, this pro-Japanese mobilization was
never simple or straightforward. On the US West Coast, for example,
the rise of Japanese immigrant nationalism was partly in response to the
Yellow Peril racism where the Issei, denied American citizenship, could
not help but identify with their country of origin. Affection for the old
country did not contradict, and indeed often coexisted with, attachment to the new country. The relief campaigns involving *imon bukuro*
and other donations were also not entirely voluntary. Participation was
expected and dissent difficult, if not entirely impossible. Putting further pressure on Japanese immigrants was intra-ethnic rivalry. Eager
to outdo each other, they competed in the quantity and quality of their
donations. The "winners" gained bragging rights, not an insignificant
matter in the tight-knit ethnic community.[4] Last but not least, the pro-
Japanese mobilization presented an opportunity for Issei and Nisei to
vindicate themselves vis-à-vis the homeland. Long stigmatized back
home as uncouth and uneducated, they could finally prove their worth.[5]

These external factors, salient among the West Coast Japanese, were also very much present in Hawai'i.

In Hawai'i, however, additional dynamics—militarism, tourism, consumerism, and indigeneity—further complicated the politics and poetics of Japanese immigrant nationalism. In the early twentieth century, the Pacific was transformed into a theater for inter-imperial competitions, a vast oceanic space Japanese and American gunboats regularly crisscrossed to demonstrate dominance. Located at the halfway point, Hawai'i—an American territory since 1900 but with a sizable population of Japanese settlers—was a popular port of call for Japanese and American naval vessels alike. Visits by the Japanese fleet sparked patriotic fervor among island Issei and Nisei eager to "comfort" the imperial seamen by gifting them *imon bukuro*. Importantly, the same Nikkei community equally welcomed the arrival of American fleets. Disembarking American sailors were potential customers whose purchasing power Issei and Nisei businesses could not easily ignore.

For American and Japanese navy men in Hawai'i, the line between "tours of duty" and "tours of leisure" often became blurred.[6] Once anchors were down, these soldiers would go ashore, try on aloha shirts, and enjoy the sights and sounds of the exotic islands. The confluence of militarism and tourism—what some scholars call *militourism*[7]—was a conspicuous dynamic, and this in turn animated Japanese immigrant nationalism. *Imon bukuro* embodied the spirit of hospitality of Hawai'i Nikkei. Inside the comfort bags, the Japanese imperial soldiers found island exotica such as Dole pineapple, Kona coffee, and hula dolls. The welcoming events for the Japanese naval fleets featured familiar tourist attractions, most notably hula.[8] Militourism was manifest not only in the American but also in the Japanese imperium. Japan's territorial acquisitions resulted in the expansion of sightseeing opportunities, and *kōgun imon*—organized tours to "comfort" the imperial soldiers—emerged to take Japanese and Japanese American tourists to the China front. Participants in these tours—among them Issei and Nisei from Hawai'i—customarily took *imon bukuro*, *imon bun*, and *senninbari* with them as gifts for those engaged in the "holy war" in mainland Asia.[9]

Circulating in tandem with militarism and tourism was yet another, quite unlikely, dynamic—a rising consumer culture. A sewing boom hit

Hawai'i in the 1930s and Issei and Nisei women flocked to Western-style sewing schools, some run by Japanese immigrants and others by American home demonstration agents.[10] Japan too experienced the dawn of "yōsai no jidai" (the era of Western sewing), and women there immersed themselves in a new domestic preoccupation.[11] More than the simple pleasure of dressmaking or a source of income was at stake. The sewing boom provided a crucial backdrop for the *imon bukuro* campaigns in which Japanese women at home and abroad functioned as handmaidens of their empire. In Hawai'i, the same skill also turned Japanese immigrant women in relatively short order into a reserve army for the "aloha wear" industry, an enterprise whose expansion took place alongside that of American empire through World War II and thereafter.[12]

Finally, weaving in and out of the multilayered dynamics of Japanese immigrant nationalism were the Indigenous islanders—Kanaka Maoli (Indigenous Hawaiians) and Uchinanchu (Indigenous Okinawans). The patriotic mobilization of Japanese immigrants—a phenomenon that was articulated at the interstices of the American and Japanese imperiums and manifest in the gendered articles handmade by *dōhō* women—directly and indirectly involved Hawaiians and Okinawans. The conditions surrounding the immigrants from Okinawa—under Japanese rule since 1879—were complex. As a minority within a minority, they were subordinated to the Japanese within the immigrant community and dominated by the White Americans who controlled the islands. In the context of this double oppression, Okinawans in Hawai'i took part in Japanese nationalism and demonstrated (or "performed") their allegiance to Japan. This strategy, often born from necessity, turned Okinawans into accomplices in settler colonial dynamics in which Indigenous Hawaiians, the islands' original occupants, were increasingly marginalized. Too often sidestepped in the discussion of settler colonialism of America, Japan, and Japanese America, Indigenous islanders were clearly part of the tangled webs of domination and subordination coursing throughout the Pacific. Their presence—often obscured by the region's dominant geopolitical forces and continuously stifled by the prevailing analytical categories in academia—must be recovered and rediscovered.[13]

To explore the dynamics highlighted above, this essay turns to the Hoji Shinbun Digital Collection created by the Japanese Diaspora Initiative, a holding of immense significance at Stanford's Hoover Institution. Immersing oneself in this archive is akin to examining a tapestry of mesmerizing hues and textures. You stand transfixed by its exceptional subtlety and complexity. Gaze long enough and manifold threads interwoven in never-before-seen patterns come into focus. Full of intriguing and sometimes befuddling tales, the collection opens new historical vistas for scholars of Japan and Japanese America. From the collection's many "treasures," the essay focuses on three journalistic gems—the *Nippu Jiji* (established in 1906), the *Hawai Hōchi* (1912), and the *Jitsugyō no Hawai* (1911). The *Hawai Hōchi* and *Nippu Jiji*, run by Fred Kinzaburō Makino (originally from Yokohama) and Yasutarō Sōga (Tokyo), respectively, were daily newspapers.[14] The *Jitsugyō no Hawai*, edited by Tetsuo Toyama (Naha, Okinawa), was a monthly business magazine whose readers included Japanese and Okinawans. The Japanese-language editions of these publications—through their texts, photographs, advertisements, and, in the case of *Jitsugyō no Hawai*, cover graphics—offer a fascinating glimpse into the history of *dōhō* nationalism in Hawai'i.

This essay first discusses a transnational genealogy of *imon bukuro* and its associated practices. An intertwined dynamic of sewing and soldiering crossed multiple borders—originating in Britain, traveling through America, and finally reaching Japan—a journey of extraordinary distance that illuminates the mobile nature of domesticity.[15] At each stop, the war front was linked to the home front to entice women to pick up sewing needle and thread, or knitting pin and yarn, to "comfort" the soldiers. The essay then turns to pre–World War II Hawai'i, where *imon bukuro*, *imon bun*, and *senninbari* emerged as the hallmark of Japanese immigrant nationalism. Two sets of events—visits by Imperial Japanese Navy fleets and the start of the Second Sino-Japanese War—galvanized the Nikkei community and mobilized *dōhō* women's hands and hearts. As militarism, tourism, domesticity, and indigeneity converged in this "untold" and "untellable" phenomenon, the crafting of Japanese immigrant nationalism acquired numerous, often hidden, layers and produced a political project of endless twists and turns.

## Sewing and Soldiering—A Brief Transnational History

*Imon bukuro, imon bun,* and *senninbari* have rarely if ever been discussed outside the context of Japan proper. As the dominant narrative goes, these relics of the past, once ubiquitous on the wartime home front, reflected the gendered and gendering logic of Japan's expansionism, something to which women willingly or unwillingly capitulated. Reminders of dark years in modern Japanese history, the handmade artifacts evoke gendered pathos under the militarist regime.[16] This national(ized) account undergoes significant revisions, however, when one looks beyond Japan and retraces the cross-border history of sewing and soldiering.

The *imon bukuro* was first introduced to Japan in the early twentieth century by members of the American Women's Christian Temperance Union (WCTU). The Japan WCTU, under the leadership of Yajima Kajiko, adopted the comfort bag as part of its organizational repertoire, a strategic move on the part of Yajima.[17] Still a fledgling entity in need of official approval, the Japan WTCU launched a series of *imon bukuro* campaigns during the Russo-Japanese War (1904–1905) in cooperation with the state.[18] As Japanese expansionism accelerated in the 1930s and 1940s, the *imon bukuro* became an indispensable part of the war machinery, and collaborations between women's organizations and the warring state continued. The Patriotic Women's Association (Aikoku Fujinkai) and the Greater Japan National Women's Defense Association (Dai Nihon Kokubō Fujinkai) played leading roles in propagating this practice, and the Rikukaigun Juppeibu—propaganda machinery of the Imperial Navy and Army—coordinated women's behind-the-lines activities.[19] The making of *imon bukuro, senninbari,* and *imon ningyō* (comfort dolls) was part of women's patriotic duties in Japan.[20] Often included in the comfort bag was a kit (thread, needles, and buttons) for the soldier's own use (see fig. 6.1).[21] Women's devotion was not driven by their love of country alone, however. The collaboration with the state, it was hoped, would pave the way for women's suffrage, a leading political priority among female leaders and activists in prewar Japan.

Prior to its arrival in Japan, the comfort bag had an equally or even more fascinating history. During the American Civil War (1861–1865), the making of care packages galvanized women in the North and the South alike. Sewing shirts and trousers, knitting socks and mittens, and

FIGURE 6.1. A sewing set for imperial soldiers (date unknown).
Japanese Subject Collection, Hoover Institution Library & Archives.

baking cakes and breads, American women sent their labors of love to the front lines to provide the soldiers with "comfort from home." Often included in these packages were tiny handmade satchels containing sewing kits, variously called *hussif*, *housewife*, *comfort bag*, *bachelor's blessing*, or *ditty bag*. These mementos from home brought exceptional pleasure to war-weary soldiers.[22] The women's relief campaigns required funding. Numerous charity events were organized where "benefit dolls"—reminiscent of Japanese *imon ningyō*—were auctioned to raise money.[23] Coordinating women's activities in the North was the newly established US Sanitary Commission, an agency whose inspiration came from the British Sanitary Commission during the Crimean War (1853–1856).[24] The commission, whose leadership was dominated by men, provided select women with opportunities to step into the public domain, develop organizational skills, and assert a degree of power and influence. For some, work with the commission became a launching pad for activism for women's suffrage.[25]

The intertwined motion of homemaking and war-making thus stretches back to Victorian England, where the Crimean War triggered a large-scale mobilization at home. Though the term *comfort bag* seemed not to have been in wide use, the practice of delivering remnants of domestic comfort to distant battlefields became ubiquitous. The military campaign in the Crimea sparked knitting and sewing drives, and the dispatch of "packages of home-worked comforts" warmed the hearts of the British soldiers stuck in a muddy war against Russians.[26] The Crimean winter was severe, so British women picked up knitting in addition to sewing. Queen Victoria, an avid knitter, helmed this gendered mobilization; with her princesses in tow, the queen, ever industrious, made mittens, socks, scarves, and comforters.[27] The link between sewing and soldiering was evident in another way. Emerging out of the war were new clothing designs, such as the cardigan (named after James Thomas Brudenell, Seventh Earl of Cardigan), the raglan coat (named after FitzRoy James Henry Somerset, First Baron Raglan), and the balaclava helmet (a knit cap originating from the Battle of Balaklava).[28] Similar to the American Civil War, the Crimean War was an occasion where the seams of gender strictures were partially loosened, as seen in the rise of Florence Nightingale, whose nursing work gave her exceptional mobility (social as well as geographical) and allowed her to take part in the affairs of empire.[29] The history of sewing and soldiering, homemaking and war-making, was complex, dynamic, and subversive.[30]

## Cheering the Warriors of the Sea

It is hard to tell exactly when and how *imon bukuro*, *imon bun*, and *senninbari* made their way to the Nikkei community in Hawai'i. Vernacular press accounts date the arrival of *imon bukuro* back at least to the start of the twentieth century. During the Russo-Japanese War, a brief article in the *Yamato Shinbun*, predecessor of the *Nippu Jiji*, reported on the making of *imon bukuro* by young female royals in Japan. To ensure that the bags' contents would suit the soldiers' tastes, the princesses dispatched their ladies-in-waiting to the entertainment district of Asakusa to discern the likes and dislikes of common men.[31] The following year, another piece, also published in the *Yamato Shinbun*, announced the visit of Yajima Kajiko. It reported that Yajima, president of the Japan WCTU, had collected nearly sixty thousand comfort bags for the Japanese soldiers fighting the Russians.[32] Japan's war was not a distant event; the gendered tales of *imon bukuko* brought this home to the immigrants in Hawai'i. Their patriotic passion, thus stirred, would continue to grow in the coming years.

In prewar Hawai'i, nothing thrilled Issei and Nisei as much as the comings and goings of Imperial Japanese Navy training vessels (*teikoku renshū kantai*). These visits—more than forty between 1876 and 1939—demonstrated Japanese naval power in the Pacific, a region also crisscrossed by American military squadrons with equal frequency.[33] The muscular silhouette (*yūshi*) of the Japanese imperial fleets "excited the flesh and blood" of Japanese immigrants and stoked their racial and national pride.[34] At the center of this politics of flesh, blood, and empire was the gendered artifact, the *imon bukuro*.

One of the earliest accounts of the convergence of imperial naval visits, comfort bags, and Japanese immigrants appeared in the *Nippu Jiji* in 1914. With the impending arrival of the battleship *Izumo*, the all-male immigrant leadership in O'ahu formed a "Comfort Bag Consultation Team" (Imon Bukuro Sōdankai) and decided to give *imon bukuro* to "comfort" (*nagusameru*) the fleet's crew. The plan—made in consultation with the Japanese Consulate in Honolulu—required women's work. Buddhist, Shinto, and Christian women's organizations were called upon to sew eight hundred cotton bags and fill them with "creative" (*shukō o korashite*) items—all within ten days.[35] In 1917, another comfort bag drive was reported in the *Hawai Hōchi*, this time for the imperial vessel *Azuma*. The schedule set by a "welcome committee," once again comprised of male leaders in collaboration with the consulate, was even tighter: more than six hundred comfort bags were to be assembled within a mere two days. The Japanese women's organizations responded in good spirit to this perhaps unreasonably challenging request and completed the task on time.[36] As fleet visits continued into the next decade, a newly formed Hawai Nihonjin Kyōkai (Japanese Society of Hawaii, established in 1921)—O'ahu-based and backed by Nikkei business leaders—took charge, and the demonstration of *dōhō* hospitality continued. The *imon bukuro* soon assumed the status of the "No. 1" (*dai ichi*) gift for Japanese naval officers, cadets, and crew calling in the islands.[37]

The 1930s were the decade of *kantai* (military vessel) nationalism in Hawai'i.[38] Under the leadership of Honolulu Nihonjin Rengō Kyōkai (United Japanese Society, established in 1932), an entity born out of the reorganization of Hawai Nihonjin Kyōkai, *dōhō* patriotism reached new heights. The visits of the combined fleets of the *Yakumo* and the *Asama* from June 15 to 19 in 1935 revealed its feverish nature. A commotion swept the Japanese immigrant community days and weeks in advance. The Welcome Committee for the Imperial Naval Training Vessels (Teikoku Renshū Kantai Kangeikai) was formed.[39] An elaborate program was devised, featuring receptions and banquets, sumo and judo matches, and around-the-island tours. Bolts of fabric bearing the logo "Welcome Comfort Bags" ("Kangei Imon Bukuro") were distributed to women to create the handmade gifts.[40] As the *Nippu Jiji* declared, the "overseas development of Yamato race" (*Yamato minzoku no kaigai hatten*) was inseparable from the Imperial Japanese Navy.[41] The *Hawai Hōchi* recounted the history of Japanese naval visitations to Hawai'i. Alongside this narrative was the statement of Seizō Yamamoto, head of the Welcome Committee and prominent member of the United Japanese Society—a statement that urged fellow *dōhō* to meet the incoming fleets with "*kangeki*" (deep emotion) and "*nessei*" (sincere passion).[42] The three "royals on the seas" (*umi no miya denka*) aboard the ships inflamed grassroots excitement, and the *Jitsugyō no Hawai*—a part Japanese and part Okinawan business magazine—published *Teikoku kantai tokubetsugō*, a special welcome issue, containing their portraits.[43]

All three media outlets were more than eager to publicize women's behind-the-scenes work. The comfort bag campaign was a "women's initiative"; a worthy pursuit triggering "the general mobilization of women's organizations" and showcasing "the outpouring of their sincere passion."[44] The names of those involved—Honolulu Japanese Women's Association, Mothers' Association of Makiki Japanese Language School, Izumo Shrine Shintō Women's Association, Japanese Midwives Association, and South King Church Women's Association, among others—were published.[45] This public acknowledgment of the women's work must have exerted pressure on anyone not yet participating. However, no matter how many accolades the makers of comfort bags received, it was nothing compared to the social prestige male leaders

FIGURE 6.2. A photo of imperial naval officers and immigrant leaders in Honolulu (*Jitsugyō noHawai*, October 27, 1939).
Hoji Shinbun Digital Collection, Hoover Institution Library & Archives.

enjoyed for their service. The *Jitsugyō no Hawai* published detailed profiles of the welcome committee's executive members and lavishly praised their work. A photograph of committee members standing next to imperial naval officers celebrated the masculine camaraderie binding the island and the homeland (fig. 6.2).[46]

Importantly, the rise of *dōhō* nationalism attracted more than one kind of woman into the sewing circle. In addition to Issei women, Nisei girls—born in Hawai'i and possessing US citizenship—also picked up needle and thread. Students at the Nuuanu Girls' Technical High School (Nuanu Jikka Kōtō Joggakō)—an establishment run by a Sōtō Buddhist sect and part of the 1930s sewing boom—volunteered to sew more than three thousand comfort bags free of charge. Impressed by the young women's actions, the *Jitsugyō no Hawai* extolled them as the model of "Japanese womanhood flourishing in the foreign soil."[47] No less virtuous were Japanese geisha. Under the leadership of Geisha Ichimatsu (Koyoko Tahara), the Honolulu Geisha Association joined the comfort bag drive.[48] The *Jitsugyō no Hawai*, whose readership included businessmen frequenting the geisha houses, could not praise them too highly. *Imon bukuro* put together by geisha, whose generosity was in stark contrast to the "stinginess of ordinary housewives," would make far better gifts for those aboard the fleets.[49] Reversing the usual social convention in which housewives represented feminine respectability and geisha the lack thereof, Ichimatsu and her urbane colleagues were lauded as exemplars of *dōhō* patriotism.[50]

Despite the talk of "stinginess," the *imon bukuro* was first and foremost a "gift from the poor" (*hinja no okurimono*) whose morale value

far outweighed its material worth.[51] The 1935 naval visit generated
media accounts that highlighted its leveling effect. Everyone on the
fleets, irrespective of rank, received not one but two comfort bags. The
handmade packages even reached the three royals, whose "commoner-
like" (*heimin-teki*) demeanors, including the unpretentious manner
with which they accepted *imon bukuro*, awed the reporters.[52] When
the contents of their packages—Prince Kuni got chocolate and
cigarettes, Prince Fushimi cigarettes and olives, and Prince Asaka
raisins and coffee—and who had made them were revealed, the women
must have been flabbergasted.[53] The *imon bukuro* suspended, however
briefly, the vast gap between officer and cadet, noble and commoner,
and created an "imagined community." The illusion of "equality"
did not stop there; the hospitality of island *dōhō* was reciprocated by
the visitors. The three royals bestowed cigarettes and confectionary
bearing the imperial insignia, an inestimably valuable gift for the
humble immigrants.[54] A reception called "At Home" (*atto hōmu*) was
held shipboard, and island *dōhō* enjoyed food, drink, and entertainment prepared by the cadets. Black-and-white photos published in the
*Nippu Jiji* and *Hawai Hōchi* captured the excitement generated by "At
Home," a well-established naval practice that celebrated the empire's
reach in a domestic and domesticating manner.[55] The jubilation did not
subside even after the ships had departed. Letters of thanks began to
arrive in bulk, and the vernacular newspapers eagerly published them.
Reminiscing about their visit to the wondrous isles, imperial soldiers
invariably expressed their gratitude toward the makers of the comfort
bags.[56]

Successful beyond all expectations, the 1935 visit set a template
for the rest of the decade. The following year, another welcome committee, again under the aegis of the United Japanese Society, formu-
lated an even more ambitious plan for the imperial cruisers *Yakumo*
and *Iwate*. The committee looked beyond O'ahu and solicited involvement of those on the outer islands. The *imon bukuro* campaign
became an inter-island endeavor; the number of participating organizations multiplied.[57] Throwing their weight behind the sewing campaign were Kimata Sewing School (Kimata Saihō Gakuin) and the
Honolulu Dressmakers Association, both strongholds of Japanese
sewers in Honolulu. The visibility of women and *imon bukuro* rose

FIGURE 6.3. Smiling soldiers each holding four (!) *imon bukuro* (*Nippu Jiji*, October 19, 1939).
Hoji Shinbun Digital Collection, Hoover Institution Library & Archives.

further with the visit of the *Yakumo*, the *Iwate*, and the *Shiretoko* in October 1939. In the aftermath of the Marco Polo Bridge Incident two years earlier, the United Japanese Society's demonstration of hospitality and loyalty intensified. The *imon bukuro* drive yielded more than seven thousand comfort bags, and the published list of contributing organizations grew lengthier.[58] A picture of smiling sailors, each holding four precious packages, confirmed the campaign's success (fig. 6.3).[59] The visibility of *dōhō* women was notable in yet another way. Japanese immigrant women in Honolulu, among them Nisei students at the University of Hawai'i, organized their own reception for the imperial seamen. Young women dressed in kimonos delighted the visitors as much as the pineapples, coconuts, and breadfruits spread across the table.[60]

Japanese immigrant nationalism clearly was a vibrant phenomenon. Yet *dōhō* patriotism was complex and more than love for the homeland fueled it. To wit, the demonstration of hospitality by Japanese immigrants in Hawai'i was not entirely selfless. They expected, even demanded, reciprocal gestures from the visiting sailors. In 1936, a small "debate" erupted on the pages of the *Nippu Jiji*. It was instigated by an unnamed reader in 'Aiea, most likely a woman.

The year before, she, like so many *dōhō* women, had made comfort bags for members of the visiting fleets. With utmost care she had chosen items for them and included personal letters. For days and weeks she had waited, but no thank-you letter, not even a postcard, had ever arrived to acknowledge the receipt of her heartfelt gift. She was perturbed. Noting that more ships were scheduled to arrive soon, she suggested that their crews should be reminded of social protocols.[61] A few days later, a rejoinder was published, this one from a resident in Nuʻuanu, most likely a man. Ms. ʻAiea's expectation was misguided, Mr. Nuʻuanu pointed out. Comfort bags were gifts for the empire's soldiers (*teikoku gunjin*), and, whether deployed in China or sailing across the Pacific, these men were dedicating their lives to the empire. Demanding a show of gratitude from them was inappropriate and would undermine the true meaning of *"imon"* (to comfort).[62] Despite this chastisement, Ms. ʻAiea's sentiment was common among Japanese immigrants. As discussed below, the *dōhō* expectation (or demand) for reciprocity would continue and in fact escalate in subsequent years.

Another factor fueling the immigrants' patriotism was *kantai keiki*— a business boom sparked by the visiting naval fleets. With each visit, women purchased goods to place in *imon bukuro*; sailors patronized ethnic stores on shore; tickets to the welcome events were bought and sold; and guides were hired and cars rented for the around-the-island tours.[63] Large sums of money circulated within the ethnic community. The vernacular press played no small part in *kantai keiki*. Under the banner "Teikoku Renshū Kantai Kangei" (Welcome, Imperial Naval Training Fleets), Japanese and Okinawan proprietors of restaurants, gift shops, gas stations, liquor stores, hotels, and inns publicly hawked their goods and services.[64] Star Brand (Mid-Pacific Kona Coffee Factory) boasted of the popularity of its product among members of the Japanese Navy.[65] Motoshige General Store promoted the sale of "Kachi Doki" (Shout of Victory)—a pesticide to exterminate ticks, flies, and bedbugs.[66] Satō clothing store—whose proprietor Taichi Satō was a leading light in the United Japanese Society and a member of the 1935 welcome committee—enticed customers to visit the shop and try on its ready-made Western clothing (sized for Japanese; navy blue in color) for "At Home."[67] The *Nippu Jiji* advertised its own product—a booklet on Nikkei history in Hawai'i (half price!)—as the best gift for Japanese naval officers.[68] The love for the homeland was inseparable from the love for profit.

The profit motive indeed often outpaced the patriotic commitment. The Nikkei community's welcome for American naval fleets was equally enthusiastic. Cheerful American sailors (*hogaraka na suiheisan*) were precious customers whose purchasing power was as valuable as that of their Japanese counterparts.[69] "Yankee sailors" dropped money at Japanese beer halls, clothing stores, and curio shops, where Japanese sewing boxes were a major hit.[70] One American naval commander, accompanied by his subordinates, visited a *gofukuya* (Japanese kimono store) not once, not twice, but three times to find souvenirs for loved ones back home.[71] The "double loyalty" of Japanese immigrants was well observed in the business magazine *Jitsugyō no Hawai*. To celebrate the Japanese naval visits, the magazine published special issues full of Japanese and Okinawan advertisements with their covers featuring a Japanese naval fleet (1935 and 1936) and the rising sun flag (1933).[72] The same magazine also embraced the *kantai keiki* brought by American naval visits and published special issues often showing the portraits of American naval commanders on their covers.[73] *Dōhō* love for sailors was not at all exclusive.

The confluence of militarism and tourism, evident above, points to the workings of a militourism in the islands that involved Japanese and Japanese Americans.[74] In it, the appropriation of things Hawaiian constituted a salient feature. The comfort bags made by Issei and Nisei women embodied the "true spirit of aloha."[75] "Kanaka (Hawaiian) dolls" were among items recommended for inclusion in *imon bukuro*.[76] The welcome program for the *Yakumo* and the *Iwate* in October 1936 featured a hula performance at the Kotohira Shinto Shrine in the immigrant neighborhood of Kalihi, where young cadets of the Imperial Japanese Navy were entertained—"comforted"—by Indigenous female performers from the Lalani Hawaiian Village (a well-known Hawaiian establishment in Waikīkī).[77] The feminization of Hawai'i was not limited to this occasion. The scene of an Indigenous man, bare-chested and barefoot, presenting a floral bouquet to Japanese naval officers in their white uniforms highlighted the gendered and gendering relationship

FIGURE 6.4. Presenting a bouquet to Japanese naval officers (*Nippu Jiji* Photo Archive).
Hoji Shinbun Digital Collection, Hoover Archives, courtesy of the Hawaii Times Photo Archive Foundation.

between Indigenous Hawai'i and imperial Japan, a relationship mediated by *dōhō* settlers in the islands (see fig. 6.4).[78]

The politics of indigeneity was visible in another way. The Japanese naval visits generated a close (discursive) encounter between two Indigenous groups, Hawaiians and Okinawans. The October 1936 special issue (*Kantai kangeigō*) of *Jitsugyō no Hawai* illuminates the interplay between the two. The issue, intended as a guidebook for those aboard visiting fleets, provided light reading on Hawai'i's history and culture. In the magazine's part-Japanese and part-Okinawan discursive space, the narratives about Indigenous Hawaiians acquired complex textures. In one piece, "Japanese Empire and King Kalākaua," an unnamed author described the indispensable role Kalākaua had played in Japan's overseas development. By opening the door to Japanese emigration, Kalākaua had laid the foundation for the propagation (*hanshoku*) of *dōhō* in the Pacific. To welcome the first contingent of Japanese immigrants, the king had even visited the immigration station and performed hula to *nagusameru* the new arrivals. Eager to build a political alliance between the two nations, the same king also had proposed a marriage of his niece Princess Ka'iulani to Prince Higashifushimi of

Japan, a career officer in the Imperial Japanese Navy.[79] Illuminating a series of "intimate connections" between Hawai'i and Japan, the piece legitimized and indeed naturalized the *dōhō* presence in the islands. Though never mentioned by name, Okinawa and Okinawans were still crucial threads in this fabricated tale of transpacific intimacy in which their subordination to Japan was offset by their settler presence and privileges in the islands.

Another piece in the same special issue, "Hawaii's Specialty Hula Dance: Hula from an Artistic Perspective," presented an even more convoluted picture of Japan–Okinawa–Hawai'i relations. Written by Sōsen (Ryōkin) Toyohira, a well-known Okinawan reporter for the *Nippu Jiji*, the article, first published by the magazine in 1933, sheds light on the origin, varieties, and religious significance of this Indigenous art form. Observing hula's degradation in the modern era—most evident in its sexual innuendoes, according to the writer—it lamented the corroding influence of tourism on Indigenous Hawaiian culture.[80] Toyohira's seemingly sympathetic gesture toward Hawaiians, whose fate was not too dissimilar to that of another group of colonized islanders, Okinawans, had a hidden layer, however. Much of the article's information came from the book *Unwritten Literature of Hawai'i: The Sacred Songs of the Hula*, a piece of imperial nostalgia written by Nathaniel Emerson. The son of American missionaries in Hawai'i, Emerson was a physician and self-proclaimed ethnologist affiliated with the Smithsonian Institution.[81] Viewing Hawaiians as a "dying race," he wrote *Unwritten Literature* to "rescue" hula from oblivion.[82] Drawing on this American settler discourse, Toyohira, another settler in the islands but one of Okinawan origin, assumed the mantle of authority and pontificated on the tragic but inevitable decline of Indigenous Hawaiians. Judged as incapable of steering their own culture first by Emerson in *Unwritten Literature* and then by Toyohira in the *Jitsugyō no Hawai*, Hawaiians were twice excluded from the ownership of their hula tradition. As this piece circulated during Japanese naval visits, it created further wrinkles in Japanese immigrant nationalism, a phenomenon animated not only by unavoidable competition between the Japanese and American empires but also by convoluted encounters between Okinawa and Hawai'i.

## Comforting the Soldiers of the Empire

Following the Marco Polo Bridge Incident in July 1937—the spark for the Second Sino-Japanese War (1937–1945)—Japanese immigrant nationalism took on new urgency. The large-scale deployment of Japanese soldiers in mainland Asia, among them young Nisei, intensified the relief campaigns. In Japan, the production of *imon bukuro*, *imon bun*, and *senninbari* accelerated, with royals, housewives, movie stars, and geisha all pitching in.[83] The donation fever in the homeland reflected "*jūgo no nessei*" (the sincere hearts behind the lines) and "broke the record" in a "spectacular" (*mezamashii*) manner.[84] Overseas, patriotic passion also soared. The first ("*ichiban nori*") to send *imon bukuro* to Japan were *dōhō* in Portland, Oregon.[85] Those in California followed suit, their commitment manifest in a picture of *imon bukuro* piled high and flanked by the Japanese flag.[86] Japanese in Hawai'i could not lag behind.

Against the backdrop of national exigency (*hijō jitai*), immigrant leadership made conscious efforts to align activities abroad with the demands of the home government. In September 1937, a notice from the Imperial Japanese Army, routed via the West Coast, reached Hawai'i to provide instructions on *imon bukuro*. Personal letters were essential, it stated, and those from small children were even better. The handicrafts of young girls, of elementary- and middle-school age in particular, would be good as well. Also on the list were canned food, postcards, pens and papers, newspapers, and magazines.[87] On New Year's Day 1939, the *Hawai Hōchi* and *Nippu Jiji* published a statement from Ishibuchi Tomosada, a fiscal officer of the Imperial Japanese Navy. Highlighting the "spiritual" values of *imon bukuro* and *imon bun*, it stated that comfort bags did not have to contain expensive objects and that comfort letters need not display sophisticated penmanship. What would touch the soldiers' hearts, Ishibuchi emphasized, was the expression of the "beautiful spirit" (*utsukushii seishin*) of overseas Japanese.[88]

The rise of patriotic fervor led to the expansion of media coverage on women's "*bikyo*" (beautiful actions). Stories of individual women, rather than women's organizations, circulated, and many accounts highlighted a new kind of mobility gained by women in the post-1937 context. As the *Nippu Jiji* reported, Koto Yamao, an immigrant midwife in rural Waialua, O'ahu, drove through the sugarcane fields and visited plantation camps to urge *dōhō* women to take part in the sewing drive.[89] More than five hundred women responded to her call for action, and nearly 1,500 comfort bags were made, a "crystallization of patriotic passion" (*nessei no kesshō*).[90] An equally exhilarating story appeared in the *Hawai Hōchi*. Members of a Buddhist women's association in Honolulu had sewn 2,500 comfort bags. Driven by their patriotic passion, however, the women could not stop. At their Sunday sermon meeting, they decided to double the number.[91] In the end, more than ten thousand comfort bags were assembled. Added to this sizable donation was the gift of six hundred loincloths (*fundoshi*), also sewn by the women.[92] Photographs of stacks of *imon bukuro* with Issei and Nisei women sitting or standing alongside them circulated on this and other occasions, a gendered "proof" of *dōhō* loyalty in Hawai'i (fig. 6.5).

FIGURE 6.5. Koto Yamao and *imon bukuro* (*Nippu Jiji* Photo Archive). Hoji Shinbun Digital Collection, Hoover Archives, courtesy of the Hawaii Times Photo Archive Foundation.

The new wave of mobilization resulted in the circulation of new practices, and the making of one-thousand-stitch amulets was added to women's to-do lists. *Dōhō* women huddling together to take turns in contributing tiny stiches—a common sight in Japan—now became part of the everyday scene in the islands as well.[93] Setsuko Nagayama, a young Nisei in Oʻahu, decided to make a protective amulet for a brother serving in the Imperial Japanese Army. Collecting one thousand stitches was not an easy task, but she was undeterred. Accompanied by a friend, she visited the headquarters of the *Hawai Hōchi* to solicit help from its female employees. All of them were happy to comply.[94] The demand for female employees became so pronounced that the newspaper had to issue an announcement asking people to avoid busy hours in the morning.[95] On the Big Island, Hawaiʻi, the making of *senninbari* was even more challenging due to its sparse population. However, as a *Nippu Jiji* story revealed, nothing could quench the women's patriotic passion. To collect enough stitches, two Nisei sisters traveled from one end of the island (Kohala) to the other (Hilo), a journey of considerable distance only the most determined would pursue.[96] Nisei women's dedication sometimes took on a startling form, as seen in the case of Toshiko Ise, who signed her *senninbari* with her own blood.[97] Okinawans too took part in the deeply Japanese practice of *senninbari*. One Okinawan mother, Uto Kamai (a pseudonym), stood on a street corner in downtown Honolulu and "begged" (*kou*) for stitches from *dōhō* women passing by, all to ensure the safety of a son who was fighting for Japan.[98]

Like *imon bukuro* and *senninbari*, *imon bun* too increased in visibility. While comfort letters already circulated during naval visits, the post-1937 mobilization pushed this patriotic practice to the forefront of the relief campaigns. Handwritten messages from young women (for romantic fantasy) as well as from boys and girls (for childhood innocence) were especially popular, and solicitations for these letters were frequent. For the Nisei, composing a letter in Japanese was not easy, but local bookstores—Kojima Shoten and Shigemori Shoseki—helped by importing *imon bun* manuals from Japan.[99] Letter writing was indeed combined with language training. For a New Year essay contest, the *Nippu Jiji* sought the submission of *imon bun* from students of Japanese-language schools across the isles. Once the contest was over, the letters would be sent to soldiers.[100] The *Hawai Hōchi* published *imon bun* written by Shizuko Murakami in its own New Year issue. Addressed to "Mr. Imperial Soldier" (*shussei gunjin-sama*), the comfort letter expressed her concern for his well-being during the bitter Chinese winter and expressed her pride as a member of the "Yamato race."[101] Murakami, a student at Tachikawa Women's High School, an immigrant establishment known for its curriculum offering classes in Japanese language, flower arrangement, tea ceremony, and Western- and Japanese-style sewing, presented an impeccable model of Nisei womanhood.[102]

Clearly, the start of the war in China intensified the expression of *dōhō* nationalism in Hawaiʻi. However, just as with the Imperial Japanese Navy visits, the post-1937 mobilization became mired in its own complexities. To begin, the patriotic zeal of Japanese immigrants had much to do with their desire to prove their worth vis-à-vis Japan. Stigmatized as "uprooted countrymen" and an "uneducated lot," Japanese immigrants hoped that their donations—generous in quantity and quality—would dispel the homeland prejudice they had long endured.[103] *Imon bukuro* were essential for rehabilitation of the islands' *dōhō* in Japanese eyes. *Hakurai imon bukuro* (comfort bags of foreign origin) were said to be so popular among soldiers that they competed for them.[104] And those from Hawaiʻi beat all others. Packed with exotic objects, the Hawaiʻi *imon bukuro* was nothing like its mediocre (*heibon*) Japanese (*naichi*) counterpart![105]

The thank-you letters from soldiers, taking up more and more space in the vernacular newspapers, gave credence to this self-serving perception. In one letter published in the *Nippu Jiji*, a Japanese soldier described how the comfort bags from Hawaiʻi delighted members of his unit in southern China. Excited beyond words, they "danced around" and "acted like children," a joyful scene captured in his drawing accompanying the letter (fig. 6.6). It showed a soldier clutching *imon bukuro* and exclaiming, "Mine came from Hawaiʻi!"[106] A "roundtable discussion" (*zadankai*) published in the *Hawai Hōchi* also attested to the exceptional quality of Hawaiʻi *imon bukuro*. A group of soldiers stationed in eastern China gave high praise to the handmade care packages they had received from Hawaiʻi. One, a father of two small children, related how the *imon bun* he found in the package—letters written by Nisei

FIGURE 6.6. A cartoon accompanying a soldier's letter (*Nippu Jiji*, August 8, 1939).
Hoji Shinbun Digital Collection, Hoover Institution Library & Archives.

children—made him weep. Another declared that *imon bukuro* from Hawai'i was simply *"nanbā wan"* (no. 1).[107]

Patriotic fever continued to soar in Hawai'i. It was no longer enough to send *imon bukuro* across the sea; the care packages had to be delivered in person. In 1938, Kōgun Shōbyōhei Imondan—a group tour to "comfort" the sick and wounded soldiers of the empire—was organized to take representatives of island *dōhō* to Japan. Announced on January 18, the tour, set to depart on March 23, would take ten thousand *imon bukuro* to the motherland.[108] The chief organizer of this transpacific tour was the Association of Japanese Innkeepers (Nihonjin Ryokan Kumiai), an influential trade group comprising Japanese and Okinawan innkeepers devoted to all things travel.[109] Joining the tour was the Hawaii Dressmakers' Association, a similarly influential women's organization whose feminine presence would surely "comfort" the convalescing soldiers. One of the tour leaders was Miyozuchi Komeya, an Issei elder, innkeeper, and member of the welcome committees for the imperial naval visits.[110] The 1938 tour was yet another variation of the militourism whose interplay between militarism and tourism animated the Hawai'i-Japan circuits.

On February 18, the tour's mission statement was published in *Nippu Jiji* and *Hawai Hōchi* under the headline "Appeal to the Sincere Hearts of All Denizens: We Urge the Donations of Imon Bukuro." In lofty language, it elaborated on the significance of the upcoming tour. Since the onset of the war in China, Japanese soldiers had made innumerable sacrifices. Many, having fallen ill or been injured during battle, were bedridden. Hawai'i *dōhō*, who shared the same bloodline, could not help but "kneel down in front of this painful sight." To express their gratitude to these "heroes in suffering" (*idainaru giseisha*), a tour was organized in consultation with Japanese authorities. Participants would visit army and navy hospitals across Japan and deliver *imon bukuro* in person.[111] Solicitations for the tour as well as for donations of comfort bags were repeated in the subsequent days and weeks, with Okinawan members of the innkeepers' association—Eishū Asato and Kiyoshi Shimabukuro—playing a visible role.[112] In the end, the number of participants exceeded one hundred, among them thirty Nisei women chaperoned by Sawano Kubota, president of the Dressmakers' Association. The *imon bukuro* campaign reached its goal as well, thanks to the hard work of women's organizations; their names were once again published in the vernacular newspapers.[113]

Celebrated as the epitome of *dōhō* nationalism, the 1938 trip in fact replaced a *bokoku kankō* (sightseeing trip in the motherland), a pleasure tour originally scheduled for the fall of 1937. In prewar Hawai'i, travel to Japan was popular among Issei and Nisei and a definite moneymaker for the innkeepers' association. The initial plan, set for the season of autumn leaves, did not materialize due to the outbreak of the war in China.[114] Rescheduled for spring 1938, the new tour promised both a different vista (cherry blossoms) and another opportunity for profit, with *dōhō* patriotism providing a gloss of respectability. For some, a trip to the motherland in a time of national emergency seemed frivolous; the *Jitsugyō no Hawai* editorialized that a visit to wartime Japan should be less about sightseeing and more about observing its social conditions.[115] Despite such advice, pre-departure excitement proliferated and another economic boom, not dissimilar to *kantai keiki*, hit the *dōhō* community. The *Hawai Hōchi* published a "Guide for Preparation for the Trip to the Homeland" ("Kōkoku hōmon oshitaku annai"). In it, Issei and Nisei proprietors advertised their travel-related merchandise—Eastman cameras (indispensable for sightseeing), coffee and cookies (perfect as souvenirs), and koa wood trinkets (ideal gifts). Joining them was the owner of a sewing machine store who announced the sales of Singer and White brands in stock.[116] The Satō clothing store, a noted advertiser during imperial naval visits, reminded travelers that the cold weather in Japan would require light spring coats.[117] The making or purchasing of new (and fashionable) clothing was essential pre-departure preparation for those heading to Japan.[118]

Once in Japan, the tour's journey was covered by Sōen Yamashita of the *Nippu Jiji* and Isao Makino of the *Hawai Hōchi*. Accounts of visits to the navy and army hospitals were published in these newspapers. At the Yokosuka Navy Hospitals, there were tearful meetings between members of the tour and recovering soldiers: *dōhō* from Hawai'i demonstrated their *sekisei* and those at the hospitals responded by bowing deeply and expressing gratitude. At the center of this transpacific exchange were *imon bukuro*, the handmade gifts emblematic of the unbreakable bond between the two.[119]

As moving as these scenes were, most press accounts in fact focused on the travelers' sightseeing and pleasure-seeking. Following their arrival in the port city of Yokohama, they visited popular spots—Nogeyama Park and Sankeien Garden in Yokohama; Shochiku Film Studio in Ofuna; and historic sites in Kamakura. In Tokyo, the itinerary included the Imperial Palace, the Nijūbashi Bridge, and the Yasukuni and Meiji Shrines. They even traveled as far as Nikko in Tochigi Prefecture, a tourist mecca enshrining the founder of the Tokugawa shogunate. In the evenings, they wined and dined with dignitaries.[120] The whereabouts of the women of the Dressmakers' Association were of particular interest to female readers in Hawai'i, so both newspapers reported "women's stories" closely. Their activities in Tokyo—a visit to the headquarters of the leading women's magazine, *Shufu no Tomo*; shopping excursions at the Shirokiya and Mitsukoshi department stores; and conferences with representatives of Tokyo Yōsai Gakuin (Western Sewing School) and Tokyo Yōsaika Renmei (Western Sewing Guild)—must have generated considerable envy among Issei and Nisei women back in the islands.[121] Though unable to join the tour, they could still experience the splendor of Tokyo and its consumerist culture vicariously. The interweaving of nationalism, tourism, and militarism gave *dōhō* women considerable mobility, whether in reality or in the imagination.

In 1940, an even larger mobilization of *imon bukuro* took place in the Japan-Hawai'i circuits, in which the confluence of gender, militarism, and tourism was once again conspicuous. The Tokyo Conference of Overseas Japanese (Kaigai Dōhō Tōkyō Taikai), held from November 4 to 8 in 1940, was part of the 2,600th commemoration of the Japanese empire, glorifying the nation's mythical founding in 660 BCE. Showcasing the empire "at its zenith," this yearlong celebration unleashed a variety of dynamics in the land of the rising sun, among them nationalism, tourism, and consumerism, all exalting the "unbroken line of the imperial reign."[122] For *dōhō* leaders in Hawai'i and other overseas communities, the congress provided an opportunity to join this unprecedented celebration. Taking place concurrently was the Exhibit of Overseas Japanese Development (Nihon Minzoku Kaigai Hatten Jōkyō Tenrankai), an event held at the famed Takashimaya department store, ground zero of Japanese consumerism. Among the exhibits showcasing the lives of Japanese immigrants were their *imon bukuro*, an irrefutable symbol of *sekisei* of overseas Nikkei whose toil had been the backbone of the thriving empire. Following the exhibition, the comfort bags were to be delivered to China by *kōkoku imondan*, a tour by select delegates from the congress whose mission was to comfort the soldiers guarding the empire's borders.[123]

The announcement of the congress reignited travel fever among Japanese immigrants in Hawai'i. Under the leadership of the United Japanese Society, calls for tour participation went out and a *kankōdan* (tour group) was organized.[124] Pre-departure preparation mobilized the ethnic business community, with the Satō clothing store once again advertising its merchandise, this time gloves and overcoats appropriate for November in Japan.[125] Another *imon bukuro* drive commenced, with the goal of assembling five thousand comfort bags within a month. Japanese sewing schools—Kobayashi, Kimata, Loyal, and Keister—did not fail to volunteer their students' labor.[126] A picture of Nisei students at the Kimata Sewing School dedicating (*hōshi*) their hearts and hands demonstrated the strength of *dōhō* loyalty (fig. 6.7).[127] The sewing drive easily exceeded its initial goal and ultimately produced nearly ten thousand comfort bags. Sōen Yamashita of the *Nippu Jiji* and Isao Makino of the *Hawai Hōchi* were pressed into service again to cover the celebration. Yamashita later published a booklet chronicling the journey of the Hawai'i delegates to the congress.[128]

FIGURE 6.7. The Kimata Sewing School (*Nippu Jiji*, September 7, 1940).
Hoji Shinbun Digital Collection, Hoover Institution Library & Archives.

The media coverage of the 2,600th anniversary was nothing but thrilling. On the congress's first day, the opening ceremony, graced by the presence of Prince Higashikuni, featured Prime Minister Konoe. He, flanked by his ministers, commended the overseas delegates on their long and difficult years away from home. A few days later, another memorable event took place: a trip by the Hawai'i delegates to the Imperial Palace. Stepping onto the sacred grounds, they had an audience with the emperor's chamberlain and received the gift of confectionary bearing the imperial insignia. Overcome by emotion, they wept.[129] The honors did not stop there. The Foreign Ministry and the Ministry of Colonial Affairs bestowed awards on *dōhō* leaders from Hawai'i.[130] An interregional conference, special meetings for women and for Nisei, and outings to military posts—Tachikawa Air Base and Yokosuka Navy Base—all added depth and breadth to the blessed occasion.[131]

The Exhibit of Overseas Japanese Development—held from November 1 to 15 on the eighth floor ("event floor") of the popular department store in Tokyo—presented a "grand panorama" of Japanese immigrant success in North and South America, the Pacific, and East and Southeast Asia. Representing the eight corners of the world (*hakkō ichiu*), the exhibition attracted nearly one million visitors and showcased the expanding borders and bounties of the Japanese empire. On display were coffee from Brazil, oranges from California, and textiles from the South Seas. Maps, posters, and photos of all kinds—later to be donated to museums and schools across Japan—provided geographical, statistical, and other information about Japanese communities around the world.[132] Strategically placed at the very end of this around-the-world tour and anchoring the "eight corners of the world" was an embankment created of *imon bukuro*, above which a banner read, "*Kaigai dōhō no sekisei*" ("Sincere hearts of overseas compatriots").[133]

Of all the displays, the Hawai'i section aroused special interest among visitors. Under the signs—"Hawai'i is the central node of the Pacific" and "*Dōhō* are opening up the treasure box, the Pacific"— unfolded a visual narrative of Japanese pioneers in the Pacific. The displays of coffee, sugar, pineapples, and koa confirmed *dōhō* productivity. Japanese-language publications, surfboards (*naminori ita*), and locally brewed sake gave a glimpse into the immigrants' daily lives. A miniature commercial ship symbolically linked the distant islands to the prospering homeland. Clearly, Japanese settlers were indispensable agents in the development of Hawai'i, but their hearts and blood still belonged to Japan. This tale of Japanese immigrant industriousness overshadowed the story of Hawai'i's Indigenous islanders. Placed on the replica of a moonlit white-sand beach, where coconut trees, pineapple saplings, and a farm tractor added ambience, was a Hawaiian hula doll (*dojin no hura ningyō*), a figure conveying bodily pleasure and native indolence.[134] Indigenous Hawaiians were not simply lagging behind; as indicated by other exhibits, they belonged squarely to the past. Stone (*sekki*) toys, lamps, and axes, all presumably remnants of the "Kanaka in the primitive age" (*genshi jidai kanaka zoku*), confirmed that the islands' original inhabitants, left outside the frame of history, were unable to take part in the march of progress.[135]

For the delegates from Hawai'i, the 2,600th anniversary marked a crucial juncture in the politics of *dōhō* recognition. Serving as a "sacrificial stone" (*suteishi*), Japanese immigrants, driven by their love for Japan, had struggled day and night; the empire's development would not have taken place without their toil. This fact, hitherto overlooked, was now fully recognized in the homeland.[136] The delegates from Hawai'i, having received a warm welcome in the motherland, could

not remain unaffected. Outpourings of emotion followed. As one delegate stated, he was amending his belief that immigrants were *"kimin"*
(abandoned people). His resolve renewed, he was all the more determined to dedicate himself to Japan's overseas development.[137] Another
delegate was also reconsidering the "insulting implications" that he
had thought were attached to the term *"imin"* (immigrants). His immigrant status, he reflected, had brought him unprecedented honors
during the congress. There was nothing shameful about being an immigrant.[138] The most important outcome of the 2,600th anniversary,
yet another delegate observed, was the fading of misperceptions about
overseas *dōhō*. Now Japanese immigrants should work even harder
to deepen the homeland's understanding of its overseas brethren, he
declared.[139] However, this affective bond between the island and the
homeland, confirmed tearfully on the occasion of the 2,600th anniversary, excluded many of the immigrants residing in Hawai'i. Those
who received awards from the imperial government during the congress were all men of Japanese ancestry, among them Yasutarō Sōga
(editor in chief of the *Nippu Jiji*), Seizō Yamamoto (president of the
welcome committees for the naval visits), Miyozuchi Komeya (leader
of the 1938 tour to Japan), and Taichi Satō (owner of the Satō clothing
store). Neither Okinawans, whose patriotic devotion and demonstration rivaled that of the Japanese, nor the women who had spent long
hours with needle and thread to craft Japanese immigrant nationalism,
appeared in the list of honorees.[140]

## Coda

Japan's attack on Pearl Harbor interrupted but did not end the politics of Japanese immigrant nationalism in Hawai'i. *Imon bukuro,
imon bun,* and *senninbari* proved extraordinarily malleable despite
dramatic changes of circumstance. Following the start of the Pacific
War, Hawai'i's *dōhō* did an about-face and began to organize *"shōri
imon bukuro"* (victory comfort bag) drives for the Allied soldiers.[141]
A Nisei soldier of the 100th Infantry Battalion, a segregated unit of
the US Army, took *senninbari* made by his niece to the Italian campaign.[142] Even after World War II, the handcrafted objects refused to
disappear from the scene. As reported by the *Hawaii Times,* successor

of the *Nippu Jiji*, with the onset of the Korean War, old *senninbari* were recycled and new ones made for Nisei soldiers, with a local kimono shop advertising the sale of bleached cotton specifically for this purpose.[143] *Imon bukuro* were put together for those deployed to the Korean peninsula,[144] but the care packages were also given to young cadets aboard the training vessels of the Japanese Self-Defense Forces calling in Honolulu. To acknowledge the kindness of their hosts in the islands, the young sailors invited them to a reception aboard the ship, "At Home."[145] Stitching across the vast divide created by the violent war in the Pacific, Japanese immigrant women continued to make *imon bukuro* and "stitch[ed] the heat of Hawai'i into *senninbari*."[146] These women thereby added numerous and often hidden layers to the fabric of *dōhō* patriotism that once flourished in the middle of the Pacific.

## Notes

1. Sakata Yasuo, "Sengo 50-nen to Nikkei Amerikajinshi kenkyū—Katararenai 1930-nendai," *Imin Kenkyū Nenpō* 1 (March 1995).

2. For the continuation of racism against Japanese Americans after World War II, see Caroline Chang Simpson, *An Absent Presence: Japanese Americans in Postwar American Culture, 1945–1960* (Durham, NC: Duke University Press, 2001).

3. John J. Stephan, *Hawaii under the Rising Sun: Japan's Plans for Conquest after Pearl Harbor* (Honolulu: University of Hawai'i Press, 1984); Yuji Ichioka, "Japanese Immigrant Nationalism: The Issei and the Sino-Japanese War, 1937–1941," *California History* 69, no. 30 (1990): 260–75; Eiichiro Azuma, *Between Two Empires: Race, History, and Transnationalism in Japanese America* (New York: Oxford University Press, 2005); Kenneth J. Ruoff, *Imperial Japan at Its Zenith: The Wartime Celebration of the Empire's 2,600th Anniversary* (Ithaca, NY: Cornell University Press, 2010).

4. Azuma, *Between Two Empires*, 166–68.

5. Ichioka, "Japanese Immigrant Nationalism," 271–73.

6. Vernadette Gonzalez and Jana Lipman, "Introduction: Tours of Duty and Tours of Leisure," *American Quarterly* 68, no. 3 (2016): 507–21.

7. Teresia Teaiwa, "Postscript: Reflections on Militourism, US Imperialism, and American Studies," *American Quarterly* 68, no. 3 (2016): 847–53; "Reading Paul Gauguin's Noa Noa with Epeli Hau'ofa's Kisses in the Nederends: Militourism, Feminism, and the 'Polynesian' Body," in *Inside Out: Literature, Cultural Politics, and Identity in the New Pacific*, eds. Vilsoni Hereniko and Rob Wilson (Lanham, MD: Rowman and Littlefield, 1999), 249–63.

8. Adria Imada, *Aloha America: Hula Circuits through the US Empire* (Durham, NC: Duke University Press, 2012).

9. Mayuka Kasai, "Shōwa senjika ni okeru imondan no jittai ni tsuite no ichi kōsatsu," *Seijigaku kenkyū* 64 (2021): 1–30; Nobuko Oshida, *Massatsusareta Nihongun Juppēbu no shōtai: Kono soshiki wa nani o shi, naze wasure sarareta no ka?* (Tokyo: Fusōsha, 2019); Ruoff, *Imperial Japan*.

10. For the Western-style sewing schools run by immigrants, see Michiyo Kitakawa, "The Making of Western Dressmaking Culture in the Hawai'i Nikkei Community before World War II," *Japanese Journal of American Studies* 31 (2020): 45–64. The 1930s "sewing boom" was also sustained by the American-side dynamic, wherein White home-demonstration agents of the Cooperative Agricultural Extension spread American domestic practices. See Mire Koikari, "Race, Nutrition, and Empire: Domestic Reform and Japanese Immigrants in Territorial-Era Hawai'i," *Gender & History* 34, no. 3 (October 2022): 771–88. For the proliferation of consumer culture among Nisei women in the islands, see Shiho Imai, *Creating the Nisei Market: Race and Citizenship in Hawai'i's Japanese American Consumer Culture* (Honolulu: University of Hawai'i Press, 2010).

11. Kazuko Koizumi, *Yōsai no jidai: Nihonjin no ifuku kakumei* (Tokyo: OM Shuppan, 2004); Miki Iida, *Hikokumin na onna-tachi: Senjika no pāma to monpe* (Tokyo: Chūō Kōron Shinsha, 2020); Andrew Gordon, *Fabricating Consumers: The Sewing Machine in Modern Japan* (Berkeley: University of California Press, 2012).

12. Christen Sasaki, "Threads of Empire: Militourism and the Aloha Wear Industry in Hawai'i," *American Quarterly* 68, no. 3 (2016): 651; Christen Sasaki, "Making Sartorial Sense of Empire: Contested Meanings of Aloha Shirt Aesthetics," *Contemporary Pacific* 34, no. 1 (2022): 31–61.

13. Eiichiro Azuma, "The Challenge of Studying the Pacific as a 'Global Asia': Problematizing Deep-Rooted Institutional Hindrances for Bridging Asian Studies and Asian American Studies," *Journal of Asian Studies* 80, no. 4 (2021): 1023–31; Jinah Kim and Natasha Tamar Sharma, "Center-to-Center Relationalities: At the Nexus of Pacific Islands Studies and Trans-Pacific Studies," and Nitasha Tamar Sherma, "Race and Indigeneity in Pacific Islands and Settler Colonial Studies," both in "Center-to-Center Relationalities: At the Nexus of Pacific Island Studies and Trans-Pacific Studies," special issue, *Critical Ethnic Studies Journal* 7, no. 2 (2021).

14. Shigehiko Shiramizu, "Hawai Nikkei shinbun no tekiō sutorateji," in *Beikoku shoki no Nihongo shinbun,* eds. Norio Tamura and Shigehiko Shiramizu (Tokyo: Keisō Shobō, 1986), 279–310.

15. Amy Kaplan, "Manifest Domesticity," in *The Anarchy of Empire in the Making of US Culture* (Cambridge, MA: Harvard University Press, 2005), 23–50.

16. For *imon bukuro,* see Annika Culver, "Battlefield Comforts of Home: Gendered Commercialization of the Military Care Package in Wartime Japan, 1937–1945," in *Defamiliarizing Japan's Asia-Pacific War,* eds. Puck Brecher and Michael Myers (Honolulu: University of Hawai'i Press, 2019), 85–103; Oshida, *Massatsusareta*; Rie Mori, "Sensō shien, hisaichi shien to 'imon bukuro': Kindai Nihon ni okeru shien katsudō no hattatsu," *Nihon kaseigaku kaishi* 70, no. 8 (2019): 543–54; Mutsumi Yamaguchi, "Senjika no zōyo: Kindai Nihon shakai ni okeru kokuminteki zōyo no sōshitsu," *Bunka jinruigaku* 73, no. 3 (2011): 237–56. For *senninbari,* see Kazuhiro Watanabe, "Senjichū no danganyoke shinkō ni kansuru minzokugaku-teki kenkyū: Senninbari shūzoku o chūshin ni" (dissertation, Sōgō Kenkyū Daigakuin, 2008), https://ci.nii.ac.jp/naid/500001013944. For a variety of sentiments women stitched into *senninbari,* ranging from ambivalence to resentment to resistance, see Namiko Mori, *Senninbari* (Tokyo: Jōhō Sentā Shuppankyoku, 1995).

17. The comfort bags were initially translated as *nagusame bukuro* or *konforuto bukuro.* Mutsumi Yamaguchi, "Saigai shien to shite no imon bukuro: 20-seiki zenhan no shinbun kiji o shiryō to shite," *Yamaguchi chiiki shakai kenkyūkai* 15 (2018): 45.

18. Rumi Yasutake, *Transnational Women's Activism: The United States, Japan, and Japanese Immigrant Communities in California, 1850–1920* (New York: New York University Press, 2004), 97–98; Culver, "Battlefield Comforts," 86.

19. Oshida, *Massatsusareta*.

20. For various patterns and designs of *imon bukuro*, see Augustin Saiz, *Nihongun sōbi daizukan*, trans. Kazuhisa Murakami (Tokyo: Hara Shoten, 2012). For regional variations of their contents, see Keiko Morita, *Senjika Aikoku Fujinkai no gunji engo katsudō (2): Kennō, imon bukuro* (Niigata: Taiyō Shobō, 2013). For the varieties of *senninbari* designs, see Michael Bortner, *Imperial Japanese Good Luck Flags and One-Thousand Stitch Belts* (Atglen, PA: Schiffer Publishing, 2008). The embroidered pieces were often turned into belts, bandannas, vests, and hats. A small handsewn fabric doll, an *imon ningyō*, usually gendered female, was also placed in the comfort bags. Ellen Schattschneider, "The Bloodstained Doll: Violence and the Gift in Wartime Japan," *Journal of Japanese Studies* 31, no. 2 (2005): 329–56.

21. Saiz, *Nihongun*, 124–25.

22. Steven LaBarre, "The American Housewife Goes to War: Sewing Kits That Accompanied the American Soldier to the Front, 1776–1976" (master's thesis, Department of History, University of Nebraska at Kearney, 2020), 26, https://www .proquest.com/openview/6415de5075b35b44749cada690a0cbe7/1.pdf?pq-origsite =gscholar&cbl=18750&diss=y.

23. Virginia Mescher, " 'Small but Mighty Host': Benefit and Fund Raising Dolls in the Civil War" (unpublished manuscript, 2007), http://raggedsoldier.com/fund _raise_doll.pdf.

24. Charles Stillé, *History of the United States Sanitary Commission: Being the General Report of the Work during the War of the Rebellion* (Philadelphia: J. B. Lippincott, 1866), 27–33, https://archive.org/details/historyofunitedsoostiluoft /page/n3/mode/2up?view=theater.

25. Wendy Hamand Venet, "The Emergence of a Suffragist: May Livermore, Civil War Activism, and the Moral Power of Women," *Civil War History* 48, no. 2 (2002): 143–64.

26. "From the Archive, 24 December 1855: Christmas in the Crimea," *Guardian Archives*, https://www.theguardian.com/theguardian/2012/dec/24/christmas-crimean -war-1855-archive.

27. Helen Rappaport, *No Place for Ladies: The Untold Story of Women in the Crimean War* (London: Aurum Press, 2007), 157–62.

28. Stefanie Markovits, *The Crimean War in the British Imagination* (Cambridge: Cambridge University Press, 2009), 7.

29. Paul Crawford, Anna Greenwood, Richard Bates, and Jonathan Memel, *Florence Nightingale at Home* (Cham, Switzerland: Palgrave Macmillan, 2020). There were others who gained mobility as a result of the Crimean War. See, for example, Ann Heilmann, *Neo-/Victorian Biographilia and James Miranda Barry: A Study in Transgender and Transgenre* (Cham, Switzerland: Palgrave Macmillan, 2018), and Sandra Gunning, "Traveling with Her Mother's Tastes: The Negotiation of Gender, Race, and Location in *Wonderful Adventures of Mrs. Seacole in Many Lands*," *Signs: Journal of Women in Culture and Society* 26, no. 4 (2001): 949–81.

30. For the use of wartime and postwar sewing as a tool of gender-sexual subversion, see Rozsika Parker, *The Subversive Stitch: Embroidery and the Making of the Feminine* (London: I. B. Tauris, 2010); Joseph McBrinn, *Queering the Subversive*

*Stitch: Men and the Culture of Needlework* (London: Bloomsbury Visual Arts, 2021); Holly Furneaux and Sue Prichard, "Contested Objects: Curating Soldier Art," *Museum & Society* 13, no. 4 (2015): 447–61; Holly Furneaux, *Military Men of Feeling: Emotion, Touch, and Masculinity in the Crimean War* (Oxford: Oxford University Press, 2016); LaBarre, "The American Housewife." What subversive stitches were made by the Japanese imperial soldiers who picked up needle and thread remains to be seen.

31. "Sawa," *Yamato Shinbun*, April 7, 1905.

32. "Yūmeinaru Yajima-joshi kitaru," *Yamato Shinbun*, August 6, 1906.

33. Stephan, *Hawaii under the Rising Sun*, 30–33.

34. "Teikoku gunkan o mukau," *Jitsugyō no Hawai*, January 1917.

35. "Imon bukuro sōdankai," *Nippu Jiji*, July 9, 1914.

36. "Gunkan Azuma e zairyū dōhō yori 630 no imon bukuro o okuru kotot o nareri," *Hawai Hōchi*, July 3, 1917.

37. "Imon bukuro no kizō wa suiheitachi ga kanarazu yorokobu," *Hawai Hōchi*, June 23, 1922; "Dōchū seikan," *Hawai Hōchi*, January 10, 1925.

38. The vernacular press extensively reported on the naval visits in 1933, 1935, 1936, and 1939.

39. "Teikoku renshū kantai kangeikai soshiki kettei," *Hawai Hōchi*, May 11, 1935.

40. "Teikoku renshū kantai kangei junjo naitei" and "Kangei imon bukuro," *Nippu Jiji*, May 17, 1935.

41. "Shasetsu," *Nippu Jiji*, May 22, 1935.

42. "Kangeki to nessei o motte" and "Hawai ni kikōshita teikoku gunkan," *Hawai Hōchi*, June 16, 1935.

43. "Umi no miya denka o mukae tatematsuru," *Jitsugyō no Hawai*, June 1935, 1-J photo.

44. The quotes come, respectively, from "Shasetsu," *Nippu Jiji*, May 22, 1935; "Zenjōin ni imon bukuro," *Hawai Hōchi*, May 9, 1935; and "Imon bukuro no nuikata o hōshi shita Nuanu Jikka Kōtō Jogakkō seito," *Jitsugyō no Hawai*, June 1935.

45. "San miya sama o hajime tatematsuri," *Nippu Jiji*, May 23, 1935; "31 dantai e," *Nippu Jiji*, May 29, 1935; Shōu Yahū, "Fujinkai to imon bukuro," *Jitsugyō no Hawai*, June 1935.

46. "Teikoku renshū kangei shunōbu to Honoruru kangei kanbu shoshi," *Jitsugyō no Hawai*, October 27, 1939.

47. "Imon bukuro no nuikata o hōshi shita Nuanu Jikka Lōtō Jogakkō seito," *Jitsugyō no Hawai*, June 1935.

48. "Norikumiin ni futa fukuro zutsu," *Nippu Jiji*, May 31, 1935; "Atashitachi ni mo to geisharen no imon bukuro," *Hawai Hōchi*, May 31, 1935.

49. "Honoruru geigi kumiai to kaigun sābisu," *Jitsugyō no Hawai*, June 1935.

50. "Geigi Ichimatsu to teikoku kaigun," *Jitsugyō no Hawai*, July 1937; "Matsuba-jō to Ichimatsu-jō no aikokushin," *Jitsugyō no Hawai*, November 1937. The relief campaigns in Japan (Tokyo and Osaka) also upheld geisha as the model of patriotic femininity. See Oshida, *Massatsusareta*, 28–31; Mikiko Kōjiya, *Sensō o ikita onnatachi* (Tokyo: Mineruva Shobō, 1985), 38–39.

51. "Kakutō yori atsumaru imon bukuro ni tsuite," *Nippu Jiji*, October 3, 1936, second edition.

52. "Hawai no gokansō o uketamawaru," *Nippu Jiji*, June 19, 1935.

53. "Imon bukuro o ukesaserare oyorokobi no sandenka," *Hawai Hōchi*, June 18, 1935.

54. "Gomonshō iri no tabako to kashi gokashi," *Hawai Hōchi*, June 21, 1935.

55. "Kinō seidai ni moyoosareta renshū kantai Atto Hōmu gahō," *Nippu Jiji*, June 18, 1935; "Dai kanrakukyō o tenkai shita sakujitsu no Atto Hōmu," *Hawai Hōchi*, June 18, 1935.

56. *Hawai Hōchi* published the soldiers' letters in four installments under the title "Imon bukuro yobun" in June 1935. See June 21, June 22, June 24, and June 25.

57. See, for example, "Renshū kantai kangei hōhō kettei," *Nippu Jiji*, August 21, 1936; "Dōhō no magokoro komoru," *Nippu Jiji*, October 2, 1936; "Teikoku renshū kantai kangei hōshiki kimaru," *Hawai Hōchi*, August 21, 1936; "Kantai kangei no imon bukuro sude ni sanzen desorou," *Hawai Hōchi*, September 18, 1936.

58. "Renshū kantai ni okuru imon bukuro no hōkoku," *Hawai Hōchi*, October 17, 1939; "Umi no yūshi ni sasageru dōhō no netsui," *Nippu Jiji*, October 17, 1939.

59. "Imon bukuro o uketotte kangeki no yūshitachi," *Nippu Jiji*, October 19, 1939.

60. "Honoruru fujinkai no kōhosei shōtaikai," *Hawai Hōchi*, October 21, 1939; "Nihonjin fujinkai no kōhosei shōtaikai," *Nippu Jiji*, October 21, 1939.

61. "Imon bukuro to reijō," *Nippu Jiji*, August 24, 1936.

62. "Imon bukuro ni taisuru reijō kisho ni tsuite," *Nippu Jiji*, August 27, 1936.

63. "Goshippu," *Nippu Jiji*, October 23, 1936.

64. See, for example, *Hawai Hōchi*, June 16, 1935. The "welcome ads" were especially conspicuous in the business magazine *Jitsugyō no Hawai*. See its special issues published in June 1933, June 1935, and October 1936.

65. Advertisement by Star, *Jitsugyō no Hawai*, May 1934, 11 J.

66. Advertisement by Motoshige shōten, *Jitsugyō no Hawai*, June 1933, 2 J.

67. "Renshū kantai kangei to haikan ni omeshi ni naru yōfuku wa," *Hawai Hōchi*, June 13, 1935; "Renshū kantai kangei to yōfuku," *Nippu Jiji*, September 19, 1936.

68. "Teikoku renshū kantai shōshi e saijō no okurimono," *Jitsugyō no Hawai*, May 1935, English cover 2. The advertisement appeared in the special issue celebrating the arrival of the American fleets.

69. "Hogaraka na suiheisan de shinai wa ōnigiwai," *Hawai Hōchi*, May 13, 1935.

70. "Wakikaeru kantai keiki," *Nippu Jiji*, May 29, 1935.

71. "Beikoku kantai to dōhō shōten," *Jitsugyō no Hawai*, June 1935.

72. For the special issues bearing the title "Kangeigō" (welcome issues), see the June 1933, June 1935, and October 1936 issues. The June 1917 issue, though not bearing the same title, still featured the arrival of the Japanese naval fleets.

73. For the *kantai keiki*, see "Kantai keiki," *Jitsugyō no Hawai*, April 1, 1939. For the *Jitsugyō no Hawai* special issues celebrating the American naval visits, see the May 1935, May 1937, and April 1938 issues.

74. For the American-side dynamics of militourism in 1920s and 1930s Hawai'i, see Imada, *Aloha America*.

75. "Renshū kantai e no imon bukuro," *Nippu Jiji*, May 22, 1935.

76. Yahū, "Fujinkai to imon bukuro," 31.

77. "Ippan kangeikai tōjitsu no yokyō puroguramu," *Hawai Hōchi*, October 8, 1936. A native enterprise, the Lalani Hawaiian Village was a (potentially) subversive site where Indigenous performers took part in the tourism economy while also striving to sustain their culture and tradition. See Imada, *Aloha America*, 159–65.

78. "Hawaii Welcomes the Imperial Japanese Navy," estimated date 1930–1941, T. 206.001, *Nippu Jiji* Photo Archives.

79. "Nihon teikoku to Karakaua-ō," *Jitsugyō no Hawai*, October 1936.

80. Sōsen (Ryōkin) Toyohira, "Hawai meibutsu fura odori," *Jitsugyō no Hawai*, October 1936.

81. Nathaniel Emerson, *Unwritten Literature of Hawaii: The Sacred Songs of the Hula* (Washington, DC: Government Printing Office, 1909).

82. Tom Smith, "History, 'Unwritten Literature,' and US Colonialism in Hawaii, 1898–1915," *Diplomatic History* 43, no. 5 (2019): 813–39.

83. "Kokoro zuyoi jūgo no mamori," *Hawai Hōchi*, July 16, 1937; "Ōfuna no sutāren imon bukuro o kennō," *Hawai Hōchi*, August 12, 1937; "Sattōsuru jūgo sekisei no kenkin," *Nippu Jiji*, August 12, 1937; "Kashikoshi san naishinnō sama kara kaigun no shōhei e," *Nippu Jiji*, February 17, 1938.

84. "Manshū Jihen o shinogu jūgo no nessi buri," *Nippu Jiji*, July 23, 1937; "Juppē kin kokubō kenkin no mezamashii rekōdo," *Hawai Hōchi*, July 28, 1937.

85. "Pōtorando kara imon bukuro ichiban nori," *Nippu Jiji*, August 26, 1937.

86. "Beitairiku no zairyūmin kara," *Hawai Hōchi*, September 6, 1937.

87. "Rikugunshō no imon bukuro chūi," *Hawai Hōchi*, September 2, 1937.

88. Tomosada Ishibuchi, "Teikoku kaigun ni taisuru Hawai dōhō no sekishin ni shasu," *Hawai Hōchi*, January 1, 1939, and *Nippu Jiji*, January 1, 1939.

89. "Fujinren sōde de imon bukuro no seisaku," *Nippu Jiji*, September 8, 1937.

90. "Waiarua chihō zen dōhō fujin," *Nippu Jiji*, September 21, 1937.

91. "Bukkyō fujinkai imon bukuro tsuika," *Hawai Hōchi*, September 6, 1937.

92. "1,2000 yo no imon bukuro kesa Taiyō Maru de hassō," *Nippu Jiji*, October 13, 1937.

93. "Jūgun no otōto ni senninbari," *Nippu Jiji*, August 28, 1937.

94. "Dai 5 shidan no nīsan ni okuru," *Hawai Hōchi*, August 16, 1937.

95. "Senninbari no irai ni tsuite kibō," *Hawai Hōchi*, August 23, 1937.

96. "Senninbari no tame," *Nippu Jiji*, September 8, 1937.

97. "Kessho shita senninbari," *Hawai Hōchi*, August 25, 1937.

98. "Shōshū no aiji ni okuru," *Nippu Jiji*, August 25, 1937.

99. Shigemori Shoseki advertisement, *Hawai Hōchi*, May 15, 1939; Kojima Shoten advertisement, *Nippu Jiji*, January 20, 1940. A variety of *imon bun* manuals circulated in Japan and provided detailed instructions on this wartime practice. For examples of the manuals, see Toshiya Ichinose, ed., *Kindai Nihon guntai kyōiku, seikatsu manyuaru shiryō shūsei, Shōwa hen, dai 7-kan: Zensen e no imon bun, shikiji aisatsu no tame ni* (2) (Tokyo: Kashiwa Shobō, 2010).

100. "Shinnengō kodomoran no kenshō sakuhin daiboshū," *Nippu Jiji*, November 21, 1938.

101. Shizuko Murakami, "Imon bun," *Hawai Hōchi*, January 1, 1939.

102. Hiromi Monobe, "Senkanki Hawai ni okeru Nikkei nisei joshi kyōiku: Nihongo gakkō kara ryōri kōshūkai made," *Ritsumeikan Gengo Bunka Kenkyū* 20, no. 1 (2008): 193–95.

103. Ichioka, "Japanese Immigrant Nationalism," 271–73.

104. "Dāhamu fukuro iri tabako o ocha to kanchigai," *Nippu Jiji*, November 26, 1937.

105. "Chintao Kaigun Rikusentai shireikan Kuwaori Hidesaburo shōshō kara," *Nippu Jiji*, August 8, 1939.

106. "Manga o soeta imon bukuro no reijō," *Nippu Jiji*, August 8, 1939.

107. "Hawai dōhō no imon bukuro to Kankō kōgun kangeki zadankai," *Hawai Hōchi*, February 16, 1939.

108. "Nihonjin Ryokan Kumiai imon bukuro ichimanko," *Hawai Hōchi*, January 18, 1938.

109. Matsutarō Yamashiro, "Nihonjin Ryokan no hensen o kataru," *Jitsugyō no Hawai*, February 1935; Noriko Fujiwara, "Kairoteki sekai o tsunagu sōchi to shite no 'imin yado': Yokohama/Honoruru o tsunagu idō no keiken no kioku," *Senshū Daigaku Ningen Kagaku Ronshū Shakaigaku hen* 2, no. 2 (2012): 155–62; Kōjirō Iida, *Honoruru Nikkeijin no rekishi chiri* (Kyoto: Nakanishiya Shuppan, 2013), 127–60.

110. "Senjika no Nihon kengaku," *Jitsugyō no Hawai*, February 1938.

111. "Ippan kakui no sekisei ni uttae," *Hawai Hōchi*, February 18, 1938; *Nippu Jiji*, February 18, 1938.

112. "Kōgun shōbyōhei imon dan," *Hawai Hōchi*, February 8, 1938; "Imon bukuro no kishin ni tsuite," *Hawai Hōchi*, February 12, 1938; "Kōgun shōbyōhei imondan," *Jitsugyō no Hawai*, February 1938, 9 J-Ads.

113. "Chichibu Maru de hassō no kōgun imon bukuro," *Hawai Hōchi*, March 24, 1938; "Ōkina kibako e," *Nippu Jiji*, March 24, 1938.

114. "Ippan kakui no sekisei ni uttae," *Hawai Hōchi*, February 18, 1938; "Ippan kakui no sekisei ni uttae," *Nippu Jiji*, February 18, 1938.

115. "Senjika no Nihon kengaku," *Jitsugyō no Hawai*, February 1938.

116. "Kokoku hōmon oshitaku annai," *Hawai Hōchi*, March 15, 1938.

117. "Nihon yuki ni owasure naku," *Hawai Hōchi*, March 21, 1938.

118. "Nihon hōmon to ryokō yōhin," *Jitsugyō no Hawai*, March 1936. This special issue was dedicated to Japan travel.

119. "Ryokan kumiai imondan ikkō," *Hawai Hōchi*, April 16, 1938; "Kōgun shōbyōhei imondan dai 3-shin," *Nippu Jiji*, April 18, 1938.

120. For the coverage of the tour in *Hawai Hōchi*, see "Nihon bare no 4-gatsu 1-nichi," April 11, 1938; "Bankoku hakurankai jimu kyoku de," April 19, 1938. For *Nippu Jiji*, see "Kōgun shōbyōhei imondan dai 1-shin," April 16, 1938; "Kōgun shōbyōhei imondan dai 3-shin," April 18, 1938; "Doresu mēkā kumiai," April 20, 1938.

121. See, for example, "Doresu mēkā kumiai," *Nippu Jiji*, April 21, 1938.

122. Ruoff, *Imperial Japan*, 1.

123. "Kaigai hatten tenrankai de," *Hawai Hōchi*, August 27, 1940; "Imon bukuro mo tenji," *Nippu Jiji*, August 26, 1940.

124. "Kaigai dōhō taikai e," *Nippu Jiji*, June 28, 1940; "Kaigai dōhō taikai e no kankōdan o soshiki," *Nippu Jiji*, July 11, 1940.

125. "Nihon gohōmon no fuyujitaku wa zehi Satō fukusōten de," *Hawai Hōchi*, September 10, 1940.

126. "Imon bukuro nuikata," *Nippu Jiji*, September 2, 1940; "Kaigai hattenten imon bukuro," *Nippu Jiji*, September 10, 1940; "Tokyo taikai no imon bukuro," *Hawai Hōchi*, September 2, 1940; "Asu 11-nichi kara," *Hawai Hōchi*, September 10, 1940.

127. "Imon bukuro hōshi," *Nippu Jiji*, September 7, 1940.

128. Sōen Yamashita, *Hōshuku kōki 2600-nen to kaigai dōhō* (Tokyo: Hōshuku kōki 2600-nen to kaigai dōhō kankō kai, 1941); "Yamashita Sōen-shi cho," *Hawai Hōchi*, June 10, 1941.

129. "Kigen 2600-nen hōshuku," *Hawai Hōchi*, November 18, 1940; "Daihyō no kangeki hitoshio fukaki," *Nippu Jiji*, November 4, 1940.

130. Yamashita, *Hōshoku*, 132–33, 147–70.

131. Yamashita, 57–76, 86–87.

132. "Nihon minzoku kaigai hatten," *Nippu Jiji*, December 3, 1940; Yamashita, *Hōshuku*, 88–90.

133. Yamashita, 91.

134. "Nihon minzoku kaigai hatten," *Nippu Jiji*, December 3, 1940.

135. Yamashita, *Hōshoku*, 91–93.

136. Yamashita, 3.

137. Yamashita, 185.

138. Yamashita, 189.

139. Yamashita, 124.

140. Yamashita, 147–70.

141. "Heitaisan no rōku o negirau," *Nippu Jiji*, May 5, 1942; "Shōri imon bukuro kansha," *Hawai Hōchi*, June 26, 1942.

142. On permanent exhibit, *Okage sama de*, at the Japanese Cultural Center of Hawai'i, Honolulu, Hawai'i.

143. "Goshippu," *Hawai'i Times*, May 5, 1951; "Goshippu," *Hawaii Times*, February 21, 1951; Marumiya Gofukuten Christmas and New Year Sales, *Hawaii Times*, December 1, 1952.

144. "Kankoku shusseihei e no imon bukuro boshū kaishi," *Hawaii Times*, February 23, 1951.

145. "Hawai no daikangei buri ni Nihon kokumin ga bikkuri," *Hawaii Times*, February 5, 1958.

146. A haiku composed by a Japanese immigrant in the islands read, "*Senninbari, Hawai no atsusa, nuikomete.*" "Shōukai sokugatsu gosenku," *Nippu Jiji*, July 10, 1939.

# CHAPTER 7

# Subjection and Citizenship

## 1930s' Nikkei Citizenry and Japanese-Language Education in Hawai'i

### Rashaad Eshack

Through education, the state defines a set of morals and responsibilities for its citizens' public life—a citizenry to which people belong. In 1930s Hawai'i, the Japanese community assumed the mantle through its own Japanese-language education system. In doing so, it reformed its educational policies in response to strife within the community, developed an education system in dialogue with Japanese imperial influence, and designed a transnational model of citizenry with local, national, and global responsibilities. Nikkei citizens, as they were called, attended Hawaiian Japanese-language schools imbued with a Nikkei citizenship demonstrative of a prewar global Japanese imperial network of education.

Believing that public education was unsatisfactory for the moral and civic upbringing of their children, Japanese-Hawaiian community leaders devised a robust system of supplementary Japanese-language schools. Although the first schools were founded at the beginning of the century, by 1919, the number of Japanese-language schools grew to more than 150, servicing over thirty thousand Nisei (second-generation immigrant) students. In 1920, the Hawaiian territorial government attempted to control these schools, citing them as teaching loyalty to Japan. This inaugurated a prolonged and fierce legal battle. In the case of *Farrington v. Tokushige*, the US Supreme Court unanimously ruled in 1927 that restrictions by the territorial government were unconstitutional, a victory for foreign-language schools across America.

The 1920s Japanese-language-school controversy has been examined by many academic works, but little is known about what comes in its aftermath.[1] The era between 1927 and 1941 was a golden age for Japanese-language schools in Hawai'i. Student attendance rates rose, new schools were built, and new educational organizations were emboldened by their legislative victory. Never would Japanese-language education be more important for the Japanese community in Hawai'i.

Despite the 1927 victory, what followed was not instant unity and success. The legacy of bitter rivalries that ripened in the 1920s fostered a state of uncertainty and competition within Japanese-language education. In the struggle for the minds of the next generation of Nikkei citizens, the Hawai Kyōikukai, or Hawaiian Japanese Educational Association (HKK), needed to reconcile its position. Fault lines that emerged included resentments over centralization of authority in Honolulu, the influence of the Honpa Hongwanji Mission of Hawai'i, and the degree to which Americanization should be emphasized in Nikkei citizenry. The few years after 1927 set the foundation for factions to emerge that would define Japanese-language education in the 1930s. In response, the HKK fostered a sustained connection to Japan to legitimize its position within the sector. It was ultimately Japan's authority that unified a fractured community. With its support, the HKK emerged as a long-lasting organization that would come to define its vision for a transnational Nikkei citizenry.

## Sowing the Seeds of Dissent: Founding the New HKK

In the aftermath of the legislative struggle over Japanese-language schools, leaders of the Japanese community were split. The HKK had ceased operations between 1922 and 1927 during the Japanese-language school controversy and needed a reformation for the post-1927 era.[2] On July 21, 1927, delegates from educational associations around the islands gathered in Honolulu to define a new, Hawai'i-wide vision for Japanese-language education.[3] With Tomokuni Iwanaga, a representative from Honolulu, serving as president, ambassadors from the different islands came together to plan for their new organization.[4] The first order of business was to define the new goals for the HKK, the first of which was to "unify, improve and advance Japanese language education in Hawai'i." The HKK was made in charge of changing education to be appropriate for "modern conditions," including the publication of new Japanese-language textbooks. Voting rights for future conferences were also planned on this first day. HKK votes would be allocated by location: the island of Hawai'i would have eleven, Maui five, Kaua'i four, rural O'ahu five, and Honolulu eight. A board of directors, with one-year terms, would be elected each year at the annual HKK conference. Their responsibilities included leading the efforts of the organization in matters of education, accounting, and anything else that was necessary.[5] By the end of the day, the stage was set for the new HKK to officially be founded.

The next day, per the bylaws of the organization, twenty-one delegates gathered to establish the new HKK. It dissolved the old organization that was founded in 1915, transferred over its assets, and elected its first board of directors. The inaugural board was made up of President Tomokuni Iwanaga as well as Ryūhei Mashimo, Shichirō Watanabe, Kenzō Murakami, and Kazuhiko Ogata. The new HKK was charged with publishing new textbooks, but in the meantime it would use Honolulu Educational Association–published books that were written during the 1920s. The Honolulu Educational Association officially ceded its publication rights to the HKK, which would take over the responsibility of textbook distribution.[6] The decisions made on these first days created a quasi-federal system where a Honolulu-based HKK would manage education in lieu of the different island educational associations. While it aimed to unify, decisions made at these meetings would plague the organization in the coming years.

The initial construction of the HKK did more to fan the flames of future controversy than to elicit true unity. The organization, which was both housed in Honolulu and overwhelmingly made up of people from Honolulu, was all but sure to elect a board of directors entirely from the capital. Each of the inaugural members came from Honolulu schools, and their positions would remain uncontested for the next three years. Despite the organization's message of inter-island unity, its actions presented another story—that it was Honolulu that would lead the charge, and power would centralize in the hands of the few who lived in the city.

Another form of exclusion that sowed the seeds of conflict was the religious affiliation of the organization. From its inception in 1915, the HKK was intimately tied to Honpa Hongwanji schools, and this changed very little in its new form. Empowered after legislative victory, and in many ways inheriting the tracks laid by the Honolulu Educational Association, the new HKK was able to push away dissenting voices in the community. While it did have to contend with defining new directions in Japanese-language education, it also went through an internal purge of those within the community who disagreed with it.[7] The targets of the purge included those who cooperated with territorial government officials in the 1920s—prominent members of society like Takie Okumura, Yasutarō Sōga, and their ilk were put to the side in this new era. By doing so, founders of the new HKK sanctioned rivalries and competing visions of Nikkei citizenry that would define the crucial first few years of the 1930s. What emerged from the 1927 inaugural HKK meetings was a powerful group that was supported by Honolulu, Honpa Hongwanji, and the *Hawai Hōchi*. Although part of its strength, these biases were reflective of the victorious factions of the 1920s era of conflict. Organizing in this manner opened the door to competing voices and marginalized opinions that grew to oppose the HKK.

## Competing Visions

Over the course of the 1930s, alternatives to the HKK-affiliated Japanese-language schools emerged. In Honolulu, over 20 percent of the Japanese-language students of the city attended one of these schools by the mid 1930s.[8] By 1939, there were as many alternative schools in Honolulu as there were HKK Japanese-language schools.[9] Honolulu was a driver of alternative voices because of its diversity and proximity to the center of power in the territory. There, the Ninhongo Kyōiku Kyōkai (NKK) was founded in 1930, leading a movement against the HKK. Its emergence ushered in an era where the HKK had to fight to maintain its dominion over the territory's language schools. It was a struggle over the issue of education and citizenry fought in the classroom and in the public sphere.

The NKK was founded by Takie Okumura, a familiar foe of the HKK.[10] It was able to gain momentum in Honolulu with support from prominent community leaders like UH professor Tasuku Harada, Iga Mōri, and *Nippu Jiji* editor Yasutarō Sōga. Its primary goal was to phase out Japanese-language schools and integrate Japanese learning into the public education system. It proclaimed that its goal was to alleviate pressures on Japanese families, who would no longer have to pay for maintaining language-school buildings or deal with long commutes for students.[11] Fundamentally, the NKK was proposing a different model for Japanese-language education, one that left citizenry out of the hands of Japanese-language schools.

In the battle over Nikkei citizenry, the rivalry was bitter. Threatened, the HKK responded in the press. In July 1931, the *Hawai Hōchi* published an editorial warning about the NKK and its goal, blaming Okumura, Mōri, Harada, and the *Nippu Jiji* for creating a smokescreen behind which was an attempt to dismantle the strength and unity of the real Japanese education provided by the HKK.[12] It also accused the NKK of belittling Japanese-language learning. The HKK saw it as a threat, particularly considering the sway that its leaders held in the wider community.[13] At the tenth-anniversary celebration of the NKK, held on April 20, 1940, with Iga Mōri and over six hundred in attendance, Okumura spoke about the organization's founding. He blamed the ills of the community on the HKK system, claiming that their Japanese-language schools were "the origin of the problem" for the Japanese community. Instead, he proposed that working with the department of education to teach Japanese served to "teach people of the true nature of teaching Japanese" and focus on writing and reading the language.[14] The NKK argued that teaching Japanese should be for the skills of the language, and everything else that came with Japanese-language schools was in fact a burden on the community. Throughout the decade, the HKK and NKK debated over who had the legitimacy to teach Japanese and what morals should be taught alongside it.

The question of morals revealed differing ideas on how citizenry education would intertwine with Japanese-language education. The NKK founders envisioned that citizenship was to be fostered in public events supplementary to Japanese-language classes. One such event was the highly publicized New Americans Conference. Running annually between 1927 and 1941, the New Americans Conference was a yearly event that brought Nisei together with high-profile members of society. Its goals included: Americanizing the new citizens, fostering political interest and involvement, overcoming feelings of inferiority from being children of laborers, and finding opportunities outside plantation work.[15] The conference represented a different model for teaching citizenship as imagined by Okumura and the founders of the NKK. Instead of integrating civic education into Japanese-language schools, making it more susceptible to Japanese imperial influence, the Japanese language alone would be taught in schools. Meanwhile, events such as the New Americans Conference would fill the void and develop Nikkei citizenry in dialogue with local leaders.

The New Americans Conference also served as a legitimization effort by the NKK. High-profile attendees, ranging from United States senators and Hawai'i governors to the Japanese consuls general attended each year. It became a way to broadcast the NKK goals to the wider Hawaiian community. It was highly publicized—held in grand, central venues like the newly built Royal Hawaiian Hotel—and it was attended by many members of the press. Making an event surrounding the future of Nisei citizens extremely public was a statement by leaders like Okumura. It stated that their vision for Japanese-language and citizenship education was the approved method if you wanted to be a "true American." To overcome the struggles that had riddled the community in the past, the NKK, alongside its events like the New Americans Conference, presented an alternative vision for Nikkei citizenry—one bound to a future in America in lieu of Japan.

The community was torn on the role of citizenry within the world of education. From the perspective of the NKK's founders, civic education with the goal of fostering integration and political participation was best left to political, educational events such as the New Americans Conference. To learn the language of their forefathers, young Nikkei citizens should study within public schools, free of Japanese intervention. While it was their intention to make the Japanese language easier to access and they believed it would help with Americanization, the NKK was an attempt to return power into the hands of those who were alienated following the 1927 Supreme Court decision.

The NKK was the manifestation of another vision of Nikkei citizenship that emerged as a direct consequence of the rivalry that came to a head in the 1920s language crisis. And while it turned "toward" America, it failed to compete with the size of the HKK, and thus was limited to Honolulu. At its prewar height, it had fewer than nine hundred students attending its schools.[16] It was, however, highly public and had a large role in shaping the image of the Japanese community for a wider audience—a symbolic threat that the HKK took very seriously. Its journey demonstrates that the 1930s were not smooth sailing for the HKK. It was mired by controversy and strife that forced it to strengthen and legitimize its own claim to Japanese-language education.

## A Coalescence of Controversy

In the summer of 1931, the fault lines present since the foundation of the new HKK came to a head. Tensions between rural and urban representatives coalesced with competing voices over Japanese-language and Nikkei citizenship education. On June 17, 1931, the first shot was fired. In advance of the fourth annual conference of the HKK (to be held between June 23 and 26), the *Nippu Jiji* published a front-page editorial criticizing the "Honpa Hongwanji Hawaii Kyoikukai." Yasutarō Sōga's paper lambasted the HKK's textbook prices, questioned the organization's accounting, and put the onus of rising education costs—and their impact on average families—squarely on the organization's shoulders.[17] Over the summer of 1931, a controversy that would determine "whether the Japanese Educational Association of Hawaii will continue or be broken up" would ensue.[18] In the face of this tumult, the HKK needed to respond, reorganize, and find a way to secure its place at the center of Hawaiian Japanese-language education.

The June 1931 conference was tense as a result of the allegations posed by the *Nippu Jiji*. The organizers attempted to ignore these attacks, but in order to assuage concerns, the price of textbooks was reduced by ten cents; additionally, an audit committee reviewed the body's accounting and revealed that all was in order.[19] Another proposal that was approved was the launch of the "Japan Educational Inspection Team"—for teachers who had not seen Japan in over a decade, or who "refused to observe various aspects of Japanese education," the HKK would pay for trips to and tours around Japan, beginning in March 1932.[20] During the conference, articles by the *Nippu Jiji* continued: in light of potential financial misdeeds, the newspaper demanded that the HKK release their accounting records to reveal the truth.[21] The costs for a large trip to Japan further aroused the suspicion of Sōga and the *Nippu Jiji*, claiming that it was an unnecessary expense for an organization supposedly in debt.[22] The HKK was under suspicion and soon parts of its own organization would join the fray.

July 1931 was a time of panic that spread around the territory. Almost daily attacks were lobbed back and forth in the press between the *Hawai Hōchi* and *Nippu Jiji*. The *Hawai Hōchi* defended the HKK, claiming that the *Nippu Jiji* accusations were false, and alleged that the *Nippu Jiji* had its own past misdeeds.[23] Rural educational associations soon joined the fight. Other representative educational associations in rural areas like Maui and the island of Hawai'i held meetings on how to respond. Meetings erupted in an uproar; it became clear that a special territory-wide conference was needed. The Maui Educational Association, most adamantly against the current structure, refused to continue further discussions without the up-front resignation of the HKK's entire executive board.[24] With its ideological rival and factions of its own organization uniting, the HKK realized it needed to make significant changes to survive.

The HKK responded to this turmoil. First, the executive board agreed to resign, paving the way for a special conference to take place, where a new election would be held. This ten-day event, which began on August 18, 1931, had hundreds of spectators in attendance.[25] On the first day, Gikai Harada, president of the Waipahu Hongwanji Gakuen, was appointed the chairman of the conference. While the financial accusations were categorically denied, the resignation of the five managing directors was finalized; "for the future welfare of the association," a new board was elected.[26] Taichi Satō, Eiichi Kishida, Shujirō Takimoto, Churaburō Nishikawa, and Futoshi Ōhama made up the new board—a more diverse body was chosen to represent different interests of Hawaiian Japanese-language education. In the new board's inaugural letter, the board reflected on how the HKK's current issues were rooted in the organization's 1927 founding.[27] However, the organization continued to defend itself against accusations of financial misdeeds. According to the board, because of "the extreme irresponsibility of the press and the excessive misunderstanding of some people, the current situation has turned into a turbulent state of affairs."[28] By holding new elections, the HKK acknowledged its own systemic flaws regarding representation in the organization but held strong against the *Nippu Jiji* and refused to back down.

Regarding the allegations of embezzlement, the delegates at the conference were divided. Delegates from Maui denied the need for an audit, while others, including Tasaka Oka, representative of the Hawai'i lower house legislature and of the Meishō Japanese-language school from Hilo, proposed an expenditure for an independent audit.[29] Meanwhile, the *Nippu Jiji* continued its demands that the cost of textbooks be made known.[30] After more than a week of deliberation, the debate was at a standstill. Harada turned to Japanese consul general Iwate Yoshio. The body submitted a request to Iwate about whether to conduct an audit and release financial information to the public. After reflection and consultation with community leaders, Iwate wrote a notice that confirmed the accusations leveled by the *Nippu Jiji* as valid but did not warrant an audit of the organization. Instead, formal accounting procedures would be initiated to prevent further issues in the future.[31] With this decision, the matter was effectively settled, and the conference was disbanded.

The controversy of the summer of 1931 was a consequence of the decisions made in the 1920s education controversy. It was a struggle that brought together competing and rural voices in conflict with the HKK. While the special conference was about the board of delegates and what to do with the accusations leveled at the HKK, it illustrated the new role played by rural parts of Hawai'i within the organization. As Honolulu was the core of the territory, it made sense that it had a certain level of authority over the rest of the islands, but it was viewed that Honolulu had grabbed too much control during the first years of the new HKK. This conference thus became a reset point for the relationship between the core and periphery in Hawai'i. Additionally, when no agreement could be reached, it fell to the Japanese consul general to make the ultimate decision. On August 28, the *Nippu Jiji* published its reaction to Iwate's ruling: Sōga criticized it, declaring that "such palliative solutions are only superficially temporary and by no means fundamental and permanent," but admitted that he "had no choice" but to accept the decision.[32] Despite his continued frustration, Sōga was unable to compete with the authority of the Japanese consul on this matter. The conference was an example of how extensions of Japan were used as a legitimization of and a unifying factor in Hawaiian

Japanese-language education. When all else failed, the reach of Japan brought together a fractured Japanese-Hawaiian community.

During the first few years after 1927, competing visions and ideals of what it meant to be Nikkei in Hawai'i materialized. In a precarious time, the HKK fought off its own missteps and competing interests to emerge as the dominant force in language and citizenship education. A large part of its strategy was its continued relationship with Japanese representation in Hawai'i. Japan was a source of legitimization for the decision made in the 1931 controversy and was integral to the strengthening of the HKK over the rest of the 1930s. As I will outline in the next section, key ties to Japan bolstered the HKK's initiatives and informed the vision for Nikkei citizenry in Hawai'i.

## Ties with Japan

In May 1929, the HKK dispatched a group of delegates, including Palama Gakuen principal and future member of the HKK executive board Futoshi Ōhama, on a tour around Japan. The delegation spent three months traveling and observing schools of all levels with the goal of importing the best of Japanese national education into its own language schools in Hawai'i.[33] This trip was one of many steps that the HKK took to solidify and justify its influence over Japanese-language education, backed by the tacit endorsement of Japan. While much academic work has been done to place Japanese-language education as a response to Americanization efforts, little has been written on the community's active links with the Japanese empire.[34] This connection was fostered by the movement of educators across the Pacific in three different capacities: 1) soliciting Japanese educators to hold education seminars around Hawai'i; 2) recruiting Kibei Nisei from Japan to become Japanese-language school teachers; and 3) sponsoring young Nisei to study abroad in Japan. Japan was used as a source of legitimization for the HKK, and sustaining this link meant sustaining its own dominion over Japanese-language schools. As the HKK turned toward Japan, the direction and design of its education—its avenue for conveying Nikkei citizenship—was developed in direct dialogue with Japanese imperial influence.

## Japanese Educators

During the initial founding meetings of 1927, the HKK expressed a need to bring over teachers from Japan to improve the territory's Japanese education standard.[35] What followed was a series of seminars that defined the education sponsored by the HKK. On June 14, 1928, Tokyo Higher Normal School professor Mabuchi Reiyū arrived in Honolulu.[36] Mabuchi was an award-winning author of Japanese textbooks in Japan, praised by the Japanese Ministry of Education for his efforts in educational research.[37] After evaluating the works of Japanese reading textbooks, he wanted to speak with as many Japanese teachers as possible to improve all aspects of their Japanese-language teaching. Using his twenty years of teaching experience, he wanted to elevate Japanese-language education for "the benefit of the Japanese race in America."[38] These seminars systematically linked teaching methods in Hawai'i to the Japanese Ministry of Education. Early in its years, the HKK aimed to demonstrate that it was able to find support for improving the standard of language teaching. As a unified body, it was able to bring over educators from Japan, creating an education teaching tree that brought Hawaiian Japanese-language instructors into a Japanese sphere of education.

As the 1930s progressed, the HKK's goals of standardization and development made way for defining the spirit of Japanese-language education. Again, the HKK turned toward Japanese educators to create this vision. In July 1934 and 1935, the HKK brought over two teachers from the well-known Tokyo Seikei Gakuen, Nishihara Keiichi and Nose Hiroaki.[39] They each did weeklong tours of Hawai'i, conducting well-attended lectures and radio broadcasts on all the major Hawaiian islands.[40] Nose, as opposed to Nishihara and Mabuchi, was an expert on moral education. Concerning the spirit of morality within Japanese-language schools, he spoke of the importance of "making children aware of the highest morals of the Japanese people" and that education "should thoroughly implement . . . in accordance with . . . today's Japan."[41] His words echoed a sentiment shared by the HKK. Despite calls for Americanization, he argued that Japanese-language education in Hawai'i should exist in congruence with the educational influences emanating from Japan itself. In the 1930s, influence from Japan remained the driving force behind how teachers taught in Hawaiian

Japanese-language schools. The HKK actively maintained its connection to Japanese imperial educational institutions, reflecting how Japanese educators acted as envoys of global Japanese education influence.

## Recruiting Kibei Nisei

To bring over teachers from Japan who could live in Hawai'i, the HKK sought out Kibei Nisei to become Japanese teachers. The term *Kibei* refers to those born in the United States who spent a significant amount of time in Japan. It was a common practice for Japanese American families to send one of their children to reside in Japan and establish roots in the homeland. Following the Immigration Act of 1924, the Kibei were some of the few individuals who could move from Japan and settle in Hawai'i. The HKK actively recruited Kibei to work in Japanese-language schools and used the Japanese consulate to coordinate placements of teachers into schools. Dissecting their experience shows how they were a key resource for 1930s Japanese-language schools and can uncover networks of Japanese Issei and Nisei educated in Japan whose backgrounds influenced Hawaiian Japanese-language education.

There are a few indicators that illustrate the increased role that Kibei played in Japanese-language education over the course of the decade. Four biannual surveys done by the *Nippu Jiji* between 1930 and 1936 reflect the proportional representation of United States citizens as Japanese-language teachers. In 1930 there were 723 teachers, of whom only 199 were "citizens," representing 28 percent of the workforce.[42] In 1932, this number was only up to 29 percent, but in 1934 it rose to 37 percent, and by 1936, over 56 percent of the teacher workforce was represented by citizens as opposed to first-generation non-US citizens.[43] This rapid increase in the number of "citizen" Japanese-language teachers is accounted for by an influx of Kibei teachers who came from Japan. Education credentials from Japan were seen as very valuable in the eyes of HKK leaders. In a 1934 trip to Hawai'i, Japanese educator Kawasaki Riichi summed up this point by stating that it was "vital to have exceptional teachers with Japanese qualifications who freely come to America."[44] As a result, over the course of the 1930s, many Japanese-educated Nisei made their way from Japan to the shores of Hawai'i to become Japanese-language educators.

One such Kibei whose story is emblematic of this trend was Shōzo Takahashi. Born on the 'Ewa plantation camp in 1914, he was sent to Japan at a young age to live with his grandparents in Fukushima Prefecture. He spent the first twenty-four years of his life in Japan and was educated as an elementary-school teacher. Around the time of the passing of his grandfather, an HKK recruiter approached him. He was told about the lack of Japanese-language teachers in Hawai'i and that he could be of good help to the community and find a good job. At that point, he made the decision to go live in Hawai'i and pursue this opportunity. Upon his arrival, he was asked by a reporter about whether he felt American or Japanese. His response was that he categorically felt Japanese; he didn't even speak English. While Takahashi didn't understand the significance of the question, as an incoming Japanese-language teacher, the Japanese daily reporter viewed it as important to classify his sense of belonging to categorize the type of influence he would have on future students, and by extension, the community.[45] His initial post at the Hawai Chūō Gakuin was given to him by the Japanese consulate. There, the principal of the school was Sakai Matsuyoshi, a graduate of Tokyo Imperial University.[46] In 1939, he got a job at the Waialae Japanese Language School, where he worked under principal Miyagi Genei, a graduate of Kyoto Imperial University.[47] In December 1941, the Waialae Japanese Language School was closed after the attack on Pearl Harbor; Takahashi later was incarcerated during the war, after which he continued his teaching career for more than twenty years.

While at the Waialae Japanese Language School, Takahashi played a part in constructing Nikkei citizenry by building civic ties to imperial Japan. In an essay compilation from the Waialae school, students wrote of the future strength of Japan and support for Japan in the war.[48] The school organized *imon bukuro*, or comfort bags, to send to the Japanese Imperial Army and demonstrate their students' support.[49] A common practice in Japan at the time, sending *imon bukuro* indicated that support for Japan remained in the consciousness of students and teachers like Shōzo Takahashi. As he wrote in his memoir, he did "change [his] way of thinking all of a sudden because [he] had lived in Japan for so long."[50] The experience of growing up in Japan followed Kibei as they left their Japanese lives to craft new ones in Hawai'i, paving a route for global Japanese educational influence.

Shōzo Takahashi's story epitomizes the role of Kibei within the dynamic between Hawaiian Japanese-language education and the Empire of Japan. Recruitment of language teachers in Japan was a common practice used by the HKK to find new teachers. Upon their arrival, the national allegiance of the Kibei came into question, and many of them maintained a stronger connection to Japan than to Hawai'i. As they developed their careers, Japanese institutions helped along the way. The Japanese consulate put people in certain positions, and networks of people educated at imperial universities facilitated further career opportunities. Although many Kibei were, on paper, American citizens who taught Japanese, a deep-rooted Japanese influence continued to inform their Japanese-language education despite restrictive immigration policies that would seek to prevent that. The HKK thus utilized Kibei to maintain its position within the wider Japanese sphere of educational influence well into the 1930s.

## Study Abroad in Japan

A dialogue with Japan over Japanese-language education meant that the exchange went two ways. During the 1930s, the HKK sponsored some of its own students to go to Japan and learn to become language teachers there. In the middle of the 1930s, "studying in Japan became a popular trend because of the growing power of Japan in East Asia."[51] The HKK followed suit by sending hundreds of students to learn at different Japanese schools. The intent was both to fill the demand for Japanese teachers in Hawai'i and ensure that the next generation of teachers would be aware of all the best Japan had to offer.

At its height, there were more than two thousand second-generation students studying abroad in prewar Japan. By 1936, over five thousand Nisei students had gone there to study.[52] Participating in this trend, the HKK sponsored several rounds of students to study in Japan with the goal of learning how to become Japanese-language teachers.[53] This method proved to be effective; by 1936, about one-third of all Hawaiian Japanese-language teachers were educated in such a fashion.[54] The future of the HKK's Japanese-language school system lay in Japan. In lieu of local language-teacher training, sending students to Japan was worth the cost. A Japanese education was a valuable asset for those who wanted to fit the mold and to properly teach the Japanese language and Nikkei citizenship. These "mental . . . and status-related circumstances that compelled people to study in Japan" were drawn from a need to cement legitimacy for leadership within the community upon their return.[55] The best way to become a Japanese teacher was to go to Japan. Though its Japanese-language schools catered to the lives of young people living in Hawai'i, an HKK concerned with fostering the future of Japanese-language education turned to the motherland in its hour of need.

As the number of Nisei grew and the relative number of Issei fell in the 1930s, the future of Japanese-language schools was at risk. If they faltered, pillars around which the community was organized would be gone. It became the responsibility of the HKK not only to empower students to become better Nikkei citizens but to ensure its survival by sending many of those students to Japan. This trend illustrates that Japan acted as the core of their world, and despite strict immigration policies, the community used that core as a continuous breeding ground for its Japanese-language schoolteachers—whether through Japanese educators, the Kibei, or those who went to study abroad in Japan.

In the aftermath of the 1927 Supreme Court decision, the HKK had to find its footing before it was able to cement its dominance over Hawaiian Japanese-language education. In its success, it relied on a sustained connection to Japan to legitimize its reign. By the middle of the decade, challenges to the HKK fell by the wayside and were limited to small pockets of Honolulu. The HKK had won largely because of its ability to connect with Japan and integrate Hawaiian Japanese education into the fold of a wider Japanese discourse. Solidifying its grasp on Japanese-language schools meant that its vision for Nikkei citizenry, formed in dialogue with the Japanese influences it welcomed, could be realized.

## Imaginations of Nikkei Citizenry

At the Waipahu Gakuen, a Honpa Hongwanji–affiliated school in rural O'ahu, teachers gave students a questionnaire for the 1940 yearbook. In it, students were asked what they wanted to be when they grew up. One student, Suenobu Fuchida, who had been an active member of the school's Boy Scout club, expressed that he desired to become a "splendid Nikkei citizen."[56] Fuchida's answer is reflective of the goal of many Japanese-language-school students—to respond to the responsibilities "one has . . . for the national society."[57] It is also an answer that their teachers wanted to hear. Following the traumatic experience of the 1920s, the HKK found it imperative to define what Nikkei citizenry meant in order to clearly convey the community's set of values and responsibilities. To understand how Nikkei citizenry was imagined, I examined policy-maker, teacher, and student writings about Nikkei citizenship. Having done so, I argue that at the core of Nikkei citizenry was a set of values ascribed as being Japanese, which was used to accomplish three goals: 1) establish loyalty to the United States, 2) demonstrate the strength of the Japanese "nation," and 3) bring peace to the Pacific. Nikkei citizenry bridged the gap between the demands of Japanese subjection and American citizenship. It created a transnational citizenry that included responsibilities to the local society, the Japanese nation, and international peace.

## The Core: Maintaining a "Japanese" Morality

While attending Japanese-language schools, students "learned Japanese culture and customs" that defined a core set of Japanese values underpinning Nikkei citizenship.[58] In an opening letter to the 1939 graduating class of the Palama Japanese-language school, Principal Kimura Toraki stressed that the key to Japanese-language education was conveying the "many good parts of the Japanese nation."[59] Cooperation, gratefulness, filial piety, et cetera, were all morals central to Nikkei citizenry. Every class at the Waialae Japanese Language School began with a "daily recitation . . . *kansha shimashō, funrei shimashō, kyōdō shimashō*" (be grateful, be respectful, be cooperative).[60] Every week had dedicated morality lessons that were informed by moral textbooks that laid out a core set of values. These Japanese values were a key component of learning in Japanese-language schools—they served to prepare Nikkei citizens for their civic responsibilities.

Symbols in schools reinforced the importance of these morals. School songs, mottoes, and daily practices all demonstrated the importance of a Japanese value set for students. In a collection of essays for the largest Hawaiian Japanese-language school, the Hawai Chūgakkō, a high school student reflected on the importance of cooperation as a Japanese value—for "in school, in sports, in work, only with cooperation will one prosper."[61] He called on students to always follow the motivating school motto: "Let's Cooperate" to strive to be a good member of society.[62] Similarly, the motto of the Waipahu Gakuen was "The Spirit of Independence and Cooperation."[63] The Japanese-language school experience began and ended with the morals that they taught. Schools were viewed as "the dojo where . . . children [were] polished" for public life.[64] To that end, Nisei were expected to represent a core set of morals emanating from Japan, with which they were expected to tackle the local, national, and global responsibilities that defined Nikkei citizenry.

## Responsibility 1: Loyalty to the United States (Local)

Loyalty to the United States meant "using the virtues of the Japanese *minzoku* [ethnic nation] to contribute to the strength of 'this country.' "[65] The HKK played an active role in encouraging US loyalty within the paradigm of Nikkei citizenry, which was perpetuated by students, teachers, and external community members. Conveying that Nikkei citizens would act with loyalty toward America was of paramount importance to the security of the community. The community had faced the wrath of anti-Japanese sentiments before and needed to prevent drawing further negative attention to itself. Loyalty to the United States was thus a responsibility of Nikkei citizens, to keep the Japanese contingent in Hawai'i safe in the face of Yellow Peril.

Messages toward students about loyalty to the United States came from all levels of the community. In the 1928 school year, Chiyeko Yonemoto, a second-grade middle-school student at the Hawai Chūō Gakuin, received her report card. In it, there was a letter—a note to all students. The letter expounded on the purpose of Japanese-language schools, emphasizing that "we put creating good American citizens first."[66] Hidden in the back of a seemingly innocuous report card was the demonstration of the position of Japanese-language schools in 1930s Hawai'i. But in the case of Yonemoto, what did her school mean by "good American citizens"? To answer that question, the reflections

of another student provide clarity. In the Palama Japanese-language
school yearbook, fourth-grade middle schooler Yoshio Komatsu wrote:

> The most important thing for a Japanese American citizen is to re-
> spect the national flag and comply with US law. A person who harms
> the public interest by disturbing or quarrelling with a person is a
> person who does not obey the law. Just because we are Japanese, it
> would be a big mistake if there were people who did not respect the
> American flag and did not follow the rules. Even Japanese people
> are citizens of the US and must comply with the laws of the two
> countries. That's why we stay in Hawaii and go to English and
> Japanese language schools to study hard. We must study hard at
> school, accumulate training, and prepare to enter society as a good
> Nikkei citizen. The American flag has three colors, each with impor-
> tant meanings. White is purity, red is bravery and blue is freedom.
> If you always keep these meanings in your heart, you will be a good
> American citizen. To become ideal Nikkei American citizens, we
> need to devote ourselves to our loyalty.[67]

Membership in the Nikkei citizenry of the 1930s entailed both following the law and understanding the spirit of being an American citizen. By doing so, Nikkei citizens would be led "along the way toward
effective and honorable citizenship in Hawai'i."[68] Additionally, in an
essay compilation for the Hawai Chūō Gakuin, another student from
the same grade wrote that "it is natural for us to be loyal to America . . .
we will learn the Japanese spirit in Japanese language schools to become
better American citizens."[69] According to students, most of whom were
born and raised in the United States, their first responsibility as Nikkei
citizens was to the US. As a part of their national belonging, students
believed that the core of attending Japanese-language school was furthering their American ideals.

Despite sentiments expressed by students, the HKK's actions demonstrated that it was chiefly concerned with fostering loyalty to the United
States so that Nikkei citizens would protect the Japanese-Hawaiian
community. In the commemorative issue for the fortieth anniversary
of the Hawai Chūō Gakuin, Yasutarō Sōga reflected on the precarious state of Japanese-language schools. He argued that to cement

their legacy as institutions within America, Japanese-language schools needed to do three things: 1) Ensure its officials and teachers believe in the mission of Nikkei citizens and are serving to make loyal American citizens; 2) Make sufficient alliances with public schools; and 3) Carry out fundamental reforms to make Japanese-language education more efficient.[70] His comments suggested that long-lasting American loyalty was to be fostered by sustained connections to educational facilities run by the state; yet, instead, the HKK spent the decade improving its connections to Japanese imperial educational institutions.

Leaders had a vested interest in how Japanese-language schools shaped the future of their community. Core to the survival of that community was loyalty to the United States—adherence to US laws and understanding an "American spirit," which was taught and understood as the first key responsibility of Nikkei citizenry. Local responsibility, however, was aimed at the local Japanese-Hawaiian community instead of solely toward a United States ethos. Due to fervent anti-Japanese sentiment, the HKK paid lip service to the Americanization movement while its actions fostered sustained dialogue with Japan. It was important that "no one who learned in Japanese schools [was] anti-American."[71] For loyalty to the United States meant security for the Japanese community in Hawai'i.

## Responsibility 2: Represent Japan (National)

Nikkei citizens were responsible toward Japan insomuch as they were expected to represent the strength of the Japanese nation in Hawai'i. To do so meant strengthening the position of the Japanese-Hawaiian community by proving Japanese racial strength within Hawai'i's heirarchy. Fusae Nichihara, a 1940 graduate of the Waipahu Gakuen, wrote an essay imploring Nisei to fulfill their responsibility to convey the strong points of Japanese people to the hearts of American citizens.[72] Japan saw itself on par with the highest level of civilization, and it was the Nikkei's duty to further that reputation. Japanese-language education was at the core of this mission; it was believed that "if Nikkei could speak English well but not speak Japanese, they would be nothing but lowly American citizens with no special characteristics."[73] Through Japanese-language schools, Nikkei citizens could learn to become fully fledged members of the Japanese nation—as a part of which they were expected to demonstrate Japanese potency for the benefit of their community.

A perceived Japanese superiority was instrumental to solidifying strength for the Japanese community in Hawai'i. In response to anti-Japanese sentiment, highlighting a connection to Japan meant defying accusations made against the community. It was believed that members of the Japanese community in Hawai'i, as visible minorities, would be seen as "different" no matter their legal citizenship; "people on the street would still refer them as 'Japanese' since they did not look American."[74] The community's marginality motivated its need to overcome biases and outperform other nationalities on the islands. Nikkei citizens were meant to understand their quasi-American status in prewar Hawai'i and consistently represent the best of Japanese morality for the security and advancement of the Japanese-Hawaiian community.

Community members feared being lumped in with other, more troublesome minorities. Hawai'i was a "showcase of the world's races" and representation of moral values espoused in Japanese-language schools meant avoiding the traps of "negative points brought by different peoples."[75] Tsukasaki Masao, a teacher at the Waialae Japanese Language School, wrote that "along with other races, [Nikkei citizens] are baptized in American culture . . . and are not inferior to others." Within the racial hierarchy of Hawai'i, it was important that Japanese people be represented well so that they didn't appear to have the faults of other minorities. For "a part of the orient [remained] in their hearts, and they [had] an admirable sensibility. This is something that the other races [didn't] have."[76] According to Tsukasaki, it was their connection to Japan that made Nikkei citizens special—even superior and a cut above the other peoples of Hawai'i. It was a responsibility within Nikkei citizenry to uphold that superiority.

Japanese exceptionalism in Hawai'i was part of a wider discourse of Japanese superiority based in prewar Japanese imperial growth. Students attending Hawaiian Japanese-language schools saw Japan to be "as good as any other foreign country," and its superiority as a reason for "why it has developed so much."[77] Community leaders also referenced the growth of Japan as evidence for Japanese exceptionalism. Sadasuke Terasaki, the chief editor of the *Hawai Hōchi*, brought to light the spectacular modern growth of Japan and its reflection of strong Japanese national characteristics, including "diligence, honesty and patience," which in Hawai'i "have allowed Japanese people to make such an impact everywhere [they went]." Japanese values tied the rapid growth of Japan to the success of Nikkei citizens in Hawai'i. Continuing the legacy of Japanese national strength was a responsibility borne by Nikkei citizens for the future of the Japanese-Hawaiian community. At the end of his remarks, Terasaki challenged students, asking them: "What characteristics do you have? Will we be an ethnic group of the future?"[78] As if the very life of every person of Japanese descent in Hawai'i were at stake, building off the strength of Japan's prewar growth meant that Nikkei citizenry played a part in the global Japanese national strength.

It was feared that if the connection to Japan were lost, the Japanese-Hawaiian community's exceptionality would fade. Eiichi Kishida, an HKK representative writing for the tenth anniversary of the Hawai Chūō Gakuin, wrote that "nothing is more unfortunate than those who have lost their awareness as a nation. Such people lose their vitality . . . and become lethargic." He stressed that Japanese-language schools were a part of buoying Japan internationally, sending a veiled warning that without their language schools, this loss of vitality could happen to the Japanese people in Hawai'i. In his mind, Japanese-language schools were crucial because "language is the only line that deepens the awareness of the people" and was needed because of its ability to empower the race moving forward. He declared: "we must pray for our descendants to forever retain their awareness as a Yamato nation."[79] Japan was the source of the overseas community's potency, and maintaining ties with it was a responsibility of Nikkei citizenry; fostering the Japanese-Hawaiian community's sense of superiority would prevent its downfall.

The Nikkei citizens bridged the gap between loyalty to the United States and being part of a Japanese nation by focusing on consequences for the local Japanese-Hawaiian community. Being Japanese was a source of strength. In an essay for the Chūō Gakuin, a second-year student wrote that "the world is paying close attention to Japan, and what would it be like if we are Japanese and can't speak Japanese." For their future, "more and more people from outside Japan are learning the language, Japanese and English will be the languages of the world, so we should learn it."[80] Japan's imperial power was used to justify a link with

Japan as a force for strengthening the Japanese-Hawaiian community. Every action it took was a representation of a global Japanese nation, and responsibility for acting on behalf of this global Japanese nation fell onto the shoulders of Nikkei citizens.

## Responsibility 3: Bring Peace to the Pacific (Global)

The responsibility of the Nikkei citizens extended from a local and national responsibility to one with global consequences for the betterment of the world. Futoshi Ōhama summarized this sentiment in 1940 when he wrote that Nikkei citizens were "an example of the civilization of America and the positive aspects of the Japanese *minzoku* that has been cultivated over three thousand years" who "not only [led] in Hawaii . . . but [could improve] the entire world."[81] As the 1930s crept forward, concerns about global circumstances including the Second Sino-Japanese War and the beginnings of World War II in Europe were placed on the shoulders of Nikkei citizens. In an opening letter from Waipahu Gakuen's Gikyō Kuchiba, fear of the world political climate prevailed when he expressed that "we are experiencing unprecedented hardships in the world, and our place demands loyalty and cooperation of all citizens."[82] The deteriorating global conditions were omnipresent in the Japanese-Hawaiian community, and attending to them entailed the third responsibility of Nikkei citizens. Their global duty included both preserving peace in the Pacific and protecting the security of the Japanese-Hawaiian community.

The global responsibilities of the 1930s became more urgent as conflict crept closer to Hawai'i's shores. In 1940, the president of the Hawai Chūō Gakuin Alumni Association wrote in its yearbook that "it is only a question of time before the United States will be affected by the great changes taking place in Europe and Asia, either by direct involvement or by changed relationships in these areas."[83] The potential for conflict was palpable, and it was expected that the Nisei in Hawai'i would foster peace and understanding as ambassadors of Japan in Hawai'i. As one Hawai Chūō Gakuin student put it, "we study both countries in their own words, so we can understand Japan better than Americans and America better than Japanese. It is our mission to help them understand each other and maintain a friendship forever."[84] The burden of peace was put on the shoulders of Nikkei citizens, as some of the few who could understand both countries; it was understood that they could communicate between them and foster international amity.

The consequences of potential conflict were a key component of why this responsibility of the Nikkei citizenry was so urgent. War between the United States and Japan was an imminent, tangible threat for the local Japanese-Hawaiian community. Fears of what would happen to members of the Japanese community in a United States territory were a large part of the Nikkei citizens' impetus to shoulder this responsibility. The Chūō Gakuin Alumni Association's president wrote that the second generation was "charged with the task of eradicating once and for all, all suspicions and doubts surrounding our loyalty to the United States," and that because of events around the world, "on the choice we make will depend our future."[85] While the responsibility of international peace was global in nature, Nikkei responsibility began as something local—to defend the security of the Japanese-Hawaiian community.

Nikkei citizenry was responsive to global conditions because the Japanese-Hawaiian community it served existed in a transnational, global state of being. The relationship between Japan and the United States defined what the goals were for Nikkei citizenship and represented a larger purpose. Nikkei citizenry was defined by the triumvirate of responsibilities that utilized a unique set of core values. Responding to the deteriorating global political climate, Nikkei citizens were placed on the border between two burgeoning empires on the precipice of conflict. It was up to them to be loyal United States citizens, represent the racial and national strength of Japan, and ultimately bring peace to the Pacific. Civic responsibilities that responded to local, national, and international affairs led to a unique, transnational conception of citizenry. Japanese-language education was crafted in direct dialogue with both United States and Japanese institutions and defined a transnational citizenry that came into its own in advance of a looming world war.

## Notes

1. For more information, refer to works such as Noriko Asato, *Teaching Mikadoism: The Attack on Japanese Language Schools in Hawaii, California, and Washington, 1919–1927* (Honolulu: University of Hawaii Press, 2006); Okita Yukuji, ed., *1920 nendai Hawai Nikkeijin no Amerika-ka no shosō* [Aspects of 1920s Hawai'i Nikkei Americanization] (Kyoto: Doshisha University, 1995).

2. Yasutarō Sōga, *Gojūnen no Hawai kaiko* (Honolulu: Gojūnenkan No Hawai Kaikō Kankōkai, 1953), 454.

3. Hawai Kyōikukai, *Hawai kyōikukai dai-50 kai daigiinkai kinenshi* (Honolulu: Hawaii Hochi, 1985).

4. Hawaii Education Association, *Hawai nihongo kyōikushi* [History of Japanese education in Hawai'i] (Honolulu: Hawaii Education Association, 1937), 319–20.

5. Hawai Kyōikukai, *Hawai nihongo kyōikushi*, 322–26.

6. Hawai Kyōikukai, 329.

7. Sōga, *Gojūnen no Hawai kaiko*, 454.

8. *Hawai nenkan dai kyū kan: Shōwa jū nen-jū ichi nen* (Honolulu: Nippu Jijisha Henshūkyoku, 1935), 175, Tokioka Heritage Resource Center at the Japanese Cultural Center of Hawai'i, Honolulu (hereafter, "THRC/JCCH").

9. *Hawai nenkan dai jū san kan: Shōwa jū go nen* (Honolulu: Nippu Jijisha Henshūkyoku, 1940), 221, THRC/JCCH.

10. For more on the rivalry between Okumura and Buddhist institutions such as the HKK, see Noriko Asato, "Issei Buddhism in the Americas: The Pioneers of the Japanese-American Buddhist Diaspora," in *Issei Buddhism in the Americas*, ed. Duncan Ryūken Williams and Tomoe Moriya (Urbana: University of Illinois Press, 2010), 45–64.

11. *Hawai nenkan dai go kan: Shōwa roku nen-nana nen* (Honolulu: Nippu Jijisha Henshūkyoku, 1931), 221, THRC/JCCH.

12. "Osorubeki kyōsōsha o mae ni shite Hawai Kyōikukai no dai dōyō," *Hawai Hōchi*, July 30, 1931.

13. For more information on the influence on education held by Takie Okumura and others, see Mariko Takagi-Kitayama, "In the Strong Wind of the Americanization Movement: The Japanese-Language School Litigation Controversy and Okumura's Educational Campaign," in *Hawaii at the Crossroads of the US and Japan before the Pacific War*, ed. Jon Thares Davidann (Honolulu: University of Hawai'i Press, 2018), 217–40.

14. "Nihongo kyōiku kyōkai sōritsu jū shūnen shukuga," *Hawai Hōchi*, April 27, 1940.

15. Jisoo Sanjume, "An Analysis of the New Americans Conference from 1927–1938" (master's thesis, University of Hawai'i at Mānoa, 1939).

16. *Hawai nenkan dai jū san kan: Shōwa jū go nen*, 221.

17. Yasutarō Sōga, "Hawai kyōikukai no kikaina taido," *Nippu Jiji*, June 25, 1931; Hawai Kyōikukai, *Hawai nihongo kyōikushi*, 370.

18. "Textbook Cost Withheld at J.E.A. Session," *Honolulu Star-Bulletin*, August 25, 1931, evening edition.

19. Hawai Kyōikukai, *Hawai nihongo kyōikushi*, 377.

20. Hawai Kyōikukai, 373.

21. Sōga, "Hawai kyōikukai no kikaina taido."

22. Sōga, *Gojūnen no Hawai kaiko*, 458.

23. "Nippu Jiji wa yōkai no shikakunashi kyōikukai mizukara kaiketsu seyo," *Hawai Hōchi*, July 21, 1931.

24. "Conference of Japan School Body Ordered," *Honolulu Star-Bulletin*, August 7, 1931.

25. "Textbook Cost Withheld at J.E.A. Session."

26. "Special J.E.A. Confab Will Open Today," *Honolulu Advertiser*, August 18, 1931.

27. Hawai Kyōikukai, *Hawai nihongo kyōikushi*, 380.

28. Hawai Kyōikukai, 381.

29. "J.E.A. Account Audit a Topic of Discussion," *Honolulu Star-Bulletin*, August 19, 1931.

30. "Fugyō tenchi ni jinu ka: Kyōikuka ni kyogi wa yurusarenu karera ga ika ni fukei o gomakasan toshite iru kono katsu jijitsu o miyo," *Nippu Jiji*, July 11, 1931.

31. George Sakamai, "J.E.A. Session Ends with New Board Elected," *Honolulu Star-Bulletin*, August 28, 1931.

32. Yasutarō Sōga, "Tatakahi no ato o kaerimite: Ichi ji no kotosaku to jōka kakushin e no dai-ippo," *Nippu Jiji*, August 28, 1931.

33. Karleen Chinen, ed., *Hawai Hōchi 100 Shūnen Kinen Hawai Nikkei Paioniazu* (Honolulu: Hawai hōchisha, 2012).

34. For some of these works on Americanization and Japanese-language education, see Hiromi Monobe, "Americanizing Hawai'i's Japanese," in Davidann, *Hawaii at the Crossroads*; Eileen Tamura, *Americanization, Acculturation, and Ethnic Identity: The Nisei Generation in Hawaii* (Urbana: University of Illinois Press, 1994).

35. Hawai Kyōikukai, *Hawai nihongo kyōikushi*, 330.

36. *Hawai nenkan dai san kan: Shōwa yon nen-go nen* (Honolulu: Nippu Jijisha Henshūkyoku, 1929), 175, THRC/JCCH.

37. "Kokugo kyōiku no kaitakusha: Nihon dai ichi no shō," *Hawai Hōchi*, July 16, 1928.

38. "Kokugo kyōiku no kaitakusha."

39. Hawai Kyōikukai, *Hawai nihongo kyōikushi*, 439–42.

40. "Hawai kyōikukai kaki kōshūkai," *Hawai Hōchi*, June 24, 1935.

41. "Gendai no shūshin kyōiku wa Nihon minzoku no jigaku ga chūshin," *Hawai Hōchi*, July 19, 1935.

42. "Hawai nenkan dai go kan: Shōwa roku nen-nana nen," 220.

43. *Hawai nenkan dai kyū kan: Shōwa jū nen-jū ichi nen*, 176; *Hawai nenkan dai jū ichi kan: Shōwa jū ni-jū san nen* (Honolulu: Nippu Jijisha Henshūkyoku, 1937), 189, THRC/JCCH.

44. "Gakkō no bunritsu o sakete tōitsu o hakare," *Nippu Jiji*, June 11, 1934.

45. Shōzo Takahashi, interview by Ted Tsukiyama and Jim Tanabe, March 12, 2004, transcript, THRC/JCCH.

46. Shōzo Takahashi, *Jibunshi* (Honolulu: Hawaii Pacific Press, 1994), 8; *Hawai nenkan dai jū ichi kan: Shōwa jū ni-jū san nen*, 192.

47. *Hawai nenkan dai jū ichi kan: Shōwa jū ni-jū san nen*.

48. "Bunshū yashi no mi," Waiarae Chihō Nihongo Gakkō Gakuyūkai, May 29, 1940, 225, THRC/JCCH.

49. "Bunshū yashi no mi," 251.

50. Takahashi, *Jibunshi*, 8.

51. Hawai Keijin Rengō Kyōkai, *Hawai Nihonjin Iminshi: Kankō Iinkai Henshū* (Honolulu: Hawai Keijin Rengō Kyōkai, 1964), 250.

52. Hawai Keijin Rengō Kyōkai, *Hawai Nihonjin Iminshi*, 250.

53. *Hawai nenkan dai kyū kan: Shōwa jū nen-jū ichi nen*.

54. *Hawai nenkan dai kyū kan: Shōwa jū nen-jū ichi nen*, 176.

55. Hawai Keijin Rengō Kyōkai, *Hawai Nihonjin Iminshi*, 250.

56. "Waipahu gakuen sotsugyō kinenshi 1940 nen," Waipahu Gakuen Kōyūkai, June 1, 1940, 10, Hawaii's Plantation Village, Waipahu, Hawai'i.

57. Kiyoshi Robert Fukuda, "Hawai chūō gakuin shūshin renshūchō," Hawai Chūō Gakuin, undated, THRC/JCCH.

58. Katherine Kawai Sano, "Childhood Memories of Our Waialae," September 15, 2007, 8, THRC/JCCH.

59. "Kinenshi 1939 Palama Nihongo Gakkō," Parama nihongo gakkō gakuyūkai, June 20, 1939, 35, THRC/JCCH.

60. Sano, "Childhood Memories," 18–19.

61. "Bunshū shokan bun 1934 nen," Hawai Chūgakkō, September 1934, 231, THRC/JCCH.

62. "Bunshū yashi no mi," 231.

63. "Waipahu gakuen sotsugyō kinenshi 1940 nen," 35.

64. "Jū shūnen kinen 1936 nen Waiarae chihō nihongo gakkō," Waialae Chihō Nihongo Gakkō, November 30, 1936, 52, THRC/JCCH.

65. "Kinenshi 1939 Palama Nihongo Gakkō." For more on the history of the term *minzoku*, see Kevin M. Doak, "Ethnic Nationalism and Romanticism in Early Twentieth-Century Japan," *Journal of Japanese Studies* 22, no. 1 (1996): 77–103.

66. "Tsūchibo," Kahului nihongo gakkō, 1928, THRC/JCCH.

67. "Kinenshi 1939 Palama Nihongo Gakkō," 46.

68. "Waipahu gakuen sotsugyō kinen 1941 nen," Waipahu Gakuen Kōyūkai, June 1, 1941, Hawaii's Plantation Village.

69. "Waipahu gakuen sotsugyō kinen 1941 nen."

70. "Hawai chūō gakuin yon jū shūnen kinen 1936," Hawai Chūō Gakuin Kōyūkai, June 10, 1936, 40–41, THRC/JCCH.

71. "Kinenshi 1939 Palama Nihongo Gakkō."

72. "Waipahu gakuen sotsugyō kinenshi 1940 nen."

73. "Kokugo kyōiku no kaitakusha."

74. "Kokugo kyōiku no kaitakusha," 225.

75. "Bunshū yashi no mi," 224.

76. "Jū shūnen kinen 1936 nen Waiarae chihō nihongo gakkō," 51.

77. "Waipahu gakuen sotsugyō kinen 1941 nen."

78. "Hawai chūō gakuin yon jū shūnen kinen 1936," 42.

79. "Hawai chūō gakuin yon jū shūnen kinen 1936," 38–39.

80. "Bunshū shokan bun 1934 nen," 225–26.

81. "Hawai chūō gakuin yon jū shūnen kinen 1936," 39.

82. "Waipahu gakuen sotsugyō kinen 1941 nen."

83. "Fuyō: 1940 Hawai chūō gakuin sotsugyō kinen," Hawai Chūō Gakuin Sotsugyō Kinen Fuyō Hensanbu, June 5, 1940, THRC/JCCH.

84. "Bunshū shokan bun 1934 nen," 225–26.

85. "Fuyō: 1940 Hawai chūō gakuin sotsugyō kinen."

# Part IV
# Nikkei and US-Japan Relations

# CHAPTER 8

# The Outbreak of the Pacific War and Japanese Companies in the United States

## Morimura Bros. & Co.

*Masato Kimura*
*Translated by Kaoru Ueda*

## Introduction

This paper aims to present a new perspective on the study of the outbreak of war between Japan and the United States by clarifying how Japanese companies in the United States, notably Morimura Bros. & Co., a trading company specializing in porcelain, responded to the war. I argue that past research failed to address two issues. The first is the micro perspective of crisis management of Japanese companies abroad. As the Japanese economy developed during the interwar period, Japanese companies, mainly trading companies and banks, expanded into the United States and China, one after another. Much research was conducted on the economic, business, and diplomatic histories of Japanese companies in China, centering on research on the South Manchurian Railway Company and Japanese textile companies in China.[1] Surprisingly, however, research on the activities of Japanese companies in the United States is limited. Although the Suitland Annex of the US National Archives and Records Administration in Washington, DC, holds collections of Japanese companies in the United States, the only study that makes full use of them is that of Mitsubishi Corporation.[2]

During the interwar period, economic relations between the United States and Japan were well balanced, with both imports and exports increasing. As a result, Japanese businesspeople and companies were at the center of economic activity. Studying to elucidate their perception and awareness will be of great value in understanding the overseas strategies of Japanese companies at the time, as well as their thoughts on overseas crisis management.

This is also an intriguing topic from today's perspective. Despite concerns about the "hollowing out of the industry," Japanese manufacturers continue expanding overseas to cut costs in the face of a strong yen. Overseas business activities accompany many risks, but among them, the country risk, or political, economic, and social conditions and events in a foreign country, is perhaps the most difficult to ascertain. Recent examples include the withdrawal of the Mitsui Petrochemical Industries plant during the Iran-Iraq War and the hostage-taking of expatriates in Iraq during the Gulf War. These recent experiences demonstrate that when a company is involved in a war in a country where it has established a presence, it faces various issues, such as how the company should respond and the perception gap in crisis that the company is facing between the Japanese and the locals. I suggest that the case of Morimura Bros., which conducted its business activities in the United States while fearing the outbreak of the Pacific War, is an excellent case study in helping answer today's issues.

Second, it will provide a new perspective on studying the Pacific War. We all know that a vast amount of research has been conducted on the causes of the outbreak of war and the path leading up to it. However, more needs to be explained about how the business community responded to the deterioration of Japan-US relations, and the process leading from the freezing of Japanese assets in the United States in July 1941 to the subsequent oil embargo against Japan and the outbreak of war on December 7, 1941.[3]

The prewar relationship between Japan and the United States is said to have been one of repeated confrontation and cooperation. The business communities of both countries maintained relatively good relations, though they faced economic friction. As Japan-US relations deteriorated after the onset of the Second Sino-Japanese War, it is clear that the business communities, which had benefited from this relationship, were seriously considering the future of Japan-US relations and attempting to take some action to improve it.[4]

Morimura Bros. Importers was founded in 1868 by Morimura Ichizaemon VI, who also became known as the founder of Morimura Gakuen (Morimura Gakuen Schools), and his younger brother Toyo.[5]

Ichizaemon was born in Edo (today's Tokyo) in 1839 into an armorer's family. The Morimura family came from Tootōmi Province (today's Shizuoka Prefecture). Still, from the mid-Edo period, they were dealers in armor and bags in Kyōbashi. They were allowed to visit the residences of *daimyo* (feudal lords) and *hatamoto* (samurai in the direct service of the shogunate). His brother Toyo was born in 1854; Toyo was fifteen years younger than Ichizaemon. In April 1876, Morimura Toyo arrived in New York and rented a room on the third floor of Dr. Bronson's house at 549 Fifty-First Street, where he began living with five others, including Satō Momotarō, Arai Ryōichirō, Suzuki Toichi, and Chūshichi Date. The cost of room and board was about twenty dollars per person per month (five dollars for room and three dollars and fifty cents for board per week).

With a letter of introduction from Fukuzawa Yukichi, Toyo immediately visited the Japanese consul, Tomita Tetsunosuke (later president of the Bank of Japan), and asked him to recommend a suitable school to learn English conversation; he began attending Eastman Business College along the Hudson River in Poughkeepsie, New York, in June. In September, he graduated from school, and in February, he rented a small store on Front Street from which to operate a general merchandise business. This store became Morimura Gumi's first base for exports to the United States.

Meanwhile, in Japan, Ichizaemon and his brother-in-law, Ōkura Magobei, traveled the inconvenient Tōkaidō Highway to Yokohama, Nagoya, Kyoto, and Osaka, and even pulled their cart to Shinbashi Station to offload goods in Tokyo, where they purchased antiques, pottery, copperware, fans, lanterns, dolls, and other products for export and sent them to Front Street. In New York City, amid scorn for "Orientals," capital was scarce, and Toyo could not rent a large store, but his stock was also small. Despite the limited space afforded by the store, Toyo often slept there after a simple supper in the evening. Finally, after much hard work, Toyo secured the services of a friendly advisor named Van Buskirk, who sold Japanese exports to him.[6]

In 1876, when the Philadelphia Centennial Exposition was held with fanfare, Toyo and his colleagues purchased the remaining exhibits and display shelves. In 1877, they rented a building at 238 Sixth Street. They operated Hinode Shōkai with Satō Momotarō.[7] However, in

1878, thinking about the future of the business, Toyo decided to go it alone. He parted ways with Satō, and established Morimura Bros. by hiring two store employees, Miyamoto and Ōtomo.

Both in name and substance, Morimura Gumi entered the New York market. Founded by Morimura Toyo, Morimura Bros. was located on New York's Sixth Avenue, near Fourth Street, the heart of the city's retail district, which was lined with Macy's and other department stores—a place where upper-class customers would take carriages to shop. In 1879, at the recommendation of Fukuzawa Yukichi, Murai Yasukata, a graduate of Keio University, joined the firm from Japan and worked closely with Toyo to expand the firm's presence in New York City. In 1880, Ichizaemon visited the United States for the first time to inspect business conditions. As a result of his careful market research, he became convinced that the ceramics business was promising.[8]

Around 1880, Morimura Bros. had annual sales of one hundred thousand dollars. The breakdown was 70 percent retail and 30 percent wholesale. Around that time, Toyo and Murai began seriously considering whether a business policy focusing mainly on retail sales would provide sufficient potential for future development. Toyo argued that it would be advantageous to continue specializing in retail for a while, but Murai maintained that the company should immediately switch to wholesaling. The two sides could not easily reach a conclusion. Since this was a significant issue concerning the future, Toyo asked for the head office's decision, instead of fixating on his own idea. At the end of 1882, the head office finally decided to specialize in wholesale sales. This change in business policy was the catalyst for the development of Morimura Gumi. The following year, Morimura Bros. moved to 540 Broadway, followed by 530 Broadway in 1890, 538 Broadway in 1894, and 546 Broadway in 1902, and each time the company expanded in size and credibility, developing into one of the leading Japanese trading companies.

Around 1885, Morimura Gumi began taking import orders based on sample products (orders sent directly to customers), and by later years, had developed to receiving large orders from the Woolworth Ten Cent Store. By 1889, sales reached $450,000—a fivefold increase over ten years. Table 8.1 compares Japan's exports to the United States starting

TABLE 8.1. Japan's Exports to the United States and Morimura
Gumi Exports to the United States (unit: one thousand yen)

| Year | Total exports | Ceramics | Morimura Gumi |
|------|------|------|------|
| 1891 | 79, 527 | 1,287 | 141 |
| 1892 | 91,102 | 1,480 | 174 |
| 1893 | 89,712 | 1,577 | 251 |
| 1894 | 113,246 | 1,484 | 157 |
| 1895 | 136,112 | 1,955 | 280 |
| 1896 | 117,842 | 1,974 | 375 |
| 1897 | 163,135 | 1,819 | 277 |
| 1898 | 165,753 | 1,990 | 308 |
| 1899 | 214,929 | 2,181 | 325 |
| 1900 | 204,429 | 2,471 | 509 |
| 1901 | 252,349 | 2,491 | 564 |
| 1902 | 258,303 | 2,461 | 662 |
| 1903 | 289,502 | 3,169 | 845 |

Note: *Total Exports* refers to Japan's total exports to the US. *Ceramics*
refers to Japan's total exports of ceramics to the US. *Morimura Gumi*
refers to the number of shipments of ceramics and sundry goods to
Morimura Bros.

Source: Nippon Tōki Kabushiki Kaisha Nippon Tōki 70-nenshi
Henshū Iinkai, comp., *Nippon Tōki shichijūnenshi* (Seventy years
of Japanese ceramics) (Nagoya: Nippon Tōki Kabushiki Kaisha,
1974), 179.

in 1891 and Morimura Gumi's shipments to Morimura Bros. stores
during the same period.

When the Morimura Bros. store was first established in New York,
it purchased and exported every piece of Japanese general merchandise
available for export. Still, when selecting products for which it could
take full responsibility, it decided it would be better to sell the products
it had made itself. Hence, it began making its own porcelain and exporting it to the United States.

In 1904, Nippon Tōki was established by Morimura Gumi.[9] Initially,
the company made tea sets and confectionery plates under the name
of *novelty line* or *fancy line*; but around 1914, dinner sets began to
be produced. Japanese ceramics became a more significant part of the
Morimura Bros. product line as these products developed.

In its porcelain business, Morimura Bros. was called the American
store. Morimura Bros., in turn, differentiated between porcelain made

for the company and that purchased from other dealers. It called the former *own products* or *own porcelain* while referring to the latter as *other porcelain* or *miscellaneous porcelain*. It focused its marketing efforts on its own products, although the amount of other and miscellaneous porcelain it handled was large.

The prewar and postwar unit prices of Noritake dinnerware of Nippon Tōki are not appropriate comparable indicators since the prices were vastly different. The number of sets sold by Morimura Bros. in the United States before the war was between eighty thousand and ninety thousand sets per year; the company strove to sell one hundred thousand sets a year. However, it was not able to achieve this goal before the war. Morimura Gumi, the head office of Morimura Bros., was located in Tokyo, and essential instructions were always received from the Tokyo head office, but all sales and manufacturing plans were made through direct negotiations between Morimura Bros. in New York and Nippon Tōki in Nagoya, and personnel exchanges also took place between the two, so the two had a de facto head office–branch relationship.[10]

In the 1930s, Morimura Bros. and Mitsui, Mitsubishi, NYK, and Yokohama Specie Bank occupied an essential position in the Japanese community in New York.[11]

## Section 1. From the Conclusion of the Tripartite Pact to the Freezing of Japanese Assets in the United States

The Treaty of Commerce and Navigation between the United States and Japan, originally signed in 1911, expired in January 1940, and while there were rumors and widespread belief that Japan-US diplomatic relations would be severed, Japanese ceramic products were selling well in the United States market.

It was in September 1940, when the Tripartite Pact was concluded between Japan, Germany, and Italy, that the course of Japan-US relations became treacherous. On September 10, a telegram from the Morimura Gumi head office stated, "Japan has made every effort to help the US understand Japan's position and to recognize the new situation in the Orient.[12] However, the US is unwilling to change its understanding but insists on its emotion and legal theories."[13] In the end, the United States' attitude did nothing but irritate Japan. The telegram continued, "It is a sincere regret that we have come to hold hands with Germany and Italy."[14] Japan's position, however, was that "from the very beginning, Japan had no ambition to invade territory, and as a neighbor and good neighbor, Japan will establish eternal peace in the Orient."[15]

While Japan was criticizing the United States for its by-the-book approach, the two countries were unlikely to reconcile unless extraordinary changes occurred. If the conflict continued, a war would be possible. As a result, New York–based Japanese companies, including Mitsui, Mitsubishi Corporation, and Yokohama Specie Bank, began preparations to ease the burden on their branches in the US by sending their employees' families back to Japan.

Mizuno Tomohiko, manager of the New York branch, who was constantly informed by the Japanese embassy and Japanese consulate in New York, determined that Morimura Gumi's head office in Tokyo, as well as Nippon Tōki, based in Nagoya, now needed to decide whether or not to engage in business activities on the premise that war would break out in the future.

A telephone call between Mizuno and Iino Ippei, a director of Morimura Gumi's head office in Tokyo, on October 23, 1940, revealed the circumstances of this decision.

After reporting on the United States economy and product sales, Mizuno said,

I am thinking of reorganizing the company, but I think it will be difficult to change it if the shareholders are the same. Selling the company to an American would be rejected due to the sales price, among others.

He pressed Tokyo about Morimura Bros.' principal policy for the future, informing Tokyo that he investigated examples in the European theater of World War II and found confiscation of assets would be likely, and that the most challenging issue was to determine whether to proceed on the premise of war or to proceed on the premise of no war.[16] In response, Iino stated that he would consider the worst-case scenario of severing diplomatic relations and responded, "I can't tell which way it is going, but do your best to be prepared."[17]

This phone call prompted Morimura Bros. to respond based on the assumption that the Pacific War was inevitable. However, opinions differed between the Japanese side, which believed that the situation in Japan made it unlikely that the Japanese military would withdraw from mainland China and make enough concessions to convince the United States that Japanese aggression in China would end, and the New York side, which believed that both governments would choose to avoid war because an open conflict would be unwise in rational terms for both countries. Nakayama Takeo of the Tokyo head office stated that the United States had been relentlessly exerting economic pressure on Japan up to the current date, and that the two remaining options were freezing funds and severing diplomatic relations.[18] Furthermore, in preparation for the worst-case scenario, he wanted to minimize the potential damage caused by frozen assets by repatriating the sales proceeds from New York as soon as possible.

Mizuno, in New York, on the other hand, would later recall,

> If Japan and the US were to fight, the impact would be so great, and since the war would be fought across the Pacific, it would be too decisive a blow to either side to deal with. Therefore, Morimura Bros. continued its business, believing that war must be averted. Back then, our thinking operated differently from today, when airplanes are more advanced, and the risk of atomic bombs is greater.[19]

In 1941, contrary to the expectations of the previous year, diplomatic relations between Japan and the United States eased somewhat. In particular, when Ambassador Nomura Kichisaburō arrived in Washington at the beginning of February, things were superficially quite calm. For example, the Morimura Bros. daily journal (*MB Shōji Nisshi*) states,

> Ambassador Nomura arrived in Washington today. The popularity of Mr. Nomura among Americans is very sympathetic. When the Ambassador arrived at Honolulu and San Francisco, he was formally escorted into ports by two destroyers, and Americans showed their favor. We feel optimistic.[20]

Furthermore, it alerted the staff to the disposal of United States inventory and urged them to be ready to repatriate to Japan at any time.

Diplomatic relations have become increasingly delicate since last year, and other companies have adopted the same attitude, so we give special consideration to inventory disposal and encourage all parties to make efforts to dispose of their stock.[21]

In addition, Nippon Tōki's director Koike sent the following message:

Tokyo and Nagoya are unanimous in the opinion that Japan and the US should adopt a policy of mitigating damage in case of emergency, and that we want Morimura Bros. (MB) to sell as many sets as possible, and that we want MB to purchase any stock left at Nippon Tōki as much as funds permit. I have received approval that MB can cancel any unpopular motifs that we still need to start [manufacturing].[22]

At this point, the New York side was also in agreement with this request and planned to cooperate as much as possible.[23] Furthermore, the head office, concerned about a potential asset freeze in the future, sent detailed instructions regarding remittances.

We are concerned about the implementation of the assets freezing order and the repercussions of the Franco-Thai peace agreement, so in this case, it would be better to send as small amounts as ¥10,000 or ¥20,000 as often as possible instead of wiring a lump sum amount. We request you take action accordingly.[24]

On the other hand, Morimura Gumi also provided a calm analysis of the future of Japan-US relations. For example,

Looking at the US-Japan relationship, both sides have different views, and discussions have reached an impasse, and now it's a matter of keeping face. However, there are absolutely no problems that cannot be solved unless both sides engage in combat and make great sacrifices. In particular, the US has no reason to start a war with Japan and cause world turmoil for Oriental issues. However, it is most important not only to make immediate decisions based on common sense, but also to consider countermeasures in an emergency.[25]

In addition, Morimura Gumi sent a telegram to New York, telling them not to be misled by rumors and misinformation, but to stick to the established policy.

The Tripartite Pact would undoubtedly drag Japan, too, into the vortex sooner or later. Even if the US were to take proactive action in support of the British, it may be focusing only on home-front efforts thoroughly and avoiding war or supporting the British to avert its surrender to Germany.

At this stage, they may have thought that the United States and Japan would not plunge into war. However, both countries would have to make rational decisions. Ambassador Nomura himself had said,

Even though I came to the US and worked hard to prevent war, if more and more Japanese trading companies sent their employees' families back to Japan, the atmosphere between the US and Japan would deteriorate further, so I wanted them to leave their families behind if at all possible.[26]

Nomura was a friend of President Roosevelt's, and his warm personality and a strong desire to improve Japan-US relations kept the bilateral relationship at a lull, if only temporarily. However, no essential solution was found.[27]

The Japanese in New York were also taking a breather from the acrimonious situation and renewing their determination to deal with the future situation as positively as possible. Mizuno was one of them.

Mizuno recounted how he felt then.

In the event of an outbreak of war, diplomats have a reciprocal guarantee of safety of life and property under customary international law. Still, ordinary civilians have no such warranty, and although diplomats are allowed to exchange ships, ordinary civilians would become prisoners of war. They might be detained by the enemy during a war that could last for who knows how many years. In this regard, Ambassador Nomura said, "I would never return to Japan without those who stayed behind to trade. If there was an exchange ship, I would definitely take them back with me." We believed Ambassador Nomura's words and were determined to remain in the United States until the end.[28]

Morimura Bros. also had a business problem. In 1941, the German offensive on the European front intensified. The British civilian economic sector turned toward military production, and in the United States, military demand took precedence over civilian demand in order to support the British. The ceramics and porcelain industries were no exception. Imports of ceramics and porcelain from the United Kingdom declined, as did domestic production in the United States, and the market began to show signs of a glut. Expressing its frustration at not being able to expand its business in response to orders from the head office despite the growing demand for Nippon Tōki products, the MB journal dated February 14, 1941, describes,

The domestic manufacturing power is under pressure to produce tableware for military use, and since production has not increased in general, the demand for Noritake ware is strong. If there is no fear of war, customers will buy more, but the demand for these products will be kept to a certain [low] level because of war concerns. In the face of a crisis in international relations, orders are likely to increase dramatically.[29]

On February 14, the monthly meeting of the New York Ceramics and General Merchandise Importers Association was held. The association's president, Langfelder; the representative of Honma Hayward, Honma Iwajirō; the vice president and treasurer of Taiyō Bōeki KK, Kondō Tamotsu; the secretary of the association; and the representative of Morimura Bros., Mizuno Tomohiko, as well as other Japanese businessmen, gathered. The lack of a system of foreign exchange and production compensation in Japan would have resulted in losses to manufacturers and exporters in the event of an emergency. For this reason, they discussed that they had no choice but be hesitant to accept orders in the United States market.[30]

Other Japanese exporting companies felt the same way. In order to continue business under these circumstances, on February 15, the Japanese Ceramics Export Federation (Dai Nippon Tōki Yushutsu Rengō) sent a message to the New York–based importers' association concerning the establishment of a company to promote the export of ceramics and porcelain, and the expansion of the export compensation system as a wartime trade measure.[31] Once these two systems were in place, the traders could continue their business activities, albeit on a limited basis. Morimura Bros. was very excited.

Meanwhile, the MB daily journal reported increased demand for Japanese ceramics in the United States, and many saw this as an opportunity to expand their business. For example, on February 27, it reported,

> Employees Hendricks and Lauterback returned from a business trip. The increase in the munitions industry in the South has more than made up for the decrease in cotton and wheat exports. The anti-Japanese mood was widely reported in the newspapers, but actually little was observed in the trading, and the people were trying their best to make emergency provisions for the shortage of goods.[32]

On March 18, the company was holding back on purchases out of concern for the prevailing situation, but significant customers such as Macy's, the May Company, Abraham & Straus, and Rothschild were experiencing shortages and were increasingly demanding autumn deliveries. The company was doing its best to allocate the necessary amount to prevent the oversupply of orders, but some customers were reluctant to accept the quotas. Considering past goodwill and future repercussions, the company had no choice but to accept the requests.[33] At the time, the war had already begun in Europe, so a military boom was underway, and the market was generally short of goods, so the products sold well.

The only concern was that the United States government might freeze Japan's funds at any moment, and since it had frozen the funds of Denmark and Norway in April 1941 and those of Germany and Italy in June of the same year, it was thought that Japan would be next. If the funds were frozen, no matter how much Morimura Bros. sold, it would not be able to remit money to Japan, so it would have to clear out its inventory in the United States as quickly as possible and remit the sales proceeds to the head office in Tokyo, and it would have to do its best to swiftly take back its US inventory in Nagoya to the US and redeem it for cash.

In addition, a special arrangement was made as an exception to Japan's foreign exchange control order; Morimura Bros. deposited the foreign exchange funds at the Yokohama branch of the Yokohama Specie Bank, to which it would transfer the funds up to the last possible penny. In case of a shortage of funds in New York, it would draw on them, so that in the event of a sudden freeze, it had every precaution in place to minimize the amount of cash that would have been seized by the United States.[34]

Although Morimura Bros. knew this in theory, there were strong voices on the ground saying,

Even though the situation has not changed, we are convinced that our efforts in business are worthwhile, and we do not doubt that it is time for Japan and the US to join forces and push forward together.[35]

Furthermore, imports from the United Kingdom began to decline. In addition, the US manufacturing industries had a discussion and decided to limit domestic private-sector demand and channel excess production capacity into the military industries.[36]

By 1941, it was certain that the import of ceramics from the United Kingdom to the United States market would not increase much due to the decline in UK domestic production capacity. The situation in the US was dependent on Japan, as its own supply capacity declined; in March 1941, the US supply, including the supply of finished goods, dropped by 8 percent. A survey of the state of porcelain production in the United States revealed that although the quality of US-made porcelain was good, production was not growing due to a shortage of labor.[37] The British wanted to increase their porcelain exports in order to earn dollars, but the rising cost of production was contributing to an increasingly inflationary trend. Although it was necessary to consider Japan as an enemy, since Japanese families in the local area were ready to pack up and leave, it was hard for salespeople to overlook the immediate supply shortage. Shortages were expected to continue and the environment to be favorable in 1941. The only concern was the threat of instability in diplomatic relations between the United States and Japan. A report explained that "women had almost no antipathy against Japanese products," making the MB staff gasp over the lost business opportunity.[38]

However, the situation on the US West Coast was different. According to the MB daily journal dated March 31–April 4, the Los Angeles store reported strong anti–Japanese product sentiment, especially since February, to the extent that pickets appeared in front of a Japanese store called Oriental in Hollywood.[39] Donations to China were also said to be flocking in. From April 5 to 11, the remaining Morimura Bros. funds in the United States were running low due to the remittance-first policy of immediately remitting sales proceeds, and the company was beginning to feel a limit to its business.

At that time, as reported by the *Journal of Commerce in New York* on April 10, the United States import licensing system had made it impossible to send munitions to Germany and Italy for British aid since more than half of the goods imported from the United States were now subject to the licensing system. The import permit system prevented the flow of dollar funds generated by imports to both Germany and Italy.[40]

Against this backdrop, Morimura Bros. was not too concerned, saying, "As long as Japan does not get any closer to Germany and Italy than it is now, it is not a problem."[41] However, the grave problems caused by the funds shortage, coupled with the reduction of cargo ships, were expanding for the company. The number of merchant vessels traveling between Japan and the United States also declined in 1941, and shipowners began to suspend their operations.[42] However, the boom in US industry, on the back of the massive defense program and reduced imports from continental Europe, resulted in a chronic shortage of goods. On May 3, the business section of the *New York Times* carried an article reporting that domestic demand had increased so dramatically that supplies could not keep up and deliveries were being delayed. In the US, a movement to help the United Kingdom by buying British products was gaining momentum. On June 22, it was announced that a price control order would be issued within three weeks. The outbreak of war between Germany and the Soviet Union made the situation even more fluid. However, US policy toward Japan continued to be hard-line. On July 9, Nakayama in Tokyo reported, "The recent rapid changes in the domestic and international situation are not very pleasing, and I am very worried."[43] He also received a telegram stating, "I can't get the shipment out of the port."[44]

## Section 2. From the Funds Freeze to the Outbreak of the Pacific War

In late July 1941, Japanese forces entered the southern part of French Indochina (present-day Vietnam). As a retaliatory measure, the US government froze Japanese assets in the US on July 26. The implementation of the fund freezing order had consequences on the freezing of assets and trade relations. Trade was placed under the control of the United States government. Japan responded by freezing British and US assets in the Japanese territories and occupied areas; as a result, the two countries lost the ways to settle bilateral trade, and commerce came to a halt. As of that day, remittances to the Tokyo head office were completely cut off.[45] Furthermore, after the *Heian Maru* arrived at the Seattle port on July 29, all imports from Japan were stopped, and Morimura Bros. in New York fell into an isolated and helpless situation.

The US government adopted strict measures to enforce asset freezing. Two government officials came to the MB office to check all the ledgers and sales slips every day.[46] They put these documents and the remaining cash into a safe in the evening and sealed it. The next morning, they came to the office at the same time as the Morimura employees to unseal the safe and take out the documents and cash. Unlike during normal conditions, MB was required to renew the license twice a month and to prepare a chart showing detailed expenses compared to the previous year's figures. They were also required to explain discrepancies between the budget and the actual expenditures. Money was neither allowed to be remitted to Japan nor to be diverted to other purposes in the United States. Therefore, Mizuno took the step of closing the Los Angeles store. The Los Angeles branch had been newly established two years earlier in anticipation of the future development of business along the Pacific coast, and Endō Yoshio was in charge of it; however, it still needed to develop fully, and Mizuno determined it would become a burden on Morimura Bros. during the challenging period when the fund-freezing order was issued.[47]

The second thing MB did was to return the Japanese employees and their families to Japan as soon as possible. On September 10, the *President Taylor* departed San Francisco and returned Yoshimoto Umezō, Kōshima Shigeo, Nagai Sukisaburō, and their families. On November 2, the *Tatsuta Maru* departed San Francisco and returned to Japan with Ueno Mareo and his family, Koike Eiji, Takema Yukio and his family, Endō Yoshio and his family, and Matsui Toshio, along with Mizuno's family.[48]

It took until November to get the second group to Japan because no suitable ship was available; Ueno Mareo's family had to wait for more than a month for a ship in Los Angeles, even though they left New York early. Despite the warnings from the head office in Tokyo and Nippon Tōki executives to return home as soon as possible, Mizuno was unwilling to abandon MB midway, given the company's history. Besides, trust had developed between the American and Japanese employees. Even when the situation deteriorated, relationships remained strong, and Mizuno was determined to stay on until the end, as he was not willing to let the American employees lose their jobs. The department stores and other business partners welcomed Mizuno's decision. They purchased the company's goods, saying that Morimura Bros. was the only firm that would take a risk and continue to provide service in a time of crisis. Out of a sense of duty to its loyal customers, MB could not say they would close the store early.[49]

Ultimately, Mizuno, Maenami Yōnosuke, and Katō Kōji stayed behind to handle the accounting and other administrative work. Maenami Yōnosuke's family did not return at his request because his relatives were living in Leonia, New Jersey. The end of the fiscal year of 1941 was approaching. However, Maenami and Katō decided to make a provisional settlement of accounts at the end of November, since it was thought that the war might start by the end of December.

If the war did not begin until the end of December and business could continue, the balance for December could be added up to make the end-of-the-fiscal-year settlement of accounts.[50]

Mizuno was also concerned that he would not be able to provide retirement benefits and year-end bonuses to his many American employees if war broke out and all of MB's assets were seized by the US government. Mizuno consulted with his lawyer and executed an escrow agreement with Chase National Bank to ensure that, in the event of war, the necessary funds would leave the hands of Morimura Bros. and go to the employees. The contract was executed.[51]

At the outbreak of war on December 7, 1941, all the MB assets were seized by the Alien Property Division, but the American employees received the severance pay and year-end bonuses in full, for which they were deeply grateful; Mizuno often received messages about it while he was in camp.[52]

On July 25, after the MB store had closed, Mizuno, Maenami, Katō, and Ueno sent a telegram to the head office stating that the order to freeze funds for Japan had finally been issued and would be enforced from July 26. Then, on the morning of July 28, all store employees gathered for instruction from manager Mizuno.

We have a glorious history of 60 years. We have been trusted by all quarters. At this time, I am taking all possible measures and have applied for permission from the authorities. We are taking all possible measures regarding employee salaries and other matters, so please do not be misled by rumors and speculation and devote yourselves to the work you are doing.[53]

Mizuno's message alleviated the employees' fears, and they felt they could begin their work as usual. Customers wrote to the company with sympathetic letters, asking if there was any way they could purchase products. On October 18, 1941, the Konoe Cabinet fell, and the Tōjō Cabinet was formed, leading Mizuno to prepare for the outbreak of the war. At the time, Morimura Bros. employed more than fifty Americans in New York, including Charles Kaiser, David Walker, and C. A. Hitchcock, many of whom had been with the company for twenty to thirty years. The company announced that thirty of these

employees would be laid off at the end of November, and all severance pay and year-end bonuses were calculated in accordance with
the company's rules and regulations. Usually, he would have given
them cash at that time, but since the funds were frozen, he only gave
them certificates, and immediately applied for approval from the US
government.[54]

For the remaining twenty employees, the company announced ten
would be laid off at the end of January of the following year and another ten at the end of February, according to their work assignments,
and he sought their agreement. He also explained that an escrow agreement had been finalized with the bank to pay its bills even if war broke
out and the company's funds were seized. Mizuno asked the employees
to remain calm and work until the end of the month.[55] The employees
understood that it was unavoidable due to the war, and none of them
wanted to leave MB, but rather, they were very supportive of Mizuno's
position and worked hard.

On November 27, 1941, executives from major companies based
in New York were summoned to the consulate, where Consul General
Morishima said,

> There is little hope for peace. On December 16, the *Tatsuta Maru*
> was scheduled to set sail from Los Angeles again, but probably for
> the last time. So those who are able to return to Japan should do so
> on this ship.[56]

After Mizuno returned to the office, John M. Geary asked him to attend a party at the Hotel Taft, to celebrate the thirty people who would
be leaving the company at the end of March and for the remaining
twenty people to bid their last farewells. Mizuno was scheduled to
have an important phone call with the Tokyo head office that evening,
but Geary insisted that he attend the party, so Mizuno left the office
at 6:30 p.m. and went to the Hotel Taft. At the hotel, a dining room
was rented out and decorated with flowers, and about fifty people
were seated at the table, including Hitchcock, Geary, J. S. Lauterback,
Gillen, Maenami, Katō, Schriber (who had left the company the prior
year), and the thirty people who had already been dismissed. Even
two examiners from the US government, who had been tormenting

Mizuno and his colleagues every day with money transfers and other problems, were seated at the top as guests of honor, waiting for Mizuno's arrival.

Mizuno said,

I cannot thank you enough for the cooperation you have given to MB and the sympathy you have shown me. Many of you have grown up at MB and know the good and bad days well. I had the misfortune of being entrusted with MB at the height of the storm, and despite having many difficulties, I was most fortunate to have such faithful friends as you. It is with unbearable sadness that I must leave you now, but I do not think that the war will last long. When the day of peace returns and we are able to do business again, please come back and help reopen this business.[57]

After the party, Mizuno returned to the MB office to a round of friendly applause. He talked to the head office at eight o'clock in the evening in New York (ten in the morning in Tokyo). At the head office, Morimura Ichizaemon VI, Ōkura Kazuchika, Yamawaki Masayoshi, and other executives answered the phone one after another to console Mizuno. In New York, Arai Yoneo clearly explained over the phone that he was prepared to help Morimura Bros. on Mizuno's behalf in the event of an emergency. Finally, Morimura Ichizaemon, the chairman, said "I trust you" to Mizuno in English.[58]

It was a sunny Sunday in New York when the Imperial Japanese Navy attacked Pearl Harbor in Hawai'i on December 7, although the clock in Japan showed 3:50 a.m. on December 8, 1941. On that day, at St. John the Divine Cathedral in New York, where the cornerstone ceremony was held in 1925 and the interior structure had been largely completed, the first Holy Communion service was to be held. Presiding Bishop Rt. Rev. Henry St. George Tucker was to officiate, and Mizuno and other members of the Anglican Church of Japan living in New York attended the ceremony.

After the sacramental service, Mizuno went to Long Island to visit an acquaintance, drove for about three hours, and returned home around 5 p.m. without knowing what was happening. The war started at 7:50 a.m. Hawai'i time, or 1:50 p.m. in New York.

New York Mayor Fiorello La Guardia told the Japanese not to step foot outside the door.

The question arose as to how to close Morimura Bros. Mizuno called the police, who had already dispatched officers to the front of the MB store and ordered him to put away the Japanese products immediately because it was undesirable to have Japanese goods on display where they could be seen from the street. Mizuno called Hitchcock, who immediately went to the company with another Morimura Bros. employee, named Glascow, and, with the help of the police, cleared out the show window during the night. The employees called him frequently. Mizuno did not feel that his surroundings were in any danger, and he felt at ease, thinking that what was expected to come actually came.

However, around 11 p.m., three FBI agents came and woke him up, and without giving him a chance to explain, Mizuno was taken to Ellis Island, where he was confined.[59] During the next five days, dozens of Japanese were transported to the island, and about 270 people, mostly from Japanese trading companies and banks in New York, were incarcerated. Maenami was taken to Ellis Island on December 8 and Katō on December 11. Given the outlook of prolonged war, Mizuno started worrying about what would happen in the future. During this period, Irving Bossawick, a certified public accountant, came to Ellis Island almost every week for correspondence, and completed all the necessary procedures for the liquidation of Morimura Bros. and to secure severance payments and year-end bonuses for its American employees.[60]

Hearings began on December 23, and the parties were summoned to the New York court to be judged. Meanwhile, in New York, about two and a half months after the outbreak of war, on February 26, when Mizuno and the others were at Camp Upton, permission was granted for the liquidation of Morimura Bros., and under the supervision of the US government, Arai, Bossawick, and Robert Hiroshi Furudera, with the cooperation of several employees, took the lead. The company hurried to liquidate its inventory, prepare financial statements, and complete a balance sheet and profit-and-loss statement as of the end of 1941.

Since the financial statements were completed quickly and it was clear that Morimura Bros. did not owe any debts in the United States, the US government allowed the payment of retirement benefits and year-end bonuses to the American employees much earlier than it did for other companies. This speedy financial-statement preparation was, of course, due in large part to Arai, Bossawick, and Furudera, but also because Maenami and Katō had prepared a provisional settlement of accounts for the end of November in anticipation of the outbreak of the war.

Mizuno organized a financial report based on this balance sheet on board an exchange ship on his way back to Japan. He handed it to President Morimura Yoshiyuki when he landed in Yokohama. A copy of this balance sheet clearly shows that the net assets of Morimura Bros. seized by the US government due to the war totaled $426,000 in the head office account alone. This amount had not changed much over the next four months, even at the end of April 1942, when the inventory of goods and other items had been further reduced. When the settlement was almost complete, the head office account had approximately $430,000—the officially approved external assets of Morimura Gumi left as an enemy asset in the United States.[61] In addition, Morimura Bros. had a fund called the MB Employees Benefit Fund, which had been set aside for the benefits of employees since 1920. This fund was wholly separate from the company's operating funds. It was entrusted to US citizens such as Arai and Bossawick at the beginning of the war, so it was not confiscated by the government. Its asset value was about $60,000 in 1960.[62]

## Conclusion

The purpose of this paper was to elucidate the crisis management of the company and its view of Japan-US relations by analyzing how Morimura Bros., which had been involved in Japan-US trade in New York since 1876, responded before and after the outbreak of the Pacific War in 1940–1941. In addition, it attempted to provide a new perspective on the study of the outbreak of the Pacific War.

First, let us consider this from a micro perspective of corporate crisis management in the United States. The Morimura Group decided immediately after the finalization of the Tripartite Pact in September 1940 to withdraw from the United States in anticipation of the outbreak of a Pacific War, and consistently adhered to the policy set forth until the outbreak of war. The Morimura Group's response to crisis management was well defined, demonstrating its excellent management. The relationship of trust between the head office and New York store manager Mizuno was also well established. As frequently mentioned in the MB daily journal, Morimura Bros. observed a great potential opportunity to expand the market share as the war in Europe intensified, domestic production in the United States was prioritized in favor of military needs, and the ceramics market was short of goods. However, it maintained its central principle. This policy should be valued highly.[63]

The company's human resources measures were meticulous. While comparable Japanese companies operating in the United States during this time dealt with the safety of their Japanese employees and their families, it is surprising that Morimura Bros. signed an escrow agreement with a trust bank to provide severance pay and bonuses to locally hired American employees. It even hired an American attorney of Japanese descent more than a year before the outbreak of war to handle the company's liquidation after the Japanese expatriates had left the United States or been detained. Moreover, it is surprising that they were preparing for the company's liquidation more than a year before the outbreak of war. Observing the experience of German and Austrian companies in the US that had their assets frozen in New York during World War I helped.

Second, I consider a macro perspective of the relationship between Japan and the United States and the outbreak of the Pacific War. The author of this chapter has long questioned why the business community could not help stopping the outbreak of the war. This study clarified some of the reasons. First, the business community had yet to truly understand what total war was all about, even though World War I had entirely changed the conventional form of warfare to total war. The companies and people in business in the United States, especially those stationed in New York, were well aware of how much stronger the US economy was than Japan's. In addition, they were mindful of the United States' hard line against Germany and Italy. Nonetheless, they believed war between the United States and Japan was inevitable due to that hard line, as well as the Tripartite Pact.

However, it was thought it would be an even match if the United States and Japan were to engage in a naval confrontation in the Asia-Pacific region. Since the United States' main forces would be directed toward Europe and the Atlantic, it was believed that the US and Japan sooner or later would restore peace or sign an armistice. Therefore, the response of the Morimura Bros. was based on the premise that the war would last only one or two years, after which they would resume business in the US again. As Mizuno recounts in "Kaisen tōji no omoide" (Memories of the outbreak of the war), the Pacific War could not have been expected to last four years, ending with Japan's unconditional surrender.[64] In this sense, the business community was fundamentally optimistic about the Japan-US relationship and American sentiment toward Japan.

As for future research agendas, confirming the whereabouts of the Morimura Bros. materials is desirable. After that, I want to gradually unveil Japanese companies' sales and information activities in the United States.

## Notes

In preparing this manuscript, I thank Tomohiko Mizuno and Robert Furudera, who agreed to be interviewed. I am also grateful to Mr. Ikuo Fukunaga, general manager of historical records and public relations at Morimura Bros., and Akifumi Nosaka, managing director of Morimura Toyoakikai, for their advice.

1. The recent studies include Ōishi Kaichirō, ed., *Senkanki Nihon no taigai keizai kankei* (Tokyo: Nihon Keizai Hyōronsha, 1992), and Peter Duus, "Nihon menbōsekigyō to Chūgoku – keizai teikoku shugi no hitotsu no kēsu sutadī," in *Senkanki no Nihon keizai bunseki*, ed. Nakamura Takafusa (Tokyo: Yamakawa Shuppansha, 1981), 189–216.

2. Kawabe Nobuo, *Sōgō shōsha no kenkyū: Senzen Mitsubishi Shōji no zaibei katsudō* (Tokyo: Jikkyō Shuppan, 1982) is an exemplary study, which made full use of the Records of the Office of Alien Property: World War II Seized Corporate Record Group No. 131.

3. Although the following publications explain the detailed process leading up to the outbreak of the Pacific War, they mention only a tiny amount of the economic activities: Nihon Kokusai Seiji Gakkai [The Japan Association of International Relations], Taiheiyō Sensō Gen'in Kenkyūbu, *Taiheiyō Sensō e no michi*, vols. 1–7 (Tokyo: Asahi Shinbunsha, 1963); Hosoya Chihiro, *Ryō taisenkan no Nihon gaikō: 1914–1945* (Tokyo: Iwanami Shoten, 1988); Hosoya Chihiro, Honma Nagayo, Irie Akira, and Hatano Sumio, eds., *Taiheiyō Sensō = the Pacific War* (Tokyo: Tōkyō Daigaku Shuppankai, 1993); and Sudō Shinji, *Nichi-Bei kaisen gaikō no kenkyū: Nichi-Bei kōshō no hottan kara Haru nōto made* (Tokyo: Keiō Tsūshin, 1986). See also Ueyama Kazuo, "Nichi-Bei tsūshō kōkai jōyaku no haki," in *Tairitsu to dakyō: 1930-nendai no Nichi-Bei tsūshō kankei*, eds. Ueyama Kazuo and Sakata Yasuo (Tokyo: Daiichi Hōki, 1994), 309–46, as an exemplary paper. It uses historical documents of Japanese companies in the United States at the time to explain in detail the perception gap between the Japanese Ministry of Foreign Affairs and

businessmen in the US over the abandonment of the Japan-US Treaty of Commerce and Navigation.

4. All the assets of Morimura Bros. were confiscated by the United States as enemy property following the outbreak of the US-Japan war on December 7, 1941. It is assumed that the company's documents and materials since its founding in 1876 were included in these confiscated assets. Still, such papers have not been found in the National Archives collections. For this reason, the records of Morimura Bros. are based on Daiyamondosha, ed., *Morimura hyakunenshi* (Tokyo: Daiyamondosha, 1986), and Nippon Tōki Kabushiki Kaisha, ed., *Nihon tōki 70 nenshi* (Nagoya: Noritake Company, 1974). See also Morimura Eiko, *Nichi-Bei bōeki o kirihiraita otoko: Morimura Toyo no shirarezaru shōgai* (Tokyo: Tōyō Keizai Shinpōsha, 2021).

5. For the formation of the Japanese society in New York, see Mizutani Shōzō, *Nyūyōku Nihonjin hattenshi* (New York: Nyū Yōku Nihonjinkai, 1921), and Zaibei Nihonjinkai Jiseki Hozonbu, ed., *Zaibei Nihonjinshi* (San Francisco: Zaibei Nihonjinkai, 1940).

6. Throughout the chapter, some non-Japanese names are written with last name only, because the Morimura Bros. journals did not always record first names. The translator used the Morimura Bros. website (https://www.morimura.co.jp/history /colum/colum10.html) to identify the original English spellings, except for the names Van Buskirk and Hendricks, which she converted from Japanese phonetics into likely English spellings.

7. For Hinode Shōkai, see Katō Ryū, Sakata Yasuo, and Akiya Norio, eds., *Nichi-Bei kiito bōeki shiryō*, vol. 1 (Tokyo: Kondō Shuppansha, 1987) and *Nihon tōki 70 nenshi*.

8. For information on Murai, see Ōnishi Rihei, ed., *Murai Yasukata den* (Tokyo: Murai Yasukata Aikyōkai, 1943).

9. For more information on Morimura Gumi's United States strategy and Morimura Ichizaemon's management philosophy, including Morimura Bros., of the late Meiji era, see Ōmori Kazuhiro, "Meiji kōki Nihon no taibei tōjiki yushutsu to Morimura Ichizaemon no keiei rinen," *Shibusawa Kenkyū* 6 (October 1993): 3–16.

10. For more information on the so-called Morimura Group, including Morimura Gumi, Nippon Tōki, and Morimura Bros., see Daiyamondosha, *Morimura hyakunenshi*, and Nippon Tōki Kabushiki Kaisha, *Nihon tōki 70 nenshi*.

11. For the status of Morimura Bros. in the New York Japanese community, see Shōzō, *Nyūyōku Nihonjin hattenshi*; and "Zai Hokubei hōjin dantai chōsa" (Bei–10 gaishi), "Hokubei Nikkei shimin gaikyō" (Bei–7 gaishi), and "Nyūyōku chihō zaijū hōjin gaikyō" (Bei–24 gaishi), Diplomatic Archives of the Ministry of Foreign Affairs of Japan.

12. Telegram from the Tokyo head office of Morimura Gumi to Morimura Bros., October 10, 1940, Morimura papers 111.8.81, held at Noritake Company Ltd., Nagoya, Japan.

13. Telegram from Morimura Gumi to Morimura Bros., October 10, 1940.

14. Telegram from Morimura Gumi to Morimura Bros., October 10, 1940.

15. Telegram from Morimura Gumi to Morimura Bros., October 10, 1940.

16. Telephone conversation with the Tokyo head office of Morimura Gumi, October 23, 1940, Morimura papers 111.8.81.

17. Telephone conversation, October 23, 1940, Morimura papers 111.8.81.

18. Telegram from Nakayama [Takeo] of the Tokyo head office to Mizuno Tomohiko, February 13, 1941, Morimura papers 111.8.81.

19. Mizuno Tomohiko, "Kaisen tōji no omoide" (unpublished manuscript, 1975), 6.

20. *MB Shōji Nisshi*, February 11, 1941, Morimura papers 111.8.81. (All subsequent citations to *MB Shōji Nisshi* in this essay also come from Morimura papers 111.8.81.)

21. *MB Shōji Nisshi*, February 11, 1941.

22. *MB Shōji Nisshi*, February 14, 1941.

23. *MB Shōji Nisshi*, February 14, 1941.

24. *MB Shōji Nisshi*, February 15, 1941.

25. Telegram from Nakayama to Mizuno, February 13, 1941.

26. Mizuno, "Kaisen tōji no omoide," 6.

27. For the American officials and public expectations in Washington and New York regarding the arrival of Ambassador Nomura, see Morishima Morito, *Shinjuwan, Risubon, Tōkyō: Zoku ichi gaikōkan no kaisō* (Tokyo: Iwanami Shoten, 1956).

28. Mizuno, "Kaisen tōji no omoide," 6.

29. *MB Shōji Nisshi*, February 14, 1941.

30. *MB Shōji Nisshi*, February 14, 1941.

31. *MB Shōji Nisshi*, February 15, 1941.

32. *MB Shōji Nisshi*, February 17, 1941.

33. *MB Shōji Nisshi*, March 15–21, 1941.

34. The Tokyo office sent detailed instructions on the money transfers to Japan around the fall of 1940.

35. *MB Shōji Nisshi*, March 1, 1941.

36. *MB Shōji Nisshi*, March 3, 1941.

37. *MB Shōji Nisshi*, March 10–21, 1941.

38. *MB Shōji Nisshi*, March 22–28, 1941.

39. *MB Shōji Nisshi*, March 31–April 4, 1941.

40. *Journal of Commerce*, April 10, 1941.

41. *MB Shōji Nisshi*, April 5–11, 1941.

42. Detailed reports on the trend of British products appear more frequently from May 1941.

43. Telegram from Nakayama [Takeo] to Mizuno Tomohiko, July 19, 1941, Morimura papers 111.8.81.

44. Telegram from Nakayama to Mizuno, July 19, 1941.

45. The freezing of Japanese assets in the United States is thought to have had a significant impact on Japan-US relations, especially Japan's intelligence activities toward the US. Still, more research needs to be conducted on the intelligence aspect. This topic deserves further study.

46. Mizuno, "Kaisen tōji no omoide," 7.

47. Mizuno, 7.

48. Mizuno, 7.

49. Mizuno, 8.

50. Preparations had been underway since October 1940 to outsource the settlement of accounts to US citizens such as Arai Yoneo and Irving Bossawick. The subject was discussed in a telephone call from the Tokyo head office to New York in October 23, 1940.

51. Mizuno, "Kaisen tōji no omoide," 8.

52. Mizuno, 8.

53. *MB Shōji Nisshi*, July 28, 1941.

54. Mizuno, "Kaisen tōji no omoide," 8.
55. Mizuno, 8.
56. *MB Shōji Nisshi*, November 28, 1941.
57. Mizuno, "Kaisen tōji no omoide," 9.
58. Many of the leaders of the Morimura Group were on the phone, indicating the high position occupied by Morimura Bros. at that time. For a valuable testimony on the situation of the Japanese community in New York on the day of the Japanese attack on Pearl Harbor, see Fujiyama Naraichi, *Ichi seinen gaikōkan no Taiheiyō sensō: Nichi-Bei kaisen no Washinton-Berurin kanraku* (Tōkyō: Shinchōsha, 1989).
59. Mizuno, "Kaisen tōji no omoide," 14–15.
60. Mizuno, 21–22.
61. Mizuno, 17.
62. As for the fact that Morimura Bros. was able to obtain considerable information on the outbreak of war between Japan and the United States, it should not be overlooked that Morimura Yoshiyuki had been a close friend of Yamamoto Isoroku since his days as a student in the US (Robert Furudera, in discussion with the author, July 14, 1993). Further research is required.
63. Mizuno Tomohiko, in discussion with the author, March 16, 1993.
64. Mizuno, "Kaisen tōji no omoide," 9.

# CHAPTER 9

# Rupture of Diplomacy

## Japan's Path to War with the United States

*Tosh Minohara*

Japan's meandering path toward the Pacific War is often understood in the context of the so-called China problem, which stems from the Japanese incursion into Manchuria on September 18, 1931. This infamous false flag event, known as either the Manchurian or Mukden Incident, became the pretext for Japanese actions that unilaterally changed the status quo of Manchuria by incorporating it within Japan's sphere of influence six months later. The establishment of the puppet state of Manchukuo was brought about by the military actions of the Japanese Kwantung Army. However, this became a slippery slope for Japan as, faced with international condemnation and diplomatic isolation, in March 1933 it withdrew from the League of Nations—of which it was a founding member. Germany followed suit in November, along with Italy in December 1937. In this way the contours of the major Axis powers began to appear in the aftermath of the Manchurian Incident.

It should be noted that Manchuria was not viewed as part of China proper at the time. Therefore, referring to this issue as a *China* problem is a misnomer in a strict sense. Moreover, hostile action over the Manchurian Incident came to a formal closure by the Tanggu Truce (Tanku Kyōtei) of May 1933, and Japan elevated its legation in China to that of an embassy two years later. In this way, Sino-Japanese relations were on a path toward normalization, helped by the fact that Chiang Kai-shek was more concerned with defeating the Communists. That said, Japanese army officers were complicit in the Shanghai Incident of January 1932 (Daiichiji Shanhai Jihen), although this occurred without the direct involvement of, nor knowledge by, Tokyo. Later in the year, Japan itself was rocked by the May 15 Incident, which emboldened the militarists and weakened Japan's democratic institutions. But what became the watershed was the North China Buffer State Strategy (Kahoku Bunri Kōsaku), launched south of the Great Wall in May 1935, as it pushed Japan to become even more deeply involved in China militarily. It therefore can be argued that from this moment onward, the Manchurian problem did indeed become a full-fledged China problem.

In order to protect its prized possession of Manchuria, the imperial Japanese government authorized the Imperial Japanese Army (IJA) to use its China Garrison Army to secure the five provinces of northern China so that they could serve as a buffer to protect Manchuria. Once this had been achieved through various political maneuverings, Tokyo proclaimed northern China to be separate from Chiang's Nationalist government. The Japanese further reinforced the China Garrison Army in April 1936, which led to increased clashes with Chinese forces. In December of that year, the Xi'an Incident took place, during which the Comintern brokered the second United Front with the Nationalists with the aim of joining hands in defeating the Japanese. In this way, the tide was beginning to turn against the Japanese; therefore, the empire now felt pressured to act decisively. It was this sense of urgency that culminated in the outbreak of the Second Sino-Japanese War (Shina Jihen), which began with the Marco Polo Bridge Incident (Rokōkyō Jiken) of July 7, 1937.

In the end, Japan would send nearly six hundred thousand troops to China in the aftermath of this incident, which would more than double to 1.3 million by the end of the Pacific War. The Chinese met the Japanese with a staggering force of 5.5 million men, so this was undoubtedly a major war by any measure. But if there ever was a defining moment in which American policy makers lost all hope that Japan would cease its path of military expansionism, it would be the Battle of Shanghai. Before this, those in Washington still had confidence that Japan's internationalist leaders, who had guided Japan during the era of Taishō democracy, would muster their collective strength to alter Japan's course. But in the aftermath of the Battle of Shanghai, attaining a diplomatic solution now seemed all but out of reach. The China problem was front and center in the minds of many Americans, and the primary issue in East Asia became how to counter and contain Japan.

In this way, it is difficult to deny that it was Japan's actions over China that became the major point of contention between the United States and Japan. This was in stark contrast to the period from the end of the Russo-Japanese War until the Manchurian Incident, when the anti-Japanese issue in the US was the main point of friction in the bilateral relationship. Although national pride and prestige had been severely injured by the US Congress through the passage of the Immigration Act of 1924 that completely excluded the Japanese, it never became a casus belli for Japan, unlike the China problem. This was because the elite Japanese diplomats who shaped foreign policy in the 1920s were ardent realists. Thus, they were cognizant of the fact that Japan could better pursue its national interests by upholding the spirit of international cooperation as established by the Nine-Power Treaty during the 1921–1922 Washington Conference. Therefore, the decision makers in Tokyo, led by the preeminent statesman Shidehara Kijūrō, were willing to overlook the anti-Japanese issue since maintaining healthy trade relations with America was immensely much more vital to Japan. From this perspective, the Japanese immigrant problem merely became a matter of national and racial pride. In other words, it had no measurable impact on Japan's national interest. Of course, it was also true that Japan was not in a particularly strong position to take a firm stand on this issue, as it was utterly dependent on the US economically—both as a market for its goods and for oil and heavy machinery imports. In this way, trade with the United States was the very lifeblood of Japan.

But most ordinary Japanese were incapable of comprehending this high-politics view of US-Japan relations. As a result, they were upset that their leaders were not taking a more forceful stand against American racial discrimination. From their view, it was clearly a slight upon a nation that had striven to modernize and that had finally obtained the status of a Big Five power amid the end of World War I. Although Japan had emerged as a global power, it felt that it was not being accorded the treatment of an equal partner.

As the racial equality clause was rejected during the Paris Peace Conference, Japanese immigrants in California had to endure even harsher measures through the 1920 Alien Land Law, which closed many of the loopholes that still allowed for landownership by Japanese after the 1913 Alien Land Law. Two years later, in the United States Supreme Court case *Takao Ozawa v. United States*, those of Japanese ancestry were deemed "aliens ineligible to citizenship" by the court, as Japanese were not "free white persons," or those of the Caucasian race.[1] On the same day, the US Supreme Court also ruled on *Yamashita v. Hinkle*, which upheld the constitutionality of the alien land law of the state of Washington that was based on race.[2] In the following year, the US Supreme Court gave its ruling on *Webb v. O'Brien*, which upheld the ban on sharecropping contracts by the California Alien Land Law.[3]

In this way, the Japanese in the United States were being treated unfairly by the highest court, but those in Japan did not react vehemently until the passage of the Immigration Act of 1924 by Congress. This was the moment that many in Japan became disillusioned with America and its self-serving version of democracy. Pro-American opinion leaders in Japan who had embraced Wilsonianism, such as Yoshino Sakuzō and Nitobe Inazō, were also now largely discredited. In their place, many Japanese began to turn their ears toward the right-wing hardliners and the militarists who had for years warned that Americans were hypocrites and that they looked down on the Japanese.

Even within the ranks of Japan's foreign ministry, or Gaimushō, a new generation of Japanese diplomats were so stunned by the behavior of a nation that they felt would always act fairly that they now began advocating for Japan to leave the West and reenter Asia (*Datsuō nyūa*). In other words, this was a reversal of Japan's prior path of leaving Asia and entering the West, summed up by the term *Datsua nyūō*, which had gained popularity in Japan in the late nineteenth century.[4] These new Asianists in the Gaimushō felt that the United States no longer could be trusted, and therefore aspired to redirect Japan's foreign policy toward the Asian continent, or *Ajia kaiki* ("return to Asia"), as they called it.[5]

This view coincided neatly with the impulses of Japan's militarists, who wanted to gain further possessions in China; since the Great Depression and the passage of the Smoot-Hawley Tariff Act in the United States, global trade was being stymied, and Japan, with its small geographic area, was placed at a distinct disadvantage because its empire did not span the globe like Britain's or France's, nor was it a large continental behemoth like the United States. It was believed that Japan needed to expand its sphere of influence and establish a yen bloc for it to survive in a world in which each nation was actively pursuing its own narrow national interests for the sake of economic survival. Furthermore, since Japanese immigration into the Americas was largely prohibited—Canada and Latin American countries like Brazil enacted their own anti–Japanese immigration legislation soon after the United States did—Japan was hard-pressed to find a way to alleviate its population explosion. Naturally, its large neighbor, China, came to be viewed as an ideal place for people to emigrate.

From this, it can be seen that the immigration problem was not overtaken by the China problem but rather that the two problems had merged. Of course, it cannot be denied that the China problem greatly overshadowed the immigration problem as the latter issue gradually faded into the backdrop. As a consequence, the China problem now became the core issue that would shape the course of relations between the United States and Japan.

But the focal point of this essay will not be the history of this bilateral relationship from the perspective of the China problem. Rather, it will closely examine why diplomacy ultimately failed in 1941, prompting Japan to go to war against the United States. As we witness the current war in Ukraine, it will be the task of the future historian to ascertain the chain of key decisions that led to the Russian invasion. In a similar vein, this essay will attempt to determine where the actual point of no return was for Japan from the perspective of diplomacy.

Although many view the attack on Pearl Harbor as the precise moment when Japan crossed the Rubicon, this understanding arises from a military perspective. From a diplomatic perspective, the true crossing point occurred the very moment that Japan's leaders had given up on peace. It was only then that the baton was passed to the military. In other words, it was the rupture of diplomacy that paved the path to Pearl Harbor. Hence, despite the Manchurian Incident, the Second Sino-Japanese War, the signing of the Tripartite Pact, and Japan's advance into southern French Indochina—which all represented pivotal moments of Japanese militarism—there was still much distance from a decision to go to war against the United States. With this in mind, this essay will argue that the prewar terminus of US-Japan relations can be pinpointed to the very moment that Japan's top diplomat, Foreign Minister Tōgō Shigenori, lost all hope for peace and reached the fateful conclusion that Japan had no choice but to rise and fight the United States to ensure its own national survival.

## Rupture of Diplomacy

The following passage from the memoirs of Tōgō Shigenori vividly reveals the enormity of the shock that the foreign minister had felt upon reading the diplomatic cable that had just arrived from the Japanese ambassador in Washington, DC, Admiral Nomura Kichisaburō.

> I was shocked to the point that I was blinded by utter disbelief. . . .
> In the end, [the United States] completely disregarded the many years of sacrifice made by Japan, forcing us to forgo the great nation status that we had striven so hard to establish in the Far East. To do so for Japan was tantamount to suicide. *We had no choice but to rise.* [italics mine][6]

As an addendum to this telegram was a note from the secretary of state, Cordell Hull, that rejected outright the latest Japanese proposal—*Otsuan* (Plan B)—which embodied Foreign Minister Tōgō's final attempt at resolving the US-Japan standoff so that war could be averted.[7] It was almost impossible not to notice the message being conveyed to Japan's leaders in the so-called Hull Note. The ball was now in Japan's court, and it needed to take the initiative and withdraw its troops from China.[8] Only then would Washington consider lifting the trade embargo that was constricting Japan. In essence, this was merely a restatement of the original Four Principles first presented by Hull at the beginning of the US-Japan talks in the spring of 1941.[9]

With this one diplomatic note of November 26, 1941, Tōgō completely lost faith that the impasse with the United States could be resolved. The significance of this was that Japan lost a leading figure in the Tōjō Hideki cabinet who steadfastly opposed war with the United States. In other words, the moment Tōgō gave up on peace, the final obstacle for Japan's path to war had been removed. It would now be the hard-liners who would dictate Japan's future course.

To be sure, Tōgō was never a pacifist. As a veteran diplomat, he was first and foremost a realist who sought to pursue diplomacy that would preserve Japan's national interests.[10] It was this firm belief that made Tōgō a staunch opponent of war with the United States, for he could not foresee any possibility of a Japanese victory over a much larger and more powerful nation. The US surpassed Japan in all economic indices, and it was this overwhelming economic might that would eventually support its enormous military production during the war. Although Japan's military prowess had undeniably increased, there was still no comparison to the real American potential in a wartime mode.

Naturally, this stark reality in national strength begs the question: Why did Tōgō fatefully conclude that Japan had "no choice but to rise"? As a realist he was clearly cognizant that Japan would be forced into fighting an unwinnable war. Then, was his decision based on the assumption, as many Japanese historians claim, that the Hull Note essentially amounted to an American ultimatum?[11] In other words, since the secretary of state had rejected outright Japan's compromise plan, the foreign minister could then only reasonably conclude that Washington had already committed itself to war. As a result, Tōgō had no hand to play but to support a war that he had sought so hard to avoid.

But this interpretation is deeply flawed, as it does not take into consideration the fact that Tōgō had never imagined from the outset that Washington would accept his diplomatic proposal in its totality. As a matter of fact, the foreign minister was not only expecting, but eager, to continue the diplomatic talks, as war was an outcome to be avoided. It should also not be overlooked that Tōgō had one more powerful card up his sleeve to slow down the hard-liners in their push for war. He could always resign from his position and force the prime minister to appoint a new foreign minister. Of course, since he was a civilian cabinet member, he lacked the ability to collapse the government by refusing to name a successor. This was a favorite tactic wielded by the IJA to quash cabinets that it felt were not toeing the line. This was possible because only active military officers could be appointed to the position of minister of the army or navy.

The foreign minister's position, as it was the head of a civilian organization, was not bound to such restrictions, so anyone could be nominated. Yet, as a member of the Goshō Kaigi (Five Ministers Meeting), the position was of paramount importance, and it was unforeseeable that Japan would make the decision to go to war without first appointing a new foreign minister. This meant that at the crucial juncture where Japan was at the precipice of war, Tōgō possessed a much greater political leverage than he otherwise would have. Thus, by resigning, at the very minimum, he would have been able to gain valuable time for diplomacy to continue while also extricating himself from the responsibility of going to war.[12]

Coincidentally, it was also on November 26 that the combined fleet of the Imperial Japanese Navy (IJN), on its mission to attack Pearl Harbor, had left Kasatka (Hitokappu) Bay. It would seem very unlikely that Tokyo would have decided to go to war with the United States with its cabinet position of foreign minister left vacant. However, since the new foreign minister would clearly be a member of a cabinet that would be going to war, it would be unfathomable that the emperor would approve this nomination lest he become culpable for the responsibility of the decision to go to war. A much more likely scenario is one where Prime Minister Tōjō pleads with Tōgō to reconsider his resignation, by which he could put himself in a position to gain more concessions from the government.

Of course, one needs to be attentive to the military situation as well. It is implausible to believe that the combined fleet would have anchored somewhere in the North Pacific while the government frantically scrambled to find someone who could fill the seat of foreign minister. In all probability, the attack on Pearl Harbor would have been called off, which in turn would have allowed more time to pursue diplomacy. Despite this, Tōgō ultimately not only decided to terminate the diplomatic talks but also chose to remain in the war cabinet. Furthermore, he expressed his utter dismay and contempt over the Hull Note. His emotion-laden words written in his memoirs indicate an individual who felt not only stunned but also betrayed by the note. Could it be that Tōgō was expecting an altogether different reply from Hull? But where there can be no doubt is that upon receiving the Hull Note, Tōgō did a complete volte-face.[13] This was a metamorphosis of the foreign minister who had hitherto striven for attaining peace, and was now defiantly proclaiming that it was "time to rise."

## Fighting Fire with Fire: The Tōjō Cabinet

It was a mere five weeks earlier that Tōgō had been tapped to become the next foreign minister in the newly formed cabinet of Prime Minister Tōjō Hideki.[14] The previous Konoe Fumimaro cabinet had been unsuccessful in breaking the impasse with the United States and paving the path to peace. By this time, Japanese assets in the US were frozen, and a complete oil embargo had been enforced since August 1, 1941. Facing such a dire situation, Prime Minister Konoe, partially out of desperation, had reached out to President Franklin D. Roosevelt with the hope of holding a bilateral summit meeting where he would attempt to directly resolve the crisis. But this was ultimately rejected by the president upon the advice of Secretary of State Hull. A despondent Konoe, also hobbled by the embarrassing arrest of Soviet spy Richard Sorge in Japan—the so-called Sorge Incident—had lost the political will to continue as prime minister. He thus abruptly resigned at an extremely critical juncture in the US-Japan diplomatic talks.[15]

As the situation with the United States was getting worse by the day, it was first decided that Japan would resort to the unprecedented measure of bringing in a member of the imperial family, Higashikuni Naruhiko, as the next prime minister.[16] But Kido Kōichi, the Lord Keeper of the Privy Seal, was staunchly opposed on the grounds that it was unwise to expose the imperial family to a position of political responsibility during a diplomatic crisis with the US. Kido's logic was that in the event that war ensued under Higashikuni, the emperor would have to shoulder part of the blame.[17] This would in turn not only tarnish the image of the imperial court but also wound the legitimacy of imperial rule.[18] Moreover, how could a living deity ever be held accountable? Unfortunately for Japan, at a crucial juncture when the fate of the nation was at stake, Kido's decision was solely driven by the instincts of self-preservation for the institution in which he was a stakeholder.

Once the plan to have an imperial member lead the government had failed, out of desperation, the elder statesmen of Japan were forced to play an even riskier hand. They would ask General Tōjō to become the next prime minister. Tōjō had been a war minister who steadfastly toed the IJA line in the Konoe Cabinet. As a matter of fact, it was his uncompromising and hawkish attitude that had led to a complete paralysis and eventual collapse of that cabinet.[19] Undoubtedly, this was a risky political maneuver, akin to fighting fire with fire. But there was one aspect of Tōjō that they felt could work in their favor. He revered the emperor, and thus it was hoped that he would be willing to rein in the hard-liners in the military and allow peace to prevail like the emperor himself wanted.[20]

The formation of the Tōjō Cabinet initially alarmed the United States. Upon learning that Tōjō had been chosen to lead the next Japanese government, President Roosevelt was concerned that control of the civilian government had now been usurped by the IJA.[21] Surprisingly, it appears that no one in Japan at that time seriously considered how this move could be interpreted by Washington. Fortunately for the elder statesmen, Prime Minister Tōjō did not act in the same manner as War Minister Tōjō had in the previous cabinet. In what historians in Japan refer to as the *Tōjō hensetsu*, or "Tōjō volte-face," upon coming to the helm of Japanese political leadership, he had quickly toned down his hawkish attitude toward the US. One explanation behind this change was that Tōjō, as prime minister of Japan, was no longer only representing the interests of the IJA. But a more plausible reason was that Tōjō had been personally requested by the emperor not only to circumvent war with the United States but also to seek a diplomatic solution to the present crisis. Possessing a keen sense of respect toward the emperor—after all, he would ultimately sacrifice his own life rather than incriminate the emperor during the Tokyo war crimes tribunals in the aftermath of the war—Tōjō endeavored to do just that.[22]

The new prime minister wasted no time in redirecting Japan's sails toward less turbulent waters. As such, he swiftly reversed the imperial edict of September 6, 1941, that had called for immediate war preparations, followed by war against the United States, United Kingdom, and the Netherlands by early October in the event that there was no breakthrough in the ongoing US-Japan talks.[23] Reversing this edict, officially known as the Imperial Policy Execution Outline, would have amounted to political suicide had it not been for Tōjō's firm control over the IJA. Thus, with one bold move, Japan could once again place diplomacy at center stage.

Tōjō was also keenly aware that he needed to alleviate the fears and suspicions that both President Roosevelt and Secretary of State Hull held toward the new leader in Japan. Therefore, Tōjō strove to reshape his former image by showing his eagerness to break the impasse with Washington. Another crucial piece of messaging was achieved by appointing a foreign minister who was not a hawk. This was how Tōgō came into the fold, as he was a highly regarded career diplomat. Furthermore, by this time Tōgō was one of a few remaining internationalists within the Gaimushō, which had undergone significant personnel changes under the nationalistic foreign minister Matsuoka Yōsuke.[24]

Tōgō was a vocal opponent of the Tripartite Pact and felt strongly that Japan's place in world affairs should be firmly among the Anglo-American camp. He also espoused the belief that entering into an alliance with Germany would only serve to further alienate both America and Britain from Japan.[25] These views contributed to Matsuoka's resentment of Tōgō as well as to the reasons why the foreign minister had recalled Tōgō as ambassador from Moscow. But Tōgō refused to go away and stubbornly remained in the foreign service out of the limelight.[26] In the end, it was this firm conviction in support of internationalism that made Tōgō stand out as the ideal candidate for foreign minister in the Tōjō Cabinet; in many ways Tōgō was the antithesis of Tōjō.

When the new prime minister first approached Tōgō about joining the cabinet, his first reaction was to decline, as it was evident that the task at hand would be an onerous one with extremely high stakes.[27] But Tōgō was also a patriot and thus felt a strong sense of duty that he needed to reorient Japan's foreign policy, which was currently on a collision course with the United States. Torn between his sense of duty and his disdain of Tōjō, he informed the prime minister that he would only accept the top diplomat position if the following three conditions were adhered to.[28] First, the new government had to agree that avoiding war with the United States would be its utmost priority. As such, the foreign minister would be given a free hand in pursuing any and all diplomatic channels. Second, the navy minister could not be a hard-liner.[29] In other words, the new navy minister would be chosen upon the advice of and consultation with Tōgō. And third, the foreign minister would be allowed to reorganize the Gaimushō. What Tōgō had in mind was the sacking of any pro-Nazi and other *kakushin* (progressive) diplomats from key positions within the foreign ministry.[30]

Lacking any other qualified candidate who even came close to his caliber, Tōjō had no viable choice but to accept the conditions set forth. But he now had a foreign minister who could greatly mitigate the impression that Japan was steadfastly pursuing a path of war. For Tōgō, his role involved much more than external perceptions; he clearly realized that it was his responsibility to mend US-Japan relations and avert a disastrous conflict that would surely culminate in Japan's defeat.

## Pursuing a Path to Peace: Plan A and Plan B

Once he was installed as foreign minister, Tōgō acted swiftly in revamping the Gaimushō. In one bold sweeping move, he reassigned three ambassadors (one was forced into retirement), five section chiefs, and a cohort of midlevel diplomats.[31] Such drastic action was hitherto unheard of in the bureaucratic system of Japan. In this way, Tōgō had effectively removed Tripartite Pact sympathizers who could prove to be an obstacle in reaching a diplomatic settlement with the United States. He also appointed diplomatic realists into the fold who would support his endeavor. A colleague he trusted, Nishi Haruhiko— also from Kagoshima Prefecture—became his deputy, and Yamamoto Kumaichi was nominated as director of the America Bureau. Kase Toshikazu became the section chief. These were all capable individuals, determined to avert a catastrophic war. Together, they wasted no time in formulating two key peace proposals—*Kouan* (Plan A) and *Otsuan* (Plan B)—that necessitated significant concessions on the part of the Japanese military.

The comprehensive and complex Plan A aspired to be an all-encompassing solution to the current points of contention between the United States and Japan. Its chief objective was to end the Second Sino-Japanese War, which had been dragging on for four years and was a major source of friction in US-Japan relations.[32] But the plan was doomed to fail from the beginning, as it stipulated that the US must permit Japan to occupy Manchuria for another twenty-five years. This absurd length was the result of political infighting. Behind the scenes, Tōgō had insisted that Japan only remain for an additional five years, but the recalcitrant IJA was adamant that its presence continue for ninety-nine years. For the foreign minister, ninety-nine years was absolutely a nonstarter; it was unfathomable that the US would acquiesce. After further bickering, twenty-five years was reached. But Tōgō knew that this duration was also much too long for the United States to stomach.

Therefore, Tōgō needed another card up his sleeve. This would be the less ambitious second proposal, *Otsuan*.[33] This plan merely sought to alleviate the immediate source of friction between the two nations: Japan's military advances into French Indochina. As such, the plan proposed that Japanese forces would withdraw immediately from southern French Indochina (Nanbu Futsuin); in exchange, the United States would suspend its oil embargo for a period of three months. This approach was a significant departure from Tokyo's policy of not withdrawing from an occupied area unless Washington agreed to lift the oil embargo first. Therefore, this concession was met with considerable ire from the IJA, and it flatly refused to permit Plan B to be presented at the negotiating table.[34] However, a resolute Tōgō persisted, even threatening his resignation in the event that Plan B was not allowed to be pursued.[35] Tōgō also reminded Tōjō that should the plan fail to see the light of day and should war then ensue, the IJA alone would have to shoulder the blame.[36]

Since the prime minister was aware that the emperor also supported Tōgō's peace initiatives, he moved to quell the opposition in the ranks of the IJA. At this moment, the gamble of the elder statesmen appeared to be paying off, as only Tōjō had the clout to convince the IJA to go along. Once the IJA was on board, getting the IJN to agree was only a matter of formality.[37] Thus, with the prime minister's support, Tōgō was able to submit his two proposals. As expected, the United States rejected Plan A from the outset, but agreed to continue talks based on Plan B.

The US-Japan talks over the second plan began in earnest on November 20, 1941.[38] It was during the same time that a group within the State Department was completing the final draft of the American compromise plan, the so-called modus vivendi.[39] While certain sections of the modus vivendi were strikingly similar to Japan's Plan B, the two had been initiated independently of each other, and the key portions of the modus vivendi had been drafted before the Japanese proposal had arrived. However, as the timing of the two proposals was so close, and as there was so much overlap in content, Tōgō misinterpreted the modus vivendi to be a direct counterproposal to his Plan B, which was not at all its intention. As this essay will show, this seemingly innocuous error by the foreign minister would have devastating repercussions in the final stages.

On November 22, Secretary of State Hull secretly showed the contents of the modus vivendi to the ambassadors and ministers from Australia, United Kingdom, the Netherlands, and China.[40] Hull then asked these ambassadors to transmit the contents of the modus vivendi to their respective governments. All the diplomats, with the notable exception of Minister Hu Shih of China, were positive about the American proposal, as it provided for a realistic means of averting a two-front war.

Australia feared that the Japanese would invade should war break out in the Pacific, and both the British and the Dutch felt strongly that the primary goal should be directed toward defeating Germany and not toward creating a new enemy in East Asia. Besides, Japan could be dealt with much more easily once the Nazis had been defeated. But Hu Shih was visibly upset, as the United States' peace proposal essentially amounted to a sellout of China. The Chinese minister quickly sent the contents of the modus vivendi via telegram to Chiang Kai-shek. When Chiang read the plan, he was furious; this was a peace that would be paid for by "barrels of Chinese blood." Ultimately, the November 22 version of the proposal would see a few more revisions before it was dropped in its entirety from the Hull Note that was submitted to Tokyo on November 26.

It should not be overlooked that the November 22 version of the modus vivendi was extremely conciliatory toward Japan.[41] It even included a passage saying that the United States government would endeavor to convince Congress to repeal the Japanese Exclusion section of the Immigration Act of 1924. This shows that even after nearly seventeen years, Washington was still keenly aware that it had slighted Japan over the issue of race.

## Fog of Diplomacy: The Perils of Intelligence

For a long time, the dominant historical narrative has been that Japan suffered a lopsided defeat in the battle over intelligence even before the attack on Pearl Harbor.[42] Furthermore, it also has been a long-standing assumption that a technologically inferior Japan did not possess the know-how to utilize a scientific method in decrypting the communications of its adversaries. This assumption is largely supported by several official assessments conducted by the United States government as well as by the lack of archival evidence that relates to Japan's SIGINT operations.

Among the existing documents, the following two are particularly interesting, as they represent the standard evaluation of Japanese intelligence capabilities. The first, dated November 1, 1944, was authorized by the Signal Security Agency, and concludes that "the history of Japanese methods of obtaining intelligence is not brilliant." It also states, "what little progress they [Japan] have made was mainly with the help they received from Germany. Tokyo's policy was to bleed others of cryptanalytic information and codebooks. . . . But when Germany agreed only to furnish information on a reciprocal basis the relationship was terminated since Japan had nothing to offer in return."[43] The second, dated September 4, 1945, was an assessment conducted in the aftermath of the Pacific War by the Military Intelligence Service, and offers a similar conclusion: "the quality of Japanese intelligence was generally poor at best, and most of the time, inaccurate spy reports comprised the core Japanese intelligence."[44] Amid the absence of other intelligence reports, this understanding of Japanese intelligence has become the generally accepted view.[45] By contrast, the United States possessed a highly effective decrypting operation toward Japan, known as MAGIC; a similar operation targeting Germany was known as ULTRA.[46]

MAGIC was successful in breaking the high-grade Japanese diplomatic traffic known as PURPLE, which were messages constructed by the Type 97 European Alphabet Printing Machine (97-shiki Ōbun Injiki).[47] Since the Gaimushō was thoroughly convinced that its most sophisticated cipher system could not be penetrated, PURPLE was used extensively to transmit highly confidential information between the Gaimushō in Tokyo and the thirteen embassies abroad. This essentially meant that even before Tokyo decided to go to war, Washington had a working knowledge of Japanese foreign policy aims and strategy during the US-Japan talks. However, the United States had no way of knowing in advance about the impending attack on Pearl Harbor, as this was a purely military operation that the Gaimushō was not privy to. As a senior minister, Tōgō knew that the IJN was planning an attack on US soil, but he was completely in the dark regarding the intended target and date. That said, Tōgō was desperate to reach an agreement with the United States, as he was well aware that the clock of diplomacy was ticking away. In this way, Japan was pursuing its diplomacy vis-à-vis the US with a set deadline, which exponentially increased the pressure on the foreign minister.

On the other hand, while American decrypting operations excelled at collecting and reading Japanese diplomatic messages, they encountered significantly more difficulty in translating the documents into English.[48] This problem was further exacerbated by the fact that Japanese Americans were initially prevented from assisting in the task until well into the war. As a result, many errors, both small and large, crept into the translations. For example, *gozenkaigi* (imperial meeting) was translated as "morning meeting" since the Japanese term *gozen*, meaning "in the presence of the emperor," was a homophone for the Japanese word for *antemeridian*.[49] Of course, errors of this magnitude are harmless and thus had negligible impact on policy. However, there were a few instances in which a simple mistranslation completely altered the content of the diplomatic correspondence.

One notable example occurred when the foreign minister sent a telegram outlining his Plan B to Ambassador Nomura Kichisaburō. In the note, Tōgō informed the ambassador that Plan B should be treated as a *saigoteki jouhoan* (final-like compromise) and thus the ambassador was to take utmost precautions not to make any unauthorized changes to the document.[50] Since the content had been cleared with the IJA, it was imperative that Nomura did not fall back onto his old habit of inserting his own thoughts and ideas that were not approved by the Gaimushō into his pursuit of diplomacy.

This crucial correspondence was intercepted and successfully decrypted by MAGIC even before it reached the ambassador himself.[51] But a grave error was made while translating the message. Tōgō's Plan B was translated as being an "absolutely final proposal," which in essence made the document an ultimatum. In fact, this was the furthest thing from Tōgō's mind.[52] What Tōgō wanted to avoid was that Nomura, out of abundant zeal to obtain peace, would revise the agreement so that it would be even more amenable to Washington.[53] As a matter of fact, Nomura had previously misrepresented the US-Japan Agreement Proposal (Nichibei Ryōkai-an) that was drafted by the so-called John Doe Associates as if it had been approved by the US government. As this proposal was extremely favorable to Japan, this excited not only the Japanese government but also the IJN. In reality, Washington had not sanctioned the agreement and was merely taking a wait-and-see attitude to gauge the Japanese response. Therefore, when Japan approached the US with the mindset that this would be the starting line for the ensuing diplomatic talks, it was in for quite a surprise when the plan was rejected outright by the Americans.

On other occasions, too, Nomura tended to digress from official instructions. He was, after all, a former navy admiral and had not been formally trained as a career diplomat. As he possessed a deep knowledge of international law, he had served as foreign minister in the Abe Nobuyuki Cabinet (August 1939–January 1940). This meant that Nomura was more senior not only in rank but also in age (by five years); being older than the current foreign minister surely would have contributed to Nomura's frequent tendency to deviate from instructions. However, at a very delicate stage in the talks, Tōgō could not allow Nomura to miscommunicate or mislead the intentions of the Japanese government in regards to Plan B. It was absolutely vital to ensure that Nomura would not make even the slightest changes— whether inferred or otherwise—to the compromise plan, as Tōjō and the IJA had signed off on it exactly the way it was transmitted to the ambassador.

If any unapproved revisions were proposed, it was likely that the IJA would disavow the plan and act to undermine the US-Japan talks. This was also the reason why Tōgō sent a seasoned diplomat, Kurusu Saburō, as a second ambassador to the United States.[54] Kurusu arrived in Washington on November 20; as a career diplomat he was expected to ensure that Nomura did not diverge from official instructions. Having two ambassadors on the same mission was a highly unusual diplomatic maneuver, but one that was necessary considering the utmost importance of this final attempt at averting war.

But despite such precautions, Tōgō had no way of knowing that the Americans had not only read his message but had made a serious error in its translation. Thus he was anxiously waiting for a formal reply from Hull. He was in high spirits because he had been able to secure a major concession from Tōjō. The prime minister had agreed to suspend all ongoing military operations, including the secret naval operations of the combined fleet—they were training in Kagoshima and planned to sail north toward Hokkaido after a brief naval exercise in Oita—in the event that the Americans made a serious counterproposal to Plan B. This shows the enormity of Tōgō's hope resting on the American response; surely, he felt that peace was now within his grasp.

Unbeknownst to Tōgō, his Plan B had been misconstrued as a Japanese ultimatum by Washington.[55] His words, *saigoteki jōhoan*, or final-like compromise proposal, had been inadvertently translated as an "absolutely final proposal." This author has examined the original decrypted documents in the National Archives, but someone—perhaps Stanley K. Hornbeck, special advisor to the Department of State—had underlined this phrase twice in pencil. From this, it is clearly evident that these three words did not go unnoticed. Unfortunately, as ensuing events show, this seemingly innocuous error in translation would set off a vicious chain of events that would end in tragedy.

It is of course possible to criticize Tōgō for not using an abundance of caution in the wording of the diplomatic note to Nomura. But then again, this message was never intended to be read by a third party. More importantly, Tōgō did not have the slightest idea that his telegrams were being intercepted and read by the Americans. He firmly believed that his lines of communication were secure. As a matter of fact, all his messages for Nomura were sent as top secret (*kancho fugo*) and intended to be read by the ambassador alone; they were not shared with anyone else in the embassy.

Moreover, in the past, when Germany had warned Japan that its diplomatic correspondence was being compromised, Japan quickly switched to a new cipher. This bolstered the foreign minister's confidence that his messages were completely safeguarded. Unbeknownst to him, however, Japan's highest-level diplomatic ciphers had been compromised due to how they were being used. Only the thirteen Japanese embassies used the latest cipher, but occasionally, a certain embassy would need to retransmit the message to a consulate based in another country. Since the consulates used an older cipher that the Americans could already read, the American codebreakers just had to work backward to determine the algorithm of the new cipher, since they already knew its content.

Despite Tōgō's enthusiasm for a diplomatic breakthrough, his Plan B was doomed to fail the very instant Washington interpreted it to be an ultimatum. An ultimatum—an "absolutely final proposal"—meant that there would be no further compromises. The United States either had to accept it in its entirety or reject it outright, in which case war would be a possible outcome. But what was eminently clear was that, according to the American position, it no longer made any sense to re-spond with a counterproposal that fell short of Japanese demands—no matter how small the gap—as it had to be a perfect match for peace to prevail. Therefore, the US had nothing to gain by submitting its modus vivendi; not only would it appear as an appeasement to Japan, but it would also show the world that America was willing to sacrifice China. Of course, if peace could be attained, then perhaps selling out China would be worth the cost. But other than that, it made much more sense to maintain a united front with China against Japan.

As Washington was under the mistaken belief that Japan would go to war if Plan B was rejected, any compromise could be ruled out. Thus, when the American response was submitted to Tokyo, Secretary Hull completely dropped the modus vivendi and merely conveyed the Four Principles that he had steadfastly maintained from the onset of the discussions. Afterward, when the Australian ambassador, Richard G. Casey, asked if Australia could attempt to broker a last-minute peace deal, Hull sternly replied that the "diplomatic stage was over."[56] From this statement, it becomes readily apparent that Hull knew very well what the ramifications of dropping the modus vivendi would be.

With this in mind, one could make a strong case that Japan crossed the Rubicon the moment the United States did not respond to its Plan B. To restate: it was the misconstruing of Japanese intentions that set into motion the tragic chain of events that would end with the utter destruction of Japan. This is why apologists in Japan view Pearl Harbor as defensive in nature: Japan was justified in attacking the United States, as Washington had decided on war first. This understanding was also utilized by the defense during the Tokyo war crimes tribunals and is grounded in the belief that had the United States not read and misunderstood Japanese diplomatic traffic, peace would have surely prevailed. But this convenient argument is based on a fallacy.

With the wealth of recent archival evidence available to researchers, it can now be concluded that Japan was equally susceptible to misreading diplomatic messages obtained through SIGINT. A 1967 CIA document uncovered by the author at the National Archives and the actual decrypted diplomatic messages tucked away in an obscurely titled folder in the Japanese Diplomatic Records Office reveal a startling truth.[57] Japan too had possessed a successful SIGINT operation, led by codebreakers from the Gaimushō, IJN, and IJA. The archival materials show that Japan was able to routinely intercept and decrypt high-grade diplomatic messages—not only those of the United States but also those of the United Kingdom and China.[58]

In addition, interviews with former Japanese cryptanalysts shed light on an alarming fact. As Chinese diplomatic messages were constructed by code rather than cipher, they were very easy to read, usually taking a mere few hours. Their contents were shared with a very select group of key policy makers by the following day.[59] The lack of sophistication of Chinese systems was not because they were inferior but because at the time there was not yet a unified way to pronounce words, and regional variances in pronunciations were quite large. Therefore, it was impossible to romanize Chinese words, and instead numbers were assigned to Chinese characters. On the other hand, the Americans and the British used a more complex system, so it took the Japanese three to four days to completely decrypt a message from these two countries.[60]

The aforementioned CIA report initially believed that Japan had simply obtained the diplomatic notes by breaking into a safe and photographing the original message prior to encryptions. This so-called direct method made sense, as even in the late 1960s it was assumed that Japan lacked any SIGINT capabilities. This hypothesis crumbled when a sharp analyst in the CIA noticed that intercepted British cables had been typed out by the Japanese using American spellings.[61] For example, *cipher* was written with an *i*, not with a *y*. Furthermore, the presence of garbled message groups in the decrypted text followed by an approximate word in parentheses indicated that Japan had successfully deciphered these messages through a scientific method.[62] This realization allowed for only one conclusion: the Japanese had been able to systematically read American, British, and Chinese diplomatic messages, and what they had been able to read was not limited to the four messages discovered by the CIA in its analysis of captured prewar Japanese diplomatic records.[63]

## The Illusion of Peace and the Reality of War

So what does this discovery tell us? The ramifications are enormous. Historians examining this period of relations between the United States and Japan will now need to reevaluate the events leading to Pearl Harbor by incorporating the revelation that Japan knew a lot more than once assumed. Furthermore, the fact that both sides could read each other's messages meant that there was a greater margin of error in misconstruing the intent of the adversary.

Hindered by the lack of archival material—most documents were destroyed in the few days before Japan's surrender—the research into Japanese SIGINT has progressed very little. But from the context of prewar US-Japan relations, it does shed light on why Tōgō gave up on peace at a critical juncture and allowed Japan to proceed on a course of war. Furthermore, it also explains why he decided to remain in the Tōjō Cabinet after hostilities with the United States had commenced. This volte-face has long baffled historians, as it was well known that Tōgō was committed to peace and only joined the Tōjō Cabinet as foreign minister to steer the nation away from a near-certain collision course with America. Thus, he could have always resorted to playing his ultimate card: resigning from the cabinet if war with the United States became inevitable.

As this essay has explored, his resignation would have assuredly wreaked considerable havoc, as it would have in essence paralyzed the government from going to war until a successor could be appointed. Moreover, this bold action would have also coalesced with his long-held belief that war with the United States needed to be averted at all costs as it could not be won. At an earlier stage, Tōgō had once threatened to resign when Tōjō had been reluctant to accept his Plan B. But in the end, he felt compelled to remain in the war cabinet; Japan now "had to rise." What happened?

The fact that the Japanese were also reading a good portion of the Chinese diplomatic traffic provides a convincing explanation to Tōgō's volte-face. This volte-face was a process that involved two distinct phases. Phase one began when Japan intercepted the November 22, 1941, telegram sent by Minister Hu Shih to Chiang Kai-shek in Chongqing. The Chinese note explained in precise detail the content of the modus vivendi as presented by Hull. Once decoded, the cable was rushed to the foreign minister, since it was believed to contain the initial American response to Tōgō's Plan B.

The American draft proposal of November 22—which was slightly revised on both November 24 and 25—contained many significant concessions that were an important departure from the Hull Four Principles, such as allowing Japan to maintain its troops in Manchuria. Thus, it is easy to imagine how elated Tōgō was; Washington was now finally flexible in its attitude and was showing a willingness to earnestly engage in diplomatic talks with Japan to ensure that peace would prevail. This was the very reason why Tōgō had accepted the position of foreign minister, and his immense efforts were finally going to reach fruition. All that Tōgō now had to do was to wait patiently for the modus vivendi, which he had already seen through the Chinese diplomatic messages, to be presented formally to Tokyo as the official United States reply. But Tōgō had jumped the gun. The ultimate decision to present the modus vivendi had not yet been made by President Roosevelt. However, as Tōgō had seen the modus vivendi, he had inadvertently connected the dots where there was actually no line.

The next phase of the volte-face occurred on the fateful day of November 26. Surely, Tōgō was anxious to receive the American reply to his Plan B.[64] What awaited him was a tremendous shock; to his "utter disbelief," when the formal diplomatic note was presented there was no trace of the modus vivendi.[65] It had simply vanished. Then, adding insult to injury, the Hull Note made no mention of his Plan B. This amounted to an outright rejection of the peace overture that he had so painstakingly negotiated with the anti-American elements in Japan. The US-Japan talks remained at the very point where they had started; the

United States would not negotiate with Japan unless its troops were first withdrawn from China proper.

With this new context, we can now comprehend Tōgō's emotionally charged words in his memoirs. It explains why he was "shocked to the point that [he] was blinded by utter disbelief." He was not expecting such a response from the United States. And to him, the absence of the modus vivendi could only mean one thing: Washington had decided to go to war against Japan. Faced with this predicament, Tōgō now felt sure that Japan had "no choice but to rise." Since the fate of the nation was now at stake, Tōgō could no longer find a logical reason to oppose war. Moreover, considering Japan's dwindling strategic oil reserves, the opportunity to strike a devastating first blow against the US made sense. Although the odds of victory were incredibly slim, it was still better than capitulating without a fight. Tōgō had been twenty-two years old when Japan went to war against Russia in 1904; Russia had been a much larger power with a formidable military. Yet Japan was able to drag it to the negotiating table and obtain a favorable peace truce after a quick and powerful initial blow. Perhaps Tōgō felt that history might repeat itself.

But the very moment Tōgō had given up on peace, the last major hurdle that lay in the path toward war with the United States had been effectively removed. As we now know, it would be the phrase "Climb Mount Niitaka (Niitakayama nobore)," and not "The weather is fine on Mount Tsukuba (Tsukubayama hare)," that would be etched forever in the annals of history of the Pacific War, along with "a date which will live in infamy."

## Notes

1. Takao Ozawa v. United States, 260 U.S. 178 (1922).

2. Yamashita v. Hinkle, 260 U.S. 199 (1922). In *Washington v. Hirabayashi*, 133 Wash. 462 (1925), the Washington State Supreme Court ruled to prohibit the transfer of stock shares in a corporation that held agricultural lands into the name of a Nisei child.

3. Webb v. O'Brien, 263 U.S. 313 (1923).

4. This term is frequently attributed to Fukuzawa Yukichi, but this is incorrect. He did pen an opinion-editorial piece titled "Datsua," but it said nothing about entering the West.

5. A prime example of this group would be Ōhashi Chūichi, who would later become the deputy foreign minister under Matsuoka Yōsuke.

6. Shigenori Tōgō, *Jidai no ichimen* (Tokyo: Hara-shobō, 1985), 253.

7. The details of the plans can be found in Ministry of Foreign Affairs, ed., *Nihongaikō nenpyō narabini shuyō bunshō*, vol. 2 (Tokyo: Hara-shobō, 1965), 555.

8. The Hull Note did not specify if Manchuria was to be included in China. However, an earlier version of the note stated, "withdraw from China (excluding Manchuria)." This phrase in parentheses was later stricken by State Department special advisor Stanley Hornbeck.

9. "The negotiation was officially launched on April 14 with the Hull-Nomura conversations." Tōgō, *Jidai no ichimen*, 167. The US principles were referred to by the Japanese as "Hull's four principles," or *Halu yon-gensoku*."

10. The standard biography on Tōgō is Nobutoshi Hagiwara, *Tōgō Shigenori: Denki to kaisetsu* (Tokyo: Hara-shobō, 1985). A more biased biography was written by his grandson, Shigehiko Tōgō, *Sofu Tōgō Shigenori no Shōgai* (Tokyo: Bungei-shinju, 1993).

11. This is the conventional interpretation appearing in most Japanese texts dealing with the outbreak of the Pacific War. For example, see Makoto Iokibe, ed., *Nichibeikankei-shi* (Tokyo: Yuhikaku, 2008), 136.

12. For details of the Meiji cabinet system, see Momose Takashi, *Showa Senzeki no Nihon: Seido to jittai* (Tokyo: Yoshikawa-kobunkan, 1990), chapter 5.

13. Tōgō, *Jidai no ichimen*, 257–59.

14. Shingo Fukushima, "Tōjō naikaku: Rikugun no yokoguruma wo tsuranuite kuni wo horobosu," in *Nihon naikaku shiroku*, vol. 4, eds. Shigeru Hayashi and Kiyoaki Tsuji (Tokyo: Daiichi-hoki, 1981), 328–29.

15. Masaki Miyake, "Dai sanji Konoe naikaku: Wasen no kantō," in Hayashi and Tsuji, *Nihon naikaku shiroku*, 308.

16. Masumi Junnosuke, *Nihon seijishi*, vol. 3 (Tokyo: Tokyo Daigaku Shuppankai), 296.

17. Isamu Togawa, *Showa no saisho: Tōjō Hideki to Gunbu Dokusai* (Tokyo: Kodansha, 1982), 152.

18. Jun Tsunoda, "Nihon no taibei kansen," in *Taiheiyō senso eno michi*, vol. 7, ed. Nihon Kokusai Seijigakkai (Tokyo: Asahi Shimbunsha, 1963), 296–98.

19. Tōjō Hideki Kankōkai, ed., *Tōjō Hideki* (Tokyo: Fuyō-shobō, 1974), 57.

20. Miyake, "Dai sanji Konoe naikaku," 308.

21. Shinji Sudō, *Nichibei kaisen gaikō no kenkyu* (Tokyo: Keiō-tsūshin, 1986), 238–39.

22. For further details, see Kamei Hiroshi, *Shōwa Tennō to Tōjō Hideki* (Tokyo: Kōjinsha, 1988).

23. For the content of the edict, see Ministry of Foreign Affairs, *Nihongaikō*, 544–45.

24. Tōgō, *Tōgō Shigenori*, 219. Tōgō was considered to be among the three chief disciples of Shidehara Kijūrō, along with Saburi Sadao and Shigemitsu Mamoru.

25. Hagiwara, *Tōgō Shigenori*, 259.

26. Tōgō, *Tōgō Shigenori*, 230.

27. Tōgō, 251.

28. For an overview of Tōgō's approach to foreign policy, see Bōeichō Bōeikenshūjo Senshishitsu, ed., *Senshisōsho daitōa senso kaisenkeii*, vol. 5 (Tokyo: Asagumo Shimbunsha, 1974), 189–99.

29. Admiral Shimada Shigetarō, a crony of Tōjō's, was appointed as navy minister. He was viewed as devoid of conviction—leading to the nickname "saloon

door," or one that swings both in and out—by his fellow navy officers. But as a lackey of Tōjō, he was not a hawk.

30. For further details on the so-called progressive diplomats, see Hiroaki Shiozaki, "Gaimushō kakushin-ha no genjō daha ninshiki to seisaku," in *Nihon gaikō no kiki ninshiki*, ed. Kindai Nihon Kenkyū 7 (Tokyo: Yamakawa Shuppansha, 1985). In the end, four senior diplomats were forced to retire from the ministry; see Hiroaki Shiozaki, *Nichieibei senō no kiro: Taiheiyō no yuwa wo meguru seisenryaku* (Tokyo: Yamakawa Shuppansha, 1984).

31. Tōgō, *Tōgō Shigenori*, 255–56.

32. For the details of Plan A, see Gaimushō Hyakunenshi Hensaniinkai, ed., *Gaimushō no hyakunen*, vol. 2 (Tokyo: Hara-shobō, 1969), 604–7.

33. Tōgō, *Jidai no ichimen*, 220–22.

34. Tōgō, 222–25. For a perspective from the IJA, see Bōeichō Bōeikenshujo Senshishitsu, *Senshisōsho*, 256–57.

35. Tōgō, *Jidai no ichimen*, 227–28. Tōgō discussed his resignation with former foreign minister Hirota Kōki, who persuaded him to remain until the US-Japan talks were concluded.

36. Gaimushō Hyakunenshi Hensaniinkai, *Gaimushō*, 598–99.

37. Gaimushō Hyakunenshi Hensaniinkai, 228–29.

38. Sudō, *Nichibei kaisen gaikō*, 268.

39. Sudō, 267. For details on the modus vivendi (final draft), see *Papers Relating to the Foreign Relations of the United States: Japan, 1931–1941*, vol. 2 (Washington, DC: Government Printing Office, 1943), 973–74.

40. Memorandum of conversation by Secretary of State Hull, November 22, 1941, *Foreign Relations of the United States, 1940*, vol. 4: *Far East* (Washington, DC: Government Printing Office, 1955), 640. (Hereafter *FRUS: Far East*.)

41. *FRUS: Far East*, 637–40.

42. For an overview, see Bessatsu Rekishdokuhon, ed., *Taiheiyō senō jōhōsen* (Tokyo: Shinjinbutsu Ouraisha, 1998).

43. Signal Security Agency, "Japanese Signal Intelligence Service," November 1, 1944, National Security Agency archives, Fort Meade, MD.

44. Military Intelligence Service, "The Japanese Intelligence System," September 4, 1945, National Security Agency archives.

45. For example, various publications by Makoto Iokibe, Shinji Sudō, and Ikuhiko Hata.

46. The decryptions have been published as Department of Defense, ed., *The "Magic" Background of Pearl Harbor* (Washington, DC: Government Printing Office, 1977).

47. Ronald Lewin, *The American Magic: Codes, Ciphers, and the Defeat of Japan* (New York: Farrar, Straus and Giroux, 1982), 36–37.

48. This point has been particularly highlighted in Keiichiro Komatsu, *Origins of the Pacific War and the Importance of "MAGIC"* (New York: St. Martin's Press, 1999), as well as in Sudō, *Nichibei kaisen gaikō*, 295–309.

49. For a thorough examination of the technical difficulties of translating intercepted Japanese cables, see Komatsu, *Origins*, 247–69.

50. Tōgō, *Tōgō Shigenori*, 232–33.

51. David D. Lowman, *MAGIC: The Untold Story of US Intelligence and the Evacuation of Japanese Residents from the West Coast during World War II* (New York: Athena Press, 2000), 60–61.

52. Tōgō, *Tōgō Shigenori*, 228. Tōjō promised that he would allow further compromises if the United States showed an interest in either Plan A or Plan B.

53. Toshikazu Kase, *Nihongaikōshi: Nichibei kōshou*, vol. 23 (Tokyo: Kashima kenkyujo-shupankai, 1970), 75–82.

54. Tōgō, *Tōgō Shigenori*, 235–36. In his memoirs, Tōgō laments that Kurusu betrayed his expectations by acting just like Nomura upon being posted in Washington. Kurusu was viewed with mistrust by Washington, as he was the diplomat who was the Japanese signatory to the Tripartite Pact. However, personally, he had been opposed to the agreement.

55. *FRUS: Far East*, 640.

56. Memorandum of conversation by Hull, November 29, 1941, *FRUS: Far East*, 687.

57. The 1967 CIA document is in "Reports on items based on material contained in the archives in the Japanese Ministry of Foreign Affairs, 1868–1965," in Herbert O. Yardley Collection, RG457 NARA II, College Park, MD, November 28, 1967. (Hereafter HOY Coll., RG457.) For a sample of the actual Japanese decryptions, see the folder "Tokushu jōhō tsuzuri," in the Ministry of Foreign Affairs DRO Archives, Tokyo.

58. "Tokushu jōhō tsuzuri," Ministry of Foreign Affairs DRO Archives, Tokyo.

59. Kazuo Kamaga (former codebreaker), interviewed by the author at Kamaga's residence in Yokohama, November 2001. Mr. Kamaga was employed by Koden Electronics at the time but has since passed away.

60. Kamaga, interview.

61. "Memorandum for SUKLO," HOY Coll., RG457.

62. "Memorandum for SUKLO," HOY Coll., RG457.

63. "Reports on items based on material contained in the archives in the Japanese Ministry of Foreign Affairs, 1868–1965," HOY Coll., RG457.

64. Australian Minister to the US Richard Casey to Prime Minister John Curtin and Minister for External Affairs H. V. Evatt, November 24, 1941, cablegram 1021, in Australian Department of Foreign Affairs and Trade Files, National Archives of Australia, Canberra.

65. Tōgō, *Jidai no ichimen*, 251–53.

# CHAPTER 10

# American Surveillance of Japanese Americans, 1933–1941

*Brian Masaru Hayashi*

Throughout the 1930s, the Japanese were among the few ethnic or racially defined groups under surveillance in the United States. Yet the American public did not fear them as fifth columnists involved in espionage or sabotage, according to public opinion. In August 1940, for example, a Gallup poll revealed that over a third of the public believed fifth columnists posed a national security threat while less than a quarter perceived that no such significant threat existed. The poll further identified agents of Nazi Germany, members of the Communist Party, and labor union organizers as security threats—not agents of Japan or Japanese Americans. In fact, even after Secretary of the Navy Frank Knox blamed the Japanese success at Pearl Harbor on a "fifth column" operating in Hawai'i, Japanese Americans did not become targets of suspicion. The National Opinion Research Center found that as late as December 24, 1941, an overwhelming majority of Americans did not fear the Japanese, but were vigilant about potential German fifth columnists in their midst. They identified Germans rather than Japanese as the main security threat by a margin of three to one—more than two weeks after the Pearl Harbor attack.[1]

In this essay, I examine the surveillance Japanese Americans were subjected to in the 1930s despite the near absence of fifth columnist fears. Previous studies, based on selective usage of documents and an underappreciation of the professionalization of counterintelligence, coupled with a public politicization of that dimension of national security, have largely skewed our understanding of why this happened to

Japanese Americans. By examining previously unused or underutilized sources written by professional intelligence officers in the Office of Naval Intelligence (ONI) and the Military Intelligence Division (MID), on the one hand, and public statements made by congressmen from the 1930s to the early 1940s, on the other, this essay illustrates a divergence of opinion regarding Japanese Americans, even though they all conducted surveillance at about the same time. Furthermore, it finds congressional leaders found more Japanese American suspects than the military intelligence officers did because they politicized counterintelligence. Under Samuel Dickstein, Martin Dies, and Guy Gillette, the Congress undertook investigations of Japanese Americans under the rubric of "subversion" and "propaganda." Despite being thwarted by the Roosevelt administration in the fall of 1941, these congressmen nevertheless paved the way for the witch hunt on West Coast Japanese Americans that began with the Roberts Commission Report of January 1942 and the Tolan Committee Hearings.[2]

Those congressional hearings, held in 1942, began with the ONI, the agency most responsible for keeping Japanese Americans under surveillance. This office gathered intelligence on other navies and prevented classified information about the United States Navy from falling into foreign hands. Established in 1882, the ONI was preoccupied with the former task and left counterintelligence to private investigative agencies to handle until World War I. Given its willingness to leave counterintelligence to private citizens, it comes as no surprise that the few security measures the ONI adopted included sweeping restrictions on "race" such as barring all Japanese from entry into the Naval Academy from 1900 onward because Japanese Americans and Imperial Japanese Navy personnel alike were "apes of the Orient." But it did not include Japanese among those to be watched when authorization was received in 1917 to "place under surveillance all citizens of the Central Powers in the Navy, or in Government employ in naval establishments, and remove them from positions which they may do possible harm." Naval intelligence had its hands full spying on aliens and their offspring from Germany, Austria, Hungary, Bulgaria, and Turkey; German Americans alone numbered over five million. Even with more than five hundred officers in its New York City office, the ONI still had to rely on volunteer help from organizations such as the American Protective League, with its quarter of a million members, to report on possible suspects engaged in espionage and sabotage. Although some German aliens engaged in sabotage, resulting in some damaged war-related factories and transport vessels, the many reports submitted to the ONI were not of sufficiently professional quality to prevent such threats to national security.[3]

Following the end of the First World War, the Office had to professionalize its counterintelligence even as its surveillance targets changed. Naval intelligence officers now perceived imperial Japan as a threat to American forces based in the Philippines, Guam, Samoa, Hawai'i, Alaska, and the Panama Canal. Although Navy officials such as then assistant secretary of the Navy Franklin D. Roosevelt began planning for the defense of Hawai'i as early as 1906, Navy planners in the decade after the Armistice was signed were aware of the near impossibility of imperial Japanese forces' invading and occupying the islands, let alone the West Coast, once the 1921-1922 Washington Treaty reduced their maximum force projection to the western Pacific. In its threat assessments, the ONI ranked the possibilities of a Japanese attack or invasion on a scale of "A" to "E," with the latter representing the possibility of an invasion, and the former the possibility of a light attack. The West Coast states, where the Japanese residents were found in not insignificant numbers, were categorized as having a low probability, from "A" to "C." The Panama Canal, vital for the rapid deployment of the Navy's fleet from the Atlantic to the eastern Pacific, was rated as "D," or subject to a major attack—the same rating as the islands of Hawai'i, where the largest number of Japanese residents in the United States were located. Only Alaska and Samoa, the two areas with very few Japanese residents, were classified as "E," or subject to invasion.[4]

The office also professionalized important parts of its counterintelligence operations in the decades following the First World War. While it had yet to establish a governing body to set standards for performance or provide a formal, rigorous education and continuous training for counterintelligence at the Naval Academy, the ONI eschewed dependence on "amateur" civilian investigators in favor of Navy Reserve personnel. It had no certification process established yet, but it quickly realized it needed personnel fluent in foreign languages—especially Japanese—and began in the two decades after World War I to regularly send officers to Japan for language training. It also created a knowledge management system to organize its files and reports related to counterintelligence, even as it tapped into the files of its Army counterpart and, to a lesser extent, those files gathered by congressional investigators. The ONI also developed systematic research methods apart from the "police" methods used by the FBI and others to build its profiles on foreign intelligence operations inside the United States and its territories. It understood that its task of counterintelligence was focused on espionage and sabotage, not internal security, subversion, or propaganda, and institutionalized some lessons learned into its district and Washington, DC, offices.[5]

By the 1930s, intelligence officers adopted some professional techniques to quickly identify foreign professional intelligence agents inside the United States. They took a functional, as opposed to a complaint-based or reported suspect–based, approach to counterespionage. The office had used the latter approach, which entailed waiting for incoming reports before beginning an investigation, during World War I; it eventually learned that the untrained civilian complainants too often provided false leads and incorrect information. With the functional approach, ONI officers selected probable targeted facilities and types of information a foreign agent was likely to seek—a method found to be more accurate and efficient in time and effort. As the District Intelligence Officer in Honolulu described it, this approach involved placing under surveillance the sites foreign intelligence agents were likely to take an interest in, such as naval or army bases, war industry–related factories, airfields, potential amphibious-landing locations, and key infrastructure. Officers ignored the idea of a suspect race or ethnic group and instead focused their investigation on those groups of Japanese most likely to engage in intelligence gathering for imperial Japan. Hence, they concentrated on the Japanese embassy and consulate officials whose diplomatic immunity provided the freedom of movement necessary for intelligence gathering and whose access to inspection-free diplomatic pouches offered a safe means for the delivery of intelligence reports to Tokyo. The office also followed military attachés' activities closely, as seen in the actions of Ellis Zacharias, who took up residence in the same building as a key Imperial Japanese Navy military attaché in Washington, DC, in 1932, to monitor the attaché's movements. Japanese military officers posing as English-language students at Harvard, Yale, and other American universities were also kept under surveillance by ONI officers. Since individuals in contact with the military attachés and language students were possible members of the Japanese intelligence-gathering networks, the office had to keep track of many individuals. To do this, the office established a Case History Section, which maintained files on thousands of people, cataloging them using the Russell Soundex system, which was readily adaptable to Japanese names. These files, each with a minimum of four reported items, contained substantive information that was evaluated by professionals before becoming accessible. Some two dozen federal government agencies consulted them, including law enforcement bureaus such as the FBI. In New York City, for example, where the Imperial Japanese Army and Navy had their inspectorate offices—and gathered tactical or operational intelligence openly—the ONI created information cards on every Japanese resident, for possible use for mass removal and internment should war break out.[6]

As a result of the office's professionalization of its practices, ONI officers gained considerable confidence by the latter half of the 1930s. They felt certain, for example, that they had a reasonably accurate sense of the organizational structure of Japanese intelligence gathering inside the United States and its territories. They also had all the known imperial Japanese military officers posing as students at Harvard, Yale, and other universities under close observation. Hence, Zacharias expressed their confidence thus: "We now had a fair idea of the scope of Japanese Intelligence in the United States: we knew the layout and the particular subjects and objects in which they were interested." They also knew there were gaps in their own knowledge, such as how the Japanese intelligence reports were transmitted back to Tokyo. When the Japanese reorganized their intelligence network, after it became clear that naval arms–limitation treaties were no longer on the horizon by 1938, naval intelligence officers scrambled to uncover who was directing Japanese intelligence inside the United States. The ONI did not discover that it was the pro-American liberal Foreign Ministry official Hidenari Terasaki, who was assigned to the embassy in Washington, DC, as its press secretary. Yet officers such as Zacharias did accurately predict a surprise attack on the fleet at Pearl Harbor; and when no further attacks on the West Coast followed immediately thereafter, they were confident that the imperial Japanese forces would not launch attacks in the eastern Pacific Ocean.[7]

With the investigation of Japanese Americans, the ONI took a measured approach. On the one hand, naval investigators initially assumed local Japanese fishermen were providing imperial Japanese officials with strategic intelligence—information on ocean currents, water depths, and coastal conditions, which was useful for planning amphibious assaults, insertions or extractions of their own agents operating behind enemy lines, and delivery of intelligence reports submitted by short-range radio transmissions. Zacharias himself believed local Japanese fishermen in Hawai'i and on the West Coast did even more—he suspected they transported agents as well. However, after carefully tracking each Japanese fishing boat and investigating each crew member, the Eleventh Naval District Office, which Zacharias directed, concluded that the Japanese fishermen were not involved in intelligence operations at all.[8]

Adoption of professional intelligence techniques also "inoculated" ONI officers from readily believing reports of suspicious Japanese activities. District intelligence officers such as Irving Mayfield, in Honolulu, maintained a healthy professional skepticism toward information on alleged spies and saboteurs received on the basis of complaints or suspects. Mayfield wrote, "Approaching the espionage problem chiefly through the investigation of reported suspects is costly in effort and largely unproductive. It represents the police detective approach to a non-police problem." Given his and his naval counterintelligence officers' skepticism toward "amateur" reports on alleged Japanese espionage, it comes as no surprise that, upon closer investigation, the ONI discovered that Japanese American fishermen probably turned over strategic intelligence to Japanese authorities but did not submit tactical or operational intelligence—the latter would have been subject to prosecution under the 1917 Espionage Act. Moreover, they recruited 142 Hawai'i-born Japanese to assist with the surveillance of the Japanese community and had included among them a Japanese American naval intelligence officer who graduated from Honolulu's McKinley High School.[9]

The other group of Japanese the office kept under surveillance were Japan's consulate officials, staff members, and volunteer helpers. In Hawai'i, these individuals were known as *toritsuginin*, whom the ONI labeled as "semi-consular agents." These community leaders were officially recognized by the consul general in Honolulu and deputized to serve as the consul general's representative to the widely scattered Japanese population throughout the islands. In the main, they handled a fair portion of the administrative functions of the consulate office, such as registering births, deaths, and marriages; they additionally prepared papers for travel to and from the United States and Japan. But occasionally the consul general requested services from them that could be construed as intelligence gathering. In a few rare instances, Buddhist priests were asked to gather tactical or operational intelligence, as happened in 1940 when the Jōdo Shinshū temple priest in Lahaina was asked to report on the US Pacific Fleet that had moved from its base in San Diego to Lahaina Roads, Maui, in May. Their counterparts on the mainland, known as Japanese Association leaders, were also under surveillance; they served a similar purpose, as far as the local consulate office was concerned. But the consular officials also tapped other Japanese accustomed to traveling far to reach the widely scattered Japanese population through the American West.[10]

The Navy was not alone in professionalizing counterintelligence operations. The Army, too, was updating its own counterintelligence group within its Military Intelligence Division. Established in 1885, the MID was already prohibited from handling domestic conflicts such as labor strikes by the Posse Comitatus Act of 1878. Yet, its officers meddled in the 1894 Pullman Strike ostensibly because the strike affected mail delivery, a federal government service. But it was not until World War I that the MID focused on counterintelligence, after the American Expeditionary Force went to France and became exposed to sophisticated tactical and operational intelligence as practiced by French and British intelligence agencies. Under the leadership of then-Major Ralph H. Van Deman (1865–1952), the MID expanded to over one thousand Army personnel by the end of the war. To assist him, he enlisted two civilian organizations, the American Protective League and the Plant Protection Service—the former with a claimed membership of a quarter million. With such a large force at its disposal, Van Deman's Western Department, Fourth Section, was able to expand the scope of his investigations to the Japanese "racial problems" in August 1918.[11]

However, by the early 1920s, the MID was unable to freely conduct domestic surveillance of the Japanese and others. The Army was reorganized after the end of World War I, and responsibility for the security of its bases was handed down to each department commander and his intelligence officer. On March 31, 1922, the commanders of American territories abroad such as Hawaiʻi, the Philippines, and Panama were all tasked with developing their own security threat assessment. But they were expressly forbidden from engaging in domestic surveillance in the absence of a clear and present danger. The division sent out a strongly worded notice to all Corps Area Commanders in December 1922 to that effect:

> The Secretary of War is much concerned at reports from time to time of the activities of intelligence offices in the United States. It is obvious that the American people are very sensitive with regard to any military interference in their affairs. Harmless and even readily justifiable inquiries arouse suspicion and opponents of the Army are very apt to quote such acts as forms of Russian or Prussian military supervision.[12]

The Division's directive was backed up by high-ranking civilian officials. The secretary of war firmly insisted that its intelligence officers should not engage in domestic intelligence. When the intelligence officer of the Hawaiian Department requested special permission to continue its domestic surveillance because of the islands' "peculiar racial conditions," the officer's civilian boss demanded conformity to the directive: "You must appreciate that both the letter and spirit of the recent instructions are opposed to investigational activities by military authorities and contemplate them only when absolutely necessary in the interest of national defense or when civilian agencies do not function." The secretary of war's admonitions were no idle threat. The year prior, an intelligence officer in Oregon had told local enforcement officials that his office would investigate the International Workers of the World, World War I veterans, the Union of Russian Workers, the Communist Party, the Communist Labor Party, the One Big Union, the Workers' International Industrial Union, anarchists, Bolsheviks, Socialists, the Nonpartisan League, the Big Four Brotherhoods, and the American Federation of Labor. He was promptly removed from his post. President Franklin Roosevelt added his voice of authority to the prohibition against Army domestic surveillance. The president called together the Army, Navy, and the FBI on June 26, 1939, to delineate the lines of responsibility for domestic counterintelligence. Known as the Delimitation Agreement and signed by the president on June 5 of the following year, it laid out that the Army and Navy would agree to restrict their domestic counterintelligence operations to their bases while giving the FBI the authority to work with civilian groups to counter fifth column activities in the United States, its territories, and the western hemisphere.[13]

The MID had its own self-imposed limits on domestic surveillance. Its budget and the low number of personnel it assigned to counterintelligence further undercut any possibility of conducting surveillance on the Japanese. The division's budget shrank from a high of $400,000 in 1920 to less than a tenth of that in 1934. It closed the decade with a higher budget of $89,450 but also with an increased workload that involved investigating and maintaining surveillance on two main groups of suspects—Nazis and their sympathizers, and communist and labor union activists. By the summer of 1940, the MID had shrunk to a low of only twenty officers and three enlisted men, assisted by forty-six civilians. The reduction in the MID's personnel was so dire that two years earlier Brigadier General George V. Strong had complained the MID had been "seriously handicapped due to shortage of funds and lack of adequate clerical and stenographic personnel."[14]

Due to these restrictions, Army intelligence came up with various measures to address the "racial conditions" posed by Japanese residents in Hawai'i and elsewhere. Lacking sufficient personnel and the budget to support a thorough surveillance of the Japanese in Hawai'i in the 1930s, departmental commanders such as Briant Wells chose to win over Japanese Americans in Hawai'i—who, by the end of the decade in question, numbered over 157,000, most with American citizenship. His Joint Defense Plan of 1933, for example, called for treating all citizens of the United States as loyal unless proven otherwise. Wells's stance pushed the Hawaiian Department further along the lines of assessing local Japanese as a low risk, a trajectory that was already finding, as its intelligence officer did in 1929, that Japanese Americans were unlikely to serve as saboteurs or collaborate with an imperial Japanese attack on the Islands:

It may be generally assumed that all Japanese born in Japan will
be hostile, but it is generally believed that Hawaiian-born Japanese
will not have the same intense feelings for Japan. In any case, it is
believed that the Japanese will not declare themselves hostile to the
United States until they are reasonably sure of the success of Japan.
They would stand to lose too much if they joined the attackers
and the attack should fail. Their attitude probably will be one of
watchful waiting until the outcome of the attack is foreseen.[15]

On the continent, the Army took a different approach to securing the
nation without direct involvement in domestic surveillance. It borrowed
data from the United States Navy and the FBI and supplemented this
with data from its own informants, who reported to Ralph Van Deman,
to assess the level of potential national security threat Japanese residents
posed. The MID believed the Japanese, unlike the communists, Nazis,
and fascists, sent out groups to gather intelligence across the nation
rather than confine themselves to certain regions to conduct propaganda and collect tactical, commercial, and strategic intelligence.
Tactical intelligence, the division believed, was gathered surreptitiously
by foreign agents such as Germans, who had the "correct racial uni-
form," or openly by Japanese officers posing as language students at
American universities. Commercial intelligence, MID officers suspected,
was gathered by various Japanese members in such business-oriented
organizations as chambers of commerce. Propaganda, they knew, was
done through the Empire of Japan's Foreign Ministry, which had in
1939 a budget of $1.5 million, half of which was funneled through
the New York City Consulate office; Japanese residents there numbered
about two thousand. Intelligence officers also learned that Japanese
propaganda was carried out by many Japanese Americans on the West
Coast and Hawai'i who were stimulated by Imperial Japanese Navy
visits. "A valuable propaganda method among the West Coast and
Hawaiian Japanese," an unnamed intelligence officer observed, "is the
regular visit of naval and government vessels. There is always a full program of reciprocal entertainment and the officers of these vessels, as a
rule, give lectures daily in schools and clubs and visit other groups."[16]
Integral to the MID's understanding of the potential threat Japanese
residents posed was information gathered from other sources. Obeying

the letter while violating the spirit of the directive against direct do-mestic surveillance, the division consulted one of the most knowledge-able former counterintelligence officers, retired general Ralph Van Deman, "the father of American military intelligence." Van Deman retired in September 1929 to San Diego, California, taking with him his voluminous card filing system and files. He exchanged information with FBI, Army, and Navy intelligence officers, and gathered intelli-gence from his own network of civilian informants who spied on var-ious suspected organizations and individuals. Some of his intelligence reports were simply collected rumors and became part of the "mess of misinformation" (his terminology) that unscrupulous politicians such as Senator Joseph McCarthy used to persecute alleged communists and labor union activists.[17]

For intelligence on West Coast Japanese residents, Van Deman tapped a well-placed journalist named Mary Oyama (1907–1994), who had broad knowledge of them due to her background. Mary was born and raised in Northern California before moving to Seattle, where she worked for several years as a social worker after graduating from high school in Sacramento. She moved to Los Angeles in the early 1930s, where she embarked upon a career in journalism after majoring in that subject at the University of Southern California. She became an im-mensely popular English-language columnist for the *Shin Sekai Asahi Shinbun*, and was a prolific writer of poetry, fiction literature, book reviews, and essays. A leading light among the American-born Japanese literati, her influence was as wide as it was deep within the Japanese American community from the mid 1930s until the attack on Pearl Harbor. She warned, "We are entering the Era of a Great Change in our Nisei and Japanese community," and urged her co-ethnics to drop the label "Japanese" from their ethnic-specific organizations. But be-fore she could convince many, she, her husband, Fred Mittwer, and their two sons, along with some 119,000 other Japanese Americans, were removed from their homes in 1942 and interned in Wartime Civilian Control Administration (WCCA) camps before being shipped to the War Relocation Authority camp, in her case, to Heart Mountain, Wyoming, where the Mittwer family remained incarcerated until early 1943. Before she was whisked away to a WCCA camp at Santa Anita, California, however, she produced at least two reports for Van

Deman as Agent B-31, warning of the risk certain individual Japanese residents might pose for national security.[18]

The reason why the MID showed little interest in direct surveillance stemmed from its view of managing sabotage. By 1936, its superiors on the general staff resisted attempts to commit the Army to the defense of industrial installations, which in turn removed the task of careful surveillance of potential saboteurs, including Japanese Americans. The chief of the general staff, Operations Branch Colonel C. M. Thiele, made it clear in a memorandum that they were not in support of such activities. "The idea that the army will be responsible for the protection of industrial installations against sabotage," the Colonel reminded staff members, "is believed to be unsound. We have religiously kept away from this commitment." Thiele pointed out that such responsibilities should be left to local state police and home guards whose forces were sufficient while the Army was concentrating on mobilizing its forces for combat duties. As for the MID officers who worked directly within the War Plans Division, their assessment of the low risk of sabotage in the continental United States was closely related to their view that sabotage was only a viable action to take if and when the possibility and opportunity to launch a significant raid or an invasion was advantageous relative to the possible losses in military personnel and equipment. In 1929, they believed the imperial Japanese forces thought a raid was impractical:

It is not considered practicable for the Japanese to make any effective descent upon any part of our home coasts, although they might attempt raids at various points. We will not have any Naval Forces, aside from submarines and aircraft, with other small craft, available for local defense purposes, so that the protection of our coasts from enemy raids will fall upon the Army to a considerable extent, once our combatant Fleet has sailed from the Pacific Coast Ports.[19]

In fact, as early as 1929, they concluded that the Imperial Japanese forces would not even contemplate an invasion of North America:

The invasion of the continental United States is beyond the capability of the Japanese in the present relative strengths and resources of the two countries, so that Japanese operations for the attainment of their two possible objectives could be, and to a large extent, probably would be, confined to the Western Pacific.[20]

But the same was not true for their estimates of necessary troop strength in the territories of the United States. Army intelligence officers in the 1930s believed significant segments of the Japanese population in Hawai'i posed a possible threat to national security. In 1934, for example, General Sherman Miles of the MID wrote a four-page report sounding the alarm on the lack of preparation for the possibility of sabotage and the inadequacy of the provost marshal's home guards in handling such matters until after the fact. Miles warned:

The plans for carrying out the mission are based on a system of registration and identification which could not be effective during the critical period of the war (the first six weeks); are based also on a very loose control under reserve officers of doubtful efficiency; are lacking in any positive measures to prevent sabotage, or anything else until overt acts have been committed; are also lacking in any measures for surveillance of the large Japanese population on the other islands or prevention of their movement to Oahu; and, above all, they emphasize enemy aliens almost to the total exclusion of American citizens of Japanese ancestry, although the latter may be equally dangerous to us.[21]

A year later, Colonel F. H. Lincoln, of the general staff, reiterated the warning that Japanese nationals in Hawai'i might cooperate with a Japanese surprise attack on Hawai'i after reviewing the war game performances of the Army and the Navy in which the "Orange" (Imperial Japanese) forces defeated the "Blue" (American) forces. According to Lincoln, "The weakness of Hawaii (to Blue) is the possibility of a surprise attack by Orange using commercial vessels plus naval forces combined with the joint effort of Orange nationals legally resident there."[22]

The possibility of many Japanese residents in Hawai'i cooperating with an imperial Japanese attacking force led Army war planners in two different directions. The first direction, planned upon as early as 1907, called for rounding up all Japanese residents and concentrating them in camps on the windward side of O'ahu. By 1924, however, the Army's Hawaiian Department shifted away from the punitive to the inducement option instead. The department's commander, Charles Summerall, worked with Hawaiian Territorial Governor Wallace Farrington to gradually bring Japanese Americans into the National Guard, justifying it on the basis that "there is no better way of securing the loyalty of such people than to incorporate them in our military forces with the environment of obligation of duty that cannot fail to win their allegiance in most, if not all cases." By the mid 1930s, Army command officers abandoned the idea of mass removal or reconcentration of Japanese Americans as impractical and morally indefensible. Adding to their belief that the islands were defensible despite their large population of Japanese Americans, they understood a successful defense of O'ahu was more than a mere possibility since they had all possible landing sites covered with preset lines of fire to create killing zones, backed with chemical weaponry ready for use. Moreover, the Army had already embarked on its own program to cultivate the loyalty of Hawai'i's Japanese, and recruited some Hawai'i-born Japanese to keep a watch on others for possible signs of espionage.[23]

In Alaska, however, the Army took a different course. The MID conceded the possibility that the imperial Japanese forces might invade and occupy Alaska. But they surmised that the Japanese aims there were to simply deny usage of the land to American forces and to provide a protected base for possible raids against American shipping and naval activities in the northeastern Pacific. Given these limited aims, the MID did not assign officers to conduct surveillance on the Japanese population in Alaska until early 1941. They chose instead to depend heavily on knowledgeable individuals who reported on the Japanese residents in the territory. Since the Japanese there numbered fewer than seven hundred, the division did not perceive them as a threat—even if some of them spent winters in Japan, affording them an opportunity to transmit intelligence reports to Tokyo with relative ease.[24]

The potential of the Japanese engaged in espionage or sabotage in Alaska was unimportant for congressional leaders. Instead, some members of the House of Representatives and the Senate focused on the propaganda and subversion components of fifth columnist activities. In the process, Senator Guy Gillette and Democratic House Representatives Samuel Dickstein and Martin Dies politicized counter-intelligence in the latter half of the 1930s. Unfamiliar with professional methods of counterintelligence, they broadened the definition of fifth columnist activities to include words rather than specific acts; took up the police method of a complaint-based, rather than a functional, approach to initiating investigations; depended on others for the requisite language skills to gather evidence instead of employing investigators fluent in Japanese; and opted for congressional hearings to expose foreign agents and rally public support rather than silently and unobtrusively identifying all members of a given spy ring before taking punitive action. Their approach built upon the broadening of the parameters of counterintelligence that began with the Espionage Act of 1917. The act they leaned on transformed the military acts of espionage and sabotage into violations of federal law at a time when German agents penetrated American borders, spied on the American military, and blew up ammunition factories on American soil to obstruct the US government's war matériel support for the Allied powers during World War I. The Supreme Court further blurred the line between counterintelligence and internal security by ruling in the 1919 case of *Schenck v. United States* that freedom of speech under the First Amendment was limited by any conditions in which a "clear and present danger" was found to exist. Chief Justice Oliver Wendell Holmes applied this concept to the draft resistance advocated by antiwar activists. In 1940 Congress further extended the internal-security reach into counterintelligence with the passage of the Smith Act, which banned advocacy or teaching of armed revolution and violent overthrow of the government, all of which made terms such as *subversion, propaganda*, and *treason* paramount.[25]

By the early 1930s, however, a new generation of congressional leaders extended the parameters of counterintelligence. Some, such as Samuel Dickstein of New York City, linked *subversion* with any activity that, in their eyes, undermined the American constitutional government. They redefined *spies* to include those who acted as "propaganda agents." A Democrat elected to the US House of Representatives in 1922, Dickstein succeeded in his reelection bids and remained in Congress into the 1930s, which is when he learned of the problem of German American organizations increasingly following in step with Germany's policy (which, after the Nazis came to power in 1932, brought with them anti-Semitism). Upon investigation of these German American groups, Dickstein came to believe they represented a significant internal security threat. He found it disturbing that German American Nazis could hold conferences and camps, study Nazi political ideology, and pledge their allegiance and monetary donations to Germany. These actions, Dickstein asserted, amounted to subversion and sabotage:

What can be done? I, too, have a tremendous lot of new matter and facts to justify a dozen investigations. Laws cannot destroy this kind of subversive propaganda. I need not elaborate for you your-self know what is going on. Recently the newspapers have been flooded with reports and pictures on Nazi activity. The Nazis are running wild. They have taken the country by storm, since they know that neither a check-up nor an investigation will be made. I will still maintain that a resolution could be passed in view of con-tinuous subversive acts and sabotage against the government of the United States and its people.[26]

Dickstein's linkage of *propaganda* to German and Italian "agitators," whose presence was far more visible in New York than the Japanese, meant the congressman was not likely to highlight the Japanese. Perhaps Dickstein never focused the attention of his House Un-American Activities Committee (HUAC) on the Japanese, as he may have viewed them as "too quiet." Or, the congressman may simply have been unaware that the Imperial Japanese Navy and the Imperial Japanese Army had offices in the city, with the latter commanded by an officer of a general's rank. Both branches of the Japanese military had their technical experts also in residence to evaluate technical data. Either way, Dickstein barely mentioned the Japanese.[27]

Under Martin Dies's leadership, however, the Japanese belatedly be-came a focal point of HUAC. He took over the committee in 1938 and launched his own crusade against the four empires he believed were in-imical to the United States government and the American people. Each of these four empires, Dies argued, shared a totalitarian ideology, a Trojan horse methodology, and a willingness to wage total war:

Four new empires have arisen upon the ruins of the world: Hitler's, Stalin's, Mussolini's, and the Mikado's. Behind each of these empires is the driving fanatical force of totalitarian ideology. Each of these empires employ the strategy of the Trojan Horse followed by the blitzkrieg of total war.

By *totalitarian ideology*, Dies was referring to the political philosophies that undergirded Nazism, communism, and fascism—the three "isms" he found objectionable. He saw in all of them the individual subservient to the State. "Under all of these totalitarian schemes the state becomes everything," Dies warned, "the individual nothing." Worse, the Texas congressman claimed, "As the state becomes supreme the individual is reduced to a mere cog in a collectivistic machine."[28]

As for Japan, the Texas congressman claimed that its government had already set up its Trojan horse inside the United States. With a totalitarian ideology, inculcated through the Japanese-language schools in California and Hawai'i, the Japanese government recruited US citizens to engage in espionage as immigrant civic organizations such as the Central Japanese Association pretended to be loyal to the United States while surreptitiously serving "the deified Emperor of Japan." Japanese merchants, by virtue of their occupation, were able to travel about, and in the process, they "collected intelligence" and "engaged in espionage activities for the Japanese Government." Japanese fishermen served as couriers for spy reports, and many Japanese Americans helped to spread the "printed Axis propaganda" which the Japanese government flooded into the United States for distribution.[29]

Dies's sense of urgency about Japanese Americans, it should be noted, did not stem from a belief that they constituted the vanguard of a Japanese invasion. In June 1940, and again in February 1941, after Pearl Harbor, the HUAC chairman made it clear he feared no invasion from singular or combined enemy invading forces:

I do not mean to imply that we in America are now in danger of invasion. As a matter of fact, there is no power or combination of powers that could ever invade the United States even if it dared to try, so long as we are adequately prepared and stand united in allegiance to the God of our fathers and the Constitution of our country.

Instead, Dies believed the danger of "treason from within" was paramount. By that he meant the American tolerance of "numerous traitorous organizations, groups, and individuals" that undermined the ideological foundations of the nation; destroyed national unity; spread destructive propaganda, dissension, and hatred, both race- and class-based; and gathered "valuable industrial and military information" useful to an enemy empire planning to subjugate the United States.[30]

After considerable investigation, HUAC under Martin Dies failed to secure a public hearing before the attack on Pearl Harbor. The Texan congressman proposed in September 1941 to hold public hearings on the alleged Japanese threat, and had already leaked some of his more eye-catching findings through newspaper outlets during the summer while he prepared fifty-two witnesses. However, the attorney general, the secretary of state, and the president strongly discouraged him; the Office of Naval Intelligence, too, did not want the hearings to exacerbate tensions with Japan, which by early fall 1941 had reached a breaking point. Moreover, by 1942, professional counterintelligence agencies had already sifted through the one-million-card index stored in 138 cabinets in the three HUAC offices and determined its overall value was low. The Army and Navy combined had submitted only about a quarter, and the State Department only 2 percent, of the total 138,807 requests for information from HUAC's massive collection of reports. Instead, it was federal government agencies with less concern for espionage and sabotage and more for internal security that had filed three-quarters of all the requests to HUAC. Those agencies included the Civil Service Commission, the Department of Justice and the FBI, the Office of Emergency Management, the Treasury Department, and the Works Progress Administration. Hence, the ONI's spokesperson confidently declared that Pearl Harbor was "all secure with everything under control," and that the Navy and Coast Guard ran "a stringent patrol at least 60 miles out" to ensure against a blitzkrieg or total war by Japan; their surveillance at sea and air was "effective considerably beyond the Hawaiian islands."[31]

Martin Dies was not the only one who politicized counterintelligence before the Pearl Harbor attack. Democratic senator Guy Gillette of Iowa also proposed in October 1941 to hold a Senate hearing on the alleged threat of Japanese Americans. He too was rejected by President Franklin Roosevelt, Secretary of State Cordell Hull, and US Attorney General Francis Biddle for similar reasons, even though the senator, unlike his House counterpart, was not known as a red-baiting politician. Rather, Gillette was a champion of the family farm, a Jeffersonian Democrat with an internationalist outlook, and a staunch critic of British imperialism to the extent that he once volunteered to fight against the British forces in the South African War (1899–1902). Highly principled, he was also known to oppose name-calling and reckless finger-pointing in the name of Americanism, in contrast to Dies. In the case of Guy Gillette, therefore, motivations outside of political opportunism better explain why he targeted Japanese Americans in the months prior to the Pearl Harbor attack.[32]

Part of the reason why Gillette went after Japanese Americans was rooted in his belief in his key informant, Kilsoo Haan. Gillette first met Haan in October 1937, when Army intelligence officer Byron Meurlott introduced him just prior to the senator's public hearing in Honolulu regarding the issue of Hawai'i's statehood. Haan spoke out against statehood, asserting such a move would only give the Empire of Japan behind-the-scenes control over the strategically important islands. He pointed to that country's successful Japanization program of the islands' Japanese nationals and American citizens, who made up 40 percent of the population. While Gillette was probably initially skeptical of Haan's claims of a Japanese government conspiracy to control the islands, by 1940 he had come to trust Haan's "intelligence" reports and public claims after the Korean American moved to Washington, DC, as a lobbyist for the Sino-Korean People's League. In January 1941, the Iowan senator wrote a recommendation letter for Haan as a public speaker on Korean independence, Japan, and Japanese Americans in glowing terms:

I have known Mr. Kilsoo Haan for about five years. I became acquainted with him in Hawaii Territory about 1937. I have been closely acquainted with him during the past two or more years that he has been residing in Washington. I have found him at all times trustworthy and dependable. He has a fund of knowledge relative to the subject matter.[33]

Gillette also accepted the testimony of Japanese American leftists as proof of the involvement of some Japanese Americans in imperial Japan's subversive propaganda campaign against the United States. He specifically called for an investigation into three Japanese American organizations advancing the Empire of Japan's propaganda aims and garnering financial support for its military campaign on the Asian continent. Gillette believed the Japanese Military Servicemen's League was subversive and potentially a fifth columnist organization, as Shūji Fuji, the leftist editor of the *Dōhō* of Los Angeles, claimed. Gillette also pointed to the Imperial Comradeship Society as another problematic organization, since it was led not by aliens but by US citizens and raised substantial amounts of monetary donations for the Japanese war machine in its imperialist drive on the Asian continent. The third organization Gillette insisted on investigating publicly reflected the antagonism some of his leftist sources felt toward some of these anti–labor unionist, Republican Party ethnic community leaders—the Japanese American Citizens League.[34]

Thus, on October 2, 1941, Senator Gillette submitted his proposal for a Senate hearing on these three alleged subversive organizations. He justified his Senate Resolution 176 based not on "race" but on assisting loyal Japanese Americans:

Out in the Western portion of the United States there are some groups of American citizens of Japanese ancestry who are doing their earnest best to prove their loyalty to America by exposing un-American Japanese governed, Japanese inspired, and Japanese controlled activities looking to possible hostilities conducted against the United States. . . . These young American citizens have been left practically alone to face the united and tremendously powerful support of these pro-Japanese organizations composed of non-quota aliens or so-called dual citizens who prefer allegiance to Japan and the so-called Kibei or United States citizens returned from Japan and all of these groups combined with the Japanese consulate agents who have been ceaseless in their activities in organizing and increasing the membership of these hostile or potentially hostile groups.[35]

In the end, however, Gillette's plea for support of loyal Japanese Americans in their struggle against these Japanese American organizations also went unheeded. As they had with Martin Dies, the president, the attorney general, and the secretary of state refused to endorse any public hearing on Japan and Japanese Americans at such a critical juncture, when relations between the two major powers at opposite ends of the Pacific Rim neared a breaking point. Secretary of State Cordell Hull telephoned Gillette that afternoon and spent about forty minutes explaining to the Iowa senator why the hearings should not be held in the interest of national security. Gillette complied, providing a four-month respite from the politicization of counterintelligence, until February 21, 1942, when John Tolan began his hearings for the House Select Committee Investigating National Defense Migration—yet another congressional examination into Japanese Americans and their alleged connections with America's enemy, the Empire of Japan.[36]

The rejection of congressional hearings on Japanese fifth column activities in the fall of 1941 was appropriate. The president rejected the two proposals, knowing they were a means to embarrass his administration. Secretary of State Cordell Hull's rejection had ostensibly higher aims—that is, to preserve his chance for a negotiated withdrawal of imperial Japan's forces from the Asian continent. The ONI and the MID too appropriately withheld their support for congressional hearings on Japanese Americans, on the grounds that the congressmen's "amateur" counterintelligence operations shifted the focus away from their primary duty to prevent espionage and sabotage, or acts of military crimes that amounted to something far more serious than words. They barely paid attention to propaganda, under the assumption such activities were legally gathered and constituted internal security matters—not the "proper" domain of professional counterintelligence operations. With their own professionally collected data, they found that only a handful of Japanese Americans posed a "real" security threat.

Conversely, congressional leaders such as Samuel Dickstein, Martin Dies, and Guy Gillette found it advantageous to politicize counterintelligence. For Dickstein, his fight against the Nazi movement at home and abroad necessitated winning public support to slow down that movement's spread in the early 1930s. To warn the public, Dickstein chose to hold hearings, call witnesses, and provide press releases, paying particular attention to German American involvement in Nazi propaganda. Given his meager budget, he supplemented its finances by soliciting support from the Nazis' archenemy, the Soviet Union. With an income of $1,250 a month from Soviet intelligence as of spring 1938, Dickstein had the money to gather documentary evidence on fascists, which both HUAC and Soviet intelligence took a keen interest in. The Jewish politician from the Lower East Side of Manhattan was viewed by Soviet intelligence as simply a corrupt politician from whom they could buy useful information. Thus, they code-named him "Crook," failing to realize that Dickstein used the money to further his struggle against the Nazis.[37]

Dies and Gillette also "profited" from politicizing counterintelligence through their focus on Japanese American propaganda. For the Texas congressman, the fifth columnist threat was primarily about propaganda and his expanded definition of *spies* allowed him to point the finger at a large number of Japanese Americans on the West Coast and Hawai'i while restricting his claims of Japanese American sabotage plotting to a small handful of residents on Terminal Island in Los Angeles Harbor. Dies did not emphasize sabotage activities since they normally precede an enemy invasion or a major attack, neither of which he believed was possible. With public hearings, Dies could then do what he excelled at—giving inflammatory public speeches rather than present carefully researched and thoughtfully articulated talks on counterintelligence. His rhetoric against the Japanese coincided with the slowdown in his committee's generating investigative reports.[38]

For the Iowa senator, targeting certain Japanese American organizations provided certain nonmaterial benefits too. On a personal level, his call for a Senate investigation into Japan's subversion of America, and Japanese American involvement therein, matched his concern for his younger brother, an admiral in the Navy who had become manager of the Navy Yard at Pearl Harbor in April 1939. On a policy and ideological level, Gillette opposed the concentration of power; his investigation would bring additional pressure on President Franklin Roosevelt not to seek a fourth term in office. Moreover, Gillette found the New Deal's lack of protection for family farms and the administration's emphasis on the military rebuilding program did not sit well with his Jeffersonian Democrat ideals.[39]

But Japanese Americans were the ones penalized rather than rewarded by the professionalization and the politicization of American counter-intelligence. Admittedly, professionalization limited the number of suspected Japanese Americans, since so few of them physically approached military bases or regularly dealt with Japanese Foreign Ministry officials. However, their failure to help avert the Pearl Harbor disaster resulted in a loss of credibility in the eyes of the American public, who were already worried about the American military's ability to halt enemy forces after the advent of the blitzkrieg on the European continent. The public's doubts opened the door for the politicization of counterintelligence by congressional leaders who made no distinction between counterintelligence and internal security, and who confused propaganda with espionage, and subversion with sabotage. Their efforts finally succeeded in two congressional hearings held in 1943. One was a House subcommittee hearing on interned Japanese Americans planning acts of sabotage once released from the War Relocation Authority camps. The other was a Senate subcommittee chaired by Senator A. B. Chandler of Kentucky, who announced during his "investigation" that 60 percent of the incarcerated Japanese were disloyal to America and were "prepared to help Japanese troops invade the West Coast right after Pearl Harbor."[40]

## Notes

1. Brian Masaru Hayashi, "Frank Knox's Fifth Column Hawai'i: The US, the Japanese, and the Pearl Harbor Attack," *Journal of American–East Asian Relations* 27, no. 2 (July 2020): 142–68; Francis MacDonnell, *Insidious Foes: The Axis Fifth Column and the American Home Front* (New York: Oxford University Press, 1995), 7–8; Lon Kurashige, "American Public Opinion about the Japanese during World War" (unpublished manuscript, 2017, private), 7.

2. Much of the writing on surveillance of Japanese Americans centers focus on the years immediately preceding the mass removal and internment of West Coast Japanese Americans in 1942; it ignores the important changes that took place at the beginning of the 1930s. See Roger Daniels, "The Bureau of the Census and the Relocation of Japanese Americans: A Note and Document," *Amerasia Journal* 9, no. 1 (Spring/Summer 1982): 101–5; Gary Okihiro, *Cane Fires: The Anti-Japanese Movement in Hawaii, 1865–1945* (Philadelphia: Temple University Press, 1991); John A. Hertzig, "Japanese Americans and MAGIC," *Amerasia Journal* 11, no. 2 (Fall/Winter 1984): 47–65; David D. Lowman, *MAGIC: The Untold Story of US Intelligence and the Evacuation of Japanese Residents from the West Coast during World War II* (Provo, UT: Athena Press, 2001); Michi Weglyn, *Years of Infamy: The*

*Untold Story of America's Concentration Camps* (New York: William Morrow, 1976), 33–53; Tetsuden Kashima, *Judgment without Trial: Japanese American Imprisonment during World War II* (Seattle: University of Washington Press, 2003), 14–42; Duncan Ryūken Williams, *American Sutra: A Story of Faith and Freedom in the Second World War* (Cambridge, MA: Belknap Press, 2019), 32–38. The exception to the rule is Bob Kumamoto, "The Search for Spies: American Counterintelligence and the Japanese American Community, 1931–1942," *Amerasia Journal* 6, no. 2 (Fall 1979): 45–76.

3. John Prout, "The Origins of the Military Attaché Corps," *American Intelligence Journal* 21, no. 1 (Spring 2002): 51; Lieutenant William L. Sachse, US Naval Reserve, "Our Naval Attaché System: Its Origins and Development to 1917," *Proceedings* vol. 72/5/519 (May 1946); Peter Karsten, *The Naval Aristocracy: The Golden Age of Annapolis and the Emergence of Modern American Navalism* (New York: The Free Press, 1972), 102–3, 215; Jeffery M.Dorwart, *Conflict of Duty: The US Navy's Intelligence Dilemma, 1919–1945* (Annapolis, MD: Naval Institute Press, 1983), 5–7; Captain Wyman H. Packard, *A Century of US Naval Intelligence* (Washington, DC: Department of the Navy, 1996), 248–51. It should be noted here that several Japanese served in the American Navy during the Spanish-American War, and that Japanese immigrants worked at the Navy Yard in Brooklyn, New York, before Navy Yard Order No. 26 was issued in 1892, which prohibited the employment of any non-US citizen as a laborer or mechanic at USN yards and stations. See Daniel H. Inouye, *Distant Islands: The Japanese American Community in New York City, 1876–1930s* (Louisville: University Press of Colorado, 2019), 123, 149–50, 196.

4. Gerald E. Wheeler, "The United States Navy and the Japanese 'Enemy': 1919–1931," *Military Affairs* 21, no. 2 (Summer 1957): 61–74; Edward S. Miller, *War Plan ORANGE: The US Strategy to Defeat Japan, 1897–1945* (Annapolis, MD: Naval Institute Press, 1991), 20–22, 27, 41, 46–47, 134.

5. See James B. Bruce and Roger George, "Professionalizing Intelligence Analysis," *Journal of Strategic Security* 8, no. 3 (2015): 7–8, for the six characteristics of a professionalized occupation.

6. Dorwart, *Conflict of Duty*, 64–65; I. H. Mayfield, Counterintelligence Section, District Intelligence Office, Fourteenth Naval District, "An Analysis of the Japanese Espionage Problem in the Hawaiian Islands," April 20, 1943, 45–46, Folder Japanese Intelligence Activities—US (Gen.), box 1, Counterintelligence Section, reports and correspondence re strike conditions, 1940–41, entry 28, Record Group 38 Office of Naval Intelligence, National Archives and Records Administration II, College Park, MD (hereafter cited as RG 38 ONI/NARA II); Ellis M. Zacharias, *Secret Missions: The Story of an Intelligence Officer* (Annapolis, MD: Naval Institute Press, 1946), 117, 147, 179–82, 205; Packard, *US Naval Intelligence*, 256.

7. Zacharias, *Secret Missions*, 178–79, 232–33, 313–33; Dorwart, *Conflict of Duty*, 66; Roger B. Jeans, *Terasaki Hidenari, Pearl Harbor, and Occupied Japan: A Bridge to Reality* (Boston: Rowman & Littlefield, 2009), 25, 29–33, 41–43, 47–49.

8. Zacharias, *Secret Missions*, 209–10; Pedro A. Loureiro, "Japanese Espionage and American Countermeasures in Pre–Pearl Harbor California," *Journal of American–East Asian Relations* 3, no. 3 (Fall 1994): 200–201.

9. Mayfield, "The Japanese Espionage Problem," RG 38 ONI/NARA II; Tom Coffman, *Inclusion: How Hawai'i Protected Japanese Americans from Mass*

*Internment, Transformed Itself, and Changed America* (Honolulu: University of Hawai'i Press, 2021), 66–68.

10. Coffman, *Inclusion*, 24; Kashima, *Judgment without Trial*, 17–42; Williams, *American Sutra*, 28–38; Yuji Ichioka, *The Issei: The World of the First Generation Japanese Immigrants, 1885–1924* (New York: The Free Press, 1988), 160–64; Eiichiro Azuma, *Between Two Empires: Race, History, and Transnationalism in Japanese America* (New York: Oxford University Press, 2005), 44–50.

11. John Patrick Finnegan, *Military Intelligence* (Washington, DC: Center of Military History, United States Army, 1998), 24–30; Joan Jensen, *Army Surveillance in America, 1775–1980* (New Haven, CT: Yale University Press, 1991), 37–38, 45, 59; Bruce W. Bidwell, *History of the Military Intelligence Division, Department of the Army General Staff: 1775–1941* (Frederick, MD: University Publications of America, 1986), 56, 236–37, 110–11, 191, 208, 241–42; United States Army, *United States Army Register Vol. III Retired List* (Washington, DC: Government Printing Office, 1968), 877.

12. Bidwell, *History of the Military Intelligence Division*, 278.

13. Bidwell, 278–80; Roy Talbert Jr., *Negative Intelligence: The Army and the American Left, 1917–1941* (Jackson: University Press of Mississippi, 1991), 256–59; James L. Gilbert, *World War I and the Origins of US Military Intelligence* (Lanham, MD: Scarecrow Press, 2012), 34–44.

14. Bidwell, *History of the Military Intelligence Division*, 258, 271.

15. Brian McAlister Linn, *Guardians of Empire: The US Army and the Pacific, 1902–1940* (Chapel Hill: University of North Carolina Press, 1997), 161–62.

16. War Department, Military Intelligence Service, Counterintelligence Bulletin no. 3, "Japanese Total Espionage in Manchuria, China, and the Netherlands East Indies," April 5, 1942, folder 2127-9; (MID), "Japanese," n.d., folder 2127-1: 5935 Japan Military Activities Abroad, box 2127, Military Intelligence Division, Regional File, 1922-44, RG 165 Records of the War Department General and Special Staffs, NARA II, College Park, MD; Zaibei Nihonjinkai Jiseki Hozonbu, ed., *Zaibei Nihonjinshi* [History of Japanese in America] (San Francisco: Zaibei Nihonjinkai, 1940), 1059–60.

17. Ralph Henry Van Deman to A. C. Wedemeyer, March 28, 1950, box 103, folder 103.24, Albert Coady Wedemeyer Papers, The Hoover Institution, Stanford, CA; Richard Halloran, "Senate Panel Holds Vast 'Subversives' File Amassed by Ex-Chief of Army Intelligence," *New York Times*, September 7, 1971; Jensen, *Army Surveillance*, 112–16, 264; Alfred W. McCoy, *Policing America's Empire: The United States, the Philippines, and the Rise of the Surveillance State* (Madison: University of Wisconsin Press, 2009), 77–82, 293–94, 297–301, 319–23, 326–33.

18. Valerie J. Matsumoto, *City Girls: The Nisei Social World in Los Angeles, 1920–1950* (New York: Oxford University Press, 2014), 23, 48, 88–90, 120, 147, 153; McCoy, *Policing America's Empire*, 330–32. It should be noted here that McCoy believes Mary Oyama's report contributed to the alleged fear and panic over the possible national security threat West Coast Japanese Americans posed in 1942. However, McCoy's claim is not supported by other evidence. The leftists, most notably Karl Yoneda, submitted reports to the FBI about the widespread support many Japanese Americans demonstrated toward imperial Japan, some of it even after the Pearl Harbor attack, which Van Deman may have seen. Yet the

retired general and the FBI recommended against the mass removal and internment of Japanese Americans.

19. C. M. Thiele, Memorandum for Lieut. Colonel J. P. Smith, G.S., May 2, 1936,
box 70, folder 238, Administrative Services Division Operations Branch, Special
Projects-War Plans "Color," 1920–1948, entry 365, Record Group 407 Record of
the Adjutant General's Office, National Archives and Records Administration II,
College Park, MD (hereafter cited as RG 407 AGO/NARA II).

20. Estimate of the Situation Joint Army and Navy Basic War Plan Orange
(1929), 19, 61, box 68, folder 226, Record of the Adjutant General's Office, 1917,
Administrative Services Division Operations Branch, Special Projects-War Plans
"Color," 1920–1948, Japan Reg. Doc. #215 to #227, entry 365, RG 407 AGO/
NARA II.

21. Sherman Miles, Memorandum for the Assistant Chief of Staff, War Plans
Division, October 22, 1934, files 3675 to 3675-5, box 145: War Plans Division
General Correspondence, 1920–1942, entry 7 (NM 84) 281, Record Group 165
Records of the War Department General and Special Staffs, National Archives and
Records Administration II, College Park, MD (hereafter cited as WDGSS/NARA II).

22. F. H. Lincoln, Memorandum for the Assistant Chief of Staff, War Plans
Division, December 24, 1935, box 70, folder 238, Record of the Adjutant General's
Office, 1917, Administrative Services Division Operations Branch, Special Projects-
War Plans "Color," 1920–1948, entry 365, RG 407 AGO/NARA II.

23. Linn, *Guardians of Empire*, 104–6, 154–57, 198, 246; Coffman, *Inclusion*,
61–65, 99.

24. Army Strategical Plan Orange red-stamped "obsolete" (1936), Annex I
Current Estimate of the Situation Annex No. 1 to Army Strategical Plan – Orange
(1936 Revision), 1–4, box 70, folder 235, entry 365, RG 407 AGO/NARA II; A. J.
Wirtz to Henry Stimson, October 3, 1940, and Sherman Miles, Memorandum to
the Adjutant General, ca. late 1940, box 565, folders 1766-Z-595 [to] 1766-Z-
606, Military Intelligence Division Correspondence, 1917–1941; C. S. Robertson,
Memorandum for Commander H. C. Davis, May 6, 1941, and excerpts from Letter,
H. B. Friele to C. S. Robertson, box 565, folders 1766-Z-595 [to] 1766-Z-606,
Military Intelligence Division Correspondence, 1917–1941; Edward W. Allen to
Mr. J. Austin Latimer, April 11, 1941, box 565, folders 1766-Z-595 [to] 1766-Z-
606, Military Intelligence Division Correspondence, 1917–1941, entry 65, RG 165
WDGSS/NARA II.

25. Dwight R. Messimer, *The Baltimore Sabotage Cell: German Agents, American
Traitors, and the U-Boat* Deutschland *during World War I* (Annapolis, MD: Naval
Institute Press, 2015); Howard Blum, *Dark Invasion, 1915: Germany's Secret War
and the Hunt for the First Terrorist Cell in America* (New York: HarperCollins,
2014); J. H. Leek, "Treason and the Constitution," *Journal of Politics* 13, no. 4
(November 1951): 617–19.

26. Dorothy Waring, *American Defender* (New York: Robert Speller, 1935),
92, 121–129; Walter Goodman, *The Committee: The Extraordinary Career of the
House Committee on Un-American Activities* (New York: Farrar, Straus and Giroux,
1968), 3–4; Samuel Dickstein to John L. McCormack, September 18, 1934, and July 20,
1937, box 3, folder 3/7 McCormack, John L.; Speech of Representative Samuel
Dickstein, over the National Broadcasting Company's Blue Network, February 18,
1938, 7:15 p.m., box 4, folder 4/1, Samuel Dickstein Papers, MS-8, American Jewish
Archives, Jacob Rader Center, Cincinnati, OH.

27. Inouye, *Distant Islands*, 38; Louis Allen, "Japanese Intelligence Systems," *Journal of Contemporary History* 22, no. 4 (October 1987): 549; Zaibei Nihonjinkai, *Zaibei Nihonjinshi*, 1062.

28. (Martin Dies), "Our Domestic Foes," Speeches HUAC, ca. 1942, 5–6, File 6 Speeches, box 158, Martin Dies Papers, Sam Houston Regional Library, Liberty, TX (hereafter cited as MDP/SHRL).

29. Committee on Un-American Activities, House of Representatives, Seventy-Seventh Congress, first session, on H. R. Res. 282, Appendix VI, "Report on Japanese Activities" (Washington, DC: Government Printing Office, 1942), 1724–26. It should be noted that Dies's Committee focused on the Japanese when their production of witnesses and testimonies fell off precipitously. See William Gellermann, *Martin Dies* (New York: John Day, 1944), 70.

30. Martin Dies, "The Fifth Column Threat to Our Basic Industries," speech before the National Association of Independent Bakers at the Edgewater Beach Hotel, June 24, 1940, reported by Jean Moore, box 157, file 26 Speeches–Fifth Column, and Martin Dies, "Trojan Horse in America," February 9, 1941, box 158, file 2, MDP/SHRL.

31. Committee on Un-American Activities House of Representatives Seventy-Seventh Congress First Session on H. Res. 282 Appendix VI Report on Japanese Activities (Washington, DC: Government Printing Office, 1942), 1728, 1730; Martin Dies, no title, n.d., ca. 1942, box 157, file 58 Speeches – HUAC, ca. 1941, MDP/SHRL; Talbert, *Negative Intelligence*, 262, note 35.

32. Obituary Service Sketch no. 609, March 11, 1937, box 1, folder 1 Stelck-Gillette—Biographical & Personal; (Guy Gillette), Text of Radio Broadcast by Senator Guy M. Gillette (D-IA) for Station WON Chicago, and WHO, Des Moines, June 5, 1952, box 3, folder 1 Stelck-Gillette—Manuscripts-Political Speeches & Addresses; S. E. McClure (Administrative Assistant), Notes on Guy M. Gillette, January 20, 1950, box 8, folder Stelck-Gillette-Subject Files–Haan, Kilsoo (Korea), Dell Stelck Collection, Special Collections, University of Iowa, Iowa City (hereafter cited as DSC/UI).

33. (Kilsoo Haan), "How Retired US Army General Wells of Hawaii of [the] Hawaiian Plantation Association, Governor Joseph Poindexter of Hawaii, and Hawaii's Delegate Samuel King Tried to Stop Me from Testifying before Hawaii Statehood Hearings in October 21, 1937," and Guy M. Gillette to Mr. W. Colnton Leigh, January 19, 1941, box 8, folder Stelck-Gillette-Subject Files–Haan, Kilsoo (Korea), DSC/UI.

34. (Guy Gillette), "Statement of Senator Guy M. Gillette, of Iowa, October 2, 1941, to be made after the introduction of the Senate Res. 176 10-2-'41 p.m.," n.d., box 8, folder Stelck-Gillette-Subject Files–Haan, Kilsoo (Korea), DSC/UI. Recent scholarship on the Japanese American Citizens League, however, contradicts Gillette's conclusions. See Bill Hosokawa, *JACL in Quest of Justice: The History of the Japanese American Citizens League* (New York: William Morrow, 1982), 69–71, 98–100, 223–27; Jere Takahashi, *Nisei, Sansei: Shifting Japanese American Identities and Politics* (Philadelphia: Temple University Press, 1997), 54–65; Lon Kurashige, *Japanese American Celebration and Conflict: A History of Ethnic Identity and Festival in Los Angeles, 1934–1990* (Berkeley: University of California Press, 2002), 29–34, 59, 62–68; Yuji Ichioka, "A Study in Dualism: James Yoshinori Sakamoto and the *Japanese American Courier*, 1928–1942," in *Before Internment: Essays in Prewar Japanese American History*, eds. Gordon H. Chang and Eiichiro Azuma (Stanford, CA: Stanford University Press, 2006), 91–126.

35. (Guy Gillette), "Statement of Senator Guy M. Gillette, of Iowa," October 2, 1941, DSC/UI.

36. Diary entry, October 2, 1941, reel 39, p. 275, Papers of Cordell Hull, Library of Congress, Washington, DC.

37. Allen Weinstein and Alexander Vassiliev, *The Haunted Wood: Soviet Espionage in America—the Stalin Era* (New York: Random House, 1999), 141–43.

38. Gellermann, *Martin Dies*, 70. For critical evaluations of the Dies Committee, see Kate Dossett, "Gender and the Dies Committee Hearings of the Federal Theatre Project," *Journal of American Studies* 47, no. 4 (2013): 993–1017; Goodman, *The Committee*, 10–11, 21, 104, 106; and John Egerton, *Speak Now Against the Day: The Generation before the Civil Rights Movement in the South* (New York: Alfred A. Knopf, 1994). For a less harsh view of Dies, see Dennis K. McDaniel, "The First Congressman Martin Dies of Texas," *Southwestern Historical Quarterly* 102, no. 2 (October 1998): 131–61; Richard Polenberg, "Franklin Roosevelt and Civil Liberties: The Case of the Dies Committee," *The Historian* 30, no. 2 (February 1968): 165–78; and Martin Dies himself in his *Martin Dies' Story* (New York: Bookmailer, 1963).

39. (Guy Gillette), "Rear Admiral Claude Sexton Gillette, US Navy," n.d.; Guy M. Gillette obituary, March 11, 1960, box 1, folder 1 Stelck-Gillette—Biographical & Personal; S. E. McClure (Administrative Assistant), Notes on Guy M. Gillette, January 20, 1950, box 8, folder Stelck-Gillette-Subject Files–Haan, Kilsoo (Korea), DSC/UI.

40. Dillon Myer, *Uprooted Americans: The Japanese Americans and the War Relocation Authority during World War II* (Tucson: University of Arizona Press, 1971), 96–97; Carey McWilliams, *Prejudice: Japanese-Americans: Symbol of Racial Intolerance* (Boston: Little, Brown, 1944), 248–49.

# Afterword

*Kaoru Ueda*

Following the publication of Yasuo Sakata's translated volume *On a Collision Course: The Dawn of Japanese Migration in the Nineteenth Century* in 2020, his scholarship continues to inspire researchers to open new avenues of studies and question established ideas. The contributing authors' enthusiasm and strong interest in uncovering untold histories of Japanese America in the 1930s are a testament to the quality of Sakata's past work. His contributions to the field of Japanese American history and relations between the United States and Japan are many. Two that stand out are his broad perspective of going beyond Japanese American history to place Japanese immigration history on a global map, and his insistence on studying multilanguage, multinational primary source documents.

The Japanese Diaspora Initiative (JDI) at the Hoover Institution Library & Archives has taken Sakata's research approach to heart and has been building and promoting its archival collections. The Hoji Shinbun Digital Collection, consisting of about one million pages from two hundred titles of Japanese-language newspapers published outside Japan, provides open access to rare historical newspapers, promoting the use of Japanese-language materials in transnational historical inquiries and offering robust research opportunities to scholars globally. Benefiting from the open-access resources, ten young scholars presented their cutting-edge research papers at the Second International Workshop on Japanese Diaspora held at Hoover on November 4, 2022. Their topics were organized into three sessions: geopolitics, nationalism, and identity; World War II and its consequences; and economy and global commodity.

Furthering the resources available in the Hoji Shinbun Digital Collection, Sakata graciously offered his transcriptions of late nineteenth-century handwritten Japanese American newspapers to be incorporated into it. He also gifted the study materials he had accumulated over time, including rare prewar surveys conducted among the Issei to reflect on their more than forty years of collective experience of living in the United States. The JDI continues to promote the scholarly and educational use of primary source documents, particularly those written at the time of the events under study, to help researchers challenge established paradigms and move the field forward.

# Glossary

| | |
|---|---|
| *bokoku kankō* | "motherland" tour of Japan for Hawaiian or American Japanese |
| *bokoku kankōdan* | "motherland" tour group of Japan for Hawaiian or American Japanese |
| *dekasegi* | migrant workers |
| *dōhō* | Japanese compatriots |
| Gaimushō | Japan's foreign ministry |
| *imon bun* | comfort letter for soldiers in combat |
| *imon bukuro* | comfort bag for soldiers in combat |
| Issei | first-generation immigrants |
| *kakehashi* | bridge of understanding |
| *kankōdan* | tour group |
| *kenjinkai* | prefectural associations |
| Kibei | lit. "go home to America," Japanese Americans who returned to the United States after receiving their education in Japan |
| *nagusameru* | to comfort |
| Nikkei | Japanese immigrant or descendant |
| Nisei | the second-generation children of immigrants (Issei) |

| | |
|---|---|
| Rikkōkai | an organization that promoted and arranged emigration from Japan |
| Sansei | the third-generation grandchildren of immigrants (Issei), children of Nisei |
| *senninbari* | one-thousand-stitch amulet believed to protect its wearer from danger in battle, popular as a hallmark of Japanese and Japanese immigrant nationalism before World War II |
| *toritsuginin* | consulate general agent |
| Yonsei | the fourth-generation great-grandchildren of immigrants (Issei), grandchildren of Nisei, children of Sansei |

# About the Contributors

**Eiichiro Azuma** is the Roy F. and Jeannette P. Nichols Professor of American History at University of Pennsylvania. He specializes in Japanese American history; transpacific migration, diaspora, and settler colonialism; and inter-imperial relations between the United States and Japan. He is the author of the award-winning monographs *Between Two Empires: Race, History, and Transnationalism in Japanese America* (Oxford University Press, 2005) and *In Search of Our Frontier: Japanese America and Settler Colonialism in the Construction of Japan's Borderless Empire* (University of California Press, 2019). Since 2019, Azuma has been involved in the Japanese Diaspora Initiative in his capacity as a Hoover Institution visiting fellow.

**Rashaad Eshack** is a PhD candidate at the University of Cambridge working under the supervision of Professor Barak Kushner. His research focuses on the transnational history of education in the Japanese diaspora, highlighting the relationship between Japan and Japanese-language teaching abroad. Eshack's scholarly focus is on the intersection between empire, transnationality, and local communities. As a historian, he aims to uncover how Japanese overseas communities positioned themselves within the tumultuous politics of the Pacific throughout the 1930s. Before beginning his PhD studies, Eshack worked as a research student in the Faculty of Economics at Kyoto University. He previously received his MA in transcultural studies at the University of Heidelberg. He has presented at the Japanese Diaspora Initiative Workshop, the World Congress on Business History, the Heidelberg Research Colloquium on Migration, and the Kyoto Next Generation Workshop. His research takes him to all corners of the Pacific world, and he regularly engages in archival fieldwork in Japan, Hawai'i, and both North and South America.

**Brian Masaru Hayashi** is a professor in the History Department, Kent State University. His current research work is on the racialist ideology known as the Yellow Peril and its effect on Asian Americans, 1894–1952. He was a visiting researcher at the Hoover Institution, Stanford University (2019–2022) and a winner of the National Endowment for the Humanities award (2022). He was previously a professor in the Human and Environmental Studies Graduate School at Kyoto University and an assistant professor at Yale University with appointments in American studies, history, and East Asian studies (courtesy). He founded and directed Yale's Ethnicity, Race, and Migration Program. He is the author of *"For the Sake of Our Japanese Brethren": Assimilation, Nationalism, and Protestantism among the Japanese of Los Angeles, 1895–1942* (Stanford University Press, 1995), winner of the Kenneth Scott Latourette Prize; *Democratizing the Enemy: The Japanese American Internment* (Princeton University Press, 2004), winner of the Robert G. Athearn Prize; and *Asian American Spies: How Asian Americans Helped Win the Allied Victory* (Oxford University Press, 2021). He also coedited, with Yasuko Takezawa, *New Wave: Studies on Japanese Americans in the 21st Century* (Kyoto University, 2004).

**Masako Iino** is a former president, professor emeritus, and trustee of Tsuda University, Tokyo, and chair of the academic advisory committee at the Japanese Overseas Migration Museum. After earning her BA at Tsuda College (present Tsuda University), Iino studied at the graduate school of Syracuse University as a Fulbright grantee, receiving her MA in American history. She taught for many years in the fields of American history and migration studies at Tsuda University, McGill University, and Acadia University and was a visiting professor at the University of California–Berkeley and Bryn Mawr College. She has also served on numerous committees and boards, including the Japan Society for the Promotion of Science and the Government Committee on the Development of Research Universities. Iino is the author or editor of many books published in Japan, including *A History of Japanese Canadians* (1997), given the Prime Minister's Award for Publication; *Another History of US-Japan Relations: Japanese Americans Swayed by the Cooperation and the Disputes between the Two Nations* (2000); *Searching Ethnic America: Multiple Approaches to "E Pluribus Unum"* (2015); and *Ethnic America* (rev. ed. 2017).

**Michael R. Jin** is an associate professor of global Asian studies and history at the University of Illinois Chicago. His areas of specialization include migration and diaspora studies, Asian American history, critical race and ethnic studies, and the history of the American West. He is the author of *Citizens, Immigrants, and the Stateless: A Japanese American Diaspora in the Pacific* (Stanford University Press, 2022), which uncovers the stories of US-born Japanese American migrants who drew the American West into the larger histories of nations and empires in the Pacific before, during, and after World War II. His current research documents the experiences of Korean survivors of the 1945 atomic bombings, which illuminate the legacies of Japanese imperialism, the shifting geopolitical dynamics of the Cold War US nuclear umbrella, and the postcolonial politics of redress. His work has been published in the *Critical Ethnic Studies Journal*, *Amerasia Journal*, the *Routledge History of US Foreign Relations*, the *Routledge Handbook of Asian American Studies*, the *American Historian*, and other scholarly venues.

**Masato Kimura** is a visiting professor at Kansai University. He received a PhD in political science from Keio University Graduate School of Law and a PhD in cultural interactions from Kansai University Graduate of School of East Asian Culture. He worked at Mitsui Bank & Co. and was subsequently a visiting researcher at the Walter H. Shorenstein Asia-Pacific Research Center, Stanford University, and the Edwin O. Reischauer

Institute of Japanese Studies, Harvard University. He later became the director of research at the Shibusawa Eiichi Memorial Foundation. His publications include *Nichi-Bei minkan keizai gaikō 1905–1911* (US-Japan private sector economic diplomacy 1905–1911) (Keiō Tsūshin, 1989); *Shibusawa Eiichi: Minkan gaikō no sōshisha* (Shibusawa Eiichi: The founder of the private sector economic diplomacy) (Chūō Kōron Shinsha, 1991); and *Shibusawa Eiichi: Nihon no infura o tsukutta minkan keizai no kyojin* (Shibusawa Eiichi: Private-sector economic giant who built the infrastructure of Japan) (Chikuma Shobō, 2020).

**Toshihiko Kishi** is a professor at the Center for Southeast Asian Studies, Kyoto University. His research covers modern East Asian history and media studies. He has extensively published on East Asian history, including *Manshūkoku no bijuaru media: Posutā, ehagaki, kitte* (Visual media in Manchukuo: Posters, postcards and stamps) (Yoshikawa Kōbunkan, 2010), *Higashi Ajia ryūkōka awā: Ekkyō suru oto kōsaku suru ongakujin* (East Asian popular songs hour: Crossing boundaries and crossing musicians) (Iwanami Shoten, 2013), *Ajia taiheiyo senso to shuyojo: Jukei seikenka no hishuyosha no shogen to kokusai kyusai kikan no kiroku kara* (The Asian-Pacific War and the internment camps: Testimonies of detainees under the Chongqing regime and records of international relief agencies), and *Teikoku Nihon no puropaganda: "Sensōnetsu" o aotta senden to hōdō* (Imperial Japan's propaganda: Political propaganda and the press fueled by "war fever") (Chūō Kōron Shinsha, 2022). He has also coedited many books, including *Yomigaeru Okinawa Beikoku shiseikenka no terebi eizō: Ryūkyū Rettō Beikoku Minsei (USCAR) no jidai* (Enlightening through TV: USCAR public diplomacy, 1950–1972) (Fuji Shuppan, 2020), and *Shijue Taiwan: Zhaori shinwenshe baodao yingxiang xuanji* (Picturing Taiwan: The Asahi Shimbun Press photo selections) (Institute of Taiwan History, Academia Sinica, 2020).

**Mire Koikari** is a professor of women's, gender, and sexuality studies at the University of Hawai'i at Mānoa. Her major publications include *Pedagogy of Democracy: Feminism and the Cold War in the US Occupation of Japan* (Temple University Press, 2008), *Cold War*

*Encounters in US-Occupied Okinawa: Women, Militarized Domesticity, and Transnationalism in East Asia* (Cambridge University Press, 2015), and *Gender, Culture, and Disaster in Post-3.11 Japan* (Bloomsbury Academic Press, 2020).

**Teruko Kumei** is a professor emeritus in the English Department of Shirayuri University (American history and culture) and was an Academic Advisory Committee member of the Japanese Overseas Migration Museum in Yokohama (2006–2015). She received the 1996 Shimizu Hiroshi Award from the Japanese Association for American Studies for *Gaikokujin o meguru shakaishi: Kindai Amerika to Nihonjin imin* (Social history of foreign workers: Modern American and Japanese immigrants) (Yuzankaku, 1995). Her studies focus on the history of Japanese immigrants in the United States, including US-Japan relations over Japanese immigration problems, Japanese-language school education, Japanese American incarceration, and Japanese immigrant literature, especially senryu, haiku, and tanka poems. Some of her works in English include *Not English Only: Redefining "American" in American Studies* (VU University Press, 2001); the chapter " 'The Twain Shall Meet' in the Nisei? Japanese Language Education and US-Japan Relations, 1900–1940," in *New Worlds, New Lives: Globalization and People of Japanese Descent in the Americas and from Latin America in Japan* (Stanford University Press, 2002); and articles in the *Japanese Journal of American Studies*.

**Tosh Minohara** is a professor of US-Japan relations at the Graduate School of Law and Politics, Kobe University, where he holds a joint appointment with the Graduate School of International Cooperation Studies. He received his BA in international relations from the University of California–Davis and his PhD in political science and diplomatic history from Kobe University. He is also the founder and chairman of the Japanese Cabinet Office–certified nonprofit organization Research Institute of Indo-Pacific Affairs and an external advisor to the Japanese Ministry of Foreign Affairs. His core academic interests are in the diplomatic, political, and security dimensions of US-Japan relations. He has published numerous monographs, edited volumes, journal articles, and op-ed pieces, including *The Japanese Exclusion Act and US-Japan Relations* [in Japanese] (Iwanami Shoten, 2002); and, as editor, *Tumultuous Decade: Empire, Society, and Diplomacy in 1930s Japan* (University of Toronto Press, 2013), *Decade of the Great War: Japan and the Wider World during the 1910s* (Brill, 2014), *The History of US-Japan Relations: From Perry to the Present* (Palgrave Macmillan, 2017), and *Beyond Versailles: The 1919 Moment in Asia* (Lexington, 2020). He has been awarded the Shimizu Hiroshi Prize (2002) and the Japan Research Award (2019).

**Yasuo Sakata** has been a leading scholar of Japanese immigration and emigration studies for decades in the United States and Japan. He received a BA in history and PhD in East Asian History from the University of California–Los Angeles. He was instrumental in compiling the Japanese American Research Project and published *A Buried Past: An Annotated Bibliography of the Japanese American Research Project Collection* (University of California Press, 1974), with Yuji Ichioka, and *Fading Footsteps of the Issei: An Annotated Check List of the Manuscript Holdings of the Japanese American Research Project Collection* (Asian American Studies Center, University of California at Los Angeles, 1992). After returning to Japan in 1990, he taught in the Faculty of International Studies, Osaka Gakuin University. He also served as the president of the Japanese Association for Migration Studies. Other notable publications include *Tairitsu to dakyō: 1930-nendai no Nichi-Bei tsūshō kankei* (Conflict and compromise: US-Japan trade relationships in the 1930s) (Daiichi Hōki, Heisei 6, 1994), coedited with Kazuo Ueyama, and *Meiji Nichi-Bei bōeki kotohajime: Chokuyu no shishi Arai Ryōichirō to sono jidai* (The beginning of the Japan-US trade in Meiji: The era of Arai Ryoichiro, a pioneer of direct trade) (Tōkyōdō Shuppan, 1996).

**Kaoru "Kay" Ueda** is the curator for the Hoover Institution Library & Archives' Japanese Diaspora Collection at Stanford University and manages the endowed Japanese Diaspora Initiative. She acquires archival materials on Japan and overseas Japanese and promotes their use for educational and scholarly purposes. She also curates and develops the Hoji Shinbun Digital Collection, the world's most extensive online full-image open-access digital collection of prewar overseas Japanese newspapers. She edited *On a Collision Course: The Dawn of Japanese Migration in the Nineteenth Century* (authored by Yasuo Sakata in Japanese; Hoover Institution Press, 2020) and *Fanning the Flames: Propaganda in Modern Japan* (Hoover Institution Press, 2021).

# Index